The Conservative Mainstream

FRANK S. MEYER

The Conservative Mainstream

ARLINGTON HOUSE • NEW ROCHELLE, N. Y.

To John and Eugene

IN HOPE

TABLE OF CONTENTS

PART I.   CONSERVATISM AND LIBERALISM

1. *What Is Conservatism?*   13
2. *Syndrome of the Liberal Establishment*   90

PART II.   POLITICAL AFFAIRS—DOMESTIC
          AND FOREIGN

3. *Issues and Institutions*   141
4. *Political Commentary 1956–1968*   224
5. *Communism and American Foreign Policy:*
    Eisenhower to Johnson   308

PART III.   IDEAS, FORCES, PEOPLE

6. *On History*   391
7. *On Education*   427
8. *On Men, Famous and Infamous*   444

INDEX   483

Introduction

For some dozen years I have been writing a regular column, "Principles and Heresies," in *National Review*, ranging widely over matters practical and theoretical, as seen from a conservative point of view. These columns, together with occasional articles and reviews written over the same period of time, constitute the substance of this book. There is, I think, in these columns and articles a continuity which justifies their presentation in this form, and where necessary I have added new material to strengthen that continuity.

The first section of the book is concerned with the underlying issue that has given the real meaning to political and social developments during the past decade—the contrasting principles of conservatism and Liberalism. The middle section builds on the basis of these theoretical considerations and discusses the unfolding events and conflicts of that period, domestic and international, from a conservative stance. The final section deals with a miscellany of ideas, institutions, and personalities less directly connected with the political. Among the subjects touched upon are education, history, and the play of ideology on the contemporary scene.

This book is possible only because of the continuing opportunity I have had to write freely in the fresh context of events, an opportunity given me by the editors of the magazines in which these writings originally appeared—in particular, William F. Buckley, Jr. of *National Review*, the late Frank Chodorov of the *Freeman*, and Russell Kirk and Eugene Davidson of *Modern Age*.

Part One

Conservatism and Liberalism

Chapter One

What Is Conservatism?

The columns and articles assembled in this chapter all have to do in one way or another with a continuing effort to define and develop ideas about the nature of American conservatism. Reading back over them, I discern two prevailing themes, not sharply separated but nevertheless distinct: the effort, on the one hand, to express and formulate the consensus of the contemporary American conservative movement, and on the other hand, to champion one emphasis within that consensus, the libertarian as opposed to the more traditionalist. More often than not, the two themes are interwoven, although sometimes, as will be apparent, one or the other predominates.

What the American conservative consensus is, I had occasion to summarize in discussing the early stages of the 1968 election campaign.

Conservatism and Republican Candidates

(National Review, December 12, 1967)

Although I do not quarrel with the spirit of political realism that has matured conservatives over the past few years, I think there is some danger of carrying that realism so far as to lose sight of conservative ends. Thus, while it is surely correct not to expect the Republican candidate to be a model of conservative purity, some conservatives go off the deep end in the other direction and talk as though the victory of any Republican would be a victory for conservatism.

When conservatives flirt, as I have heard them do during the past year, with the idea of Charles Percy as Republican nominee or with that ultimate monstrosity in cynicism, a Rockefeller-Reagan ticket, they are making Republicanism per se, instead of conservatism, their end. It seems to me that to deserve conservative support, a candidate should hold broad views which are in general consonant with the conservative consensus in America today. Such consonance does not demand agreement on every specific issue but only a broad outlook that is conservative in its essence.

For want of a better definition of the conservative consensus, I offer a summary of my own definition of it, which I presented a year or two ago in a paper on conservatism for the Public Affairs Conference Center. It may serve as something of a rough test for conservatives in their consideration of candidates.

The following attitudes, I maintained, outline the American conservative position.

1) Conservatism assumes the existence of an objective moral order based upon ontological foundations. The conservative looks at political and social questions with the assumption that there are objective standards for human conduct and objective criteria for political theories and institutions, which it is the duty of human beings to understand as thoroughly as they are able and to which it is their duty to approximate their actions.

2) Within the limits of an objective moral order, the primary reference of conservative political and social thought and action is to the individual person. There may be among some conservatives a greater emphasis upon freedom and rights, as among others a greater emphasis upon duties and responsibilities; but, whichever the emphasis, conservative thought is shot through and through with concern for the person. It is

deeply suspicious of theories and policies based upon the collectivities that are the political reference points of Liberalism—"minorities," "labor," "the people." It rejects the ideological concept of associations of human beings as collective entities and the collectivist politics based upon this ideology.

3) Conservatism is profoundly anti-utopian. While it recognizes the continuing certainty of change and the necessity of basic principle being expressed under different circumstances in different ways, and while it strives always for the improvement of human institutions and the human condition, it rejects absolutely the idea that society or men generally are perfectible. It is perennially suspicious of the utopian approach, which attempts to *design* society and the lives of human beings.

4) On the basis of concern for the individual person and rejection of utopian planning, conservatives believe in a strict limitation of the power of government. They are firmly opposed to the Liberal concept of the state as the engine for the fixing of ideological blueprints upon the citizenry. They stand for freedom of social and personal action as against government-directed action, and for a free economic system.

5) From these positions American conservatism derives its firm support of the Constitution of the United States as originally conceived—to achieve the protection of individual liberty in an ordered society by limiting the power of government. Conservatives support the preservation of the elements of the structure thereby created: restriction of government to its proper functions; within government, tension and balance between local and central power; within the Federal Government, tension and balance between the coordinate branches. They strive to reestablish a federal system of strictly divided powers, as far as government itself is concerned, and to repulse the encroachment of government, federal or state, upon the economy and the individual lives of citizens.

6) In their devotion to Western civilization and their firm American patriotism, conservatives are deeply aware of the danger of Communism as an armed and messianic threat to

the very existence of Western civilization and the United States. They believe that our foreign and military policy must be based upon recognition of this reality. As opposed to the vague internationalism and the wishful thinking about Communist "mellowing" that characterize Liberal thought and action, they see the defense of the West and the United States as the overriding imperative of public policy. It is in this light that they regard a successful conclusion of the Vietnam war as vital to the over-all struggle against Communism.

There is nothing here on specific issues—no conservative "party line" on urban questions or tax structure or the detailed strategy and tactics of Vietnam. Nor will any candidate politically likely under current circumstances present himself as the philosophical exponent of such a theoretical conservative position. But in the minds of conservatives that position can act as a criterion by which men and their stand on issues may be adjudged—not only positively as to whom a conservative might most desire as a candidate, but negatively also as to who must be opposed at all costs.

Within the consensus of American conservatism, however, there exist strains and tensions, the origins of which are both historical and intellectual. Or perhaps it might be better to say the consensus is itself the result of tensions. I touched on these questions in a number of columns in National Review *but the most systematic analysis appeared in an article in* Modern Age.

Freedom, Tradition, Conservatism

(Modern Age, Fall, 1960)

The last half-dozen years have seen a development of conservative thought in the United States unparalleled in a century. It is ironic, although not historically unprecedented, that such a burst of creative energy on the intellectual level should occur simultaneously with a continuing spread of the influence of liberalism in the practical political sphere, to the point where it has now captured the decisive positions of power in the Republican as well as in the Democratic party. But ironic or not, it is the fact. For the first time in modern America a whole school has arisen that consciously challenges the very foundations of collectivist Liberalism; two intellectually serious journals, *Modern Age* and *National Review*, have established themselves integrally in the life of the nation; and an increasing number of the newer generation of undergraduates, graduate students and young instructors in the universities openly proclaim themselves conservatives. Most important, perhaps, an intense and far-ranging discussion has been taking place among conservatives on the meaning and matter of conservatism in the circumstances of mid-twentieth-century America.

It is to this discussion that I want to address myself. In the course of it there have developed doctrines apparently sharply opposed to each other, and sometimes presented as mutually incompatible, but which I believe can in reality be united within a single broader conservative political theory, since they have their roots in a common tradition and are arrayed against a common enemy. Their opposition, which takes many forms, is essentially a division between those who abstract from the corpus of Western belief its stress upon freedom and upon the innate importance of the individual person (what we may call the libertarian position) and those who— drawing upon the same source—stress value and virtue and order (what we may call the traditionalist position).

But the source from which both draw, the continuing consciousness of Western civilization, has been specifically distinguished by its ability to hold these apparently opposed ends in balance and tension; and in fact the two positions which confront each other today in American conservative discourse both implicitly accept, to a large degree, the ends of the other. Without the implicit acceptance of an absolute ground of value, the pre-eminence of the person as criterion of political and social thought and action has no philosophical foundation; and freedom would be only a meaningless excitation and could never become the serious goal of a serious politics. On the other hand, the belief in virtue as the end of men's being implicitly recognizes the necessity of freedom to choose that end; otherwise, virtue could be no more than a conditioned tropism. And the raising of order to the rank of an end overshadowing and subordinating the individual person would make of order not what the traditionalist conservative means by it, but the rule of totalitarian authority, inhuman and subhuman.

On neither side is there a purposeful, philosophically founded rejection of the ends the other side proclaims. Rather, each side emphasizes so strongly the aspect of the great tradition of the West which it sees as decisive, that distortion sets in. The place of its goals in the total tradition of the West is lost sight of, and the complementary interdependence of freedom and virtue, of the individual person and political order, is forgotten.

Nevertheless, although these contrary emphases in conservative thought can and do pull away from each other when the proponents of either forsake one side of their common heritage of belief in virtue as man's proper end *and* his freedom under God as the condition of the achievement of that end, their opposition is not irreconcilable, precisely because they do in fact jointly possess that very heritage. Extremists on one side may be undisturbed by the danger of the recrudescence of authoritarian status society if only it would enforce the doctrines in which they believe. Extremists on the other side may care little what becomes of ultimate values if only political and economic individualism prevails. But both extremes are self-defeating: truth withers when freedom dies, however righteous the authority that kills it; and free individualism uninformed by moral value rots at its core and soon brings about conditions that pave the way for surrender to tyranny.

Such extremes, however, are not the necessary outcome of a dialectic between doctrines which emphasize opposite sides of the same truth. Indeed, a dialectic between different emphases based upon the same fundamental understanding is the mode by which finite men have achieved much of the wisdom contained in tradition. Such a dialectic is in the highest degree necessary today between the libertarians and the traditionalists among conservatives. It cannot fail to achieve results of the greatest significance, if only the protagonists, in pressing that aspect of the truth which each regards as decisive, keep constantly in their consciousness other and complementary aspects of the same truth.

The tendency to establish false antitheses obstructing fruitful confrontation arises in part from an inherent dilemma of conservatism in a revolutionary era, such as ours. There is a real contradiction between the deep piety of the conservative spirit towards tradition, prescription, the preservation of the fibre of society (what has been called "natural conservatism") and the more reasoned, consciously principled, militant conservatism which becomes necessary when the fibres of society have been rudely torn apart, when deleterious revolutionary principles ride high, and restoration, not preservation, is the order of the day. For what the conservative is committed to conserve is not simply whatever happens to be the established conditions of a few years or a few decades, but the consensus of his civilization, of his country, as that consensus over the centuries has reflected truth derived from the very constitution of being. We are today historically in a situation created by thirty years of slow and insidious revolution at home and a half-century of violent open revolution abroad. To conserve the true and the good under these circumstances is to restore an understanding (and a social structure reflecting that understanding) which has been all but buried, not to preserve the transient customs and prescriptions of the present.

It is here that the dilemma of conservatism affects our present doctrinal discussion. The need in our circumstances for the most vigorous use of reason to combat the collectivist, scientistic, amoral wave of the present tends to induce in the libertarian an apotheosis of reason and a neglect of tradition and prescription (which he identifies with the prevailing prescriptions of the present). The traditionalist, suspecting that he sees in this libertarian tendency the same fever to impose upon men an abstract speculative ideology that has characterized the revolution of our time—as well as the French Revolution and its spiritual forbears—tends to recoil, and in his turn to press a one-sided position. Too often he confounds reason and principle with "demon ideology." Rather than justly insisting upon the limits of reason—the finite bounds of the purview of any one man or any one generation, and the responsibility to employ reason in the context of continuing tradition—he seems sometimes to turn his back on reason altogether and to place the claims of custom and prescription in irreconcilable opposition to it.

Both attitudes obscure the truth; both vitiate the value of the dialectic. The history of the West has been a history of reason operating within tradition. The balance has been tenuous, the tension at times has tightened till it was spiritually almost unbearable; but out of this balance and tension the glory of the West has been created. To claim exclusive sovereignty for either component—reason or tradition—is to smirch that glory and cripple the potentialities of conservatism in its struggle against the Liberal collectivist Leviathan.

Abstract reason, functioning in a vacuum of tradition, can indeed give birth to an arid and distorting ideology. But, in a revolutionary age, the qualities of natural conservatism by themselves can lead only to the enthronement of the prevailing power of the revolution. Natural conservatism is a legitimate human characteristic and in settled times it is conducive to good. It represents the universal human tendency to hold by the accustomed, to maintain existing modes of life. In settled times it can exist in healthy tension with the other equally natural human characteristic, the impulse to break beyond

accepted limits in the deepening of truth and the heightening
of value. But this is only possible before the fibres of society
have been loosened, before the "cake of custom" has been
broken. Then these two human tendencies can be held in just
proportions, since men of all conditions believe, each at the
level of his understanding, in the same transcendent Ground
of truth and value, eternal and dynamic. But when, through
whatever cause, this unity in tension is riven, when the dynamic
takes off into thin air, breaking its tension with the perpetual
rhythms of life—in short, when a revolutionary force shatters
the unity and balance of civilization—then conservatism must
be of another sort if it is to fulfill its responsibility. It is not
and cannot be limited to that uncritical acceptance, that uncomplicated reverence, which is the essence of natural conservatism.
The world of idea and symbol and image has been turned
topsy-turvy; the life-stream of civilization has been cut off
and dispersed.

This is our situation. What is required of us is a *conscious*
conservatism—a clearly principled restatement in new circumstances of philosophical and political truth. This conscious conservatism cannot be a simple piety—although in a deep sense
it must have piety towards the constitution of being. Nevertheless
in its consciousness it necessarily reflects a reaction to the
rude break the revolution has made in the continuity of human
wisdom. It is called forth by a sense of the loss which that
cutting off has created. It cannot now be identical with the
natural conservatism towards which it yearns. The world in
which it exists is the revolutionary world. To accept that, to
conserve that, would be to accept and conserve the very denial
of man's long-developed understanding, the very destruction of
achieved truth, which are the essence of the revolution.

Nor can the conscious conservatism required of us appeal
simply and uncomplicatedly to the past. The past has had
many aspects, all held in measured suspension. But the revolution has destroyed that suspension, that tradition; the delicate
fabric can never be re-created in the same identical form; its

integral character has been destroyed. The conscious conservatism of a revolutionary or post-revolutionary era faces problems inconceivable to the natural conservatism of a pre-revolutionary time. The modes of thought of natural conservatism are not by themselves adequate to the tasks of a time like this. Today's conservatism cannot simply affirm. It must select and adjudge. It is conservative because in its selection and in its judgment it bases itself upon the accumulated wisdom of mankind over millennia, because it accepts the limits upon the irresponsible play of untrammeled reason which the unchanging values exhibited by that wisdom dictate. But it is, it has to be, not acceptance of what lies before it in the contemporary world, but challenge. In an era like ours the existing regime in philosophical thought, as in political and social actuality, is fundamentally wrong. To accept is to be, not conservative, but acquiescent to revolution.

Situations of this nature have arisen again and again in the history of civilization; and each time the great renewers have been those who were able to recover true principle out of the wreck of their heritage. They were guided by reason—reason mediated, it is true, by prudence, but in the first instance reason. Like Socrates, Plato, Aristotle, confronting the chaos in the body politic and in the minds of men created by the overweening pride of the Athenian *demos*, we do not live in the happy age of a natural conservatism. We cannot simply revere; we cannot uncritically follow tradition, for the tradition presented to us is rapidly becoming—thanks to the prevailing intellectual climate, thanks to the schools, thanks to the outpourings of all the agencies that mould opinion and belief—the tradition of a positivism scornful of truth and virtue, the tradition of the collective, the tradition of the untrammeled state.

The conservative today, like the conscious conservative of all revolutionary eras, cannot escape the necessity and the duty to bring reason to bear upon the problems that confront him. He has to separate the true from the false, applying basic principle to the task of cutting through the tangled mass of con-

fusion and falsehood; he has the responsibility of establishing
in new circumstances forms of thought and institutional arrangements which will express the truth of the great tradition of the
West. Respectful though he is of the wisdom of the past and
reverent though he is toward precedent and prescription, the
tasks he faces can only be carried out with the aid of reason,
the faculty which enables us to distinguish principle and thus
to separate the true from the false.

The projection of a sharp antithesis between reason and tradition distorts the true harmony which exists between them and
blocks the development of conservative thought. There is no real
antagonism. Conservatism, to continue to develop today, must
embrace both: reason operating within tradition: neither ideological *hubris* abstractly creating utopian blueprints, ignoring
the accumulated wisdom of mankind, nor blind dependence
upon that wisdom to answer automatically the questions posed
to our generation and demanding our own expenditure of our
own mind and spirit.

Closely related to the false antithesis between reason and
tradition that distorts the dialogue between the libertarian
emphasis and the traditionalist emphasis among conservatives is our historical inheritance of the nineteenth-century
European struggle between classical liberalism and a conservatism that was too often rigidly authoritarian. Granted
there is much in classical liberalism that conservatives must
reject—its philosophical foundation, its tendency towards
utopian constructions, its disregard (explicitly, though by no
means implicitly) of tradition; granted that it is the source of
much that is responsible for the plight of the twentieth century:
but its championship of freedom and its development of political
and economic theories directed towards the assurance of freedom
have contributed to our heritage concepts which we need to
conserve and develop as surely as we need to reject the utilitarian ethics and the secular progressivism that classical liberalism has also passed on to us.

Nineteenth-century conservatism, with all its understanding of the pre-eminence of virtue and value, for all its piety towards the continuing tradition of mankind, was far too cavalier to the claims of freedom, far too ready to subordinate the individual person to the authority of state or society.

The conservative today is the inheritor of the best in both of these tragically bifurcated branches of the Western tradition. But the division lingers on and adds to the difficulties of conservative discourse. The traditionalist, although in practice he fights alongside the libertarian against the collectivist Leviathan state of the twentieth century, tends to reject the political and economic theories of freedom which flow from classical liberalism, in his reaction against its unsound metaphysics. He discards the true with the false, creating unnecessary obstacles to the mutual dialogue in which he is engaged with his libertarian *alter ego*. The libertarian, suffering from the mixed heritage of the nineteenth-century champions of liberty, reacts against the traditionalist's emphasis upon precedent and continuity out of antipathy to the authoritarianism with which that emphasis has been associated—although in actuality he stands firmly for continuity and tradition against the rising revolutionary wave of collectivism and statism.

We are victims here of an inherent tragedy in the history of classical liberalism. As it developed the economic and political doctrines of limited state power, the free-market economy and the freedom of the individual person, it sapped, by its utilitarianism, the foundations of belief in an organic moral order. But the only possible basis of respect for the integrity of the individual person and for the overriding value of his freedom is belief in an organic moral order. Without such a belief, no doctrine of political and economic liberty can stand.

Furthermore, when such a belief is not universally accepted, a free society, even if it could exist, would become licentious war of all against all. Political freedom, failing a broad acceptance of the personal obligation to duty and to charity, is never viable. Deprived of an understanding of the philosophical foundations of freedom, and exposed to the ravening of conscience-

less marauders, men forget that they are fully men only to the
degree that they are free to choose their destiny, and they turn
to whatever fallacy promises them welfare and order.

The classical liberal as philosopher dug away the foundations
of the economic and political doctrines of classical liberalism.
But however much he may thereby have contributed to our
misfortunes, he himself continued to live on the inherited moral
capital of centuries of Christendom. His philosophical doctrines
attacked the foundations of conscience, but he himself was
still a man of conscience. As Christopher Dawson has said:
"The old liberalism, with all its shortcomings, had its roots
deep in the soil of Western and Christian culture." With those
roots as yet unsevered, the classical liberal was able to develop
the theories of political and economic freedom which are part
of the conservative heritage today.

The misunderstandings between libertarian and traditionalist
are to a considerable degree the result of a failure to understand the differing levels on which classical liberal doctrines
are valid and invalid. Although the classical liberal forgot—
and the contemporary libertarian conservative sometimes tends
to forget—that in the *moral* realm freedom is only a means
whereby men can pursue their proper end, which is virtue, he
did understand that in the *political* realm freedom is the primary
end. If, with Acton, we "take the establishment of liberty for
the realization of moral duties to be the end of civil society,"
the traditionalist conservative of today, living in an age when
liberty is the last thought of our political mentors, has little
cause to reject the contributions to the understanding of liberty
of the classical liberals, however corrupted their understanding
of the ends of liberty. Their error lay largely in the confusion of
the temporal with the transcendent. They could not distinguish
between the *authoritarianism* with which men and institutions
suppress the freedom of men, and the *authority* of God
and truth.

On the other hand, the same error in reverse vitiated the
thought of nineteenth-century conservatives. They respected

the authority of God and of truth as conveyed in tradition, but too often they imbued the authoritarianism of men and institutions with the sacred aura of divine authority. They gave way to the temptation to make of tradition, which in its rightful role serves as a guide to the operation of reason, a weapon with which to suppress reason.

It is true that from their understanding of the basis of men's moral existence, from their reverence for the continuity and precedent that ties the present to the past, contemporary conservatism has inherited elements vital to its very existence. Yet we can no more make of the great conservative minds of the nineteenth century unerring guides to be blindly followed than we can condemn out of hand their classical liberal opponents. Sound though they were on the essentials of man's being, on his destiny to virtue and his responsibility to seek it, on his duty in the moral order, they failed too often to realize that the *political* condition of moral fulfillment is freedom from coercion. Signally they failed to recognize the decisive danger in a union of political and economic power—a danger becoming daily greater before their eyes as science and technology created apace immense aggregates of economic energy. Aware, as the classical liberals were not, of the reality of original sin, they forgot that its effects are never more virulent than when men wield unlimited power. Looking to the state to promote virtue, they forgot that the power of the state rests in the hands of men as subject to the effects of original sin as those they govern. They could not, or would not, see a truth the classical liberals understood: if to the power naturally inherent in the state, to defend its citizens from violence, domestic and foreign, and to administer justice, there is added a positive power over economic and social energy, the temptation to tyranny becomes irresistible, and the political conditions of freedom wither.

The tendency of the traditionalist conservative to insist that the crystallization of a conservative outlook today requires only that we carry on the principles of those who called themselves conservatives in the nineteenth century oversimplifies and confuses the problem. That the conservative is one who preserves tradition does not mean that his task is arid imitation and repetition of what others have done before. It is true that in ultimate terms, upon the basic issue of human destiny, truths have been given us that we cannot improve upon, that we can only convey and make real in the context of our time. Here indeed the conservatives of the nineteenth century played a heroic part in preserving in the teeth of the overwhelming tendency of the era the age-old image of man as a creature of transcendent destiny.

In the political and economic realm, however, these truths establish only the foundation for an understanding of the end of civil society and the function of the state. That end, to guarantee freedom, so that men may uncoercedly pursue virtue, can be achieved in different circumstances by different means. To the clarification of what these means are in specific circumstances, the conservative must apply his reason. The technological circumstances of the twentieth century demand above all the breaking up of power and the separation of centers of power—both within the economy itself, within the state itself, and between the state and the economy. Power of a magnitude never before dreamed of by men has been brought into being. While separation of power has always been essential to a good society, if those who possess it are to be preserved from corruption and those who do not are to be safeguarded from coercion, this has become a fateful necessity under the conditions of modern technology. To the analysis of this decisive problem and to the development of political and economic solutions of it, classical liberalism contributed mightily. If we reject that heritage, we should be casting away some of the most powerful among our weapons against socialism, Communism, and collectivist Liberalism. The traditionalist who would have us do so because of the philosophical errors of classical liberalism, like the libertarian who rejects tradition because it has sometimes been associated with authoritarianism, seriously weakens the development of conservative doctrine.

The historical fact is—and it adds to the complexity of our

problems—that the great tradition of the West has come to us through the nineteenth century, split, bifurcated, so that we must draw not only upon those who called themselves conservatives in that century but also upon those who called themselves liberals. The economists of the liberal British tradition, from Adam Smith through and beyond the vilified Manchesterians, like the Austrian economists from Menger and Böhm-Bawerk to Mises and Hayek, analyzed the conditions of industrial society and established the principles upon which the colossal power that it produces can be developed for the use of man without nurturing a monstrous Leviathan. Without their mighty intellectual endeavor, we should be disarmed before the collectivist economics of Marx, Keynes, and Galbraith. And in the sphere of political theory, who has surpassed the nineteenth-century liberals in their prophetic understanding of the looming dangers of the all-powerful state? Conservatives today can reject neither side of their nineteenth-century heritage; they must draw upon both.

Differences of emphasis between libertarian and traditionalist cannot be avoided and should not be regretted. Conservatism has no monolithic party line. Our task is to overcome the nineteenth century bifurcation of the Western tradition in fruitful dialogue, not to perpetuate it by refusing to understand the breadth and complexity of our heritage, out of a narrow historicism that unearths outworn party emblems.

I am well aware that what I have been saying can be criticized as eclecticism and attacked as an effort to smother principle. But it is not the laying aside of clear belief, either by the libertarian conservative or by the traditionalist conservative, in order to present a front against contemporary collectivist Liberalism, that is here conceived. Rather, it is the deepening of the beliefs which each holds through the development of their implications in a dialectic free of distorting narrowness. That deepening—and the development of a common conservative doctrine, comprehending both emphases—cannot be achieved in a surface manner by blinking differences or blurring intellectual distinctions with grandiose phraseology. It can only be achieved by a hard-fought dialectic—but a dialectic in which both sides recognize not only that they have a common enemy, but also that, despite all differences, they hold a common heritage.

As Americans indeed we have a great tradition to draw upon, in which the division, the bifurcation, of European thought between the emphasis on virtue and value and order and the emphasis on freedom and the integrity of the individual person was overcome, and a harmonious unity of the tensed poles of Western thought was achieved in political theory and practice, as never before or since. The men who created the republic, who framed the Constitution and produced that monument of political wisdom, *The Federalist Papers,* represented among them as great a conflict of emphasis as any in contemporary American conservatism. Washington, Franklin, Jefferson, Hamilton, Adams, Jay, Mason, Madison—among them there existed immense differences on the claims of the individual person and the claims of order, on the relation of virtue to freedom. But their dialectic was conducted within a continuing awareness of their joint heritage. Out of that dialectic they created a political theory and a political structure based upon the understanding that, while truth and virtue are metaphysical and moral ends, the freedom to seek them is the political condition of those ends—and that a social structure which keeps power divided is the indispensable means to this political end. The debate from which our American institutions arose is a fitting model for our debate.

In the course of defending this interpretation of the conservative view as both traditionalist and libertarian—a position labelled by Brent Bozell "fusionism"—I found myself from time to time in dispute with other conservatives, either with traditionalists, who objected to my emphasis on freedom, or with "pure libertarians," who objected equally vehemently to my respect for tradition and my insistence upon the claims of an objective moral order.

One of the first of such disputes was with Russell Kirk, who on the occasion of John Stuart Mill's 100th anniversary had written a sharp attack upon Mill in the pages of National Review.

In Defense of John Stuart Mill

(National Review, March 28, 1956)

It is an unfortunate result of the quasi-monopoly of the major organs of discussion held by the collectivist Liberals for the past generation, that those who hold to the great tradition of Western civilization have been deprived of the means to carry on the dialectic between the different strands of that tradition. Inhibited by the lack of a forum, and also by an understandable reluctance to divert energy from the primary endeavor of resisting the marshalled hosts of error, we have tended to gloss over differences, the clarification of which can only strengthen our common purpose and enrich the tradition for which we stand.

For that tradition is not a monolithic "party line." Its very existence takes the form, in large part, of a long discourse between man and man and between God and man. The maintenance of that tradition requires a continuation of discourse, pursued with respect for the accumulated wisdom of the past and with responsibility toward the dictates of reason. Such discourse strives toward Truth with the humility to realize that while Truth is objective and eternal, the quest for it by man's finite understanding is unending; that while Truth is not available anew to each generation and each man, independent of the support of tradition, neither has it been at some point in the past given once and for all, so that there is nothing left to do but pass it on from generation to generation.

Thus, as we approach the one-hundredth anniversary of the publication of John Stuart Mill's *On Liberty,* I would maintain

against the view of Russell Kirk (*National Review,* January 25)
that the aspect of the nineteenth century which that book
reflects—its character as an Age of Discussion and its love of
liberty—is the respect in which it is most glorious and most
resembles such high points in man's strivings as fifth-century
Athens and thirteenth-century Christendom. This is not to
defend the materialism and scientism of the nineteenth century,
any more than to salute John Stuart Mill's defense of liberty
is to overlook the confusion and errors of his philosophical
position. But it seems to me that Mr. Kirk attacks both Mill
and the Victorian Age for those qualities from which we have
the most to learn and which, despite all the shortcomings of the
man and the age, we must cherish against the blank conformity and power idolatry of our day. Likewise, from Mill's
antagonist, the complex James Fitzjames Stephen, he appears
to select for praise those ideas which Stephen's imagination
drew from the Romantic pagan-Teutonic *mystique* of folk,
community, force and power. All too familiar, they presage
the nightmares of the twentieth century, with which the nineteenth century was so sadly pregnant.

Both Mill and Stephen were nurtured in the bosom of utilitarianism, a position not only philosophically unsound, but
historically disastrous in its effects; nor did either of them
ever free himself from its influences. Nothing in the writings
of Bentham or either of the Mills, it seems to me, is any
more blatantly utilitarian than Stephen's discussion of liberty,
which Mr. Kirk adduces in condemnation of Mill:

> To me the question whether liberty is a good or
> a bad thing appears as irrational as the question
> whether fire is a good or a bad thing? It is both good
> and bad according to time, place, and circumstance ...

Mr. Kirk himself, after all, calls liberty "the quality which,
after divine grace and right reason, lifts man above the brutes."
Surely, such a quality cannot be considered "both good and
bad, according to time, place, and circumstance." And if it

might seem that I am drawing a strained implication from
Stephen's words, to confirm its cogency it is only necessary to
dip at random into his answer to Mill's essay, his *Liberty,
Equality, Fraternity,* an essay that glorifies force and power
against reason and moral truth. The most fundamental questions
of right and truth are reduced to a calculus of power:

> Is there or not a God and a future state? . . . the
> attitude of the law and of public authority generally
> towards the discussion of this question will and *ought*
> to depend upon the nature of the view which happens
> to be dominant for the time being on the question
> itself . . . [my emphasis]

Granted that the foundations of Mill's position are no less
utilitarian than Stephen's. Granted that with him, as with
Stephen, morality is equated with utility until, strictly considered, the very possibility of standards by which experience
is to be judged and conduct inspired is swept away. Granted,
in short, that for many of the most powerful minds and spirits
of the mid-nineteenth century, the tradition of the West lay
in a pile of shattered debris. The fact remains that John Stuart
Mill was one of the first to challenge the impending results
of the tidal wave that had been set in motion; to struggle
mightily, in his own way, as R. P. Anschutz has shown in *The
Philosophy of John Stuart Mill,* with the doctrines in which
he had been raised. It is true that he never succeeded in breaking loose from that barren system; but in vindicating the individual person as the measure of value over against the
collective instrumentalities of state and society, and in demanding that the worth of a society should be judged by the degree
to which it makes possible the freedom of the individual, he
vindicated the first principle of morality (for no man can
act morally unless he is free to choose good from evil). He
posited against the state centralism that was developing along
with unrestricted and total democracy, the fundamental social

and political derivative of the natural law: the inalienable
rights of the individual.

His fault is not in his conclusions, but in his mode of arriving
at them. He did not understand the source of man's rights
in the realm of value beyond history. A fundamental philosophical error, which is the essential error of utilitarianism, of
positivism, of all monism, vitiates his thought: the confusion
of fact and value, the erection of man's history into a standard
by which that history is to be judged. As Eric Voegelin in *The
New Science of Politics* and Percy Newcastle in *The Heresy
of Democracy* have both in their different ways so cogently
demonstrated, this is an error which has possessed a large
section of Western thought—theist as well as atheist, conservative as well as radical—to the great detriment of the
wisdom and peace of our civilization. To be sure, it has been
possible, as we have seen over and over again, for noble minds
to cling to false systems and to make nevertheless substantial
intellectual contributions. Men—even philosophers—do not
always think with logical rigor. More streams than one enter
their consciousness and help to form their product. Edmund
Burke, for example, whose thinking was corrupted through
and through with this historicist, expediential outlook (one
which, as Richard Weaver has demonstrated, showed through
his very rhetoric), played a glorious role during one of the
greatest crises in the history of the West.

To attack Mill for his philosophical errors, even to stress
the decisive effect which in his case those errors had at an
important moment in the development of thought, is legitimate
enough, and in fact of great value in clarifying some of the
most confused issues of the day. To condemn him, however,
not as having unsound foundations for his defense of liberty,
but for that defense itself; to champion against him an antagonist
as unsound as Mill philosophically, as utilitarian as Mill himself,
one who can be caught blatantly attacking the ideal of the
freedom of the person through glorification of the sword; to

hold that the triumph of the mailed tyrannies of the twentieth century "refutes" and "dates" Mill's ringing vindication of liberty; this, it seems to me, is to put forward the claims of power over spirit, blind force over right reason, matter over man, what is over what ought to be.

The basis of Mill's defense of the liberty of the individual is unsound not because the liberty of the individual is anything less than the first (although not the only) political principle of a good society, and certainly not because the victory of totalitarianism and welfarism in the twentieth century makes liberty an "outdated" ideal; it is unsound because the grounds of his defense, far from being too absolute, are not absolute enough, and, secondarily, because of the unclarity of his concept of society, and his tendency to equate society with the state.

I am myself prepared to defend a position more absolute than Mill's, because I assert the right of individual freedom not on the grounds of utility but on the grounds of the very nature of man and the nature of the drama of his existence. He lives between good and evil, beauty and ugliness, truth and error, and he fulfills his destiny in the choices he makes. No social institution, not even the conglomerate of such institutions we call for convenience "society" can make the least one of these choices. In that sense they are neither free nor unfree. Only the individual person, whose fate it is to choose, can be free, for freedom is no more nor less than the possibility—and responsibility—to choose. Freedom is the essence of the being of man, and since all social institutions are subordinate to men, the virtue of political and social institutions should be judged by the degree to which they expand or contract the area of freedom. Force, which Mr. Kirk, with Stephen, seems to regard as the great mover of history that confounds reasonable discussion and refutes the ideal of liberty, surely has no moral character of its own. It is controlled by men, for evil or for good; and the ideal of the utmost liberty for each individual man to make his choice is the end to which force should be directed. It is in this sense that Mill's championship of the individual against the state and society must, I believe, be accepted as an important part of our heritage.

The only alternative to the moral rule of liberty of the individual is to enthrone the sad tendency of human history as right, to glorify with James Stephen "the man of genius who rules by persuading an efficient minority to coerce an indifferent and self-indulgent majority . . ." The use of force against those who propound error is wrong, not because it is inexpedient but because it is an outrage upon the freedom of man and, in that, upon the very nature of man. Liberty is the political end of man's existence because liberty is the condition of his being. It is for this reason that conservatism, which in preserving the tradition preserves this truth, is only constant to itself when it is libertarian.

Conservatives in Pursuit of Truth

(National Review, June 6, 1956)

A correspondent in the May 16 issue of *National Review*, commenting upon Russell Kirk's article on John Stuart Mill and my rejoinder thereto, raises an issue of the most serious moment. My difference of opinion with Mr. Kirk on the place of the concept of liberty in political thought, he sees as representing a "fundamental—and irreconcilable—ideological division among those who call themselves conservatives."

That this issue is fundamental, I agree, but I do not think it is irreconcilable. There is no question but that in the ranks of those who are dedicated to the conservation and revitalization of the great tradition of the West, there exist diverse emphases upon different aspects of that tradition. More particularly, there is a very sharp division between those who emphasize continuity and authority and those who emphasize reason and the autonomy of the person, as the basis of their opposition to the prevailing relativism and value-nihilism, collectivism and statism. But these emphases are not irreconcilable, even if they are sometimes so one-sided as to lose sight of their mutual interdependence.

The one emphasis, traditionalist and authoritative, stressing the values expressed and maintained in the tradition of Western and Christian civilization, tends to regard economic and political forms as comparatively unimportant, and to underestimate a great insight of that tradition, that those values cannot be compelled, that they can only be freely chosen by each individual person. Or, to the degree that it does recognize the importance of freedom, it tends to assume that freedom will automatically prevail and that the economic and political forms necessary to safeguard it will spontaneously arise, if only the moral ends of human existence and the traditional prescriptions in which they are incorporated are maintained. Deeply aware that truth and good are the ends of man's existence, it too easily loses sight of the essential condition of man's pursuit of those ends: he cannot choose the good and the true unless he is free to choose, and that must mean as free to reject as to accept.

The other emphasis, individualist and libertarian, puts at the center of its consideration the prime *condition* of the search for truth: freedom. Concerned by the fearful threat to the pursuit of value that concentrated power constitutes, particularly under the circumstances of modern technology, it stresses the political and economic prerequisites of freedom. It insists upon the limitation of the state to its essential functions of defense, the preservation of order, and the administration of justice, and upon the untrammeled operation of a capitalist market economy, as the incommutable foundations of that freedom in an industrial society.

Concentrating upon the safeguards of freedom and the power of reason to arrive at any understanding of freedom, it sometimes tends to forget that reason is well-grounded only when it operates within tradition, that is, in the light of the accumulated wisdom of the generations; and, in its concern with the preservation of the freedom of the individual person, it can

lose sight of the philosophical values which are at the same
time the ends which freedom serves and the very foundation
of that respect for the innate dignity of the individual person
upon which the defense of freedom rests.

Although these two emphases in conservative thought can
and do pull away from each other, and although there is
serious danger of their so doing when the proponents of either
forsake their common heritage of belief in immutable value
as man's proper end, and his freedom under God as the condition of the achievement of his end, it is precisely because they
mutually possess that very heritage that their division is not
"irreconcilable." Extremists on one side may look with equanimity upon the recrudescence of an authoritarian status society
if only it promulgates the doctrines in which they believe.
Extremists on the other side may care not what becomes of
ultimate values if only their political and economic individualism
prevails. But both extremes are self-defeating: truth withers
when freedom dies, however righteous the authority that kills
it; and free individualism uninformed by moral value rots at
its core and soon surrenders to tyranny.

Such extremes are not the necessary outcome of the principled pursuit of the truth. Discussion, dialectic, between different
emphases based upon the same fundamental understanding, is
the mode by which finite men have achieved much of the
wisdom contained in tradition. Through it they can attain today
a common position to which "the wise and the honest may
repair"—if only the protagonists, in pressing that aspect of
the truth which they regard as decisive, do not totally exclude
from their consideration other·and complementary aspects of
the same truth.

The essence of the problem is, in my opinion, the confusion
of the metaphysical with the moral-political levels. Thus, the
aforementioned correspondent accuses me of being "in love
with the 'freedom to choose,' not with the truth that that
freedom may lead to." But the point is that the "truth" is a
metaphysical end and "the freedom to choose" is, so far as

human beings are concerned, the *moral-political condition* of achieving that end.

There is no more logic in the conclusion that a love of freedom implies a disbelief in, a lack of enthusiasm for, ultimate values, than there is in the Liberal canard that a belief in ultimate values makes impossible a belief in freedom. The reverse is the case: the belief in ultimate values and the belief in freedom are dependent one upon the other, integral aspects of the same understanding. The love of liberty and the love of truth are not the hostile standards of irreconcilable parties; rather they form together the twin sign of any viable conservatism.

Another dispute had an ironic outcome. I set out to criticize the "pure libertarians," in defense of the element of tradition and concern for virtue in the conservative tradition. But that article was answered not by a libertarian, but by Brent Bozell, the most traditional of traditionalists, who attacked me on the other flank for the libertarian content of my own position.

My original criticism of extreme libertarianism and my answer to Mr. Bozell's counterattack follow.

The Twisted Tree of Liberty

(National Review, January 16, 1962)

In the spectrum of American conservatism there are and have been many different groupings, holding varying positions within the same broad outlook. Some have emphasized the menace of international Communism; others have emphasized the danger of the creeping rot at the heart of our own institutions. Some stress the corrosion of tradition, and with it of the natural law and justice, as the source of our afflictions; others, an intellectual failure to grasp the prime importance of freedom in the body politic. Nevertheless, whatever the differences in emphasis, there has been general agreement in the practical political sphere on the necessity both to resist the collectivism and statism that emanate from indigenous Liberalism and simultaneously to repel and overcome the Communist attack upon Western civilization, which—though it has its subversive detachments operating domestically—is primarily based upon the armed power of a foreign enemy.

There have been, of course, tendencies to overstress one aspect or another to such a degree that those who do so tend to move right out of the spectrum. There have been some who concentrate so wholeheartedly on the menace of domestic Communism that its international character is lost sight of and the true role of Liberalism is only cloudily understood. There have been some with such concern for the deterioration of the philosophical foundations of virtue and justice that they neglect almost totally the corollary—that in the political realm freedom is the precondition of a good society. But whatever strains these one-sided emphases have created in the growth towards a mature political and philosophical American conservative position, there has not been until lately any grouping which directly and explicitly opposes itself to the defense of freedom from either its domestic or foreign enemies.

Recently, however, there has arisen for the first time a con-sidered position, developed out of the "pure libertarian" sector of right-wing opinion, which sharply repudiates the struggle against the major and most immediate contemporary enemy of freedom, Soviet Communism—and does so on grounds, pur-portedly, of a love for freedom. These "pure libertarian" paci-fists applaud Khrushchev, support the Fair Play for Cuba Committee, join the Sane Nuclear Policy Committee, and toy with the tactic of a united front with Communists "against war." They project themselves as the true representatives of the Right, attacking the militantly anti-Communist position of the leadership of American conservatism as moving towards the destruction of individual liberty because it is prepared to use the power of the American state in one of its legitimate functions, to defend freedom against Communist totalitarianism.

It might seem that there is no point to discussing a view of reality so patently distorted that it can consider appeasement of Communism, disarming ourselves before the Communist armed drive, and alliance with those who ease the road to Communist victory, as essential to the defense of the freedom of the individual. But although those who profess these absurd opinions are small in number, they do influence a section of the right wing, particularly in the universities, and they may, if not combatted, influence more, for they offer tempting flesh-pots: the opportunity at one and the same time bravely to proclaim devotion to individual freedom, championship of the free-market economy, and opposition to prevailing Liberal wel-fare-statism, while comfortably basking in the sunshine of the Liberal atmosphere, which is today primarily the atmosphere of appeasement and piecemeal surrender.

Shocking though they are, the practical results of this pacifist strain in the right wing are minimal; more important is the light that the development of such a monstrous misapprehension of reality casts upon the dangers inherent in the "pure liber-tarian" approach to the problems of freedom in society. It is a tendency which, followed unchecked, can be as harmful to the development of a mature American conservative position as the counter-tendency in the conservative penumbra—con-cerning which I have written previously in these pages—to look upon the state as unlimitedly constituted to enforce virtue, thus abnegating the freedom of the individual.

Of course, in any healthy growing movement there are bound to be clashes of opinion, differences of emphasis, within over-all agreement on basic principle. This is particularly to be expected in the burgeoning American conservative movement of today— and for two reasons. In the first place, the tone of the con-servative mind, with its aversion to the narrowly ideological and its respect for the human person, is alien to the concept of a "party line" and so is generous to individual differences of stress on this or that aspect of a general outlook. But more specifically, the principles which inspire the contemporary

American conservative movement are developing as the fusion of two different streams of thought. The one, which, for want of a better word, one may call the "traditionalist," puts its primary emphasis upon the authority of transcendent truth and the necessity of a political and social order in accord with the constitution of being. The other, which, again for want of a better word, one may call the "libertarian," takes as its first principle in political affairs the freedom of the individual person and emphasizes the restriction of the power of the state and the maintenance of the free-market economy as guarantee of that freedom.

Before the challenge of modern collectivism, hostile alike to transcendent truth and to individual freedom, traditionalist and libertarian have found common cause and tend more and more to work together on the practical political level. But further, the common source in the *ethos* of Western civilization from which flow both the traditionalist and the libertarian currents, has made possible a continuing discussion which is creating the fusion that is contemporary American conservatism. That fused position recognizes at one and the same time the transcendent goal of human existence and the primacy of the freedom of the person in the political order. Indeed, it maintains that the only possible ultimate vindication of the freedom of the individual person rests upon a belief in his overriding value as a person, a value based upon transcendent considerations. And it maintains that the duty of men is to seek virtue; but it insists that men cannot in actuality do so unless they are free from the constraint of the physical coercion of an unlimited state. For the simulacrum of virtuous acts brought about by the coercion of superior power, is not virtue, the meaning of which resides in the free choice of good over evil.

Therefore, the conservative—who understands also that power in this world will always exist and cannot be wished out of existence—stands for division of power, in order that those who hold it may balance each other and the concentration of overweening power be foreclosed. He stands for the limitation of the power of the state, division of power within the state, a free economy, and prescriptive protection of the rights of individual persons and groups of individual persons against the state. But he does not see the state as an absolute evil; he regards it as a necessary institution, so long as it is restricted to its natural functions: the preservation of domestic peace and order, the administration of justice, and defense against foreign enemies.

In the political sphere the conservative consensus presently emerging in the United States regards freedom as an end; but, although it is an end at the political level, it is a means—as is the whole political structure—to the higher ends of the human person. Without reference to those ends, it is meaningless. While that conservative consensus regards the untrammeled state as the greatest of political evils, it does not regard the state itself as evil so long as it is limited to its proper functions, so long as the force it wields is effectively limited by a constitutional understanding of the bounds beyond which that force may not intrude upon the sacred sphere of the individual person, and so long as that understanding is enforced by division and balance of powers.

The American conservative today, therefore, although he owes much to the libertarian stream in Western thought— its deep concern with freedom, its analysis of the political structure in terms of freedom, its understanding of the vital importance of the free-market economy for a free modern society— cannot accept the fundamental philosophical position, sometimes rationalist, sometimes utilitarian, which is the historical foundation of pure libertarianism. He cannot posit freedom as an absolute end nor can he, considering the condition of man, deny the role of the state as an institution necessary to protect the freedoms of individual persons from molestation, whether through domestic or foreign force. He is not, in a word, a utopian. He knows that power exists in the world and that it must be controlled, not ignored with wishful utopian thinking.

The contemporary American conservative not only rejects the authoritarian extremes of nineteenth-century conservatism and the extremes of nineteenth-century rationalist and utilitarian liberalism, but, in a sense, he goes behind the so often sterile nineteenth-century conservative-liberal controversy, to found his outlook upon that earlier synthesis of belief in transcendent value and in human freedom which the Founders of the Republic embodied in their lives and actions, discursively expressed in their writings and their debates, and bequeathed to us in the body politic they constituted.

Their political concern was the establishment of freedom and its preservation, but they understood that freedom is meaningless unless founded upon "the laws of Nature and of Nature's God." The protection of the free energies of free individuals, so that they might in liberty strive to live according to those laws, was their most intimate concern. But they knew that in the defense of liberty a properly constituted state is necessary, not only to "establish Justice [and] insure domestic Tranquility" but also to "provide for the common Defense." They did not content themselves with abstract analyses of liberty; they proclaimed in unambiguous tones, "Give me liberty or give me death." To that wager of fate, "with a firm reliance on the Protection of Divine Providence," they pledged "our Lives, our Fortunes, and our sacred Honor."

"Providence," "honor," "valor," are concepts that the dry utilitarianism of the "pure libertarian" cannot compass. The pity is that when the soul cannot respond to those words, all the brave intellectual structure turns to cobwebs; and the champion of a freedom unfounded on the deep nature of man and the constitution of being pipes out: "Give me liberty if it doesn't mean risking war; give me liberty, but not at the risk of nuclear death."

Why Freedom

(National Review, September 25, 1962)

In reply to Brent Bozell's article, "Freedom or Virtue?" (September 11), I should like first to plead innocent to his friendly indictment that I have "labored earnestly in recent years to promote and justify modern American conservatism as a 'fusion' of the libertarian and traditionalist points of view." Rather I (and others with whom I share a common outlook—he mentions Stanton Evans by name) have been attempting something very different from an ideological—and eclectic—effort to create a position abstractly "fusing" two other positions. What I have been attempting to do is to help articulate in theoretical and practical terms the instinctive consensus of the contemporary American conservative movement—a movement which is inspired by no ideological construct, but by devotion to the fundamental understanding of the men who made Western civilization and the American republic.

That consensus simultaneously accepts the existence of an objective moral and spiritual order, which places as man's end the pursuit of virtue, *and* the freedom of the individual person as a decisive necessity for a good political order. From the first of these principles it draws as corollaries its opposition to positivism, relativism, and materialism; from the second, it draws its demand for principled limitation of the power of the state, for the strictest guarantees that the power of the state will be foreclosed from interference in the moral and spiritual sphere, in the economic sphere, or with the liberties of individual persons—so long as they do not by force or fraud coerce others.

That this double allegiance to virtue and to freedom is the over-all consensus of contemporary American conservatism, the most cursory acquaintance with the conservative movement demonstrates. Mr. Bozell, I am sure, would agree that this is the actuality, no matter how much he may disapprove of it.

Every important publication of the movement exhibits the two motifs; so do the platforms of both conservative youth organizations, the Intercollegiate Society of Individualists and the Young Americans for Freedom; and the most widely read conservative book of the century, *The Conscience of a Conservative*, is an epitome of that unity.

If I have "labored" to demonstrate the potential congruity

of the "traditionalist" and "libertarian" positions, it has not been because I was "attempting to promote . . . a fusion," but because I have thought that the rigid positions of doctrinaire traditionalists and doctrinaire libertarians were both distortions of the same fundamental tradition and could be reconciled and assimilated in the central consensus of American conservatism. It is only when virtue or freedom is wrenched out of the intrinsic interdependence in which they have existed in our tradition that ideological opposition arises.

I have recently dealt in these pages with some of the results that occur when virtue is denied as an end for men and freedom raised to the sole end of man's existence. In "The Twisted Tree of Liberty," I tried to demonstrate that freedom, essential though it is as a condition for the virtuous life, is by itself without content or purpose if the existence of an objective moral order which men should strive to understand and move towards is not accepted. The results of such ideological abstraction of freedom from its functional foundation in the human condition are observable again and again as the pure libertarian develops his position—in the craven retreat before Communist tyranny of the pure libertarian of the nuclear pacifist breed, as in the arid subhuman image of man and the calculated cruelties of Ayn Rand.

If on the other hand, freedom is denied as a necessary condition of a good political order, and the state is endowed with the right to endorse virtue upon individual persons, a parallel distortion occurs. Virtue, which is only virtue when freely chosen (this Mr. Bozell at bottom admits—as, being a Christian, he must admit), is made inaccessible to the coerced citizen, wherever and to the degree that the state compels his action. His actions may look like virtuous actions, but they are the actions of an automaton and cannot be truly virtuous, because being unfree to reject virtue, he is unfree to choose it. Even this assumes, however, that the men who hold the power of the state will use that power to enforce actions that are the simulacrum of virtue. But Lord Acton's insight still remains true, that there is in power a tendency to corrupt, and the more absolute the power, the more absolute the corruption. The experience of mankind has demonstrated this sad truth, however different may have been the philosophical foundations of those who held power that approached the absolute. Diocletian and Constantine, Inquisitionist and Cromwellian, Nazi and Communist—all have exhibited the corruption that power brings in its train. Each had a vision of how men ought to live and was determined to force that vision upon those subject to their will. If the state is endowed with the power to enforce virtue, the men who hold that power will enforce their own concepts as virtuous.

Such a state of affairs is the opposite pole—and as great a distortion—as the anarchistic worship of freedom as an absolute good without purpose or end. It is theocracy. That is, it is giving to some men the right and the power to enforce upon other men their own particular, limited and perforce distorted, finite view of the Infinite—of God's will. And this remains true whether their God is the pagan god of Diocletian, or the Christian God of Constantine, Philip II and Cromwell, or the *Volk* of the Nazis, or the dialectical materialist History of the Communists.

Mr. Bozell denies that his is a theocratic outlook, and indeed the positions he has taken in practice are far from theocratic, far from authoritarian. But the theoretical presuppositions put forward in *Freedom or Virtue?* nevertheless lead directly to theocracy. Whenever he wishes to justify his accord with practical measures conducive to freedom, he falls back upon the safeguards of "prudence." In *his* prudence I would have great confidence; but prudence is an art inherent in the men who exercise it. To hope that the men who exercise theocratic power will be prudent is a slender reed on which to base the defense of the freedom integrally necessary to a virtuous society.

For men imbued with the certainty of their vision of reality it will always be difficult to restrain the temptation to enforce

that vision upon others and thus to deprive them of the right
freely to choose the good. It is the glory of Western civilization,
with its Christian understanding of the shimmering tension
between freedom and virtue, that it has in its essence held
firm to its insistence upon both—although to the doggedly
rational mind, the paradox of virtue in freedom is as much
"a folly to the Greeks and a scandal to the Jews" as the Incarnation itself, which is the ground from which the strength to hold
this paradoxical belief proceeds.

Mr. Bozell attacks "humanism" as the sin which pervades
the belief in freedom, but there is a humanism implicit in the
glorification of man by the Incarnation. It is his rejection of
the humanist element in the Western and Christian tradition
that leads Mr. Bozell to his insistence upon the radical opposition
of the good society to the free society. The humanist side of that
tradition has always held in check the Puritanical and Jansenist
drive towards a conception of man as a totally corrupt creature.
Realizing his tendencies towards corruption, the balanced tradition of the West has seen him at the same time as a son of God,
who by the aid of Grace and of the reason implanted in him
possesses the highest of potentialities.

Therefore, it has conceived virtue not merely in the negative
terms of subduing evil inclinations, but also in positive terms—
in terms of achievement of potentialities which, although finite,
are immeasurably great. Rejecting the Manichean disdain for the
things of this world, it has considered the joy of created being
as a high good. Its concept of virtue is positive, the performing
of acts honorable, noble, valorous, glorious, generous. The free
law of love is its highest command, not the meticulous performance of scheduled actions, the chalking up of gold stars
and black marks in the records of a Divine Scorer.

Freedom, then, is a necessary political condition of a virtuous
society, not only because the high likelihood is that the standards imposed by men with the power of the state would not in
fact be virtuous standards; but also because, even if they were
virtuous, to impose them upon individual persons would im-

mensely reduce their ability to act virtuously at all and absolutely destroy their potentiality for active, creative, positive
virtue.

The key to the preservation of freedom is the limitation of the
state. Political freedom can be defined as freedom from coercion
in life, limb, liberty, or property, by force or fraud; it has
nothing to do with the ideas, the persuasions, the customs
which go into forming every human person. To refuse to see,
as Mr. Bozell seems to do, the differences between coercive acts
against the person and the civilizational influences which help to
form the person, is to deny the difference between the authoritarian imposition of human power and the persuasive authority
of truth and good.

Furthermore, political freedom has no relation to the definition Mr. Bozell imposes upon the libertarian conservative, that
is, "the freedom to participate in the making of public policy."
This is emphatically *not* what is meant by political freedom.
What is meant by political freedom is the limitation of the
power of the state to the function of preserving a free order.
It demands that the state be prohibited from positive actions
affecting the lives of individual persons, except insofar as such
action is necessary to prevent the freedom of some from being
exercised to limit the freedom of others.

Political freedom emphatically has nothing to do with who
governs or who chooses the governors, but only with the strict
limitation of the powers of the governors, whoever they may be.

The contradiction which Mr. Bozell posits between "political
freedom" and "economic freedom" is a contradiction created out
of his own misunderstanding. The freedom of the economic
sphere from state interference is but one aspect of the freedom
of persons in other spheres of their life from state interference.
It is not possible for men to "exercise their political freedom
against their economic freedom," as Mr. Bozell maintains; it is
only possible for an overweening state to exercise its power
against men's free activities in the economic sphere. A free
economy is a condition of political freedom because it is an

aspect of political freedom—exactly as are freedom of persons in their daily lives, freedom of thought and press, and speech, freedom of worship.

If the goal of a free political order is accepted, there is no mystery of the sort Mr. Bozell professes to find in the principle that the state should be limited to the triple functions of defense against foreign enemies, preservation of internal order, and the administration of justice between man and man.

In fact, the derivation of this proposition is really no mystery to Mr. Bozell, as he makes clear a few lines later. He knows that it can be derived when freedom *is* considered as a political end, and certainly he is right that it could never be derived when society is considered as an "organism," of which men are cells. But to clear up whatever "mystery" there may be, I shall here briefly summarize how it is derived when men are thought of as persons for whom political freedom is morally vital. (For a further and more exhaustive consideration, I refer him, and any other readers who may be interested, to my book, *In Defense of Freedom: A Conservative Credo,* which will be published next month.)

Briefly, then: 1) There is great danger to human freedom, and thereby to the achievement of virtue, if any more power than that which is absolutely necessary is lodged in the same set of hands. 2) The state *is* a necessity as an institution to preserve the freedom of men from infringement by other men through domestic or foreign force or fraud; and to settle the disputes that occur when rights clash with rights. 3) From this necessity are derived the legitimate powers of the state: defense, the preservation of domestic order, the administration of justice. 4) The exercise, however, of these necessary functions requires a dangerous concentration of power—the monopoly of legally and socially accepted force. Any additional control over individual persons in any sphere of their lives adds dangerously to this already dangerous concentration of power. 5) No other activities of men, except these three legitimate functions of the state, require the monopoly of force. All others can be performed by individual persons and voluntary associations of persons. 6) Since the power of the state is dangerous to begin with, and since all other functions beyond its essential three can be performed by men otherwise, the preservation of a truly free political order demands the limitation of the state to these functions.

To summarize: The principle that the political order must be a free order if men are to have the maximum possibilities of achieving virtue is, I maintain, inextricably linked, in the tradition of the West and the tradition of the American republic, with the principle that the goal of men is virtue. They are both essential principles of conservatism—which by definition is devoted to the preservation, maintenance and extension of that tradition. Conservatism, therefore, unites the "traditionalist" emphasis upon virtue and the "libertarian" emphasis upon freedom. The denial of the claims of virtue leads not to conservatism, but to spiritual aridity and social anarchy; the denial of the claims of freedom leads not to conservatism, but to authoritarianism and theocracy.

When these attitudes are only emphases, differences of stress among conservatives, they can produce a fruitful and healthy dialogue. But neither the libertarian nor the traditionalist can totally deny the ends of the other without moving outside of the conservative dialogue and breaking continuity with the Western tradition. That tradition bears onward from generation to generation the understanding—rooted in the Christian vision of the nature and destiny of man—of the primary value, under God, of the individual person. From his nature arises his duty to virtue and his inalienable right to freedom as a condition of the pursuit of virtue.

Neither virtue nor freedom alone, but the ineluctable combination of virtue *and* freedom, is the sign and spirit of the West.

The West is in decay not, as Mr. Bozell asserts, because "the free society has come to take priority over the good society"; but because freedom has declined as virtue has declined. The recovery of the one demands the recovery of the other; the recovery of both is the mission of conservatism today. *Virtue in freedom*—this is the goal of our endeavor.

Professor Walter J. Berns in his book, Freedom, Virtue and the First Amendment, *had somewhat earlier taken a position analogous to that of Mr. Bozell. The column which follows was largely inspired by my differences with that book.*

Freedom, Virtue, and Government
(National Review, October 12, 1957)

It is a curious fact that certain justices of the Supreme Court have in recent years been dubbed "libertarian," while, except on certain very special questions, their political philosophy is in fact the very opposite of libertarian. Justices Douglas, Black and Warren would come very low indeed on any scale that measured the intensity and breadth of their devotion to the liberty of the person. And lower still would come their admiring constituency among those who write and teach and influence opinion on these matters.

Where the issue is one of licensing a Communist to engage in activities directly conducive to the destruction of all freedom (and therefore criminal *per se*), they press the concept of individual freedom beyond the limits of elementary reason and prudence. But where no criminal construction could conceivably be placed upon the free action of the individual person, they and their predecessors again and again have ruled in destruction of the foundations upon which individual freedom is possible: impairing the freedom of contract in the gold-clause cases; upholding the social-security acts that prevent a man from providing for his future—or not providing for it—as seems proper to him; forcing a citizen of the United States under the rule of an alien court.

The history of the past quarter of a century is a continuing record of government conducted in the image of the social worker, of the probing busybody, who knows better than the man who is living it how each citizen's life should be lived. Since 1937 the Supreme Court has happily gone along striking down constitutional guarantees against this kind of government. Lately it has taken to originating the game itself—as in the integration decisions. When the hunt is up to find some new area in which to eliminate the freedom of individuals to act outside of government control, Black, Douglas and Warren show the quality of their "libertarianism" by joining the New-Dealing Frankfurters and the Moderate-Republican Burtons in sealed and sacred unanimity.

Nor is this to be wondered at. The so-called libertarians share with their New-Deal and Moderate-Republican colleagues the belief that it is possible for government to enforce the good. The calamitous socialization which has descended upon these United States in the years since 1932 is grounded in the very situation against which the framers of our Constitution sought to guard: the use of government to impose upon men positive rules of action.

It has been argued by some conservative opponents of the tendency of contemporary thought and politics that the mischief does not arise at all from the use of government for the purpose of enforcing a putative good, but only from the imputation of good to ends which are in fact evil. Government, they maintain, is the proper agency for the enforcement of proper ends upon individual men. It is only that Liberals use it for the wrong ends. Those who argue thus are saying in effect that if only governmental power can be seized and held by governors imbued with true principle, men can be forced to be virtuous.

But, in fact, the only "virtue" that can be so enforced is virtue defined in one of the ways the contemporary relativists define it (acceptance of custom, adjustment to the norm). External coercion could only make men "virtuous" if virtue consisted of conforming one's behavior to the kind of behavior those with power prescribe as good. But if virtue is the movement of a man toward an absolute Good exhibited by reason and by love, then by its very nature it cannot be forced, it must be chosen. If I may be permitted to quote Aristotle, since opponents of the position I am maintaining sometimes adduce his authority: ". . . in order to be good one must be in a certain state when one does the several acts, *i.e., one must do them as a result of choice* and for the sake of the acts themselves." (My emphasis.)

Truly to be able to choose good, however, demands a freedom and autonomy which unfortunately also makes it possible for men to choose evil. Otherwise there is no meaning to choice, and virtue in the true sense is impossible. Therefore, the *power* of government is a necessary power to prevent the freedom of one man from interfering with the *freedom* of another. But individual and corporate *teaching* of the truth and the good is the only activity whereby men can influence other men toward *virtue*.

The limited government that the founders of the Republic established presupposed a devotion to a common heritage, a common understanding of virtue and the good, based upon tradition and reason. The repudiation of the heritage by the Liberal pseudo-libertarians of the day transforms their boasted devotion to personal liberty into wanton presentation of privilege to the beneficiaries of approved intellectual fashion.

But indignation at their misuse of the concept of freedom in the service of the instinct for amoral power will help little if it leads to contempt for freedom and disdain for the concept of limited government which is the political foundation of freedom.

Only men who choose the good freely can be virtuous. It is true that the nature of virtue is not such that men will always bid highest for it in "the free market place of ideas"; but neither is it a cultural badge, like the pigtail of the Chinese of the Manchu dynasty, or the social-security number of the American worker, which can be imposed upon the person by the authority of the state. It is best nurtured by the teaching and example of family and church (one could add the school, if our schools had not become creatures of the state); and it is best exercised in a social situation where government limited to the preservation of order and the administration of justice has as its essential aim the guarantee of the maximum of possible freedom to each individual person.

From a very different angle, Professor Morton Auerbach, both in his book The Conservative Illusion *and in an article in* National Review, *attacked the consensus of contemporary American conservatism as an inchoate contradiction of classically conservative and classically liberal assumptions. I, among others, replied to him.*

The Separation of Powers

(National Review, January 30, 1962)

In his reply to Stanton Evans' review of *The Conservative Illusion,* Professor Auerbach restates more succinctly the central contentions of the book itself: 1) that a belief in transcendental truth is incompatible with a belief in individual human freedom, and 2) that therefore the rapidly growing American conservatism of today is an intellectual monstrosity rent by contradictions.

What Professor Auerbach fails to understand is that the Christian understanding of the nature and destiny of man, which is the foundation of Western civilization, is always and everywhere what conservatives strive to conserve. That understanding accepts the existence of aboslute truth and good and at the same time recognizes that men are created with the free will to accept or reject that truth and good. Conservatism, therefore, demands both the struggle to vindicate truth and good and the establishment of conditions in which the free will of individual persons can be effectively exercised.

Conservatism sees two overriding evils in society. On the one hand, it fights against determinist philosophies, which equate truth and good with whatever happens historically to succeed, and against relativist philosophies, which deny the very existence of truth and good. On the other hand, it resists the growth of a monopoly of power, usually exercised through the state, which suppresses or distorts the exercise of free will by individual persons. It believes, further, that such a monopoly of force can be as thoroughly and evilly exercised by a "democratic" majority as by an "aristocratic" minority or by a single tyrant.

Professor Auerbach is right when he says that conservatives oppose the contemporary aggrandizement of the state and its movement towards totalitarianism (what he so gently characterizes as "the administrative state"), for the aggrandizing state is the enemy of the freedom of the person. He is wrong when he regards such opposition as incompatible with "medieval" belief in "natural law and religious orthodoxy." Indeed, the Middle Ages maintained a separation of powers both through the geographically decentralized institutions of feudalism and through the balance of powers between church and state. That separation of powers placed feudal Europe, as Professor Wittfogel has demonstrated in his *Oriental Despotism,* among the freest societies in the history of man.

American conservatives do not wish to return to medieval conditions. They do wish, in modern conditions, to preserve and develop the tension between the transcendent ends of man and the freedom through which he can attain those ends, the tension which Western civilization has always expressed. They will not be diverted from pursuing that course by semantic or historicist arguments based upon the struggles between nineteenth-century conservatives and nineteenth-century liberals. The nineteenth century, heir to the disruption of the French Revolution, was a brief and distorted era in the long history of Western civilization. In its struggles there was truth on both sides, and from both sides the contemporary American conservative can learn. But it is the authentic tradition of the West which he is striving to recover, a tradition which goes far deeper than the parochial disputes of the nineteenth century.

The American conservative has indeed a special heritage, the discussions and the achievements of the Founders of the American Constitution (Madison pre-eminently), men who established the highest political form the West has yet created to express the tension of transcendent truth and human freedom. The political structure they left us has its contradictions, no doubt; but, like the contradictions Professor Auerbach finds among American conservatives today, they reflect the imperfect state of man and the tension within which he must live if he is to be true to his nature, striving towards transcendent ends in freedom.

In many ways similar to that of Professor Auerbach was the criticism of conservatism by Professor William J. Newman.

Caricature of Conservatism

(National Review, June 17, 1961)

It is a continuing mystery how the contemporary Liberal, committed as he is to political concepts and programs that aggrandize the coercive state, can continue to pose as the champion of freedom and to castigate conservatives as its enemy. This is a feat that can be accomplished only by blindly embracing ideological shibboleths and totally ignoring reality. Yet it is a feat that is accomplished constantly—one which is repeated more and more often as the challenge of a resurgent conservatism forces upon the Liberal Establishment an attempted confutation, in place of the bland ignoring of serious conservative thought which has been its tactic until recently.

Within the past year or two, innumerable articles in the scholarly journals and the magazines of opinion, as well as a number of books, have been devoted to this endeavor. The most recent example of the *genus*, a book called *The Futilitarian Society*, written by William J. Newman, a professor at Boston University, will serve to typify others. Although it is a partic-

ularly silly and flatulent example, Professor Newman's very
verbosity and naiveté bring the salient points of the general
thesis into clearer relief.

The intellectual strategy of the endeavor can be readily identified—although the premises on which it is based are never
quite openly stated, being rather assumed and implied. They are
assumed as the obvious beliefs of anyone who does not accept
obscurantist nonsense about eternal values and that sort of thing.
They are implied as the necessary corollaries of the humanly
directed "change" which is constantly projected by Mr. Newman
as the only alternative to the static society bereft of freedom for
which he insists conservatism stands. But that "change," which he
regards as the only criterion of freedom and which is to be created
by conscious human will, can only be the social engineering
dear to the collectivist mind, whether in its Marxist or Liberal
incarnation.

Here is the absurdity. Conservatives are branded as enemies
of freedom—because they insist upon an eternal order of being
and a fixed goal of virtue, which is the goal towards which free
men will move if they are to fulfill their destiny as beings created
with the freedom to accept or reject that destiny. Mr. Newman, and those whose critique of conservatism he represents,
fly in horror from the thought that freedom can have any
meaning unless it is absolutely free-wheeling; unless it is choice
with no consequences, no responsibility; unless it is nothing
but a free act of choice suspended in vacuum. But since in
the real world freedom must be freedom to choose between
concrete alternatives, the Liberal critic of conservatism is left
with change itself as an absolute. Since, however, impersonal
change as an absolute is itself intolerable to the human mind
because of its anarchic, formless meaninglessness, he falls back
upon directed change, change directed by collectivities, which
by their very nature utterly destroy the freedom of the individual person.

Within the "limitations" of reality, of the constitution of being,
within the "limitations" that the duty to virtuous action imposes

upon men, the conservative view of the human situation places no curb on human freedom. It insists upon the authority of truth, but by its very recognition of that authority it insisits equally upon the sanctity of the individual person's freedom to accept or reject that authority. It does so because it knows that virtue cannot be imposed by external earthly power; because it knows that freedom has nothing to do with "change," with "innovation," with "creative acts," with "invention" (as Mr. Newman would have it), but is a necessity integral to the God-given choice of virtue or evil, of Heaven or Hell. Therefore, the conservative strains toward a society in which the freedom of the individual person in all its aspects will be protected to the highest degree possible, while at the same time every energy of the leaders of society, of its educational system and its influential organs, will be devoted to persuasion towards virtue.

This central understanding of contemporary American conservatism, which is being worked out in the live and growing movement of recent years, Mr. Newman succeeds in avoiding by never looking at that movement as a whole; by mushing together in a single conspectus true conservatives with men like Walter Lippmann, Louis Hartz, Daniel Boorstin, Daniel Bell (because they like Locke, or talk of "the end of ideology" and lack the true radical fire); and by projecting something called "a conservative mood," symbolized by Eisenhower and the Eisenhower years.

National Review is never mentioned in his compendious pages. Of the proliferating conservative movement on the campuses and among the young generally, of the Sharon Statement which confutes his caricature of conservatism, he has nothing to say. He does mention *Modern Age* and *The Conscience of a Conservative*, but only to sneer or to quote out of context isolated passages from the intense and serious discussion that has been proceeding among conservatives.

He utterly ignores the understanding the West has painfully and gloriously achieved of the eternal tension of virtue and freedom, in order to establish a simplistic ideological diagram

on the basis of which to categorize conservatism as the enemy
of freedom. This is not the intellectual discourse Liberals maintain they champion; it is a caricature of discourse.

Father Stanley Parry in Modern Age *had maintained that the
sickness of our civilization was so profound that it was beyond
recovery. Only a new age of prophecy, which could lay the
foundations for a new civilization, he insisted, could recover
fundamental values, and therefore conservatism as well as
Liberalism was irrelevant.*

Conservatism and Crisis: A Reply to Fr. Parry

(Modern Age, Winter 1962–63)

There is a sense in which Disraeli's dictum on "the two nations"
is true of the United States today. But it is true not in Disraeli's
—or in Karl Marx's—sense of a profound gulf between a poor
and frustrated majority and a powerful and wealthy minority.
The opposition between "the two nations" that constitute the
United States today is characterized by spiritual and intellectual
differences, not by differences of wealth and economic power.

A profound chasm has come into being between the beliefs
and instincts of the solid citizenry of the country and the ideology of the dominant section of those whose powers and talents
determine the tone and direction of our national life. For some
decades now, the tradition of Western civilization—both generally and in its specific American form—has been under concerted attack from a corrosive and nihilistic ideology, which has
perversely seized upon the century's broadening in factual
knowledge as a charter for frontal attack upon the age-old
wisdom of the civilization concerning the nature and destiny of
men. Positivist in its epistemology, relativist in its ontolgy (if
ontology is a proper category for such metaphysical nihilism),
utopian, to the point of *hubris* and beyond, in its conviction

that human beings can be manipulated and "structured" like beams of steel to sastisfy an engineer's blueprint, this ideology takes political form in what today is called Liberalism.

It is this outlook which characterizes the presently predominant intellectual and governmental leadership of the nation. But, although that leadership maintains itself in power upon the basis of a quasi-monopolistic control of the channels of communication and by proposing speciously attractive programs, appealing to apparent immediate interests of sections of the electorate, it has not succeeded in seriously establishing its ideology in the minds and souls of the American people.

Making free with Toynbee's phrases, I would maintain that there is indeed a "schism in the body politic," but that there is not so far in the generality of Americans a "schism in the soul." It is here that I would begin to take exception to Fr. Stanley Parry's consideration of the present state of our society ["The Restoration of Tradition," *Modern Age,* Spring, 1961].

His analysis of the forms of social crisis is brilliant. In particular, his discussion of the deepest form of social crisis, what he calls "civilizational crisis," is profound and accurate; but I challenge his premise that we in the United States are in the grip of a crisis of this type. Such a crisis Fr. Parry defines as involving "a falling out of the area of experience of large segments of previously held truth"—that is, the destruction of fundamental traditional beliefs in the minds of the people who make up the civilization.

No one can deny, of course, that the impact of the views and attitudes of the intellectual leadership has affected and distorted the form in which traditional truths are held and understood by the American people; but all evidence points to the essential survival of that tradition in the *ethos* of the people. And when I say "the people," I do not mean only "the man on the street"; I mean also the great majority of professionals and businessmen and community leaders, of Congressmen and state senators and legislators and municipal officials. The other "nation," powerful though it is, is a limited and shallow stratum; sometimes described as the Liberal Establishment, it is constantly horrified and constantly thwarted by the refusal of the solid strata of American society to acquiesce in its outlook. To give but a few random examples: its "sophisticated" moves towards appeasement of Communism have brought into existence a widespread and deeply rooted anti-Communist movement; its flossy "educational" projects—projects without substance and totally unrelated to true education—are being defeated in bond vote after bond vote in communities all over the country; the socializing projects of the bureaucracy and the Executive again and again are thwarted by the Congress; and, most offensive to the Establishment, a strong and solid conservatism with firm intellectual foundations is arising to challenge it at every level of American life.

These are not the symptoms of a dying civilization. This is not Fr. Parry's "change in the very structure of the community's experience of truth in history." This is not Toynbee's "schism in the soul"; it is more akin to Spengler's figure of "pseudomorphosis." The essential health of the American tradition remains vigorously alive; but it is imprisoned in the mould that a dominant Liberalism has for a time succeeded in imposing upon it. Whatever the case may be in the other provinces of Western civilization, in the United States our crisis is not of the "dissolution" of tradition; it is a crisis brought about by the sad fact that those whose duty it is to articulate the tradition have betrayed it. Our crisis calls not for a new concept of truth to form a new tradition, but for intellectual, moral and political leaders who can articulate again and develop in contemporary terms a tradition that in its essence is still doggedly defended by the people.

Therefore, the opposition of conservatism and Liberalism is not, as Fr. Parry maintains, irrelevant to the decisive issue; it *is* the issue. Were our crisis a "civilizational crisis" in his sense, a deep-going "change from order and truth to disorder and negation," a change shared in by the whole of society, then it would be true that conservatism is simply a "formula for escaping inevitabilities in history." For then the conservative effort to vindicate the fundamental spirit and understanding of our civilization, its "shared participation of truth," would be meaningless. If the civilization were indeed so dead in the hearts of the people, then the only adequate response *would* be to drive free of the civilizational debris and devote all energies to proclaiming essential truth in timeless terms, without respect or piety towards the shaped forms and the rich heritage in which, as citizens of Christendom and of the American Republic, our understanding of truth lives.

If this were so, then Fr. Parry's "prophetic response," not conservatism, would be the stance of a man who was a man. There are times when so deeply revolutionary a response *is* demanded —for the "prophetic response" is a revolutionary response. It challenges not merely the perversions and distortions of truth which have grown up in the civilization's perception of truth and in its body politic, but it challenges the very form the civilization's perception of truth has taken. It says, not only that the vision of the civilization has been perverted, but that at its best it has become outmoded before a higher vision; that its very way of understanding and of guiding human life is no longer a way to truth and good, but has become an inhibiting limitation upon the spirit.

It is true that the prophetic *tone* has many levels. And when the conservative movement is embarked upon the course of combat against the perversion of a civilization, upon the course of restoring the civilization, that tone may well be necessary. There is something of the revolutionary, or, if you wish, counter-revolutionary, in the endeavor to wipe out the perversion of a civilization, to return to the source of its virtue, to re-assert and bring to fruition its pristine glory. But it is not in this sense that Fr. Parry, following Eric Voegelin, writes of "prophetic response." He means (this is why he regards the conservative enterprise as irrelevant) that our civilization has passed the point of no return. It has, to use his phrase, "fallen out of existence."

While I will not deny that such things have happened in history—to Sumeria, to Egypt, to the Classical world—I do not believe that Western Christendom has run its course. Whatever may be in store for it in the European land of its birth, I do not believe that in the United States, the most forward thrust and strongest bastion of the West, thirty years of Karl Marx, John Dewey, and Franklin Roosevelt have cast us adrift, "out of existence" in a civilizationless void.

Therefore, the contemporary American conservative effort is far from irrelevant. Rather it is directed with precision towards overcoming the actual spiritual, moral and political crisis we do face today—not Fr. Parry's systemic "civilizational crisis," but a schism in our society between the outlook, the "perception of truth," of those who hold decisive political and ideological power and that of the people as a whole. Having said this, I must add that a "civilizational crisis" in Fr. Parry's terms is not impossible in the not-too-distant future; if the leadership of our society remains much longer in the hands of those who hold it today, it is possible that they will succeed in totally destroying the Western consciousness, the instinct for virtue and freedom, which still informs the *ethos* of Americans beyond the direct influence of the Establishment. The problem can be stated in the starkest terms: can the men of the rising conservative movement in America expel the dominant Establishment from its positions of control before they succeed in bringing about the corruption of the American people in the image of their own corruption?

This is not simply—perhaps not primarily—a political problem. It is a confrontation at every level: intellectual, moral, social, political. The conservative task would seem to be a heroic task. All the heights of our society—with the partial exception of the Congress and the state legislatures—are occupied by forces inspired by a Liberalism philosophically nihilistic to the genius of Western civilization. That task would be more than heroic, it would be a valiant but hopeless Lost Cause, were it not that the attacking conservative forces can draw upon the energies and vitality of those who make up the body of the social order.

Fr. Parry's insistence upon the deep and final character of the crisis of our civilization, and his insistence upon the irrelevance of the conservative-Liberal polarity, stems, I believe, from his failure to understand the specific genius of Western civilization which inspired our Constitution and the men who created it and guided the Republic in its early years. They created a political instrumentality congruent with the deep Western fusion of belief in the authority of absolute truth and good with belief in the dignity and freedom of the individual person. This was an epochal leap forward in the development of the Western and Christian vision of the majesty of God and the freedom of man. Fr. Parry condemns the contemporary American conservative devotion to this breath-taking vision of human potentiality under God (he calls it "spiritual individualism") as a hopeless and fatal "refusal to consider the issue of substantive truth." He ranges it alongside of Liberalism and reaction and economism as a "partial response" to our crisis—a response doomed to disaster because it does not come to grips with the truth of the human condition.

He fails completely to understand that the great social and political problem of Western civilization—how to establish an order that makes possible the flowering of devotion to truth and good and simultaneously preserves the freedom of the individual person—is here solved in principle for the first time. The key is the limitation of the power of the state—that is, of the power of some men to impose their beliefs on other men—while to the natural leaders of the social order is given the duty of leading and persuading their fellow men in the paths of justice and truth. Where has there ever been a society at once so noble and so free as the American Republic in the first half century of its existence? And what destroyed the promise of that idyllic spring but the successive infringements upon the concept of divided and limited governmental power, which are historically symbolized (each time more catastrophically) by the development of mass democratism in the 1830's, by the undermining of the sovereignty of the several states in the 1860's, and by the naturalization in this country of the theory and practice of twentieth-century collectivism in the 1930's?

Because Fr. Parry conceives freedom only as a by-product, not as a primary condition, of a good social order, he does not understand the character of the sickness of our society: the displacement of freedom in behalf of what those with power think the good to be. It does not matter here that I would agree with Fr. Parry that their concept of the good is disastrously wrong, totally out of accord with the constitution of being; the evidence of historical experience confirms what the founders of the Republic drew from the insight of the West: if the freedom of individual persons is not guaranteed by the arrangements of the political order, power always corrupts, even when the motives of those who use it to enforce their beliefs are beneficent. This is not to deny the necessity of devotion to virtue in the persons who make up a social order, and particularly in those who hold positions of influence in it, if such an order is to survive. But to affirm the necessity of virtue as an end for men does not require the subordination of freedom. Rather, if individual persons, who are the only spiritually significant entities in the social order, are to achieve virtue, they must be free. The responsibility for recognizing the demands of virtue, articulating the modes of virtue, and inculcating virtue cannot rest in any social organism, but only in individual persons. The coercive organs of society cannot establish or enforce virtue, since by its nature virtue must be the free choice of persons. The attempt to enforce it by power turns gold into dross.

The deep understanding that the Founders of our Republic derived from the essential Christian and Western recognition of the mutual interdependence of virtue and freedom, they made socially actual in the institutions and the *ethos* of the Republic. Fr. Parry rejects that high point in Western history; he maintains that to posit virtue and freedom as interdependent necessities of the social order, and to place the responsibility for virtue upon   the individual, is to neglect "the problem of right social order and in doing so [to neglect] the central problem of civilizational crisis." But this "spiritual individualism" *is* our tradition. It is this understanding that still remains in the hearts of the American people, inarticulate, instinctive perhaps, but firmly held. And it is to the articulation, the renewal, the development in contemporary conditions of their vision that the rising American conservative leadership is devoted.

There is no certainty that this leadership will in sufficient time achieve the intellectual and political victory necessary to insure the triumph of the spirit of Western civilization it embodies. But if it does not, that will be its failure; it will not be because it has embarked upon a hopeless endeavor. For the West is not dead in spirit; its glorious vision—the highest ever achieved by men—remains.

It is not only from the collectivist riders of power abroad and at home that defeat can come. The tenuous tension between the claims of virtue and the claims of freedom can be upset as well by men who—although they hate tyranny and collectivism with a fierce hatred—blind themselves to the central truth of the West, that neither virtue nor freedom can be made the end in a social order at the expense of the other without spiritual disaster.

Fr. Parry's Spenglerian pessimism on the fate of Western civilization rests on other foundations than Spengler's own; and he, basing himself upon a Rock firmer than any civilization, has hope, where Spengler had only grim fortitude. Civilizations have been born and civilizations have died; and it may be that ours will turn out to have been at the point of death in this mid-20th century. But whether this will be so or not depends upon our understanding and our energies. It depends upon our strength to recover the essence of our past, upon the imagination and vigor with which we can create the forms in which that essence can be realized under contemporary conditions. It depends upon the stamina and the courage we can summon to fight for the Western vision against the perversions that assail us from every side.

We may, I repeat, be defeated. But only then—after we have tried with our deepest energies to vindicate the truths of the West, when in our defeat the Western forms of truth no longer live in the hearts of men—only then will Fr. Parry's "prophetic response" be the part required of men devoted to truth and good. That day has not come. The West still lives. Today our need is not for "prophets" in Fr. Parry's sense—men who, with everything destroyed behind them, delve deep into reality to re-establish a form for truth when all forms lie in shards. In every aspect of human endeavor—philosophical, social, political, military—what we need are fighters for the reasoned and re-vealed incarnation of truth, virtue, freedom that Western civilization has been and can again be.

Two reviews of very different books enabled me to explore some relevant aspects of conservatism. The first was one by Peter Viereck, whose early reputation as a "New Conservative" gave him authority on conservative matters even after he had become a Stevensonian Democrat; the second was Barry Gold-water's The Conscience of a Conservative.

Counterfeit at a Popular Price

(National Review, August 11, 1956)

Peter Viereck writes, beyond doubt, the most breathless prose the English language is capable of accommodating. The style is the man. Frenetic, undisciplined, impulsive, and the sport of every eddy of the prevailing wind, he would seem to be asking only for derisive laughter when he puts himself forward as a conservative. Yet in the public eye he has achieved and retained that reputation. His publishers proclaim him "the leading spokesman of a philosophical new conservatism." And all the proper intellectual journals delight to confirm the title. Titillated by their daring, they present his "conservatism" just as proudly, and almost as often, as the more orthodox offerings of Arthur Schlesinger, Jr. or George Kennan or Richard Rovere.

The risk, indeed, is not very great. If it involves a speculative flutter on the long side in Metternich or Burke, it is always well hedged with short commitments in whatever is particularly obnoxious to the Liberals on the contemporary scene. Against Taft in '52 and McCarthy in '54, Mr. Viereck blossomed out as the conservative champion of "a better and wiser future under the better and wiser intellectualism of Stevenson."

His scent for the Enlightened Attitude is remarkably keen. That, however, is a trait which he shares with many other hucksters of the fashionable idea. What sets him apart is his versatility. One can distinguish in general between the less adept and the more adept players of this game, in that the common or garden pundit expands upon the fashion of the moment, while the accomplished expert is always a step—but not too long a step—ahead of it. Peter Viereck, with a truly astonishing ability which bodes well for his future, has acquired the knack of doing both at the same time.

On the one hand, he runs with the hares of the established fashion which writes off all opposition to the prevailing Liberal orthodoxy as the psychological resentment of unadjusted neurotics. Following T. W. Adorno, Richard Hofstadter and David Riesman (although with a peculiar elegance of diction all his own) Mr. Viereck attributes everything that is wrong in the land—the Stubborn Refusal of the Backward to accept the Social Humaneness and Social Democracy of the New Deal, or to understand and support the Sober Conservatism of Acheson and Harriman and Stevenson—to a psychopathological combination of "Midwest hick-Protestant revenge against [the] condescending East" with "the resentment of lower middle-class Celtic South Boston against Harvard."

But at the same time he hunts with the hounds on the trail

of next year's fashion, celebrating "the unadjusted man"—not too unadjusted, mind you, but just enough to get him in on the ground floor when the bull market in "adjustment" levels off and the smart operators shift to "the aristocracy of the expert" or "the personality of leadership" or whatever will be our next psychological panacea.

Perhaps one should not be too hard on Mr. Viereck. The game has to be played if one wants success upon the terms within which the Establishment is prepared to grant success. His tortured interpretations of Metternich as the *alter ego* of Franklin Roosevelt, and Burke as the model of Adlai Stevenson; his passionate affirmations that whatever else conservatism may be— socialist, statist, organicist—one thing it can never be is capitalist; all this may serve well enough to add a fillip to the pages of the Liberal journals. There they do little harm.

But when it comes to foisting Mr. Viereck upon the young and the uninstructed as an authority to whom they may turn to find out what conservatism is—this is carrying things too far. And his recent manual in the *Anvil* series, *Conservatism from John Adams to Churchill,* is a book explicitly designed for instruction of "the serious general reader and the college community." To represent, as the *Anvil* editors do, his confusion, inconsequence and Liberalism as the last word of a "distinguished scholar" of conservatism, is inexcusable. The book is no better than, and no different from his usual product; and it not improved by the addition of seventy-five pages of read-as-you-run snippets ripped out of context from the writings of thirty-one conservative authorities of the last century and a half. As a manual of conservatism, it is a counterfeit.

In an age in which grammar, rhetoric and logic are no longer taught, the mass production of counterfeits is likely to continue apace. Viereck is not the first, nor will he be the last, to succeed in passing off his unexceptionably Liberal sentiments as conservatism.

To make it completely impossible to bring off such preposterous masquerades would be, given the present state of critical intelligence, a utopian hope. But if only all those who speak seriously in the name of conservatism would come to see that reverence for tradition, essential though it is to any conservative tradition, is not by itself enough. The tradition is diverse and varied. Only a definite core of principle which, while fully respectful of the wisdom of our ancestors, provides a criterion for distinguishing their wisdom from their folly, can—among much more important results—snuff the pretensions of a Viereck.

A Man of Principle

(National Review, April 23, 1960)

When leading political figures can be distinguished one from the other mainly by their haircuts, and Presidential candidates are packaged and repackaged like cigarettes and automobiles (the New This and the Dynamic That), it is rare indeed to find a man in high office who stands for clear-cut principle and presents himself to the public on the basis of principle. It is rarer still when that principle is conservative principle.

But Senator Barry Goldwater, in his new book, *The Conscience of a Conservative* has dared to challenge the conventions of contemporary politics and the careful self-seeking calculations of the poll-peepers who rely on a boyish grin or a "sincere" personality to get them by, year after year, playing both ends against the middle.

Barry Goldwater, an outstanding Senator, a national leader of the Republican Party, has won his spurs in practical politics in two eminently successful campaigns in his native state. And his fellow Senators have a high enough regard for his knowledge of how to win elections to choose him as chairman of the Senate Republican Campaign Committee. When, therefore, he cuts across the shuffling double-talk of contemporary political discourse to speak sharply and clearly for a principled conservative program, he cannot be shunted aside with the noises about "the art of the possible" which the call for a clear conservative program usually evokes from those who put all their faith in the sovereign virtues of slick propaganda and "smart operating."

Forthright and solidly conservative, Senator Goldwater's book, from its foreword on the perennial truth of the conservative position to its last chapter on the Soviet danger, is a pleasure to read, for it is written with a lucidity and power that has long been missing from published statements designed to satisfy everyone and offend no one. At the very start he drives to the heart of the contention that conservatism is an impossible position to hold today because it is irrelevant to contemporary reality: *"Conservatism, we are told, is out of date. The charge is preposterous and we ought boldly to say so. The laws of God, and of nature, have no deadline. The principles on which the conservative political position is based . . . are derived from the nature of man, and from the truths that God has revealed about His creation."*

Nor is he content with stating this idea in general terms. He comes directly to grips with those "conservatives" who continually apologize for their conservatism; who dilute their championship of conservatism with fundamental concessions to the Liberal position; who compromise the conservative doctrine of limited government by accepting the essential premise of the welfare state with such specious phrases as "government with a heart"; or who blur the issue of freedom from the Leviathan state with cloudy affirmations about being "conservative when it comes to economic problems, liberal when it comes to human problems." Senator Goldwater cuts sharply through these confusions: *". . . the conservative has learned that the economic and spiritual aspects of man's nature are inexorably intertwined. He cannot be economically free, or even economically efficient, if he is enslaved politically; conversely, man's political freedom is illusory if he is dependent for his economic needs upon the State. . . . Throughout history, true conservatism has been at war equally with autocrats and with 'democratic' Jacobins. . . . Today [it] is at odds with dictators who rule by terror and equally with those gentler collectivists who ask our permission to play God with the human race."*

Having established these foundations for his positions, Senator Goldwater proceeds to an analysis of the dangers of centralized power, and then, in a series of succinct, hard-hitting chapters, to the development of a program for the extension of freedom at home and for the defense of freedom against Soviet aggression.

Justly and acutely he distinguishes the problem of states' rights from the problem of civil rights, vindicating the classical constitutional doctrine of state sovereignty while simultaneously supporting the enforcement of specifically asserted constitutional rights, such as the right to vote. Where the two problems have been confounded and the issue obfuscated by Liberal demagogy and judicial usurpation—as on federally enforced school integration—he patiently disentangles the confusion and firmly asserts basic principle: *"It may be just or wise or expedient for Negro children to attend the same schools as white children, but they do not have a* civil *right to do so which is protected by the federal constitution or which is enforceable by the federal government."*

On labor, his position is, of course, well known: the return of labor unions to their legitimate function of representing employees in bargaining with their employers over terms of employment; voluntary unionism; restraint of unions from corporate political activity; and the prohibition of industry-wide bargaining.

On the farm problem, he proposes uncompromising adherence to the principles of the free market and calls for "prompt and final termination of the farm-subsidy program."

Summarizing his domestic program, Senator Goldwater hits sharply at the concept of the welfare state, which has in recent years replaced the concept of socialism-through-nationalization as "the currently favored instrument of collectivization." Castigating the idea that there is some innate virtue in the expenditure of resources by government rather than by private individuals, he argues that the direct opposite is the case, that freedom is threatened even by present levels of government expenditure; and he proposes a "staged withdrawal" of the federal government from all areas that lie outside its constitutional mandate. Furthermore, he calls for abandonment of the graduated principle of taxation of incomes, estates and gifts (an aspect of fiscal policy which is directed not towards the raising of revenue, but towards redistribution of wealth, bringing in, as it does, less than $5 billion of the government's $80 billion current intake).

Turning from domestic to foreign policy, Senator Goldwater begins: *"And still the awful truth remains: We can establish the domestic conditions for maximizing freedom . . . and yet become slaves. We can do this by losing the Cold War to the Soviet Union."* And that war, he maintains, we are losing and will continue to lose until we recognize that we cannot have *"a peace in which freedom and justice will prevail . . . given the nature of Communism [until] Soviet power will no longer be in a position to threaten us and the rest of the world. A tolerable peace, in other words, must* follow *victory over Communism."* Which does not mean that we should provoke open war, but does mean that we should always be willing to risk war rather than surrender, and that our basic strategy should be devoted to pushing back the Soviet Empire, with the aim of eventually bringing about its disintegration.

To this end he proposes, among other measures: the strengthening of our military stance to achieve decisive military superiority; the restriction of foreign aid to true military allies; a formal declaration that we consider "the world Communist movement an outlaw in the community of civilized nations," and severance of diplomatic relations with all Communist governments, including that of the Soviet Union; encouragement and prudent, well-planned support of revolt by captive peoples against the Soviet Empire; aid to "friendly peoples that have the means and desire . . . to undertake offensive operations for the recovery of their homelands"; and the exploitation of enemy weaknesses by "military operations against vulnerable Communist regimes" in such situations as that which occurred in Hungary in 1956.

This is a startling program—both domestically and in foreign affairs—in the present atmosphere of don't-rock-the-boat contentment with aggrandizing bureaucracy at home and complacent faith in coexistence abroad. A startling program indeed —but nothing less would express the dictates of conservative principle in this crisis of the Republic. By stating it with such clarity and force, Senator Goldwater has placed himself in the first rank of American statesmen.

Friedrich A. Hayek is one of the great economists of the twentieth century. He is as well an opponent of socialism and contemporary Liberalism in all their manifestations; but he rejects certain aspects of the conservative position, calling himself not a conservative but a "Whig." In a review of his The Constitution of Liberty, *I analyzed as I saw them the strengths and weaknesses of his position.*

Champion of Freedom

(National Review, May 7, 1960)

Friedrich A. Hayek has weathered the storm of three decades of collectivist domination of economic thought, the hero of engagement after engagement, and has survived to survey a battlefield on which the tide of battle has begun to turn. The influence of economist-publicists like John Kenneth Galbraith on public policy is certainly still enormous; but in the academic world, the Keynesian and quasi-Marxist doctrines which reigned supreme for so long are today under the sharpest criticism among economists. The up-and-coming men in the profession, the most brilliant contributors to the journals are more and more economists of the Chicago School and of the Austrian School—followers of Hayek, of Frank Knight, of Ludwig von Mises.

Professor Hayek's new book, *The Constitution of Liberty,* is a monumental summation of the ideas for which he has fought and of the analysis through which he has arrived at those ideas. It is a fitting successor to the volumes of economic analysis (*Prices and Production* and *The Pure Theory of Capital*) which established him as the outstanding theoretical critic of Keynes in England in the thirties; to *The Road to Serfdom*, which struck a clarion note against British socialism and American welfarism alike in the forties; and to *Individualism and Economic Order* and *The Counter-Revolution of Science*, which dug deep to the roots of the scientistic and collectivist ideology of the twentieth century.

Of all these books, *The Constitution of Liberty* is nearest in theme to *The Road to Serfdom*. But *The Road to Serfdom* was—by its nature as a burning polemic directed against immediate encroaching dangers—brief in scope, primarily critical in manner, and essentially practical in approach. *The Constitution of Liberty* immensely expands the theme. It is rounded and deeply based; it is more positive in its prescription than polemical in its critique; it is a thoroughgoing effort to establish a theoretical foundation for the concept of a free society.

The first section, "The Value of Freedom," develops the philosophical ground of Professor Hayek's defense of freedom. The second section, "Freedom and the Law," is an historical and analytical examination of modern Western institutional efforts to guarantee a political basis for freedom. And the third, "Freedom in the Welfare State," discusses the most pressing dangers to freedom in contemporary society. Each section is developed with admirable logic and clarity. If I find myself in the fullest sympathy with the third section, and rather critical of the argument in the earlier part of the book, particularly the first section, it is not because of any shortcomings in Professor Hayek's treatment, but rather for reasons of philosophical difference in viewpoint.

His criticism of the progressive income tax and the use of that tax for purposes of social redistribution is a classic confutation of the taxing principles and practices which are almost universally accepted today, and upon which the entire structure of the welfare state rests. Equally powerful is his criticism of the social security system as established in all the major countries of the West. We in America, as he points out, are only at the beginning of the process, which has now reached the stage in Germany, for example, where 20 per cent of the national income is handed over to the social security administration. No society, Professor Hayek shows, no matter how "affluent," can afford such a diversion of national income into the hands of the bureaucrat, nor can it long remain affluent under such circumstances. He is likewise powerfully convincing on the built-in tendencies of the welfare state toward inflation, on the evils of the coercive aspects of labor unionism, on the bias of state education toward decay of quality.

I agree so strongly with almost all of Professor Hayek's analysis of contemporary social and economic problems, that it may seem somewhat churlish to note my disagreements with his theoretical position. I do so with the more diffidence— indeed with something approaching a sense of impiety— because I owe so much personally to his *Road to Serfdom,* which I read at a crucial moment in my life and which played a decisive part in helping me free myself from Marxist ideology. But I do not think that the utilitarian foundation upon which Professor Hayek bases his defense of freedom is either philosophically valid, or a bulwark strong enough to withstand the assaults of collectivist ideology.

That, empirically, freedom is the circumstance in which men can best achieve the ends they have chosen; that freedom is necessary for progress; that freedom minimizes the arrogant power of those who think they can engineer a solution to all social problems: all these arguments of his are undoubtedly true. But they are persuasive only to the degree that hypostasized ends of "society" are not preferred above the ends of individual men; or that equalitarianism is not preferred above progress; or that the "wisdom" of an elite of social engineers is not regarded as preferable to the choices of individual human beings.

Professor Hayek's defense of freedom is based upon preferences which we may share. But freedom as an essential right of men is founded not upon preferences, but upon the nature of men and the very constitution of being. It is inalienable and indefeasible as a right, not for any reasons of utility but because it is the true condition of man's created being. In the argument with collectivism, utilitarian reasons can always be answered with alternative utilitarian reasons. The final struggle with collectivism (at the deep level at which Professor Hayek invites us to consider the problem) can only be waged in terms of an understanding of the nature of man. It is because freedom is the truth of the order of things that the conservative, who is first of all one who respects the inborn constitution of creation, stands for freedom.

Freedom, indeed, cannot by itself define the end to which the conservative is devoted; but in the growing shadow of the collectivist state, it is the most pressing object of his actions. Professor Hayek, however he may differ with the conservative world view, stands for freedom and has fought valiantly for freedom. Justly he describes himself as a "Whig," in the postscript to his book, "Why I Am Not A Conservative." He is a Whig, with all the moral and intellectual power of eighteenth-century Whiggism, infinitely superior to its French Revolutionary and Liberal successors. But he is a Whig with the flaw of Whiggism, its fear of acknowledging the absolute transcendent values upon which its strength is founded.

The next three columns, written at widely different times from 1958 to 1965, are concerned with various aspects of the development of the conservative movement in the United States.

The Horizons of Conservatism

(National Review, March 9, 1965)

Every action has a reaction, and the recent intense concentration of conservatives on strictly political matters has engendered certain subjective attitudes among them that bear serious consideration. I am not referring to the critique of the 1964 campaign and the proposals for more effective use of conservative resources in the future, which I and others have discussed in these pages. Rather I am concerned with widespread manifestations of a spirit that would narrow down the sweep and meaning of the conservative movement to total concentration on the techniques and methods that can lead to victory at the polls.

There is nothing wrong, of course, with the effort to attain professional competence politically. Indeed, in the past conservatives have badly neglected these skills, and it is a great step forward that they have learned to appreciate them. But there is great danger presently of forgetting that they are just that—skills, and no more. Too much concentration on them leads inevitably to opportunism (elect a new duplicate of Eisenhower and hope he turns out all right) or demagogy (frighten the people by telling them that the natural working out of the Liberal world view is a Communist conspiracy, or a "Fabian" conspiracy, or a plot hatched out in the cellars of *Foreign Affairs*). The skills and techniques of political organization have their place in our society, but they are only secondary auxiliaries for a movement whose duty it is radically to transform the consciousness of an age.

This is what the contemporary American conservative movement exists to do. It has no other excuse for being. If it allows fascination with methods and techniques to become primary in its thinking, it will inevitably succumb to the temptation of gaining power for the sake of gaining power. If it wins, those who achieve power will be the prisoners of their methods, little different in essentials from the men who hold power today. Concentration on method without the greater emphasis on transforming popular consciousness can only lead to rivalry with the Liberals in appealing to the baser instincts of the people. The conservative movement has a more difficult task: to appeal to the higher instincts and beliefs that survive, half smothered, in the American people. This is the only foundation for a victory worth winning.

This is a different problem from the one of developing concrete programs expressing the conservative position (about which I have written recently), although the two problems are somewhat interconnected. The working out of concrete programs is essentially an aspect of political activity. But it is also connected with the problem I am here discussing, because it is not possible to develop programs with meaning, depth, and appeal which goes beyond the lower instincts of the electorate, except upon the basis of a broad and profound development of the conservative world view.

That world view is the world view of Western civilization. Conservatism in a revolutionary age, like the one we are living through, cannot simply stand for a series of received opinions. Too much has been shattered for it to be possible ever simply to return to the forms and modes of the past. Conservatism must be something more than preservative; it must restore, and it must create new forms and modes to express the essential content of our civilization. That requires an activity far wider than the political, for the political is the sphere of struggle, struggle *for* a vision that is articulated. Conservatives today have the double task of simultaneously fighting for a position and articulating it. And this latter task is not secondary, but decisive. It is a task which is both moral (in the broad sense of living by high standards) and intellectual (in the broad sense of using reason to apply tradition to new circumstances).

We attack the Establishment, and justly; but we have not met its pretensions area by area and point by point at the level that *our* pretensions to be the heirs of Western civilization demand. We have made a good beginning, but an enormous amount remains to be done, and there is serious danger that present tendencies to concentrate narrowly on the political will obscure the breadth of our obligations.

We cannot be content with slogans, with oversimplifications of complex reality, with neat formulae to capture votes. As the defender of the tradition of the West, the conservative movement must stand for excellence—and excellence at every level of human endeavor. This means that political victories achieved in shoddy ways are not conservative victories, but only insubstantial ripples on the surface of events. It also means that in deepening its championship of Western civilization, the conservative movement must go far beyond the limited area of politics and economics.

In the outlook of a society—and, by the same token, in the outlook of a movement devoted to transforming a society—politics and economics only reflect an underlying understanding of the nature and destiny of men. But such understanding involves the broadest considerations, considerations that go as far afield from the political as the areas of philosophy, the sciences, literature, and history. At every point along the entire gamut of human consciousness, the fundamental insights of contemporary conservatism have the utmost relevance, but they will not come to bear effectively if one-sided effort narrows the potentiality of conservatism. Political action will have true significance only if it is backed by the broadest development of conservative potentialities.

The Conservative Movement: Growing Pains

(National Review, May 6, 1961)

I write this column directly upon my return from a speaking tour which took me in a week's time through the East, the Midwest, the South, and the Southwest. Such a conspectus is somewhat dizzying (the mind has its difficulties adjusting to the abrupt transitions of the jet plane); but in this case two conclusions impressed themselves upon me with unmistakable force: first, the conservative movement in the United States is growing with startling rapidity; second, as it grows it is coming up against problems which threaten its health and continued development. It is, in brief, experiencing the phenomenon of success; it is suffering from growing pains.

There are a number of these difficulties, and they will have to be solved if the movement is to achieve the goals urgently demanded of it in the present historical situation of the United States and Western civilization: to wrest political power from the Liberal Establishment and to lead the nation and the West to victory over international Communism.

Ideologically, the major question facing the conservative movement would seem to be the continuing problem of reconciling and uniting those who place the defeat of Communism as the first necessity of action and those who minimize the danger of Communism as against the danger of the relentless advance of collectivist Liberalism. Each of these positions at its extreme tends to become blind to the danger the other stresses. Thus, some libertarian opponents of the aggrandizement of the federal bureaucracy refuse to recognize the imminently threatening quality of the offensive of armed Communism; on the other hand, some of those most deeply concerned with the Communist threat are willing to overlook any degeneration of the conditions and institutions of freedom in the United States if only they believe it conduces to greater efficiency against the Communist enemy. From these distorted emphases, other distortions arise. For some, any professed anti-Communist, no matter how socialist his views, is regarded uncritically, while for others the distinction between Communists and Liberals becomes blurred, so that anyone whose actions objectively weaken freedom becomes *ipso facto* a Communist.

A proper understanding of the double enemy we face—Communism and Liberalism—and of the interaction between them is essential if these disparate emphases are to be brought together and united in a single movement in defense of a free republic against internal and external enemies. It must be understood that Liberalism weakens the fiber of society, but that Liberals are not, as are Communists, conscious enemies, conspiratorially organized for the conquest of world power. They must be fought in different ways: Communism with *every reserve* both of the individual and of voluntary associations of individuals *and* of the state; Liberals by the methods of education, political organization and action.

But the two struggles, different though they are, are equally important. The defeat of Communism is, of course, necessary for the very physical preservation of the nation and its institutions. On the other hand, quite apart from the tragic consequences if Communism were defeated only to have the collectivism projected by Liberals triumphant at home, the evidence of two decades would seem to show that it is categorically impossible for Communism to be defeated under Liberal leadership.

Parallel to the need for rapidly consummating a unification of the movement's diverse ideological emphases, there is another set of problems, which can best be described as organizational. What is at stake here will be in part resolved as the ideological emphases I have discussed are reconciled; but it is not so easy to see today the forms that resolution will take. Here again, two contradictory emphases, each of which expresses an aspect of a correct position, exist. On the one hand, there is a tendency —correct only in its understanding of the decisive importance of achieving political power—to subordinate the principles and the organic growth of a conservative movement to the electoral victory of the Republican Party. On the other hand, the natural impatience of hard conservatives with this position tends to narrow the movement and to insist upon a doctrinal purity which can repel many who are today becoming conscious of the appeal of conservatism and moving towards it.

The problem is to find forms of organization which will assert the independence of the movement over against any political party's corporate interests or the interests of any political leader, no matter how appealing he may be, while avoiding inflexible demands for uniformity of detailed programs. The solution demands a fine balance between strict loyalty to fundamental principle and a prudential understanding that precisely the individualist nature of conservative Americans necessitates the greatest flexibility and personal initiative in the development of concrete action.

Conservatives cannot by their nature imitate the organizational forms of totalitarian movements. But neither can they afford to be so loosely organized that the principles of the movement are subordinated to the leadership of a political figure. The movement must set the pace, and subordinate whatever leaders come forward to its principles. The forms of organization which will meet these necessary requirements are yet to be found. But found they must be if conservatism is to triumph in America—and the present growth and vigor the conservative movement is displaying is a good omen that they will be found.

On What Ball?

(National Review, January 4, 1958)

In a recent letter to *National Review* (December 21, 1957), Ralph de Toledano, concluding an exchange with L. Brent Bozell, writes:

> Moral: Democrats win elections because they keep their eye on the ball. Republicans, like Trotskyite splinter-groups, get their kicks from ideological purity.

It is clear from the context of this particular exchange of letters, and from other things he has written, that what Mr. de Toledano is talking about is not the sins of Republicans as such, but of conservatives. He is not a Republican out of prescriptive loyalty to the Grand Old Party, but because he regards the Republican Party as the vehicle of opposition to the Liberalism of which the Democratic Party, since the days of Franklin Roosevelt, has been the carrier. It is conservatives with whom he is concerned, and it is conservatives whom he is attacking because they "don't keep their eye on the ball," but "get their kicks from ideological purity."

In this pragmatic age, "ideological purity" is a powerful rhetorical "devil-term"; we admire the practical, the successful; the tone conveyed by his phrase suggests an amused contempt for the impractical, and obscures the meaning of what is being said. Placed in juxtaposition to "winning elections," however, it can have only one meaning . . . devotion to principle. The captive of the rhetoric of the time, Mr. de Toledano here does himself a serious wrong. I esteem him as a writer and a fighter, and know him as a friend; and one thing I can be sure of: when the chips are down, he will always be found on the side of true principle.

But, even from his assumed stance of the practical man, he is wrong. As a matter of fact, Liberalism and the Democratic Party (which in its national leadership is the party of Liberalism) have won their victories through a broadly consistent devotion to principle—if false principle. And conservatism has lost ground, and is losing ground, precisely because, in its effort to keep its eye on Mr. de Toledano's ball, it has consistently compromised principle—whether it has lost elections with Willkie and Dewey, or won them with Eisenhower.

Here is the real moral for conservatives: the tide is running, and to stand still or make slight advances is to be swept back. Winning elections with an Eisenhower and barring out a Stevenson (at the cost of toning down and disintegrating the principled right wing of the Republican Party) has to no discernible degree modified our course towards appeasement and defeat abroad and statist erosion of our institutions at home. The present Administration does not perhaps swim so enthusiastically with the tides as its predecessors; but this is a minor difference of mood; it is not a difference of principle.

The point of the matter is that we are living, and have been living for some decades, in the midst of a revolution which is directed towards the destruction of Western civilization. Conservatives are by definition defenders of that civilization; and in a revolutionary age this means that they are, and must be, counterrevolutionaries. Anyone has the right not to be a conservative, but no one has the right to call himself by that name who is not prepared to recognize the harsh reality that compromise with the dominant forces of this age is not possible. Against the most advanced and hideous form of that revolution, Communism, the terms and conditions of this uncompromising struggle are laid down by the revolutionaries themselves: it is a fight which will have to be conducted with every available weapon, and to the death. We have to recognize what the Communists know and openly proclaim, that Communism and Western civilization cannot both survive.

Our domestic form of the revolution of the twentieth century is less hideous, less advanced in its development, and it has proceeded thus far without violence and within legal forms. The struggle of conservatives against it is a struggle not with weapons, but for the minds of men. The constitutional framework still exists, however battered, within which it is possible to resist and defeat the revolutionaries.

But, make no mistake about it, these are two forms of the same phenomenon. In a fundamental sense the dominant forces in American life today are revolutionary, that is, they are directed towards the destruction of the principles of Western civilization and the American tradition. The politics of New Dealism, Fair Dealism, and New Republicanism are directed towards the strengthening of the State and the diminution of the person. The prevalent quasi-Marxist and Keynesian economics are directed towards the substitution of a state-controlled, ever less "mixed," economy for the free economy of capitalism. The positivist and materialist philosophy of our educational theory and practice, of our radio and television and press, of our academic and intellectual circles, eats away at the fabric of principle and belief which is Western civilization. Everywhere the same revolutionary spirit expresses itself. For the conservative to compromise with it is to give up his reason for being.

However much the forms and the methods may vary, however numerous the points of ideological difference, Communism and collectivist Liberalism are both expressions of one worldwide revolution. Its contemporary political forms were described, and their underlying unity perceived, sixteen years ago by James Burnham, who called it "the managerial revolution." Its historical and philosophical meaning has been drawn forth and powerfully presented by Eric Voegelin, who calls it "gnosticism." Its concrete reality in the United States was displayed in action during the Hiss case, and interpreted by Whittaker Chambers in his great autobiography, *Witness.*

In opposition to this revolution, the "ideological purity" of conservatives is justly of the greatest concern.

In late 1960 National Review *celebrated its fifth anniversary, an event at which I was one of the speakers. The column with which I end this chapter was based upon what I said at that celebration. More than seven years have passed, the greater part of a decade. The Sixties are almost over. Much that I hoped for in 1960 has come about. Much more remains to be achieved. But the tempo of development apart ("Hope for the '60's" should have been "Hope for the Future"), I would write it today as I wrote it then. I end this chapter with it because it expresses what I believe to be the conservative vision of the future of America and of Western civilization.*

Hope for the '60's

(National Review, January 14, 1961)

The Liberal Republican Administration of Dwight D. Eisenhower is drawing to an end; in a few days the Liberal Democrat John F. Kennedy will be inaugurated as the 35th President of the United States. As we enter the seventh decade of the twentieth century under continuing Liberal auspices, it may be worth pausing to ask: What are the prospects for conservatism in the years ahead?

On the political scene itself there are few hopeful signs— except the emergence of a principled conservative figure in the person of Senator Barry Goldwater. But there is a development of the highest importance which has been taking place over the past decade and is now coming to fruition, a develop-

ment which is not directly political in itself, but which can be
the foundation of immense changes in the political scene. This is
the revival of conservative thought in the United States that
has taken place over the last half decade, an intellectual movement unparalleled in the last hundred years. It promises to
reverse the whole trend of American intellectual history from
the days of Lincoln to those of Franklin Roosevelt and Dwight
Eisenhower, and to call a halt to the steady retreat of the
Western tradition, and its political doctrines of freedom and
constitutionalism, before scientism, positivism, and the Liberal
collectivist idolatry of the state.

It is paradoxical, although it is not totally unprecedented
historically, that such a burst of conservative energy on the intellectual level should occur simultaneously with a continuing and
accelerating spread of the influence of Liberalism in the practical political sphere. But although it is a paradox, it is the case.
For the first time in modern America, the rising influence among
intellectuals is the influence of conservatism. Liberalism is on the
defensive—in economics, in political science, in history, in the
study of literature, even in the citadel of positivism, the
philosophical faculties of our universities.

I do not want to exaggerate. I am not maintaining that the
stranglehold of the arid and nihilistic doctrines which for three
generations have increasingly permeated American thought is
broken—or even that it is on the verge of being broken. That
consummation will be achieved only after a long, hard fight.
What I do maintain is that the tide has turned and turned unmistakably. No matter how black the progress of events may seem,
as the barbarian hammers on the gate from Laos to Cuba, from
Berlin to the tower of infamy on the East River; as within our
walls principle seems lost in our political life; as we slip
bemusedly into acquiescence in collectivism and the tyranny
of bureaucracy at home and into acquiescence in appeasement
and dishonor in the face of our implacable enemy abroad—the
hope of the future is being born before our eyes.

It is ideas and beliefs that decide how men will act. I do not underestimate the hard, steel strength of power. Whether for good or evil, it is power which has the next to the last word in the affairs of men—but not the last word. Power is wielded by men, controlled by men, limited by men, as they are guided and inspired by the ideas and beliefs they hold. And this I submit as the truth of the human condition—in the teeth of the prevailing mythology of our century, in the teeth of the behavioral scientists, the psychoanalytic delvers, the Machiavellian calculators of pure power, who stifle the thought of the era with their epicene "research" and masochistic obeisance to whatever ideas or whatever men possess for the moment transitory influence and authority. It is ideas and beliefs that truly reflect the nature of man and his destiny that will in the end decide our future.

Such ideas, such beliefs are on the ascendant. The turn has come. This is no guarantee of victory. It is not for temporal success that we are promised that the Gates of Hell shall not prevail against us. For final certainty we can only know that we fight for the right. But the possibility of temporal victory is taking shape; the weapons are being forged; the issue rests in our stamina and courage.

The West and freedom have been at bay before. Persian and Carthaginian, Arab and Turk, as they have felt final victory in their grasp, have been flung back and destroyed, when the West, reinvigorated in its inborn love of freedom, has struck out and conquered. Thermopylae and Salamis, Poitiers and Lepanto, tell the tale.

For men of courage, it is never totally black. We can take example from many a battle against high odds in our long heritage. The Spartans who defended the pass at Thermopylae against the countless myriads of Xerxes died at their post—and saved the West. Calm, firm, with ultimate courage, they stood against the Persian host—and won though they lost. In Housman's lines their example echoes down the centuries:

The King with half the East at heel is marched from lands
of morning;

> *Their fighters drink the rivers up, their shafts benight the
> air.*
> *And he that stands will die for nought, and home there's no
> returning.*
> *The Spartans on the sea-wet rock sat down and combed
> their hair.*

Our situation is no more desperate, our enemies no more
powerful, than the situations our spiritual ancestors faced,
than the enemies they conquered. The great tradition of the
West is rising again in idea and belief and image. The weapons
with which to fight are in our hands. The future lies in our
determination, in our firmness of principle, in the courage
with which we gird our will to rise to our destiny.

Chapter Two

Syndrome of the Liberal Establishment

As will be clear from the last chapter, the pervasive influence against which contemporary American conservatism contends is what has come to be known as Liberalism, far removed though this ideology of the twentieth century is from that liberalism of the past which held freedom as its central tenet. As I wrote in an essay in Left, Right and Center,* reviewing the genesis of today's conservative movement and its relation to Liberalism:

"The crystallization in the past dozen years or so of an American conservative movement is a delayed reaction to the revolutionary transformation of America that began with the election of Franklin Roosevelt in 1932. That revolution itself has been a gentler, more humane, bloodless expression in the United States of the revolutionary wave that has swept the globe in the twentieth century. Its grimmest, most total manifestations have been the phenomena of Communism and Nazism. In rather peculiar forms in late years it has expressed itself in the so-called nationalism typified by Nasser, Nkrumah, and Sukarno; in Western Europe it has taken the forms of the socialism of England or that of Scandinavia. Everywhere, however open or masked, it represents an aggrandizement of the power of the state over the lives of individual persons. Always that aggrandizement is

* Edited by Robert A. Goldwin (Chicago: Rand McNally & Company, 1965).

cloaked in a rhetoric and a program putatively directed to and putatively concerned for 'the masses.'

"The American form of that revolution differs little in its essentials from Western European democratic socialism. But, by an ironic twist of history, it has become known as 'liberalism.' (So far is it removed from the classical liberalism of the nineteenth century, with its overriding concern for individual liberty and the limitation of the state, that clear discourse requires some mode of differentiation; and I shall for that reason, through the rest of this essay, refer to this twentieth-century American development as Liberalism, with a capital L, reserving the lower case for classical liberalism.) Ushered in by the election of 1932, so thorough was the victory of Liberalism that for many years afterwards it met with no concerted resistance, in either the intellectual or political spheres. True, islands of resistance remained—in the Congress, in the academy among some economists and humanists, in the business community, in the endemic mass anti-Communist movement among some strata of the population. These were rear-guard actions; by and large, Liberalism dominated the scene, took over the academy and the organs of mass communications, controlled the Democratic Party, and slowly penetrated the Republican Party. Only in recent years has there emerged a consistent, cohesive conservative movement, based upon a broad consensus of principle, challenging Liberal assumptions and Liberal power all along the line."

Liberalism, however, is not a rigid monolithic creed; it is made up of many strands, but it has a clearly recognizable physiognomy. It has become as a view of life inextricably bound up with the elements of power that make up the American Establishment.

Profile of the Establishment

(National Review, October 11, 1958)

"What is this Establishment you keep writing about?" In conversation and correspondence I have been asked this question a dozen times. The implication is, of course, that we at *National Review* have created a straw man against whom we inveigh; that it is ridiculous to speak, as *National Review* does, of a unity of outlook that so closely binds together the powerful and decisive figures in every sphere of American life that on all important questions their opinions and action can be predicted within very narrow limits. But that is what an Establishment is: not a conspiracy, not an organized and disciplined body, but men inspired by so essential a unity of belief on fundamental matters that consultation, organization, detailed agreement, is unnecessary.

If anyone thinks that it is an exaggeration to speak of such a unity of view, I challenge him to suggest, however quietly and modestly, at any dinner party or cocktail party representative of the elite of our society that the traditional values of the West are absolutely and without compromise superior to those of any other civilization; or that John Dewey has had a maleficent influence upon twentieth-century American society equal to, if not surpassing that of Karl Marx; or that the political theory and practice of Grover Cleveland and William McKinley represented a norm infinitely nearer to the norm of a free society than the political theory and practice of Franklin Roosevelt and Dwight Eisenhower. Try it and see what happens. You will expose, as with a powerful x-ray, the firm skeleton of dogma that makes the Establishment what it is, however many the surface differences that, on inessentials, divide it into cliques and groups.

Differences do exist—between Stevensonian Democrats and Modern Republicans, between "life-adjustment" educationists and "social-reconstructionist" educationists, between New York *Times* publicists and New York *Herald Tribune* publicists. But, underlying these differences, a broadly consistent and delimitable body of dogma pervades the consciousness and shapes the actions of the decisive and articulate sections of our society.

Philosophically, this body of dogma is relativist, pragmatic, positivist, scornful of absolute criteria, of all strictly theoretical thought, of all inquiry not amenable to the methods of the natural sciences.

Socially, it assumes the existence of an organism, "society," as the being to which, and to the good of which, all moral (and by the same token, political) problems finally refer. Sometimes this principle is modified, but never by intrinsic reference to the individual person, only by reference to collectivist images of specialized groups of individuals: "minorities," "the under-privileged," "the elite," "scientists," "gifted children," "backward children," "labor." Concern is never for, there is no moral reference to, a man who is a Negro, a poor man, a rich man, a well-born man, an able man, a biologist, a child, a carpenter.

Politically, it attributes virtue in strict proportionality to power. Actions are best, and best performed, when the state performs them; and within the governmental structure, best when the act of the federal government rather than of the several states; and within the federal government, best when the action of the executive rather than of the legislative. And if it cannot be the act of government, better that it be the act of an organization than that of an individual, better that of a large organization than that of a small one.

Economically, it takes for granted that the several energies of men expressed through the functioning of a free-market economy can lead only to disaster (although it was with the growth of that system that the great leap in human productivity of the last 150 years occurred). Considering centralized direc-tion and regulation the desideratum of economic systems, it either looks towards state ownership of all productive facilities, in a Marxist or quasi-Marxist manner, or, in a Keynesian manner, it demands that the statist section in a "mixed economy" control all the decisive sectors of the economy and receive a lion's share, through taxation, of the product. In either case it insists that only "socially desirable" production shall be encouraged; and that the decision as to what is "socially desirable" shall be made not by the individual consumers through the market, but by the bureaucrats and social workers through the power of regulation and taxation.

Emotionally, it prefers psychoanalysis to the dark night of the soul, "adjustment" to achievement, security to freedom. It preaches "the end of ideology," admires experts and fears prophets, fears above all commitment to value transcending the fact.

These are the dogmas that bind together those who constitute the Establishment. They determine what the Establishment is and what it stands for in every sphere from the philosophical to the practical. And these dogmas constitute a view of man diametrically opposed to the dogmas upon which Western civilization and American freedom are founded.

So long as the Establishment that is inspired by this view is in the ascendancy, there are only two historical alternatives: that our civilization will be destroyed from within, by the gradual triumph of the regnant anti-Western principle; or that it will be destroyed from without by Communist conquest, against which the votaries of this destructive relativist principle have in the end no defense, having no rock of ultimate defiance upon which to stand against Communism.

This is why it is necessary to recognize that there *is* an Establishment and to discern its lineaments clearly. For only if it is seen to exist and seen for what it is, is it possible to fight to unseat it.

At various times in my column in National Review *I have commented on some of these specific strands of Liberal doctrine. The three columns which follow are concerned: the first, with sociological perversion of the psychoanalytic approach; the second, with some curious transformations in the doctrine of Liberalism; the third, with unreasoning worship of the scientific method, exclusive of all other modes of human understanding.*

Symptoms of Mass Delusion

(*National Review,* February 8, 1956)

It is, I hope, with all due modesty that I present this month an original clinical finding of some significance. The available evidence has forced me to the conclusion that the social scientific profession, particularly those of its members who lean upon psychoanalytical theory, have been for a number of years suffering from a clearly defined malady that exhibits the classical symptoms of mass delusion.

A delusion is characterized, in general terms, first by the inability to recognize the true character and cause of some aspect of reality, and secondly, by the substitution of a fantasy that is often very elaborate, well-knit and self-consistent. Thirdly, both the rejection of reality and the insistence upon the fantastic explanation are highly charged with emotion and maintained with great intensity. Nor is a delusion less a delusion if it is held by a large number of people; it becomes a mass delusion.

The concept of mass delusion is, indeed, freqently called upon by social scientists and psychoanalysts to explain actions and attitudes which are, or seem to them to be, irrational. They should, therefore, be able to avoid falling victim to delusion themselves. The fact of the matter, however, is that over the past few years, sociologists, political scientists and psychologists have been developing, elaborating, and earnestly improving a theory about the political behavior of the American people that has all the attributes of a fantastic explanation of a phenomenon, the true nature of which is as plain as the nose on your face.

Millions of Americans followed Taft's leadership; millions admired MacArthur; millions supported McCarthy's drive against Communism; and millions exhibit a desire for an alternative to the dominant Liberal control of both political parties. And the very existence of this phenomenon (which they call McCarthyism) has a traumatic effect upon the consciousness of the social scientists. After twenty-five years of the welfare state, of Deweyite education, and of control of press and radio and television by the "enlightened," it simply should not be. Like the individuals or peoples whose delusions they dissect, the social scientists of the Establishment have run into a brute fact of experience which controverts their whole vision of the world.

Unable to accept the clear and obvious explanation, that tens of millions of Americans are in principled opposition to their position, they have constructed an explanation which will account for the facts, which they cannot escape, without disturbing their emotional equilibrium. Not ideas, not principles, nothing by which a reasonable man could be affected, could possibly be the cause of this intractable resistance to the good, the true, and the beautiful. It is only the unfortunate fact that a certain "personality structure," a sort of psychoanalytical original sin—"the authoritarian personality"—has affected a large number of our fellow citizens, if not from birth, at least from the period of weaning and toilet training. Since all political, economic and social propositions that form the accepted corpus of Liberal thought are beyond intellectual doubt or question, the only explanation of dissent must be, in the Liberal fantasy, a psychological defect, approaching, it is often hinted, paranoia.

Even Margaret Mead, who has done her share to bring about the present attitudes of the behavioral sciences, seems to have misgivings at the length to which this development has gone. Writing in *The American Scholar* (Summer, 1955), she observes of an article typical of this trend (Richard Hofstadter's "The Pseudo-Conservative Revolt," in the same journal, Winter, 1954-55), that he, like others, ignores "the state of the world in favor of parochial explanations which invoke individual personalities—McCarthy, McLeod—or less specifically identified Texas millionaires; or, more diffusely still, old-Americans losing ground, or new-Americans worrying over just having won it . . . Hofstadter invokes the psychoanalytically oriented, German-modeled, authoritarian personality study, in which the character structure of lower-middle-class Americans is equated, with a disregard of cultural differences, with the character of lower-middle-class Germans as prone to victimize the weak . . . There might be no atom bomb, no hydrogen bomb, no explicit insistence on a polarized world, no Communist China to alter the attitudes of the American people . . ."

It is this triumphant production of a deep-psychological explanation for the obvious which gives one the sensation of dealing with the victims of a mass delusion as one reads the papers of the "psychoanalytically oriented" social scientists. With a sickening reversal of meaning, which reminds one dismayingly of "newspeak," every sign of individualist or traditional resistance to the tyranny of contemporary conformity is attributed to "the authoritarian personality."

This concept, which dots the pages of the journals of sociology and political science, is derived from the study published in 1950, to which Miss Mead refers, *The Authoritarian Personality*, by T. W. Adorno, Else Frenkel-Brunswik *et al.* The study utilized the most approved and up-to-date techniques of clinical psychology—psychological interviews, "projective" questionnaires, etc.—interpreted in the light of psychoanalytic theory. The "projective question" is an engaging little device. It is designed to trap the interviewee into revealing his unconscious personality through questions apparently directed toward his conscious beliefs. The psychoanalytic investigator, knowing the secrets of the human heart, manipulates the answers, with card index and IBM machine, in the light of his interpretive theory, and emerges with a conclusion. The conclusion is always in the form of a "correlation."

Correlation is the ritual word, and its action is supposed to derive truth from the collected data. The difficulty is that so few of the infinite factors which go to make up any human personality can be "tested," that the selection of the factors to be tested and of the correlations to be measured are completely at the mercy of the theoretical attitudes, implicit or explicit, with which the investigator begins. This is one of the reasons why the study of man in society can never be a science. The real issues of importance are inherent in the presuppositions; and it is at this non-scientific, philosophical, intuitive level that discussion is most valuable. But this is the one level at which the truly "scientific" social scientist refuses to discuss. He prefers to correlate.

Thus, the authors of *The Authoritarian Personality* begin with the assumption that anyone who is opposed to the welfare state is likely to be "unenlightened" about science and religion; to accept the authority of an organic moral order; to hate Jews and Negroes; to have an unconscious desire to grind the faces of the weak; and to respect his parents. And, Glory be, after all their exercises with projective questionnaires and clinical interviews, with the intercorrelation of their PEC (political and economic conservatism) scale, their AS (anti-Semitism) scale, their E (ethnocentrism) scale and their F (implicit pre-fascistic tendencies) scale, out pops the stereotype built into the system from the beginning: "the authoritarian personality," composite of the above traits—complete with a moral upbringing and strict toilet training.

I am primarily concerned, however, not with the weaknesses of the study itself, but rather with the way in which the concept of "the authoritarian personality" has become the answer to the social scientist's need of a construct to explain to his emotional satisfaction the "irrational" obstinacy of those who do not accept the blessings of the welfare state. I shall, therefore, not here develop in further detail my criticisms of the methodology and validity of *The Authoritarian Personality*. As a matter of fact, so dubious are its procedures that aspect after aspect of the study is constantly being criticized by the sociologists themselves. A book recently published, *Studies in the Scope and Method of "The Authoritarian Personality,"* edited by Richard Christie and Marie Jahoda, contains devastating analyses of almost every element of its methodology. The various contributors attack its sampling procedures, bias in the setting of questions, bias among the interviewers, theoretical distortion of the results. Yet, somehow they maintain throughout a tone of enormous respect for the study and its conclusions. This is an interesting point, and one characteristic of the multifarious articles which take those conclusions as a major premise in further discussion. They lean upon the thesis that conservative political and economic attitudes today have no relation to rational ideas, but are simply the result of a personality structure which is characteristic of the Nazi, although they are admittedly well aware of the scholarly shoddiness of the study from which that thesis is derived.

Richard Hofstadter, for example, in "The Pseudo-Conservative Revolt," already referred to, coolly says: "While I have drawn heavily upon this enlightening study, I have some reservations about its methods and conclusions. For a critical review, see Richard Christie and Marie Jahoda, eds., *Studies in the Scope and Method of 'The Authoritarian Personality'* . . ."

But that critical review contains such statements as this: "a major finding of *The Authoritarian Personality*—the demonstration of a syndrome of attitudes of political conservatism and authoritarianism, as revealed by the formal statistics of a correlation between the numerical scores—could instead reflect the mere fact that the PEC scale and the F scale both contain questions which are basically similar in content."

And it is exactly upon the conclusion that such a syndrome exists, that the political and economic conservative ranks high on the F scale, has fascist leanings, is an "authoritarian personality," that Mr. Hofstadter's whole exercise in exorcism of the right-wing opposition in America depends. Even if the establishment of the stereotype of an "authoritarian personality" rests on shaky foundations, it plays too great a part in the delusionary system of Mr. Hofstadter and his fellow Liberals for them to give it up.

While one finds "the authoritarian personality" turning up in all sorts and varieties of articles, it is in discussions which impinge directly upon problems raised by the survival of an opposition, where the Liberal psyche has most at stake and where its delusionary system is most desperately needed, that it becomes omnipresent. Over the past year or two a number of such articles have appeared. Now the most touted of them have been collected in a book called *The New American Right,* edited by Daniel Bell, where anyone with a morbid interest in the pathology of the Liberal social-scientific mind may read them at his convenience. I recommend it as an objective confirmation of my analysis of the neurotic plight of that mind. Every contributor to this collection—Richard Hofstadter, David Riesman, Peter

Viereck (that sterling conservative), Talcott Parsons, Nathan Glazer, S. M. Lipset, Daniel Bell—blandly ignores the possibility that there could be any real issue of a rational kind in American politics today which would justify the existence of an opposition, and proceeds to a sociological-psychological analysis of the extraordinary fact that there is one.

The book is haunted by "the authoritarian personality," sometimes manifesting itself directly, sometimes disguised as "status anxiety." It explains everything and makes it possible for a group of leading scholars to write essays which ignore every important substantive question in the field with which they are dealing. So anxious have they been to close and seal the controversies of the last twenty-five years, to fix the nation once for all in a Byzantine New Dealism, sanctified by the canon, "You can't turn the clock back," that they have convinced themselves that in very fact the issues *are* closed. When, then, overwhelming evidence to the contrary accumulates, reality becomes too much for them to support. They take refuge in a collective neurosis, conjuring up the demon of "the authoritarian personality" to give substance to their delusion.

Individual delusions, or even such harmless mass delusions as Millerite adventism or flying-saucer cults hurt no one but their devotees. A mass delusion like this one, however, which affects the corporation of intellectuals so widely, is a matter of general concern. This ferocious maternal protection of what they want to believe, in irresponsible defiance of reason and understanding, is the true *trahison des clercs*. It creates between the intellectuals and the rest of society a schism which portends ill for civilization.

Retreat from Relativism

(National Review, December 14, 1955)

A curious mutation is occurring in the relativist doctrine which for a generation has dominated the thought of the intellectual

Establishment of the academic world. Again and again in the scholarly journals, even in those closest to such shrines of relativism as Columbia University, one reads categorical repudiations of what was but recently received dogma. Clyde Kluckhohn of Harvard, an outstanding anthropologist, roundly asserts:

> Few anthropologists would today defend without important qualification Ruth Benedict's famous statement: ". . . the co-existing and equally valid patterns of life which mankind has carved for itself from the raw materials of existence." (*Journal of Philosophy,* November 10, 1955)

David Easton of the University of Chicago's Department of Political Science writes:

> Not so many years ago the image held by the social scientist about his discipline permitted him to be clear and unambiguous about its relation to ethics. Today the situation has radically changed. We can detect a feeling of uneasiness in social science about its earlier conceptions. . . . We must ask: . . . What *ought* social science to say about values? By its very formulation, this is a moral, not a factual question. (*Antioch Review,* Spring, 1955)

In ethics, in jurisprudence, in political science, even in sociology and psychology, Mr. Easton's "uneasiness" is manifest. The heirs of Dewey, Veblen and Holmes have begun to turn the dissecting knives of the "revolt against formalism" upon their own relativist assumptions. It is always good to see error dissected, especially by those who have been error's votaries; but before we sing hosanna for the conversion of the heathen, we might be sure that one error is not being replaced by another, even more disastrous.

That, I am afraid, is what is happening. It is true that among those who are becoming disillusioned by the philosophical emptiness of relativism and disturbed by some of its practical results, there are some who are searching for truth uninhibited by the blinkers of scientism and the behavioristic view of the human person. But these are few and far between. Much more characteristic of the general line of thought is Mr. Kluckhohn's article in the *Journal of Philosophy*, to which I have referred. Prepared for the American Philosophical Association, Eastern Division, as a contribution to a symposium on "Ethical Relativity in the Light of Recent Developments in Social Science," this paper is most revealing.

There can be no doubt that Mr. Kluckhohn, who is a recognized leader in the "behavorial sciences," speaks with authority. But if there were any question, the footnote which introduces his paper will set the uninitiated reader straight. I quote it not only to establish Mr. Kluckhohn's credentials beyond doubt, but also because it is so arresting an example of the apparent fear among contemporary scholars of standing on their own feet, of their need to run in a pack (a well-heeled pack, of course, suitably maintained by Rockefeller and/or Ford):

> This paper arises rather directly out of my participation in the Comparative Study of Values in Five Cultures of the Laboratory of Social Relations, Harvard University. I express my gratitude to my colleagues in this project and to the Rockefeller Foundation who supported it through the Foundation's Division of Social Sciences. . . . The writing of the paper was made possible by a fellowship at the Centre for Advanced Study in the Behavioral Sciences [Ford Foundation].

The difficulties of ethical relativism have become apparent, Mr. Kluckhohn says,

> in part [as] a reaction to the observation of social consequences. If one follows out literally and logically the implications of Benedict's words, one is com-

pelled to accept any cultural pattern as vindicated
precisely by its cultural status: slavery, cannibalism,
Nazism, or Communism may not be congenial to
Christians or to contemporary Western societies, but
moral criticism of the cultural patterns of other people
is precluded. Emotionally and practically, this extreme position is hardly tolerable—even for scholars
—in the contemporary world.

True, indeed, although it might be pointed out that during
the twenties and thirties, decades in which ethical relativism was
riding high, both Communism and Nazism were certainly in
existence—and for that matter, that cannibalism and slavery
are "culture patterns" probably as old as the human race.

Fundamentally, I am afraid that it is not a new-found awareness of the direction in which human nature, unguided by
absolute moral truth, may go, that motivates the retreat from
extreme relativism. After all, the relativists of the twenties and
thirties did know *something* about cannibalism and slavery,
about the possibilities of depravity in the human being; but
they thought that the social engineer could keep under control
the aspects of that depravity not instrumental to their ends.
They were striking for power, and relativism in its most extreme
forms served to destroy the barriers of traditional loyalty to
truth which stood in their way.

Now they have power. They have become the guardians of
a new orthodoxy, which requires firmer foundations than the
shifting sands of relativism. Mr. Kluckhohn finds that among
psychologists:

> there appears to be a growing trend toward agree-
> ment [that] there are panhuman universals as regards
> needs and capacities that shape, or could rightly
> shape, at least the broad outlines of a morality that
> transcends cultural difference.

He finds that "sociologists have similarly been placing greater

emphasis upon the universals"; and, as an anthropologist, he
proclaims the astounding discovery that:

> While the specific manifestations of human nature
> vary between cultures and between individuals in the
> same culture, human nature is universal.

Obvious though this is, the common possession of common
sense and of the great philosophical tradition, it is, formally
at least, a step forward from the obscurantism of the positivist
methodology which has pervaded the social sciences. It implies
a bare acceptance, at any rate, of the concept of truth. To look
for the sources of ethical obligation, of what man *ought* to do,
in the universal nature of man would seem to be an approach
toward the tradition of natural law. F. S. C. Northrop, as a matter of fact, in another paper in the same symposium, attempts
explicitly to claim that tradition, whittling its noble dimensions
down to the measure of his own scientistic eclecticism.

Actually, however, the "uneasiness" which dictates a search
for some stronger foundation than pure relativism is a motivation at far remove from the love of truth that inspires the
natural-law tradition. And the universal human nature which
is here recognized is a far cry from that image of man, free and
responsible, which is, in its different modes, a common element
in the classical, the Christian and the humanist traditions. The
universal human nature of Mr. Kluckhohn's thought is a poor
truncated thing. Man's being is stripped of all qualities not
accessible to the scientific method; and that which makes him
truly man, the tragedy and the glory, the tension between the
freedom which is the law of his inner being and the necessity
which the external world presents to his consciousness is accessible to the scientific method only in very small part.

That method has performed wonders in the fields to which
it is adapted, and it undoubtedly can contribute to the understanding of man, but by itself it is helpless to expose the human
person in his complexity. To reject all the other resources of
the understanding—the non-scientific uses of reason of the

historian, the philosopher, the theologian, the insights of the aesthetic sensibility, intuition, faith—is to present universal human nature as a sad, thin scarecrow, deprived of life and substance.

Man, the person, plays no greater part in this more objective behavioral science than he did in the relativistic dispensation. Men do not create culture, but an hypostasized Culture creates men. Mr. Kluckhohn quotes approvingly the sociologist Kolb:

> The basic field conditions for the emergence of the human psyche have been relatively the same since man has been man: society, culture, symbolic inter-action, and the potentialities of the biological or-ganism interacting [to form] the universal emergent: human nature . . .

Jack London of the University of California in a review in the *American Journal of Sociology* (March, 1955) says:

> This reviewer rejects [the] assumption that the power structure is resident in individuals qua indi-viduals. . . . Rather, power is organized through the medium of special-interest groups or collectivities which transcends the wishes, beliefs, attitudes, and opinions of the individuals in them. Such collectivities develop a life of their own, with their own series of functions, claims, and expectations and are not a mere aggregation of inert individuals. . . . As a result of being acting organisms, they work out their beha-vior in the process of acting within the human con-text.

To the sociologists Hans Gerth and C. Wright Mills, as Benjamin Schwartz shows in a biting review of their *Character and Social Structure: The Psychology of Social Institutions,*

> . . . isolated individuals are mindless. Here most of the contents and activities which are ordinarily attrib-

uted to mind and spirit inhere, in some fashion, in the
social structure. It is the social structure which has
its values, *its* symbols, and *its* roles. (*World Politics,*
October, 1955)

Such a view of man finds itself hard put, when in the retreat
from relativism it attempts to take account of values, particularly
of ethical values, of the "ought." The scientific and engineering
methodology cannot deal with any realm beyond the "is." Mr.
Kluckhohn writes: "The 'oughts' in all cultures . . . are observable and formulable in 'is' terms"; and he proceeds to reduce
the very meaning of the "ought" to the "is."

The difficulties into which this approach plunges the scientistic student of man are manifold; but they can best be discussed in relation to the critical areas in which they arise.
The journals have exhibited the problem recently in a number
of controversies, most notably in the discussion aroused by
Walter Lippmann's *The Public Philosophy,* in the examination
of the rationale of the Justices of the Supreme Court in recent
years, and in the beginnings of a discussion of the recent Congress for Cultural Freedom at Milan. I hope to examine one or
more of these topics in future columns in this department.

The Bigotry of Science

(National Review, March 8, 1958)

Despite the ingrained certainty of the contemporary intellectual
world that there never has been so flexible and so tolerant a
society as ours, the truth of the matter is very nearly the opposite. Never, perhaps, has the intellectual imagination been held
so tightly within a strait jacket as in these "enlightened" times.
The bigotry with which Liberalism systematically attempts to
destroy any person or idea or attitude that asserts the existence
of a many-chambered universe, outside the arid and sterile cell
in which the Liberal mind would confine the human imagination, becomes day by day more and more obvious.

But there is another aspect of contemporary bigotry, a buttress to the constraining power of Liberal ideology, but also independently a heavy yoke upon the human spirit. This is the bigotry of science: the demand that all activities of the intellect which do not follow the methods of the sciences, and all intellectual conclusions which do not square with the conclusions of that methodology, be cast into outer darkness as infantile and/or superstitious.

The influence of this bigoted assumption, that only the scientific method is valid and that all other methods achieved by men have been but the fumblings of children, can be observed in every area of intellectual endeavor. The rich tradition of the ages is discarded left and right—in philosophy, by the logical positivists and the analytical philosophers; in literary criticism, by the devotees of a desiccated New Criticism; in political and social theory, by the "policy scientists" and the "behavioral scientists." The heritage of metaphysics, literary sensibility, moral and political theory, is thrown on the waste heap to make place for a methodology that is satisfactory enough for the study of the regularities of the behavior of physical matter, but which becomes totally inadequate either for the consideration of ultimate truth or for the study of situations involving men—sentient beings endowed with consciousness, will, and the faculty of moral understanding.

The ability to grasp concepts that can neither be derived from the empirical observation of nature or society, nor deduced by mathematical means from such observations, has degenerated to so pitiful a level that those pages of scholarly quarterlies and Liberal-oriented magazines of opinion which attempt to deal with such questions, partake of the tantalizing nature of double-talk.

Nor is this to be wondered at. The assiduous denial of the existence of realms not reducible to understanding by the scientific method produces minds that are functionally incapable of intelligible discourse about matters that by their nature exist only in such realms. When a Nestor of contemporary political science like Harold Lasswell, or a theoretical astronomer like Fred Hoyle, or an exponent of the new control-science, cybernetics, talks about such a transcendentally-based concept as value and attempts to contain it within the modes of apprehension of the scientific method, it is like a congenitally blind man discoursing on the sunset.

More immediately and practically, the effects of this science-worship are reflected in the cry that arises as the Soviet threat mounts: "Science will save us"—when our deepest problems are defects of moral understanding and will, defects which the scientific methodology can do nothing to correct.

If I attack the presumptions of scientists and show a regard for the body of scientific knowledge that is rather less than it usually receives these days, it is not because I underestimate the validity and the power of the scientific method in its proper sphere. The accelerating control of nature, achieved over the past 150 years, is witness to its power; and it would be obscurantist indeed to separate those triumphs from the method upon which they are based.

Nor certainly would I suggest that there is anything wrong *per se* in the continuing development of scientific control over nature. Quite apart from the fact that the very survival of Western civilization depends at least partially upon a high rate of scientific and technological development, there is something deeply immoral about any effort, whether that of an individual person or of a civilization, to solve fundamental problems at a lower level than that of highest capability. The development of the scientific faculty creates problems for an unbalanced civilization, it is true. But to suppress one faculty in order that the underdeveloped ability of another faculty may have its problems cut down to size is to stunt spiritual growth—which is to move rapidly down the road to fossilization and death.

This is not the problem; it is not the scientific method in its own sphere that is wrong. What is wrong is its application to areas unamenable to its characteristic virtue, the ability to analyze recurrent sets of regular activity of phenomena and to deduce the causal principles at work. What is wrong is its use in areas where conscious subjective freedom enters: whether it be the activities of men, or the universe as a whole.

Art, politics, psychology, ethics, philosophy—the whole gamut of knowledge outside of the knowledge of how to predict and control the reactions of physical matter—are intrinsically un-amenable to the scientific methodology. Abstract reason, intuitive apprehension, the method of analogy, the creative symbolism of art, the tradition of revelation: it is through these modes of understanding that men know most of the important things they know. The mode of the sciences has its place, and an important one, but only when it takes its proper position in the ranked hierarchy of knowledge, so that in the control of nature it becomes a useful servant, not a disintegrator and disorganizer of the truly human understanding.

Conservatives as well as Liberals are concerned with the preservation of the rights of human beings; but they have a very different view of what these rights are and of their philosophical foundation. The two columns that follow explore some aspects of this question.

Rights and "Rights"

(*National Review*, August 2, 1958)

One of the most unpleasant aspects of the political scene in these Liberal decades is the mixture of whine and threat with which politicians, social workers, trade-union leaders, and leaders of so-called minorities insistently demand that the state decree and enforce special privileges for all and sundry. Worse, the privileges demanded—material security from the cradle to the grave, equal economic treatment despite differences of ability, equal education irrespective of ability and at the tax-payers' expense—are dubbed "rights." Thus a concept vital to the existence of a free society, the concept of the unalienable rights of men to life, liberty and property, is brought into disrepute.

The true rights of men are not claims to material and social privilege; they are rights in their persons, rights to live uncoerced by other men or groups of men, rights derived from the nature of men and from the moral law. What such rights mean in detail has been spelled out in the Constitution of the United States and in the principles of the common law; and understanding and respect for them has been fundamental to the political structure of our Federal Republic in its best days.

Nevertheless, so repellent has the contemporary clamor which dresses out a garb for special privilege in the language of "rights" become, that some conservatives, throwing out the baby with the bath water, would deny the very existence of rights independently and unalienably adhering to the individual human person. Substituting the concept that the rights of the individual person *vis-à-vis* society and the state are conditional to and dependent upon the person's performance of his duties to society and the state, they proclaim the doctrine: no rights without corresponding duties.

Now, granted that the duties that impinge upon human beings derive from the same moral law from which their rights derive, nevertheless duties and rights do not depend directly upon one another. The individual person lives in a social milieu constituted of other persons and of the groupings of persons which make up social and political institutions. However much awe and reverence may become associated with these institutions, they cannot *as such* have any moral claims upon him. Only insofar as they represent the moral rights of other persons, that is, only secondarily, does he have duties to them. The Great Commandment, which is the cornerstone of the structure of Western moral thought, reflects this hierarchy of values, ignoring utterly everything but God and individual persons: "Thou shalt love the Lord thy God with all thy heart, and with all thy soul, and with all thy strength, and with all thy mind; and thy neighbor as thyself."

"Society," which is simply an abstraction meaning the sum total of all the relations between persons, cannot be a primary source of obligation in moral and political thought. To insist that it is, is either actually to believe that society is a living organism endowed with a soul and constituting a third term that should be added to the Great Commandment; or it is to talk nonsense. Only if one is willing to take the former position, is it possible logically to defend as an axiom of political theory the proposition: no rights without corresponding duties.

This doctrine depends upon the belief that society is a being, almost a person, who in reciprocal relationship with individual persons hands out rights as they fulfill their duties to it. In such a scheme of things, rights would obviously be dependent upon duties performed; but they would not be rights, they would be rewards for good behavior.

The rights of human beings, however, are not the gift of some Leviathan; they are inherently derived from the nature of men. The duties of human beings are not tribute owed to Leviathan; they are moral imperatives grounded in objective value. Each is independent of the other; it is not a matter of *quid pro quo.*

Rights are moral claims which every individual person has upon other persons, and upon all associations of other persons, including in particular the state; and they remain valid whether he is a good man or an evil man, whether he performs his duties or fails to perform them. Duties are obligations morally binding on each person, whatever his situation, whether other men, groups of men or the state respect his rights or trample upon them. No man can give as an excuse for failure to carry out a duty that others have failed to respect his rights. No man, no group of men, no state, can give as an excuse for depriving an individual person of his inherent rights, that he has failed to perform a duty.

Duties and rights both derive from the same source, the moral ground of man's nature. But if they are made directly dependent one upon the other, they cease to be rights or duties. Losing their moral autonomy, rights become rewards dispensed to the individual by society or the state and duties become obediences extorted by power.

The *form* that the duties incumbent upon any individual person will take will depend, first, upon the position in life and the endowments of the person concerned, and secondly upon social circumstances; but the essential content of his duties— to obey the moral law—remains the same, whatever his position and capability, whatever the customs of society or the laws of the state. Similarly, the forms in which a man's rights are expressed may vary with time and place and custom, but the content remains the same—the right to live uncoerced by force in possession of life, liberty and property.

These rights are as essential to a free society as is the performance of moral duties. Conservatives, however appalled by the prostitution of the noble concept of human rights to materialist ends, cannot deny the independent status of rights without destroying their defenses against the great enemy of our time, the Leviathan state.

"Open Society" or Tyranny: False Dilemma

(National Review, January 16, 1960)

One of the most effective weapons of Liberal thought is the use of false antithesis: if you are opposed to socialized medicine, you don't care if the streets are full of wretches wracked with lung cancer dying in the gutter; if you cast a critical eye on the social security system, you want millions of indigent aged to spend their declining years on a diet of bread and water in bleak and cheerless garrets; if you do not bleed with the social worker's heart of an Eleanor Roosevelt, you have no heart at all.

These antitheses are not only vicious in intent, but false in fact. They are vicious because they are directed to enlisting the store of human benevolence and pity in the service of the pitiless purposes of the social engineers. They are false because —difficult though the human condition is—we are not faced with the harsh choice of accepting the arid antiseptic world of the Liberal ideologues or else condemning mankind to misery.

The immense potentialities for the creation of wealth inherent in a free economy operating in a free society, associated with the ancient and sacred virtues of family loyalty and personal charity, would destroy the false dilemma imposed in these antitheses. It is the Liberal ideology itself that is responsible both for the shackling of the productive powers of a free economy and for the corrosion of the virtues without which the life of men in society becomes intrinsically horrible, however excellent the political and economic institutions are.

The problems posed by the Liberals are in the main of their own creation. They are not natural to the human state, still less are they derived from the central tradition of Western Civilization. It is the distinguishing sign of Liberal thought to split asunder the unity in tension by which the West has been able to preserve the freedom of the person and the authority of truth and good, liberty in society and order in society, the searching spirit and the discipline of tradition.

At the very foundations of our political theory and practice, the disintegrating weapon of Liberalism against the balance of freedom and order the West has achieved has been the concept of the "open society." That concept I cannot define better than was done by Brent Bozell in a recent column in *National Review Bulletin* (December 12, 1959), when he described the "open society" as a society whose "supreme law . . . is that *all* questions are open questions—open to constant re-examination and re-evaluation, according to the empirical data on hand at any given moment. In such a society, there is no place for immutable principles and made up minds."

All questions must be open questions or all questions will be closed questions—the open society or tyranny: this is the antithesis which is insistently drummed into our consciousness at every level of Liberal indoctrination. In the day-to-day teaching of the public schools, in the accepted modes of thought of the colleges, in the rarefied atmosphere of the academic journals, as in the substantive content of all the avenues of communication— lowbrow, middlebrow and highbrow—the challenge is posed in strictly exclusive terms. Any hint of adherence to absolute truth at any level—it is argued or insinuated or propounded as self-evident—leads inexorably to a closed and absolute tyranny.

But the antithesis is false. We are not faced with the alternative, on the one hand, of a society without values, without standards of truth and beauty and good, of a philosophy without an end or ultimate purpose, of an ethos at the mercy of prevailing majority opinion; and, on the other hand, of a society under iron control from top to bottom by tyrants armored with absolute authority, a Byzantine philosophy deprived of freedom to explore and think, an ethos bound in multitudinous regulations.

The history of the West has been the history of a third way, a way that has held in shimmering balance the authority of truth and the freedom of men. And it has done that, sometimes less perfectly, sometimes more perfectly, by recognizing a hierarchy of truths in the intellectual and spiritual realm and a division of function among the institutions of men. It has distinguished—in turmoil and strife, it is true, but in the end it has always distinguished—between the fundamental truths which constitute the structure of man's being as a creature with a supernatural destiny living in the natural world, and those questions where truth is uncertain, where men who agree upon essential truths may differ with good will.

Furthermore, the West has always recognized, until the era of Marxism and Liberalism, that the ultimate guardians of its essential truths were not those who constitute the state, with their power to enforce and their susceptibility to the corruptions of power, but the learned, the priestly, the prophetic, skilled in the tradition and devoted not to power but to truth.

In societies of the West as far apart as that of the Middle Ages (with its multitudinous centers of political power naturally grown from the soil of the decay of the Roman Empire, but united upon fundamental truths) and that shaped by the Founding Fathers of the United States (with its conscious separation of political power, but still united upon less precise but as firmly held general truths), the balance, the tension has been proclaimed.

That balanced society is our heritage. It is the answer to the false antithesis pressed upon us by Liberalism. It is a society neither "open" nor "closed," a society open to truth and freedom, closed to positivist nihilism and statist tyranny. This is the concept that must be flung in the teeth of the Liberal who poses the false dilemma of "open society or tyranny."

One of the areas of sharpest conflict between conservatives and Liberals is foreign policy and .in particular the estimate of Communism and of the necessities of American foreign policy in relation to it. I have from time to time commented on various facets of the Liberal approach to world affairs.

Moral Coexistence

(National Review, April 23, 1960)

Reading the March issue of *Encounter*, I was impressed to the point of shock by the unlikely conjuncture of two articles which together startlingly manifest the progressive corrosion of Western intelligence by relativism and ethical neutralism. Both showed a total absence of the intellectual ability to make distinctions and differentiations, and the unhappy disappearance of any sentiment of just pride and firm belief in the inheritance and civilization of the West.

There was no surprise in itself in one of the articles, an interview with George Kennan, who, like Robert Oppenheimer, exiled from the opportunity for substantive political mischief has for some years contented himself with grandiose pseudo-metaphysical mining and sapping of the foundations of his civilization. He is a certified sage of the Establishment, and one expects from him neither pride in the West nor the ability to make elementary distinctions.

What caused the shock was to find juxtaposed to the interview with Kennan an article by Michael Polanyi, a man who is generally regarded as being in opposition to the doctrines of established Liberalism—an article which displayed the same implicit refusal to make sharp distinctions and the same lack of pride in the heritage of the West. I do not want to imply that the two men have at all the same tone or that their aims and ends are the same; they undoubtedly diverge widely, both in their philosophical tone and in the solutions they would propose to specific political and social problems. What is frightening is that when it comes to the bedrock of fundamental belief and loyalty, they share an implicit set of concepts which can only be described as neutralism in the struggle between the values of the West and the revolutionary values Soviet Communism expresses and champions.

Neither of them distinguishes in essence between the imperfections of Western and American society, on the one hand, and Communist society, on the other. Both equate the moral significance of "Communist revisionism" of the Djilas type with sociological criticism of American life of the Riesman type. Neither is willing to make absolute moral and spiritual distinctions between Western civilization and Communist society. Both show themselves devoid of devotion, loyalty, piety to the West which nurtured them.

Kennan makes it directly obvious that he regards that loyalty to America and that pride in our institutions which until recently characterized the American ethos, as sinful: "Somehow we Americans have made ourselves guilty over the course of decades of great arrogance . . . a sort of childish arrogance about the virtues of our own society." And he goes on to con-

gratulate us for having overcome this "romanticism of the nineteenth century" and having reached the high level of "maturity"
on which he sits, where the weaknesses of American society
criticized by the sociologists are rhetorically equated with the
weaknesses of Soviet society, criticized by the "revisionists."

He himself has some valid and some decidedly invalid criticisms to make of certain aspects of materialism and conformism
in the United States, but none of those criticisms points toward
recovering our heritage of freedom. They all end, as might
be expected, in a call for a *dirigisme à la Galbraith*, where
a bureaucratic elite, through manipulation of the tax system,
could dictate the disposition of national income, not according
to the desires of those who earn it, but according to the plans
of social engineers.

But whatever might be expected of Kennan, it is distressing
to find Michael Polanyi, who has from time to time in the
past written very well on aspects of the Western ethos, accepting the same kind of moral equivalence between the West
and Communism and exhibiting the same debilitation of loyalty
to the West.

In some ways, indeed, he says it more clearly; early in his
article he writes: "The idea that morality consists in imposing
on ourselves the curb of moral commands is so ingrained in
us, that we simply cannot see that the moral need of our time
is, on the contrary, to curb our inordinate moral demands, which
precipitate us into moral degradation, and threaten us with
bodily destruction." Which means, as what follows shows, that
we must stop feeling superior to Communism and recognize
that virtue today rests in the joint effort of the "revisionists"
of the Communist world and the critics of our own society to
achieve an uncommitted neutral unity. The struggle between
Communism and the West must be overcome, as the religious
wars of the seventeenth century were overcome, by a bland
ethos, neutral to ultimate value, "a civic partnership united in
its resolve on continuous reform."

The end achieved by the resolution of the seventeenth-century struggle was, in Polanyi's words, to establish "for the first time since the rise of Christianity the foundations of a secular society." He does not describe the society which would make the struggle between Communism and the West irrelevant. But as the solution to the religious wars was the founding of a secular, that is, an irreligious society, may we not surmise that a society which would tamp down the burning Western belief in the freedom of the person would be an inhuman society?

This is not solution, but suicide. The West has always been able to look on itself critically, to recognize its imperfections and strive to overcome them. But when faced with an enemy, alien to its basic beliefs, threatening its existence, it has rejected compromise and scorned hesitation. The enemy we face today is the most alien and the most deadly in our history, one with whom accommodation means surrender. We need now not lofty disinterested counsels, but the cry that rang out at Roncesvalles and Lepanto: "We are right! They are wrong!"

Commonweal Puts the West in its Place

(National Review, October 7, 1961)

One thing the Liberal mind cannot stomach is the concept that some things have greater values than others, that there can be among human beings, nations, and civilizations a higher and a lower. So it was predictable that when Brent Bozell in "The Strange Drift of Liberal Catholicism" (*National Review*, August 12) dared to say that Western civilization has a unique and transcendent value, and that our war against Communism is a holy war, Liberalism would rise in its wrath.

It is somewhat disconcerting, however, that the attack has been spearheaded by a Liberal journal which is also a Catholic journal, *Commonweal*, and that the attack has the content that it has. Were it not for that content, and for the further fact that the editors of *Commonweal* attack not only the article, but the "professional competence" of the editors of *National*

Review, the non-Catholic as well as the Catholic editors, "in dealing with the relation between Catholicism and socio-political matters," I should leave the matter to Mr. Bozell, who is perfectly capable of defending himself and his article, and to my Catholic colleagues on the editorial board.

But the issue is wider. *Commonweal* not only challenged the several and individual competencies of the editors of *National Review*, who strongly approved of the article, whatever their faith; it drove a knife to the heart of any man who, recognizing the fearful potentialities of modern warfare, is nonetheless willing to stand up and fight for his country and his civilization. Obviously, the horrendous potentialities of nuclear warfare would give pause to any sane man if all that were at stake between surrender and resistance were moderate preferences between one civilization and another, varying shades of gray that held nothing approximating black and white.

But Communism, in actual and objective fact, does represent an absolute black, and the West as a civilization is *in its essence* as close to an absolute white as is possible in the subdued light which illuminates this imperfect world. Sharp and vivid extremes do exist in reality, no matter how much the Liberal and relativist mind strives to cloak the real presence of glorious and desperate alternatives. As Brent Bozell wrote: "*God is involved in the Cold War; but more to the point: God's civilization is involved. The West makes this claim over against the rest of the world: that it has been vouchsafed the truth about the nature of man and his relationship to the universe, and has been commissioned to construct and preserve an earthly city based on this truth.*"

This statement it is which so scandalizes *Commonweal*. Blinding in its simple directness, it blazes upon the gimcrack structure of "if, and, and but," of "maybe and perhaps," of "everything is relative," behind which the Liberals take refuge from reality. So sharp a confrontation of good and evil is too painful for them. The West is nice, they concede, "of high merit and great value," and Communism is nasty; we are right to conduct "a continuing and unremitting opposition to Communism." But Heaven forbid that the issue be placed too sharply or too clearly: "To speak of the West as God's civilization is almost blasphemous. . . ." To assert that the West's war against Communism is a holy war is "to enlist God as the Supreme Commander of our natural forces [and] hopelessly to confuse the sacral and the secular order."

Of course, "to enlist God" for a human end would be immeasurably blasphemous; but what if God has enlisted us, through the heritage of our long history and His revelation of good and truth, to resist to the utmost, to bend our every energy to destroy, an incarnate evil? It is sad to have to remind Catholics, even Liberal Catholics, that this is a sacramental, not a Manichean world, that our secular actions as ordinary men partake of the sacred when we act with good faith and motive and grace towards truth and good.

With all the human imperfections that attended their wars, were the Crusaders who defended the West against the tide of Islam "hopelessly misguided," "almost blasphemous," as they fought for the Honor of God and for the West which carried that Honor and that Truth? We may be more historically sophisticated than they, but if we are not blinded by historical relativism, the essence of their understanding of the role of the West remains true for us—that, in Cardinal Newman's words, *"this commonwealth [is] pre-eminently and emphatically human society, and its intellect the human mind, and its decisions the sense of mankind, and its disciplined and cultivated state civilization in the abstract . . . [It is] the state also of that supernatural society and system which our Maker has given us directly from Himself, Christian Polity. . . ."*

If to fight for this civilization with the belief that we do God's will is blasphemous, then not the Western but the Buddhist view of the things of this world is true: they are but shadows to which no man should give a moment's allegiance. But this the West has always denied. Its Christian vision has seen this sentient world as reflecting and embodying, however imperfectly, issues of transcendent significance.

It is only this understanding that can strengthen and justify us against the hazards of these fearful times. *Commonweal* may raise its hands in horror if we see a divine sanction for our mission; the patriots of the early Republic had a more profound view of the relations between things divine and human:

> *"Then conquer we must,*
> *For our cause it is just,—*
> *And this be our motto,—*
> *In God is our trust!"*

Paths Towards Surrender

(National Review, November 4, 1961)

With all his weaknesses, Dwight Eisenhower had one strength as President of the United States: the voices of the Establishment, which dominate the intellectual life of the nation, reached him only in muffled tones. Kennedy, unfortunately, is under constant and direct bombardment. Not only is he surrounded by a choice assortment of its leading figures, but also it is rumored that he reads—and from the publicity given to what he reads, it is largely, if not entirely, the product of that same Liberal Establishment. It is the pressure of this accumulated opinion which goes far to explain the pusillanimity Kennedy—whatever his native inclinations may be—has displayed on Cuba, on Berlin, on nuclear testing, on the manifold issues of resistance to the Communist drive for world conquest.

As James Burnham pointed out in a recent column in *National Review* (October 21), in order to form a policy it is necessary to decide whether war or Communism is the main enemy; and those who speak with authority in the Liberal Establishment are, with honorable exceptions, committed to the thesis that war is the main enemy. Not clearly and consciously committed, however. Most of these men have managed to live in a blur in which they assert their equal hatred of war *and* Communism, although their operative conclusions have for the past fifteen years by and large expressed their underlying mood—that at bottom war, not Communism, is the main enemy.

Not until fairly recently has the logical outcome of this choice of enemies been openly and radically expressed by any influential segment of the Establishment. Only with the foundation of the Committee of Correspondence at Harvard, among whose leaders are David Riesman, H. Stuart Hughes and Erich Fromm, has the position which considers surrender as preferable to nuclear war been publicly espoused. Under the double impact of the tightening of the world situation and the emergence of a conscious conservative insistence upon the defeat of Communism as the first imperative of American policy, this stark movement towards surrender has been steadily gaining influence. A process of polarization is setting in, which, as issues sharpen, is making it more and more difficult to maintain the impossible juggling act of equating the risk of war with the risk of Communist world domination as equal dangers. A choice of enemies is imposed by reality, and the lines are becoming clarified.

One of the most startling developments in the emergence of a clear position from the murk of Liberal double-talk has been the transformation of *Commentary*, perhaps the most intellectually influential of American monthlies. Under its previous editor, Elliot Cohen, it was a bulwark of anti-Communism. Under its present editor, Norman Podhoretz, it is steadily moving towards defeatism—despite isolated rearguard anti-Communist actions by Moshe Decter and Sidney Hook.

The general outlines of the position *Commentary* has been developing were sharply enunciated in two articles in its September issue, which, if their double thesis were true, would denominate anyone willing to *risk* nuclear war in resisting Communism a madman. It is the more troubling that one of these articles is by Hans J. Morgenthau, who has long held a reputation as a tough "realist" in the field of foreign policy, and the other is by Robert A. Nisbet, who both in his stewardship of the University of California, Riverside, and in his sociological writings has earned the plaudits of conservatives.

Professor Morgenthau, under the title "Death in the Nuclear Age," devotes himself to denying the moral foundation of valor, nobility of soul, determination to resist evil at whatever cost. There was a time, he writes, when death in defense of ideals made sense; but "we" no longer believe in immortality, and in the nuclear age "we" can no longer believe in its humanist substitute, immortality in the memory of future generations, because nuclear warfare would destroy civilization and the memory of men. That to do what is right is right, is a concept inaccessible to him: "To die with honor is absurd if nobody is left to honor the dead."

With the vision of Thermopylae destroyed for us down-to-earth moderns, Dr. Nisbet's article quiets any remaining qualms. Associating himself with the soporific "wisdom" of George Kennan, John A. Lukacs, Louis J. Halle, Edmund Stillman and William Pfaff; playing heavily on the myth of the end of messianism in a managerial, non-aggressive, Khrushchev era; insisting that Communism as a world movement does not exist, he reduces the Soviet threat to that of "a dangerous military nationalism." He inveighs against "the ideologist of the right . . . who sees in the world around us . . . ethical and metaphysical problems posed by an absolute Evil."

The conclusion to be drawn from Morgenthau's article and Nisbet's, taken together, is clear. If nuclear warfare poses the threat it does—and no sane man would deny its fantastic horror; if death with honor in defense of the true and the good has lost its meaning; and if Communism is just another militant imperialism, like Wilhelm II's Germany, then accommodation is obviously the right and politic course.

But in the real world, this is a course that can lead only to surrender and Communist world domination. For Communism *is in reality* an armed messianic force that will be contented with no less than world domination. To consider it as less evil, while holding to biological survival as the *summum bonum,* is to insure its victory.

As yet the logic of the blurred refusal to face the issue of liberty or death has not, in the thinking of the great majority of those who make up the Establishment, led to so dangerous a conclusion. Within the blur, there is still hope of a different clarification: that Communism is indeed an evil which must be resisted at all costs if the United States and Western civilization are to survive, that Communism, not war, is the main enemy. It is the first task of the growing conservative consciousness to bring about this resolution of the dominant contemporary confusion, by pressing home upon the Establishment and its President the realities of Communism and the validity of our ancient beliefs which elevate truth and honor and valor far above the ignoble blackmail of death.

The Liberal Veto

(National Review, February 27, 1962)

Contemporary American conservatism as a conscious movement has come into existence largely in reaction to the development of the Liberal revolution of the last few decades. Nevertheless, despite these origins and despite the fact that, almost universally, conscious conservatives condemn Liberalism, there seems to be among many conservatives a certain lack of understanding of what Liberalism essentially is.

This leads to practical political problems of the utmost immediate importance—and in diverse quarters. It is clear how the lack of understanding of Liberalism that sees actual Communists or conscious Communist supporters in every American activity that objectively helps the Communists (when in actual fact usually it is not Communist ideology but Liberal ideology that is responsible), can disorient conservatives in their double battle against Communism and Liberalism. But at a pole of the conservative temper far removed from this outlook, there is another, and in the long run perhaps even more self-defeating form of blindness to the nature of Liberalism. This expresses itself in the idea that because of the pressing immediate danger from Communism, the main task of conservatives is to make an alliance with important sectors of the Liberal establishment, sinking all their conservative principles except anti-Communism. It is the kind of thinking which places high hopes in the anti-Communist stance of a Romney or a Rockefeller, or in persons within and around the Administration who are a little more aware of reality than those who comprise its blatant appeasement wing.

Considering the immediate menace of Communism, there might be some practical political wisdom to this if Liberals *as Liberals* were capable of understanding the character of the struggle with Communism and of concerting an effective anti-Communist policy. Indeed, since Liberals are not, like Communists, men whose whole person is cast in the image of their ideology and since their instincts and their underlying upbringing are essentially at war with their Liberal ideology, many of them may very well one day adhere to a clear anti-Communist policy—but only after such a policy has been developed by non-Liberals on premises other than the premises of the Liberal ideology and when that policy has achieved substantial political support.

This is not to deny that in the intervening period it may be possible from time to time to gain the support of Liberals on specific issues in specific situations. Even on such specific issues, however, the initiative is not likely to come from Liberal quarters. And certainly the Liberals are not able to develop an effective over-all anti-Communist policy, nor even to participate in the development of such a policy under any circumstances in which the fundamental premises of Liberalism would come to bear.

For the underlying assumptions of the Liberal mind are such that they continuously veto the necessary principles for the

conduct of a successful struggle against the horror of Communism—as they did not veto a successful struggle against the
horror of Nazism. I use the word "horror" advisedly. As one
reads the Liberal journals or the statements of Liberal spokesmen; as one studies the sort of thing that Liberal censors,
following the Fulbright Memorandum, have cut out of the
speeches of our military officers; as one observes how they
seize on every will-o'-the-wisp, from the "agrarian reformer"
myth of the thirties to "Sino-Soviet enmity" today, which can
distract attention from the reality of Communism—and then
thinks back upon the kind of language the Liberals were using
in 1938 and 1939 and 1940 about Nazism, it is clear that the
equal monstrosity and the greater threat of Communism does
not and cannot inspire in them a deep conviction of the kind
they held about Nazism. They simply do not feel about Communism, as they did about Nazism, that this is an enemy
so thoroughly alien and so threatening to Western civilization
that it must be defeated if freedom and truth are to survive.

This incapacity of the Liberal mind to understand Communism in its full horror is the essential tragic cause of the
devastating retreat of the United States and the West before
Communism. The reasons why this is so—why the Liberals
cannot lead the fight against Communism—are not far to
seek. To consider only a few of them: The Liberal commitment to positivism destroys belief in the transcendent values
upon which Western civilization is based. The Liberal commitment to relativism cuts away the foundation of that loyalty
unto death to Western values which is essential if, under the
somber conditions of modern technology, the reality of the
onslaught of Communism is to be faced without flinching,
without pretending to ourselves that what is there really isn't
there. The Liberal commitment to collectivism and social engineering, to the priority of "society" and the state over the
freedom of the person, leads to a feeling deep down that,
after all, however deplorable their means, however frightful

their *Schrecklichkeit*, the Communists are black-sheep brothers under the skin.

Conservative principles are not a luxury to be put aside for the overriding emergency of the struggle against Communism; it is only on the basis of these principles that this struggle can be effectively pursued. As appeasement develops naturally out of the Liberal assumptions, anti-Communism develops naturally out of the principles of conservatism. Not their watering down, but their intensification is the necessary basis for a successful fight against Communism.

Us Simple Americans

(National Review, July 31, 1962)

It is time to take stock. Seventeen years of steady advance of Soviet power, and the continuing failure of American leadership to concert an effective counterstrategy, inevitably create increasingly dangerous situations in world affairs. Today we live in conditions created by the collapse of any effective American policy in the post-Dulles years of the Eisenhower Administration and the first years of the Kennedy Administration.

The beginning of this phase was signalized by the Khrushchev visit to the United States and the conferences at Camp David. The years since have seen accelerating deterioration of Western resistance: the steady attrition of our stance on Germany in the face of Khrushchev's ultimata; the agonized collapse of Western power in continental Africa and on the southern shores of the Mediterranean; the continued strangling of Chinese Nationalist power and the negotiated advance of Communism into Southeast Asia; the establishment of a firm Communist base in the Western Hemisphere, aided and abetted first by American complacence, then by American hand-wringing and bumbling.

These are a few of the surface events; but even more devastatingly significant than these clear notes of retreat has been the steady underlying theme of "coexistence" and appeasement, heralded by Eisenhower's "war is unthinkable" and rising to a crescendo in the settled policy of the Kennedy Administration that victory is a "simplistic idea." But "in war there is no substitute for victory," and it is war in which we are engaged—war declared by the international Communist enterprise at its inception many years ago, war in which, at least since 1945, the United States has been the main enemy, indeed the only serious enemy. Every strategy, every tactic, every action of that enterprise has as its guiding aim the defeat of the United States, for only the United States stands in the way of its messianic drive to conquest of the world.

These are the simple sober facts of the situation in which we find ourselves—facts confirmed both by the explicit witness of the corpus of Communist doctrine and by the record of the history of our time. But the Establishment brands anyone who dares to state this central blinding truth as "simplistic." When Barry Goldwater writes, "Our job, first and foremost, is to persuade the enemy that we would rather follow the world to Kingdom Come than consign it to Hell under Communism," or when Robert Pell, the senatorial candidate of the Conservative Party of New York, says, "It has become almost treasonable to speak of the enemy as the enemy," it fills the air with verbiage about "Americans who are unable to accept the complicated adjustments necessary in our time," and "the responsibilities and nuances entailed in world leadership."

Our policies and our actions over these years—policies and actions concerted by connoisseurs of nuances—are evidence of what failure to recognize simple, stark reality brings in its train. Our blind pressure for disarmament, which can only improve the enemy's position; our long cessation of nuclear testing; our craven abandonment of the U-2 flights; our absurd cooperation with the Soviet Union (can anyone imagine such cooperation with Nazi Germany?) in "cultural exchange"; our wasting of the substance of America on economic aid to countries that never have and never will support us in the war with Communism; our leaders' fantastic wishful thinking about "polycentric Communism" and "national Communism"; our insults—and often worse than insults—to our firmest allies: all are witness that the "nuances" of the Establishment are but elaborate rationalizations of a refusal to face reality and fulfill the solemn duties that morality and patriotism alike dictate to those who guide the fortunes of the United States in this perilous hour.

When one shakes his mind free of the verbal gymnastics and super-sophisticated "analyses" of which most discussion of foreign policy consists today, when one steps back and soberly takes stock of the world as it actually is, the truth *is* simple. It is that only the power of the United States prevents the instant domination of the world by Communism; and that, because of our power, it is upon us and us alone that the duty of leadership and the authority of decision rest.

The "nuances" which the various factions of the Establishment can find to evade this truth are inexhaustible. If the intellectual bankruptcy of Rostow, Stevenson, Bowles with their blatant refusal to recognize the reality of Communism, becomes glaringly obvious, then the stark responsibility of the United States can be shrugged off and our proud sovereignty putatively traded away by Lippmann and Fulbright (and now Rockefeller, in his new book *The Future of Federalism*) in some gimmicky dream of an Atlantic Union or a "federation of free nations," which will relieve us of the burden and the glory of manhood. The Europe of a tragically torn France, an effete Britain, an Italy "opening to the left," a Germany hanging upon the life of a great octogenarian, is held by the slenderest threads from full socialism and outright accommodation with Communism. It is only from the United States that the will and the power to defend freedom can come; but it will only come from the United States when the nerveless hands of the tergiversating experts in "nuances" are replaced at the helm by the hands of men who are wise enough to be able to see simple things—

that Communism is evil; that it threatens to destroy us; that it must be defeated; and that on the United States rests the duty, as we have the power, to bring about its defeat.

World Government: Last Refuge of Liberalism

(National Review, March 12, 1963)

As one observes the continuing series of decisions that shape our foreign policy, the question inevitably arises: what is the purpose, the goal, the end, towards which those who make these decisions think they are moving?

We have seen the enfeeblement of our manned air power by the quashing of the RS-70 and Skybolt; the withdrawal of our advanced missiles from Turkey and Italy; the decision to phase the B-47 out of Europe; the hammer blows calculated to bring to power neutralist forces in France, England and Canada; the support given to every anti-Western force in Africa, from the shore of the Mediterranean to the Cape of Good Hope; to say nothing of our continued toleration, in flagrant repudiation of the Monroe Doctrine, of an armed and hostile base in the Caribbean—or of the continuing cozy correspondence between Kennedy and Khrushchev.

What do the men who perpetrate these policies think they are doing? In the light of the sworn and dedicated, openly expressed and confirmed, Communist determination to conquer the world, what other alternative than the apocalyptic choice the Communists insist upon—victory or defeat—do they foresee in the still hours of the night when all men with power, even Liberals, come face to face with ultimate responsibility?

These men are not Communists, nor are they Communist-sympathizers. They cannot and do not accept Communist control of the world; but they will not and they do not take the patently necessary steps to bring about the defeat of Communism.

Nor is this inconsequence a peculiar stigma of the Kennedy Administration. The same question must be raised about those who stood by when half of Europe and all of China were swallowed up by Communism while we held a monopoly of nuclear weapons; who halted our victorious armies on the Yalu; who proclaimed the principle that "war is unthinkable" when the Communists think of nothing day and night but war in one form or another; who gave Khrushchev a triumphal tour of the United States, who stopped the U-2 flights, who let the Hungarian people bleed to death. This is not a Kennedy disease, nor is it a Democratic disease; it is a disease of Liberalism, Democratic or Republican.

Push any argument with a Liberal about world politics to fundamentals, and you will find the assumption that enables him to ignore reality. The Liberal mind, abhorring the prospect of a Communist world, but shrinking from the hard necessity— the only real alternative to that prospect—of girding ourselves for the defeat of Communism, takes refuge in the concept of World Government. Like a child hiding behind its mother's skirts, it finds its comfort in the concept of a mechanism (Heaven knows who will control it, or what god-like creatures will justly administer it) that will abolish all tension and remove all responsibility from our shoulders, while everyone lives happily ever after in peace and prosperity. This is the myth that emerges as final solution to all problems, as much from the tough-minded analysis of Herman Kahn (*On Thermonuclear War*) or the Modern Republicanism of Nelson Rockefeller (*The Future of Federalism*), as from the ideological Liberalism of William Fulbright (speeches, *passim*).

Most of the time—as with so many of the articles of the Liberal credo—the virtues of World Government are simply taken for granted as self-evident. If any doubt is expressed, it is only about the possibility of achieving this end "in time," never about its desirability. Kahn is typical of a whole school of "realistic" analysts of modern warfare, as Fulbright with his scorn for American sovereignty is typical of Liberal ideologists. They neglect not only the chasm which separates Western civilization from Communist neo-barbarism, but also the profoundly different moral concepts that underlie Western, as distinguished from Indian or Chinese or Islamic, civilization, or from African pre-civilization—to say nothing of the lesser but still profound differences of *ethos* that separate one nation from another within the West, most particularly those that separate the American constitutional doctrine of limited government from European doctrine and experience.

It is easy to understand why such slipshod thinking prevails. Emotionally, World Government is the *deus ex machina* that saves the Liberal from the harsh reality of Communism. Intellectually also, unity, uniformity, hatred of diversity are the unexamined premises of men who have turned the verb "discriminate," once a hallmark of civilized thought, into a swear word.

So viscerally indeed, so uncritically, are these beliefs held that when an effort is made to argue the case for World Government, rather than just assume it, the arguments presented suffer from elementary historical and political confusions. An example is Nelson Rockefeller's *The Future of Federalism*, mentioned above, which projects the necessity and desirability of World Government by analogy with the necessity and desirability of the unification of the thirteen American Colonies. Blindly he ignores the common origin, historical tradition, political experience, and moral outlook which laid the basis for our federal union, in order to make of the success of that union a moral mandate for world federalism.

The contemporary myth of World Government remains what it has been since Franklin Roosevelt created the United Nations—the last refuge of men unwilling to face the reality of messianic Communism, unwilling to accept their moral responsibility to beat it down.

As Willmoore Kendall once said, the Liberals, despite their vaunted openmindedness, are by and large unwilling to participate in the "discussion process." If one refuses to accept their underlying assumptions, discussion is ruled out. Whether they preach a "moderation" without principle or indignantly excommunicate from the intellectual world those who challenge their assumptions, the result is the same—the stifling of fundamental discussion.

The New Moderation

(National Review, October 20, 1956)

Moderation is the vogue of the hour. Arthur Larson and all the New Republicans intone its praises, and the New Stevenson agrees. It has even produced the New Nixon—and what bids fair, at this writing, to become the dullest and most meaningless Presidential campaign of all the forty-three the Republic has seen.

But the election campaign is only the most immediate of the spheres of human action and thought in which the spreading fungus of "moderation" is dampening the joy of nations and ossifying the intellect. In the phantasmagoric world of "mass communications," where controversy would seem to be essential if freedom is to survive, the really damning judgment upon a man is that he is "controversial." A pro-Communist is not condemned, as he should be, because he is a pro-Communist, but because he is "controversial." By the same token, a firm anti-Communist is also "controversial"; that he fights for good against evil, that he is an advocate of the truth, is unimportant. All that matters is that nothing shall be said that might disturb anyone's complacency. To take truth and principle seriously, to insist that some things are right and other things are wrong, is to be an "extremist"; and extremists are not only upsetting to complacency, they are by definition evil when moderation is the good.

The scene is the same in the scholarly world. From the Milan Conference of the Congress for Cultural Freedom to the maiden book review by the newest arrival in the scholarly journals, everything breathes of moderation. And why not? Since truth is only relative, and good no more than the prevailing custom of the tribe, what is the use of getting excited about differences of opinion? There is nothing so important that it cannot be handled with a little common sense, good will, and accommodation. Besides, the big bad hydrogen bomb is threatening in the background; and if anybody makes too much of a fuss about good or truth or principle, it might get angry, and go off. And as everyone in our enlightened age knows, nothing, nothing at all, is more important than sheer survival. It is better to live on your knees than to die on your feet.

Now that the scientific method has been applied to the problems of philosophy and ethics, we know that principles and firm beliefs are superstitious hangovers from the Dark Ages or rationalizations of the unpublishable yearnings of the id: only the instrumental is "meaningful." There is, of course, no point in taking seriously anything that isn't meaningful. But, since only the instrumental is meaningful, and since the instrumental changes like a chameleon with each moment of the changing situation, *it* can't be taken too seriously either. So the sensible man will take no idea, no position, seriously enough to risk anything for it; moderation will be his watchword.

Thus was developed the new god-term which has descended upon us in the last couple of years. Here, as in so many other cases, it is in the intellectual world that the source and fount of prevailing attitudes is to be found. What begins in the cloister ends in the public arena. We have become so moderate that the school child who would emulate famous men rather than adjust to his "peer group," is anxiously submitted to the psychiatric counselor as dangerously abnormal. And the baseball player who throws his bat on the ground in disgust at an umpire's decision is heaved out of the game as a threat to baseball's public relations in an era of television and moderation.

Actually, of course, what is being inculcated as moderation is an ideology of nihilistic relativism that has little relation to the true meaning of the word. Moderation, as it has been understood in the philosophical tradition of the West, implies something very different from this contempt for value. It has meant the rational and prudential control of the passions and the will so that the ends of truth and good might be more clearly seen, and action more evenly directed towards them. Moderation in this traditional sense has a close relation to Aristotle's doctrine of virtue as a mean between the vices of excess and the vices of defect.

This is a far cry from the "moderation" that is preached for us today, which knows neither virtue nor vice and condemns principle in the name of the instrumental, of "what works." The Aristotelian doctrine of the mean, for example, denominates courage as a virtue—the mean between rashness, the vice of excess, and cowardice, the vice of defect. But our disciples of moderation, the leaders of both parties, steadily and consistently exhibit both the vice of defect and the vice of excess. Charged with the foreign policy of a nation upon which the future of the world depends, in words they rashly promise or threaten whatever comes to mind; but in action, with unexampled cowardice, they retreat and retreat behind a smoke screen of platitudes, surrendering position after position to bluff and blackmail.

Moderation in its true meaning is a virtue in any man or any people. But what is being promulgated today under that name is not temperance of judgment and firmness of action. It is contempt for principle; it is blind refusal to face the real and compelling crisis of our affairs, domestic and foreign; it is cowardly fear of taking a position and standing by it with resolution. This is not moderation, but the surrender of human dignity. As a principle by which to live, it leads straight to moral and spiritual suicide.

A Specter Is Haunting Yale

(National Review, February 15, 1958)

Professors Cushing Strout and Charles L. Black Jr. are luminaries in the Yale firmament. Now, though a Princeton man myself, I am not one to maintain that no good can come out of New Haven; Bill Buckley, Brent Bozell and John Chamber-lain are products of Yale, and Willmoore Kendall, if not out of it, is at least deeply in it. But, judging from two recent articles, one by Dr. Strout in *Partisan Review*, the other by Dr. Black in the *New Republic*, something is afoot at Yale.

The ideology is not particularly new, but the emotional tone that accompanies it is: a sort of combination of "The devil is dead, may the new devil soon die" with "Who's afraid of the big bad wolf?" One underlying concern seems to dominate both Dr. Strout and Dr. Black: Senator McCarthy, as the latter puts it, "was insignificant" compared to the immense danger to Liberalism from the invasion of the intellectual community by a conservative critique of Liberal fundamentals.

The specific phenomenon which disturbs Dr. Black is Walter Berns' book, *Freedom, Virtue and the First Amendment* (which was discussed in *National Review* by Willmoore Kendall—November 16, 23 and 30, 1957); and what particularly disturbs Dr. Black about it, is that a man whom he has to recognize as a fellow intellectual can have so little regard for the household gods of Liberalism.

> He [Berns] would, I judge, be happy and at home in just about the same kind of world as would most of the people he stigmatizes. . . . The same kind of world, that is, with one variation. Freedom, in his world, would no longer have intrinsic value. It would be guarded only insofar as it was judged effi-caciously to serve other ends.
>
> This, I take it, is the philosophical bedrock of the book. When such a man assumes such a position, we rub our eyes—in astonishment, but also in the gesture of waking.

Let us be clear as to what it is that gives Dr. Black such a shock. I have my disagreement with Dr. Berns' position: I think he places freedom at too low a level of the political process; I think he gives to the state a role in the propagation of virtue that is not its function, but the function of church and family and of the intellectual leaders of society. But this is not Dr. Black's criticism. What shocks him is not Dr. Berns' position on the social *loci* of responsibility for the preservation of freedom and for the propagation of virtue. What shocks him is the blasphemy against relativism (openly uttered in the very halls of the academy) that asserts the existence of absolute value, of virtue and justice as ultimate ends.

After all, "we are so built and placed as never to be able to know for sure whether our values, or any values, have validity —or even what validity means in this sense." We are awash in a great sea of uncertainties—"Everything we know about is a process." Dr. Black "can only state some thoughts that make [him] willing to act on the belief that freedom, as a thing in itself, is worth our attachment." But he "disclaim[s] any private wire to the front office of ethical certitude, and [doesn't] think anybody else has one."

Presumably, in this whirling process that cuts off communication with "the front office of ethical certitude," Dr. Black's affection for freedom has no more moral validity than Jack the Ripper's affection for murder, or Stalin's for liquidating the kulaks, or Hitler's for gassing and disassembling Jews. It is all a matter of what passing bit of the Process any of us thinks "is worth our attachment."

These are the standard arguments of Liberalism and relativism. What is new and different is the note of indignation and alarm that respectably bound books, written by respectable citizens of the academy, should dare to challenge the hallowed dogmas of the academy.

Dr. Strout is not so straightforward as Dr. Black. He is compulsively and nervously concerned with the same phenomenon, but through most of his article, "Liberalism, Conservatism and the Babel of Tongues," he tries to pretend that the specter isn't there. Liberalism, to be sure, isn't doing very well intellectually at the moment; but that is only the result of too much overconfidence, after twenty-five years of power. All that is necessary is to recognize that the nice conservatives are really saying much the same thing as the nice Liberals, and there isn't too much to worry about if the nice conservatives and the nice Liberals would only get together. The pattern for their unity is expressed in practice by the present Supreme Court and the "conservative senators who finally brought McCarthy to book," and is outlined in theory by Edward Shils in his attack upon all security measures, *The Torment of Secrecy*.

There is a danger, of course (life is never safe), but, like the savage who will not give the demon he fears a name, lest it have power over him, Dr. Strout sedulously refuses to name his fears aright. Instead, he adopts the current sociological fashion of attributing all serious opposition to Liberalism to a backwoods "populism," to an unwashed envy and hatred of Eastern Ivy-League Liberals, and thus leaves his argument with an immense empty center. For if it is only the populist mob that is challenging the basic assumptions of Liberalism, why has Liberalism anything to fear intellectually?

His emotion is reserved for the "angry pages of William Buckley's *National Review*." But it is not anger that is upsetting him; there has been for many years an angry opposition to the Establishment. What is disturbing Dr. Strout is the same thing that disturbs Dr. Black, who, more honest or more courageous, refuses to take refuge behind the swirling skirts of sociology. *National Review*, and the movement of thought it represents, has called the Liberals to account in terms that have to be met intellectually—and the Liberal mind, accustomed for years to the unchallenged reign of its dogmas, cannot face the reckoning.

Part Two

Political Affairs–
Domestic and Foreign

Chapter Three

Issues and Institutions

The material of the last two chapters represents an effort to clarify the meaning of conservatism and of the Liberalism against which conservatism is arrayed. By the very nature of a magazine of opinion the larger amount of my periodical writing has been concerned with the application of these principles to events and situations as they have occurred and taken form. This chapter and the two following contain material of this type: (1) discussion of political issues and the development of American political institutions; (2) commentary on practical politics; and (3) commentary on American foreign policy.

The subject of this chapter is the first of these—a series of discussions of broad political issues that have arisen, and of the constitutional and political development of the organs of American government. There is, I think, no sharp line between my treatment of these more practical issues and the more theoretical discussion of conservatism and Liberalism. Rather, in what is included in this and the following chapters, I have tried to show in concrete circumstances the living meaning of the conservative outlook.

Underlying the conservative political attitude is the assumption that politics is not simply a power struggle, the meaning of which is determined by the possibilities of victory for party, group, or individual, but is always to be judged, however remotely, by its relation to the endeavor to achieve a good society. Of course, the tactical problems of winning power loom large—and correctly so—but in the end a conservative insists that tactics be subordinated to principle.

Politics and Responsibility

(National Review, April 4, 1956)

Political men in a representative republic have always had to consider the opinions of their constituencies. And sometimes the sheer love of power has led them to an extreme pampering of the whims of those constituencies against the dictates of morality and their own better judgment. But, by and large, until recent times it was thought the duty of those elevated to positions of legislation and administration to act as a "creative minority," to guide and educate the opinion upon which they were dependent. Thus, the appeal to the electorate was, on large issues at least, an appeal to choice on the level of principle.

It would be idle to idealize the past or to deny that, even at the best, principle in politics has always been mixed with a large element of interest and advantage, that it has always been more or less heavily larded with pork from the barrel. But it has been left to our enlightened time to make a virtue of opportunism, to deny the very place of principle in politics, to make of sensitive and immediate reaction to the mood of the voter, skillful interpretation of public-opinion polls, the highest quality of the rising public man.

The result is that political decisions which are fraught with moral implications of the most far-reaching significance are, in every Western country, taken on the grounds of the sheerest expediency, to satisfy the appetites or satiate the thoughtless passions of whatever collections of voters are believed powerful enough to affect an election.

It is this kind of "leadership" which, at its extreme, has been

one of the major factors in creating the French political im-
broglio, from which Americans and Englishmen are accustomed
to extract so satisfactory a sense of political superiority. But any
serious consideration of the content of the rivalry between the
Conservative and Labor parties in Britain at the present time,
or between the Republican and Democratic parties here, will
quickly remove the grounds of self-satisfaction. That we are
in better case than the French would seem to be due to the
survival, though in a battered state, of institutions we owe to
the wisdom of our ancestors; to the fact that we have not as
yet exhausted the moral capital bequeathed us by past generations; but not to any profound differences in the caliber of our
present political leadership.

As the London *Spectator* said recently, remarking upon an
editorial in the *Daily Telegraph* that posited public opinion as
a sovereign reason for political action on a moral question:

> The argument from public opinion has neither
> moral nor intellectual validity. As Burke said to the
> electors of Bristol, "Your representative owes you not
> his industry only but his judgement; and he betrays
> instead of serving you if he sacrifices it to your
> opinion." Perhaps it is too much to hope that Con-
> servatives should pay as much attention to Edmund
> Burke as they do to Dr. Gallup.

Nor, either on domestic or foreign issues, is the spectacle of
American politics any more edifying. Samuel Lubell, who,
despite his Liberal bias, is a most astute analyst of the political
scene, sums the matter up with an image no less ludicrous
than disgraceful:

> With both the Democrats and Republicans com-
> mitted to preserving the gains of the last generation
> [read: collectivist developments], our parties have
> become, as one voter pictured them, "like two fat
> men in a narrow hall." They cannot squeeze past each

other. Either they move in the same direction or remain stuck in unbudging deadlock. [*Commentary,*
March 1956]

Those who are called to the positions of natural leadership
within the constitutional structure of the Republic forfeit
their role, while fearful issues of domestic and foreign policy
are manipulated to secure the approval of the lowest common
denominator of the electorate. In such a vacuum, it is obvious
that when the raw presence of crisis penetrates to the consciousness of the people, they will look elsewhere for leadership;
and there are, as the twentieth century has amply shown,
totalitarian demagogues, quite outside of the traditions of the
West, ready to give them leadership. What is not so obvious
is this: even as things are, the attitudes and desires of "the
people," to which political leadership panders, are by no means
the simple views of simple people, but the creation of irresponsible elites who shape and "represent" public opinion.

The tremendous power of the mass-communications trades
(particularly since the advent of television, but long developing
in multi-million-circulation magazines and newspapers, and in
radio and the movies) plays first part in the shaping, although
the government departments, the trade unions, the so-called
voluntary organizations interact and coordinate with the publicists proper through their own public-relations activities. And
it is these latter—organizations like the League of Women
Voters, the American Association for the United Nations, the
various associations and leagues pretending to speak for "minority groups"—which are considered as "representing" the public
opinion to which the politician defers.

I am in no way questioning the propriety of the existence of
such organizations in a free society, nor the right of those who
speak and write to influence opinion, to do so. What I am
saying is that these groupings, as things are today, function
with total irresponsibility, in that the nominal holders of power,
thinking to serve public opinion, are in fact merely executing

the policies of these elites, whom no one can call to account. The situation would be bad enough with such groupings exercising their power without public accountability; it is made much worse, worse to a decisive degree, by the fact that those who hold this indirect power have in their immense majority no more conscious responsibility to truth and principle, which should go with power, than have the politicians themselves.

It is true, of course, that a few among them have the clear and distinct aims of the Communist conspiracy. A good many more hold on principle to the objectives of a Fabian socialism. In the inchoate atmosphere of principle-less opportunism, both of these groups, by default of opposition, exert an influence far beyond their numbers and give a sinister direction to the formation of opinion and policy. But the great majority of those who compose the determining elites believe in nothing and have no conscious direction—except the fashions accepted by their fellows, the overriding need to be in the intellectual swim, in a word, conformity each with each. As our political leadership looks to what it fatuously conceives to be the will of the people to know what it should do, so those who make that opinion look to each other.

Yet for all the danger they pose to the Republic, indeed to civilization itself, these are not evil men—neither the real nor the nominal holders of power. Although—to borrow from another context the pat phrasing of William F. Buckley, Jr.—there is in their pronouncements "not a word said, not an inflection intentionally turned loose, having to do with the political or social or philosophical imperatives" that might for good or ill denote and define something to stand for or to fight against, they are, by and large, not "traitors, or adventurers, or charisma-conscious political evangelists or, even, cynics." They are neither hot nor cold. And they cannot be responsible because no one has ever taught them to see the difference between good and evil, to define and to differentiate, to know a hawk from a handsaw. It is not possible to be responsible without the ability to define and separate good and duty from interest and passion. And the teaching which has molded the outlook of the past two generations has been such that these necessary foundations for responsible leadership have on the whole simply not been available to those in power.

It is those who deal with fundamental ideas, with philosophy and theology (or, in our day, anti-theology) who in the end shape the way in which men live. The politically powerful, while they may be held accountable for the goodness or maliciousness of their will, for their personal character, are not accountable for the limitations of their training, for the intellectual atmosphere of society. Neither the discipline of definition and differentiation nor the very existence of values, of standards by which action can be judged, has been taught them. Reason has been subordinated to the flow of experience; distinction and differentiation mocked at as pedantic medievalism; and values reduced to the taste and choice of each man's natural and untutored desires. And for this state of affairs the blame rests upon the intellectuals, upon those who taught them and who taught their teachers.

The political life of our time reflects the intellectual trend of decades, of a successively more radical devaluation of values, culminating in a positivism, a pragmatism, an instrumentalism which have spawned the shapeless motivations of the practical man. Even these philosophical positions, however, while they were the culmination of a process of attack upon the traditional foundations of knowledge and understanding, carried with them in their very negativity certain intellectual demands that could stimulate the mind. Today, however, if a perusal of the learned journals is any indication, a dead level of mediocrity where nothing is different from anything else, a sort of intellectual entropy, rules. As a conservato-liberal and libero-conservative mishmash pervades our political life and the vast majority of the "middle-brow" organs of opinion—the programs of Ed Murrow, *Time* and *Life,* and the *Reporter*—so the outstanding characteristic of the "highbrow" organs is vapidity.

An important philosophical journal prints as its leading article an essay entitled "Against Wisdom"—and means it. (*Philosophy and Phenomenological Research,* September, 1955). In Milan there assemble 150 intellectuals, the most touted carriers of the ideology of the non-Soviet world, called together by the Congress for Cultural Freedom to discuss "The Future of Freedom." And what, to judge from the public reports, was their consensus? I quote from an article of Edward Shils in *Encounter* (November, 1955). He is not the most detached of witnesses, but nothing else I have read, either in reportage of the Congress or in published papers there delivered, contradicts him. The title of his report is "The End of Ideology?" and by ideology, his context clearly shows that he means not the Marxist or Mannheimian concept of ideology as the rationalization of group interest, but all firm principle. The Congress showed, he believes, that "We no longer feel the need for a comprehensive explicit system of beliefs." It demonstrated the "growing hollowness of the conventional distinctions between socialism and capitalism . . . the vanity of the claims of simon-pure socialists and free-enterprise liberals," the futility of continuing "to argue along the old lines as if the crucial distinction in economic policy was between socialism and capitalism." The "belief in a higher law found no support, either."

If these, the cream of the recognized intellectuals of the day, collaborated to create such an impression, how can one blame the poor political man who takes "the voice of the people," whatever ventriloquist that voice may echo, as the only standard to which he can repair?

Our ills cannot be cured on any surface level. It is at the source of evil that evil must be fought; and that means that in the fight for truth and responsibility, the decisive front is the field of ideas. This, it might seem, is a sorry hope when one surveys the condition of contemporary intellectual life. But its very vapidity creates an opportunity.

The one thing that men at their best cannot tolerate is nothingness, and that is what the thinking of the accepted intellectuals of the West has reduced itself to. A false philosophy, coming at last to the dead center of its own mediocrity, can not long continue to give form to men's ideas.

The field is open, and the hope for the future lies with those who, caring deeply for truth and unable to face the emptiness of accepted thought, stand forth to revindicate value. So doing, they can make possible the rebirth of an individual, a social, a political life founded upon value.

One of the most devastating results of the politics of expedience which has prevailed these last few decades is a dramatic distortion of the relation between state and society—a distortion which I characterized in 1959 as an inevitable outcome of the violation of a "political law of parity." Almost a decade later, the reader will, I think, see only a further and more disastrous development of the process described.

A Political "Law of Parity"?

(National Review, January 17, 1959)

Libertarian conservatives have with justice concentrated their attention upon the cancer-like growth of the State, as its malignant cells invade the body of society ever more widely. But as our attention has been concentrated upon this primary danger, upon the massive destruction by the State of the independent functioning of individual persons in a free society, another phenomenon, the obverse of this and yet integrally connected with it, has been less remarked. Or, when it has been noticed, it has been seen in its several parts, as a series of separate and disconnected problems, not as a single phenomenon.

I am speaking of the increasing inability of the State to fulfill its true functions. Its failure to fulfill these functions (functions which can be fulfilled by no other institution or organization) contributes to the decay of our civilization and our country almost as much as the overweening extension of its power beyond its natural bounds. Defense against external enemies; the preservation of internal order and the protection of the individual citizen in his life, liberty and property; the administration of justice: it is to provide for these necessities of the human condition that the State exists. But these functions, the State's reason for being, are deteriorating day by day and year by year in parallel proportion to the growth of the State's usurpations outside its rightful arena of activity.

If this seems paradoxical, consider:

Defense against external enemies? As military budgets grow to massive proportions and their toll upon the citizen in taxation and inflation mounts and mounts, as frivolous projects of "foreign aid" add their totally unnecessary weight to the burden, as millions of men are conscripted in the decisive years of their preparation for life, what has the State done to protect us from our enemies? At the end of World War II and for a half a decade after, we possessed overwhelming military and material strength—and our enemies advanced one-third of a world closer to our jugular. In the years since, we have possessed, and we possess today, superior strength, and the enemy comes closer and closer without serious let or hindrance.

Preservation of internal order? Protection of the citizen in his life, liberty, and property? The State, with its systems of compulsory schools and its network of "social agencies," backed by the power of taxation and the unchecked sanctions of administrative tribunals, penetrates into the nooks and crannies of personal and family life, laying down the norms of conformity and driving out the traditional morality of the West to make place for a relativist ethic of adjustment. Where it does not belong, it enters; but where it should be acting, signs of breakdown multiply. Our great cities are becoming jungles where no man can go about his business or stroll in the public park in safety, and even inside the schools themselves our children are terrorized, knifed, and raped.

Administration of justice? While the multifarious measures of the Welfare State spawn tribunals with quasi-judicial power, dealing with every concern of the citizen, the very concept of justice based on principle is systematically being done to death in the courts of the land. In place of the immemorial counsels of jurisprudential and legal principle, expediency and the climate of fashionable opinion (always, of course, unconscious factors bearing upon judges, but now consciously and unashamedly invoked) become the bases of judicial decision. With the sanction of positivist philosophy, enforcement of the prejudices of the Establishment becomes the norm, while the idea of evenhanded and impartial administration of justice is scorned by the enlightened as a fairy tale from the Dark Ages.

Thus the valid functions of the State decay with the growth of its tyrannical power over areas which should not be its concern. I think I do not exaggerate the direction of the trend and the accelerating helplessness of the State in dealing with the problems for whose solution it exists. Even though our Establishment has not yet brought about here that combination of vast social penetration with utter inability to fulfill the true functions of the State which destroyed the French Fourth Republic and made Gaullism necessary and possible, the same *direction* of development is clearly marked.

A "law of parity" would seem to be operating whereby, as the State enlarges its claims and directs its power towards the total domination of society, it fails more and more to be able to do that for which we must depend upon the State: to preserve our order internally and against external enemies. If anything is to be learned from modern history, there would seem to be only one alternative to respecting this law of parity. Men cannot live without order of some kind, and there appears to be only one set of circumstances in which order—of a sort—can be maintained when the State establishes its power over the whole social process and over the lives of individual persons: that is the method of total terror and total conditioning, the method of Communism.

This is order; but it is a Hellish order—the stasis imposed upon human existence when the harmonious balance of function among human institutions is destroyed and power is loosed from the control of reason and morality. And it is the order we are likely to get if we do not drive the State back within its limits. Conservatives who stress the danger to freedom from the growth of State power and conservatives who stress the danger to freedom from the weakness of will of the American state in the struggles against Communism have much more in common ideologically than they sometimes think. The cause of limiting the State to its proper functions and the cause of maintaining and defending civilized order through a State strong in its proper sphere are in fact not two causes, but one.

The health of the Republic has always depended upon maintenance of the balance and tension between the tripartite constitutional powers—the legislature, the executive, and the judiciary. For a good part of this century that balance has been deeply disturbed—and always at the expense of the Congress, first by the growing power of the Presidency and more lately by the usurpations of the Supreme Court. The three articles which follow were written some eight years apart, but all are concerned with the increasing debility of the Congress and with modes of restoring its power.

The Revolt Against Congress

(National Review, May 30, 1956)

In the devious way in which revolutionary changes are engineered in this age of mass communications, the public is presently being conditioned to accept a constitutional transformation of fateful import. At stake is the survival of sufficient congressional power to balance the enormously swollen power of the modern Executive; and therewith, the survival of the most fundamental principle of American government—an effective system of checks and balances.

The pressure upon the Congress to yield all real powers to the President and his appointees is not, as it would have been in the brighter days of the Republic, the subject of an open national debate. Rather it is developed indirectly in the course of the arguments and the tactics employed in connection with successive passing political controversies: the demand for a ten-year *carte blanche* to the Executive in the dispensation of foreign aid; last year's open assault, and this year's flank-attack, upon the Bricker amendment; the Administration's outrageous dictate under which the McClellan Committee and the Congress were denied information available to foreign governments (information vitally necessary if the Congress was to know how its own directives, specified in the laws on the export of strategic materials to Iron-Curtain countries, were being carried out).

The same issue underlay the hurly-burly of the controversy around Senator McCarthy two years ago. And the backwash of that controversy is now working its slow way through the courts in the form of decisions upon the powers of investigating committees. The legal issue has been raised in a number of cases—most particularly in the Icardi case and the Watkins case. But it has not by any means been definitely settled. There are strong signs that a judicial doctrine is being developed in the lower courts—one which may well appeal to the present membership of the Supreme Court—which would emasculate Congress' investigatory powers.

The courts in this respect, of course, are following, not, as in Mr. Dooley's simpler age, the election returns, but the attitudes and prejudices of the intellectual Establishment—the filtrate of those attitudes and prejudices as it is expressed in the product of the "opinion makers" of press, radio and television. And these almost to a man are champions of the Executive. Under cover of the slogan of "legislative encroachment," they have disseminated a theory of Executive power unknown to the Constitution.

Such theories, of course, since they involve the exercise of power, never remain idle speculations. It was a political man, an ex-President of the United States, who a year or two ago put the doctrine at its clearest, declaring that the whole people look to the President "for leadership, *and not confined within the limits of a written document.* Every hope and every fear of his fellow citizens, almost every aspect of their welfare and activity, falls within the scope of his concern—indeed, within the scope of his duty." (My emphasis)

But whether in the blunt accents of Mr. Truman, or in the subtler language of the academy, or in the constantly repeated formulas of the columnists, a view of the Constitution is being put forward which would destroy the balance of powers and center authority in a plebiscitarian Leader-President. That Mr. Truman's practice, and the practice of his predecessor, was based on such a theory, the history of the twenty years between 1932 and 1952 confirms. And the four years since have done little to reverse the trend.

In practice and in theory, Presidential supremacy is asserted, not as a proposal for a change or "improvement" of the Constitution, but as *in fact* the law of the land which must not be changed without inviting anarchy and threatening the security of the nation. And to add insult to injury, the proponents of Presidential supremacy have set up a drum-fire of accusation that it is the Congress which is stepping beyond its proper bounds, that the balance of powers is threatened by "legislative encroachment."

It was at the climax of the McCarthy controversy that executive arrogance received its most detailed formulation. In President Eisenhower's directive to the Department of Defense, severely limiting the testimony of members of the Administration, and in Attorney General Brownell's memorandum submitted therewith, a very specific and time-honored set of precedents (directed toward preserving the privacy of the President's personal counsels) was juggled to cover a very different contemporary situation; namely, the activities of a widespread and populous bureaucracy. The extension of secrecy to the activities of some 2,000,000 federal employees, and the exclusion of the

Legislature from information concerning those activities, raises an entirely different point, the spirit of which is in no way covered by the earlier precedents.

Mr. Brownell's memorandum cites twenty-six instances of refusal of information to the Congress, fifteen of which occurred during the Administrations of Roosevelt and Truman. But in all the Administrations from Washington to Hoover there were only eleven such instances. Furthermore, each of the earlier precedents cited had to do with a single occasion of refusal to submit to the Congress papers, either of the President himself or of one of his immediate advisors; while a number of those cited from the last two Administrations were blanket orders, cutting off the Congress from access to information in wide areas of the governmental bureaucracy for an indefinite period.

This indeed is the heart of the matter. The developments of the past thirty years have brought into existence a tremendous new power—a far-flung bureaucracy that enforces administrative law upon tens of millions of citizens every day. The hothouse development of that bureaucracy and of the administrative law which has grown apace with its growth, makes comparison with the limited executive establishments of Washington or Buchanan or Cleveland absurd.

A true balance of powers cannot exist in the abstract. It is a concept which in its very nature is concrete and empiric. If one power is strengthened, the others must also be; or they inevitably become totally subordinated to the strongest. Because of the character of its function, the Executive has harvested most of the power accruing to the federal government from the unconscionable growth of state power over recent decades.

A reduction to constitutional limits of the activity of the federal government would be the quickest way to redress the balance. But that is an unlikely immediate event—and, in fact, one which will never take place on the initiative of the Executive. Therefore, to the degree that the power of the Executive cannot immediately be cut, the power—and particularly the negative power, the restraining power—of the other branches must be increased.

The Judiciary lacks the independent sanctions to resist over any considerable period of time the pressure of a powerful Executive, with congruent strength from the Legislature. The legislative branch, accordingly, must exploit its reserves of constitutional power and match the increased strength of the Executive.

Traditionally, as in the classical example of the struggle of the British Parliament against the Stuarts, the strength of the Legislature has lain in control of the purse-strings and in the power of impeachment (or, in its British analogue, the bill of attainder). But impeachment, like the hydrogen bomb, is a weapon whose very strength inhibits its use except in the most extreme situations. And control of appropriations has become, with the far-flung operations of modern government, a restraint exceedingly difficult to bring to bear. This is particularly the case when so large a portion of expenditure is associated with measures of defense. Besides, a few hundred Congressmen and Senators simply cannot keep up with the ramified activities of a federal bureaucracy of two-million odd.

Likewise, the power of law-making, once the state has entered the field of *positive* activities (a condition which is the result of welfare-state ideas, one never foreseen in the Constitution) becomes less and less effective as a means of control by the Congress over the actions of the Executive. The sort of law envisaged by the makers of the Constitution was fundamentally regulative in character—rules of the game, so to speak—laying down the conditions for the interrelationships of citizens. Whereas the laws of which we have had so many in recent years empower the government to act in multitudinous ways directly affecting individuals. Whatever the Congress does in drafting legislation, the effective meaning of the law is determined by those who enforce it. This modern phenomenon substantially transfers from the Congress to the Executive a large measure of the legislative power.

So much has this come to be accepted that Arthur N. Holcombe, in *The Yale Review* (March, 1954), writes without blinking an eyelash: "After all, the function of the Congress under the Federal Constitution is not to dictate legislative policy to the President. It is rather to insure that the policies of the Administration will not be carried into execution without substantial evidence of the consent of the people in different parts of the country." An interesting idea! But the federal Constitution states in Article I, Section 1: "All legislative Powers herein granted shall be vested in a Congress of the United States. . . ."

The danger to the constitutional concept of divided powers and mutual checks upon single authority would be grave enough with the growth of the executive power proper. But, with the arrogation of a large part of the judicial and legislative powers by that same Executive, the danger becomes a hundred-fold more serious. If the Constitution is to be preserved, the Congress must find the means to redress the balance.

It is primarily in the actual day-to-day administration that the usurpation occurs. Hence it is there that the power of the Congress must be exerted. And the Congress *has* reserves, firmly based in constitutional practice, by which it can influence this only sphere in which it can come to grips with executive aggrandizement.

The investigatory powers, and only these powers, enable the Congress to examine and take appropriate measures against executive usurpation in the concrete circumstances in which it occurs. Without them, the right to legislate and appropriate becomes a hollow formality. With them, the Congress may once again be able to attain its constitutional prerogatives as an equal of the Executive. Far from being restrained, as the current hue and cry demands, the investigatory powers will have to be much expanded, if the fundamental constitutional concept of checks and balances is to survive.

One does not have to agree with the pragmatic cynicism of Mr. Justice Jackson's opinion in the steel-seizure case, when he said: "If not good law, there was worldly wisdom in the maxim attributed to Napoleon that 'The tools belong to the man who can use them.'" But one can wholeheartedly agree with his next sentence: "We may say that power to legislate . . . belongs in the hands of Congress, but only Congress itself can prevent power from slipping through its fingers." And only Congress can defend the Constitution when Executive and Judiciary fail.

The Attack On the Congress

(National Review, February 11, 1964)

In recent weeks, an endemic concern of Liberalism has taken on epidemic proportions. Liberals have never liked the Congress. The Presidency, the bureaucracy, and more lately the Supreme Court, have been their chosen instruments. The Congress too often refuses to go along with their bright new schemes, or if it goes along, does so only halfheartedly, scrutinizing too closely, enacting this and rejecting that, sticking a dozen monkey

---

All legislative Powers herein granted shall be vested in a Congress of the United States, which shall consist of a Senate and House of Representatives. (Art. I, sec. 1, Constitution of the United States)

---

wrenches into the planners' well-oiled machinery. But, although Liberal disdain for the Congress is not new, the intensity of the attack today is creating a major political issue.

As if a conductor had waved his baton, a swelling orchestra has taken up the theme. As I write, I have in front of me a column by Walter Lippmann, "Government Unworkable"; an article from the New York *Times Magazine,* "It Is The People Who Face the Test: They Will Determine Whether the New President Can Overcome Standpattism in Congress"; an article from *Commentary,* "Non-Rule in America"; and an editorial from the New York *Times,* "Cobwebs in Congress"—and these are but a sampling of the many-voiced outcry.

Why this attack on the Congress? It is my opinion that it is not an ephemeral journalistic campaign or a reaction to the actions of the present Congress, but rather is a much more deep-going issue—an issue which can be understood only in the light of an analysis of the factors making up the constitutional crisis of these years.

They built well, those men of 1787. Thirty years of the Roosevelt revolution, double or more that time of incessant centralizing theory and pressure and propaganda—and still the constitutional barriers stand firm, if battered. They thwart the plans and ambitions of the acolytes of the streamlined state, where the Executive decides, the bureaucracy acts, and the blueprints of the Liberal ideologues are imposed upon the citizen.

The barriers have been penetrated, it is true; in area after area governmental measures alien to the constitutional tradition have prevailed, limiting our freedoms and weakening our posture before the world. But these are only bits and pieces of the Liberal Grand Design. The Design itself remains unimplemented. Free action for planners, operating uninhibited by the beliefs and desires of the men who are the objects of the plan (a state of affairs which is the prime necessity for collectivism, Liberal or Socialist or Communist), has never been achieved.

The entire constitutional structure has stood in the way: the multifarious local centers of power still, despite the growth of federal power, maintain a large measure of independence; the guarantees of the Bill of Rights, although evaded again and again, still continue to hobble the arrogance of office; the continuing independence of the state courts and the lower federal courts, despite the subservience of the Supreme Court, slow up and hamper the growth of centralized power. But the main impediment has been the Congress. Never since Franklin Roosevelt carried it by storm in the first flush of the New Deal has it been willing to rubber-stamp the projects of the Executive. Measure after measure has been rejected, transformed, cut down. And, as Willmoore Kendall has pointed out, the restraining influence of the Congress upon the progress of the Liberal revolution has been effective not only because of these actions, but because of the proposals the Executive would like to make but does not dare to, in view of "its certain foreknowledge of the impossibility of getting the proposals through Congress."

Why the intensification of the Liberal attack on Congress has occurred at just this time is not entirely clear. If I may hazard a speculation, I would say that there are several factors which have combined to bring it about:

1) The development of the "civil rights movement" has, for the first time since the days of the sit-down strikes in the thirties, presented the ideologues with a militant extra-legal mass movement which potentially could be used as a club to beat the Congress into submission.

2) The growth of a powerful and articulate conservative criticism has made them feel that time is short, that it is no longer possible to rely upon the passage of time for the steady attrition of constitutional understanding. This has sent a shock of alarm through the Liberal community; it throws serious doubt upon their hitherto complacent assurance that they have complete control of the centers of power for an indefinite period, that therefore they can afford to wait for the cumulative results of slow and steady progress towards their goals, through the circumventing of Congress by the Executive and the Judiciary.

3) It has become predictable that, without the shackling of the Congress, the usurpation of legislative power by the President and the Supreme Court is likely to produce diminishing returns. In late years it has been mainly in areas related to foreign policy that the President has been able to exert such powers, and the Congress has shown its firm intention of riding herd on him here, as the recent gutting of the foreign aid bill shows. In other areas, the extreme exasperation of the Liberals with Kennedy before his death because he did not sufficiently "give leadership"—that is, blackmail the Congress strenuously enough—bears witness both to Kennedy's astute awareness of political possibilities and to the increasing intransigence of the Congress in the exercise of its legislative prerogatives. Johnson,

who has to put his whole honeymoon prestige on the line to get over even the truncated foreign aid bill, is in the course of learning the same lesson.

As far as the Supreme Court is concerned, its forays over the past few years in the usurpation of legislative power have radically weakened its prestige as a constitutional organ respected by all factions—so radically that the time is fast approaching when the Congress could exercise its constitutional powers to clip the wings of the Court without the danger of deeply alienating its constituency. This, I believe, the Liberal analysts sense, although the Congress itself has as yet shown no serious signs of moving towards such action. The immense emotional and political pressure which is currently being generated around the Civil Rights Bill seems otherwise inexplicable. The Court, with the support of the Presidency, has till now been able quite effectively to carry through a similar program of drastic debilitation of the sovereignty of the states and of the rights of individual persons, for the aggrandizement of federal executive power and the imposition upon the citizenry of the blueprints of Liberal ideological dogma.

It is, in fact, the emotion created by the Civil Rights Bill upon which the Liberal ideologues are depending to forward their attack upon the Congress and the Constitution. (This is not to deny the right of Negroes to equal treatment and dignity before the law. But no clause in that bill is concerned with such old-fashioned American rights. They are concerned, rather, with federal enforcement of special group privileges.) Almost every section of the bill, as James Jackson Kilpatrick has lucidly demonstrated (*National Review*, September 24, 1963), is directed toward destroying the constitutional balance of power and centering control over the lives of citizens in the hands of the chosen instruments of Liberalism, the Executive and a subservient Supreme Judiciary.

While it is around the fate of this bill and in the penumbra of the passions generated by it that the present clamor against the Congress is arising, the attack is much more general. It is

directed specifically at every aspect of the functioning of the
Congress that enables it to act in the spirit of the Constitution
as a creator of consensus. The doctrine that underlies these
attacks is a doctrine alien to the Constitution, a doctrine impatient of consensus, demanding crushing of differences, of minority rights and customs. It is a majoritarian doctrine masquerading as American constitutional democracy. Its proponents would
do away with the daily give-and-take of congressional ironing
out of the conflicts of interest between diverse groups. They
would substitute the uncontrolled power of a President elected
with a specious quadrennial "mandate"—that is, supposedly
executing the desires (if, indeed, they are the desires when one
considers all the factors that go into a Presidential election) of
51 per cent or 52 per cent or 53 per cent—or even 55 per cent
or 60 per cent—of the electorate.

Hence, the attack on the modes of procedure worked out
over the years in consonance with the constitutional spirit of
consensus: the committee system, seniority, the shifting coali-
tions of the Congress, the freedom of congressmen and senators
from party discipline of the European style. The ideal image
in which the Congress would be remodeled, if the pressures
presently being exerted were to be successful, is one where an
opposition party would still exist and discussion would still take
place, but where, when the President spoke, a disciplined party
majority in the Congress would more or less automatically implement his desires, with "all deliberate speed."

When the New York *Times* writes: "The scandalous lag in
the legislature is out in the open for all to see. Congress has a
constitutional obligation to function as a legislature," it never
seems to occur to its editors that refusal to pass a Presidential
program is as much a legislative act as passing it. Indeed, the
Congress might legislate even more effectively than it has so
far done, in its resistance to Presidential directives, by further
extending its negative legislation and repealing some of the
legislation presently on the statute books. The superstition that
has developed in recent years that Congress is somehow obli-

gated to pass into law whatever the President proposes, is a gross distortion of the President's minimal constitutional relation to legislation. Apart from his veto power, all the Constitution grants him in relation to legislation is the right "from time to time [to] give to the Congress Information of the State of the Union, and recommend to their Consideration such Measures as he shall judge necessary and expedient. . . ." (Art. II, Sec. 3). *Recommend* means *recommend,* not *demand,* not *pressure,* not *go to the people* to arouse demagogic pressures against the Congress. It means *recommend,* and no more. The first substantive words of the Constitution, Article I, Section 1, state explicitly: "All [*all!*] legislative Powers herein granted shall be vested in a Congress of the United States. . . ."

If Congress chooses to be a "do nothing" Congress—that is, if it chooses to reject Presidential proposals and to see no need for additional legislation, that is its prerogative. If it chooses so to organize itself as, in its opinion, best implements its constitutional duty of establishing consensus, that is its prerogative. And we may thank Heaven for the wisdom of the Founders who gave it its prerogative—and for the wisdom of the Congresses which have "done nothing" to fasten tighter the yoke of governmental power on our necks.

The Court Challenges the Congress

(National Review, March 24, 1964)

Usurpation of power when allowed to go unchallenged breeds arrogance, irresponsibility and further usurpation. The history of the Supreme Court in our generation is far too apt a case in point.

When the Liberals first gained control of that branch, as a result of Franklin Roosevelt's pressures and Charles Evans Hughes' surrender, they moved reasonably cautiously. They utilized the Court primarily as a second echelon, supporting the President and his bureaucracy in their assault on the Constitution. In these years, also, the foundation for the present Court's constitutional irresponsibility was thoroughly laid, as the cynical legal positivism of the dissenting minority of the era of Justice Holmes became the guiding doctrine of the Court in its majority. That doctrine, which has frequently been summed up in the adage, "The Constitution is what the Court says it is," takes on a more sinister hue when it is carried from the genial cynicism of the law school lecture room into the precincts of actual power. In the hands of the *epigonoi* of the Anglo-American legal tradition who make up the present Supreme Court majority, it means quite simply: "Ignore both the written word of the Constitution and the tradition of precedent. Do whatever your prejudices or your ideology lead you to do."

During these years the Court was never effectively chastised either for its participation in the Presidential distortion of the constitutional balance with the Congress and the several states, or for its more and more open substitution of its own ideological prepossessions in the stead of juridical interpretation of the Constitution, as the stuff of its decisions. So, when the time was ripe, its initial usurpations unchallenged, it proceeded to major usurpations. When the tempo of the revolution was slowed down by the steady refusal of the Congress to enact into law the ideological blueprints demanded of it by President after President, the Court took over. Ten years ago, in *Brown* v. *Board of Education,* it boldly usurped the legislative powers reserved by the Constitution to the Congress and the legislatures of the several states and promulgated a dictate affecting the lives of individual citizens, the sovereignty of the states, and the prerogatives of the Congress.

Neither of the coequal powers of the federal government opposed this rape of the Constitution. The Congress remained quiescent; Eisenhower and Kennedy—in sharp contrast to Jefferson, Jackson and Lincoln in parallel situations—hastened to enforce the Court's palpably unconstitutional edict. Usurpation breeds usurpation. In a series of decisions in the last two or three years, the Court has legislated God out of the public school system; in *Baker* v. *Carr* it tore from the states their control over their own legislative processes. Still Congress remained quiescent and Presidents put the massive power of the federal executive at the disposal of the Court's legislative usurpation.

Last month, swollen with pride and power, the Justices turned their attention to legislating for the Congress itself. In the Georgia case on apportionment of congressional districts, the Court thrust aside with hardly a glance the unconditionally explicit language of Article I, Sections 4 and 5 of the Constitution, which gives to the Congress sole power over the conditions of election of Representatives—excepting only (Article I, Section 1) that the electors "shall have the qualifications requisite for electors of the most numerous branch of the State Legislature" and that Representatives "shall be apportioned among the several States . . . according to their respective numbers." Dragging up from the depths of their egalitarian ideology the concept— laughable to any student of the Constitution's formation—that in the minds of the Framers this meant "one man, one vote" in mathematically precise style, the majority of the Justices are attempting to seize from Congress its constitutional control over elections and to impose upon the country their prejudices in favor of box-like congressional districts in place of established constitutional practice. As Justice Harlan said in his eloquently reasoned dissent, the decision of the majority is "manufactured out of whole cloth."

The irresponsibility of this decision is manifest in its challenge to the legitimate tenure of nine-tenths of the present Representatives and in the potential chaos into which it throws the congressional elections of 1964. But these are secondary evils. The primary question facing the country is the principled question whether the Court is to be allowed to continue upon its course to the total destruction of constitutional balance of powers. That balance of powers, magnificent political concept though it is, has never been self-enforcing. It has depended upon the utilization by the coordinate branches of government of the power invested in each of them to prevent any other of them from getting out of hand.

The gage is now sharply thrown down before the Congress— and the Congress has the constitutional power to accept the challenge and cut short the Court's usurpations. In the present instance of the Georgia case, the Congress can by joint resolution affirm its constitutional powers and nullify the decision. Further, as far as the general usurpation of the Court is concerned, the Congress has the power to bring it under control. Article III, Section 2 of the Constitution clearly limits the Court's appellate jurisdiction to such bounds as the Congress may ordain. That jurisdiction, as presently exercised, has become a menace to the constitutional balance of powers. It is up to the Congress to right the balance.

It is indeed the Supreme Court that has most arrogantly during the past few years moved beyond its constitutional powers and in general ignored fundamental principles of law to establish in their place the Liberal prejudices of the Justices. I have had occasion to comment on a number of aspects of these activities of the Court.

Confusion in the Court

(National Review, January 11, 1956)

At the risk of trespassing on the terrain of this magazine's legal expert, I should like to discuss a controversy about the rationale of latter-day Supreme Court decisions, which has been sputtering away in the journals of political science for the past year or two. I do so because this controversy involves considerations that go far beyond the strictly legal sphere. At a point of immense practical importance, it reflects the radical moral philosophical crisis of contemporary thought about man and society.

So far as political scientists are concerned, the issue was joined, and the problem most cogently and honestly stated, in two articles by Earl Latham of Amherst—"The Majoritarian Dilemma in the United States Supreme Court" and "The Supreme Court and the Supreme People," which appeared respectively in *Confluence* and the *Journal of Politics* a year or two ago. Mr. Latham writes:

> Since 1937, the Suprme Court . . . has tried to distinguish between the rights of economic minorities and those of non-economic minorities. The Court has attempted to subordinate the first to the desires of legislative majorities; and to exalt the second above legislative majorities. Because it has surrendered authority on the first, it has had difficulty holding its authority on the second. . . . It is probably more than a cliché that freedom is whole and indivisible; and that a policy of freedom for some but not for others makes partisans out of jurists. [*Confluence*, December, 1953]

He describes with sharp sardonicism the confusion of doctrine in the Court, which has ensued in recent years from its effort to find a conceptual basis upon which it could defend non-economic rights when it has given up the conceptual basis upon which it had previously defended both economic and non-economic rights.

Mr. Latham does not, however, in my opinion, recognize the character of that confusion. At best he skirts the real issue, which is a philosophical one, basing his criticism on the surface level of minority versus majority, and ignoring almost altogether the underlying moral question of the ground from which rights derive. For the origin of the confusion is purely philosophical: the pragmatic denial of immutable moral principle as the basis of jurisprudence. Therefrom arises the continuing attrition of the constitutional doctrine that the basic rights of life, liberty, and property are integral to the individual and beyond the just power of any government to abrogate.

But although Mr. Latham avoids the fundamental issue, he has, at any rate, stirred up the dovecotes. The challenge he has presented has evoked an indignant and varied Liberal reaction, whether avowedly directed toward his articles or not. The pragmatic chickens hatched by a generation of jurists in the ethically relativist tradition of Justice Holmes have come home to roost. The concept of fundamental law grounded in moral principle and standing above the will of a popular majority was fair enough game when it stood in the way of welfarist raids upon private property. But when the decay of that concept produces a Supreme Court vacillating and unsure in its approach to "the civil rights of minorities," it becomes a different matter.

Now I am not minimizing the importance of "the civil rights of minorities," if by that is meant the basic liberties of the persons who make up such minorities, and not simply the rights of minorities who constitute powerful enough voting blocs to enforce special privilege for themselves over against the liberties of other individuals and to the detriment of the rule of law that makes all liberties possible. But there is a certain grim humor— or would be if what is at stake were not so portentous for the survival of freedom—in the wrigglings of the Liberal mind groping for a firm foundation in the bog of moral relativism it has itself created.

Typical of the kind of argument I have in mind, and of the reaction to Mr. Latham's analysis, are the articles of John P. Roche of Haverford, "Judicial Self-Restraint" (*American Political Science Review*, September, 1955); of Loren P. Beth of the University of Florida, "The Case for Judicial Protection of Civil Liberties" (*Journal of Politics*, February, 1955); and of Donald Meiklejohn of the University of Chicago, "Labels and Libertarians" (*Ethics*, October, 1955).

Mr. Roche disposes of the whole matter by sneering with scientistic superiority:

> Every society, sociological research suggests, has its set of myths which incorporate and symbolize its political, economic, and social aspirations. Thus, as medieval society had the Quest for the Holy Grail and the cult of numerology, we, in our enlightened epoch, have as significant manifestations of our collective hopes the dream of impartial decision-making. . . . While this dream of objectivizing political Truth is in no sense a unique American phenomenon, it is surely true to say that in no other democratic nation has the effort been carried so far and with such persistence. . . . the greatest hopes for injecting pure Truth-serum into the body politic have been traditionally reserved for the federal judiciary, and particularly for the Supreme Court.

Mr. Beth and Mr. Meiklejohn, however, represent another point of view, one less simply relativist, more consonant with the new search for some "objective" foundation for the *demi-vierge* "democratic welfare state." They want a theory that will firmly establish the right kind of rights while smothering unprofitable questions about the wrong kind. They argue that, while majorities and social engineers may "modify" the rights of property and of the due process of the Fifth and Fourteenth Amendments, the rights of the First Amendment are "preferred rights"—"not that [God save the mark!] free speech is a great philosophical value in the abstract; it is instead that no democratic society can endure without such freedom: a supremely practical consideration." (Beth, *Journal of Politics*)

For many years, pragmatic political and juridical theory has subordinated the rights of property to the higher judgment of the masses, or of those who demagogically speak for the masses, in the name of a clear-sighted realism which dispels the fogs of metaphysics. Now, therefore, it is a little hard to vindicate the rights of personal freedom on philosophical grounds. But some foundation firmer than the will of a passing majority is needed, so they are vindicated on the grounds of their usefulness to the continuity of the democratic process.

It is in vain that Donald Meiklejohn, who places his defense of the "preferred rights" of the First Amendment on this same basis, inveighs against C. H. Pritchett's insistence "that the American Constitution is a pragmatic affair." His own position, like Mr. Beth's, is itself grounded in a hardly less pragmatic differentiation between democratically expendable rights of property (which, Mr. Beth implies, are but formulas that "enjoin us to preserve competition, or poverty, or unemployment, or segregation") and contemporaneously useful, therefore valuable, rights of personal liberty.

The Liberal, then, now wants a higher status for certain parts of the Bill of Rights than the merely pragmatic role of "counsels of moderation" to the legislature, which Judge Learned Hand assigned it. And this poses a problem. For without judicial review, how can even the First Amendment be protected from legislative majorities? But if the assumption of an underlying moral standard expressed in the Constitution, by which all positive law is to be measured, is pragmatically rejected, whence can the Court derive justification for judicial review?

Essentially, Mr. Meiklejohn's answer is that the standard is to be found in the social norm. Since we all believe in democracy and since the political scientists can tell us that without the guarantees of the First Amendment "the community does not achieve that wise and representative quality in its judgments which is the heart of self-government," the First Amendment has a "preferred status" denied to other Constitutional guarantees. What this comes to is that neither the dictates of the moral law nor the express prescriptions of the written constituent law of the nation, which incorporates them, have authority sufficient to override the majesty of majorities; but any dogma to which the social scientist gives the accolade of his behavioral investigation *has* that authority.

Thus, the Supreme Court itself in the school desegregation case based its decision not upon moral truth and constitutional prescription, but founded its rejection of the "separate but equal" doctrine largely upon the expertism of half a dozen sociologists and psychologists.

In analyzing the mechanisms of this rationale, I neither want to depreciate in any way the rights of the First Amendment nor have I intended here to take a position on the complex problem of desegregation. What I am trying to emphasize is the speciousness of the scientific concepts of objectivity which underlie that sociological jurisprudence that seems to be replacing legal positivism.

In substance Mr. Meiklejohn's argument is based upon the assumption that democracy is a good, since it can be sociologically determined that the people of the United States want it; that the guarantees of the First Amendment are essential to the continuance of democracy, while the rights of property, by implication, are not; that therefore, whatever the Constitution may say, there is an objective basis for one set of rights and not for the other.

The difficulty is, however, that the standards based on this kind of "objectivity" are without force or substance, because a moral concept of what ought to be, as distinguished from what is, is totally lacking. The standards by which the acts of executive and legislature are to be judged under the Constitution become nothing but the assessments by social scientists of what majority consensus *is*. Surely that consensus could be better determined by elections and plebiscites; and if a dictatorship of the majority over the individual and the minority is what we want, it might just as well be arrived at directly, without the interposition of social scientists.

But the rule of law, based upon principles of justice morally derived, is the principle of free constitutions, most especially of the American. It is not necessary to hold to any particular metaphysic or theology to recognize the intrinsic problem: that the positive experience which the scientific method investigates cannot by itself be the source of standards, of values, of ideals, by which all conduct (including government conduct, even the conduct of democratic governments) can be judged. As Henry S. Kariel of Harvard writes in the *Western Political Quarterly* (September, 1955):

> Any theory . . . which makes the ideal and real synonymous eliminates the tension between . . . fact and value. To dispel this tension is to make it impossible to advance a political theory as ideal, as true, as just. Indeed the very notion of justice becomes irrelevant . . . the very pursuit of truth becomes an irrational endeavor. Once metaphysics providing terms by which troubled individuals might assess moving events, historical states, and political behavior has been dismissed, man's claim to make meaningful distinctions, ascribe values, and exercise his reason becomes impertinent.

If the only defense of rights rests upon standards derived from the scientific investigation of society, then the rights of political and civil liberty will be completely at the mercy of social-scientific modes as the rights of property have been. The winds are indeed blowing that way. Much of sociological theory, much of the theory of "interpersonal psychiatry" would eliminate the individual completely from consideration, since, as B. F. Skinner, Professor of Psychology of Harvard, puts it:

> In turning to the external conditions which shape and maintain the behavior of men, while questioning the reality of inner qualities and faculties to which human achievements were once attributed, we turn from the ill-defined and remote to the observable and manipulable.

His article, entitled "Freedom and the Control of Men" (*The American Scholar*, Winter, 1955-56), is an outright call for the rejection of traditional ideas about freedom. We must reconsider "our attitude toward freedom—or its reciprocal, the control of human behavior." It is old-fashioned and prevents us from following the dictates of science. It stands in the way of our accepting "the fact that some kind of control of human behavior is inevitable," and impedes "wise decisions," misleading us so that "we refuse to engage in control when valuable results might be forthcoming."

This is the direction in which sociological objectivism as a basis for law and morals leads. There is no middle position. Either standards derived from the moral order by reason operating within tradition will protect the human rights that stem from that order; or everything is in neutral flux, to be moulded for expediential reasons by the high priests of a "science of man," guided by nothing but their itch for control in the testing of successive hypotheses.

Hypocrisy—or Prudence?

(National Review, November 10, 1956)

I have always thought there was a good deal to be said for what the more logical nations call "Anglo-Saxon hypocrisy." Time after time it turns out that what is meant by "hypocrisy" is no more than a happy exercise of prudence—prudence being the virtue that applies principle to circumstance.

A case in point is the doctrine of clear and present danger. Through its operation, a totalitarian conspiracy that attempts to mask itself as a legitimate expression of freedom of speech has been brought within the scope of the criminal law, without endangering the essence of the constitutional guarantees of freedom. For some time under attack from the Left as a hypocritical evasion of the issue of freedom of speech, this doctrine has recently been condemned also by certain voices on the

Right—with a different object, of course, but in much the same tenor.

As might be expected, the Left, with its Jacobinical heritage of abstract rigidity, attacks the doctrine on the grounds that freedom of speech is a right overriding the claims of all other rights. Thus, it completely disposes of any function for prudence in mediating conflict *between* rights or in implementing them in practice.

Only the exercise of prudence can bridge the gap between the absolute claims of metaphysical values and the contradictory demands to which they give rise in the concrete world in which we live. Without the exercise of that virtue it would be necessary, for example, in the case of the Communist conspiracy either to allow it to go unchecked until it encompassed the destruction of the very memory of the principle of freedom; or, in order to check it, to reduce freedom of speech from a principle to an expendable luxury, scrapping the Constitution to defend the Constitution.

It is undoubtedly true that Justice Holmes, who in *Schenck v. U.S.* promulgated the doctrine of clear and present danger, was himself largely motivated by philosophical considerations of a pragmatic cast. But the arguments he used are equally susceptible to interpretation in the light of a philosophical position that accepts the objective existence of truth and value, relying upon prudence to work out the rival claims of differing values in the shifting and transitory circumstances of history. It is hard to see how any reasonable man can disagree with Holmes' dictum: "The most stringent protection of free speech would not protect a man in falsely shouting fire in a theatre and causing a panic."

Yet the position of the Left, as expressed in its criticism of the doctrine of clear and present danger (and particularly of the developments of that doctrine in recent years in the Dennis case and elsewhere) would seem to imply that the right to cry fire in a crowded theatre *does* take precedence over the right of the spectators to preserve their lives. The theory of

"preferred rights," which asserts that the guarantees of freedom of speech are superior to all other parts of the Constitution—and to the Constitution as a whole—makes short work
of the need for prudence, by denying the validity of all other
rights and therefore of the possibility of a clash of rights.

This is not the first time that the concept of rights grounded
in the nature of man has been perverted by the Left into an
arbitrary fiat sanctifying the particular slogans by which the
drive to power was to be consummated. The Jacobins confined the claims of rights to what was consonant with the
needs of "the revolutionary nation"; the Bolsheviks, to the
demands of the dictatorship of the proletariat and the greater
glory of the Party. Our welfare-statist champions of "preferred
rights" not only subordinate the whole complex structure of
the constitutional order (that guarantees all individual rights)
to a single set of rights, but further limit the applicability of
these latter to those groups they favor, so that while the rights
of free speech apply to Communists and union organizers, they
do not apply to segregationists and anti-union employers.

Such simplification is understandable enough coming from
the Left, which has never recognized the anti-Utopian truth
that life on this earth can never more than arduously strive
to approximate to the ideal, and which, therefore, is scornful
both of the necessity and of the possibility of prudence as a
mediator between the ideal and the actual. But it is disturbing
to find notions being disseminated on the Right that reflect
the same kind of simplification, although with opposite
conclusions.

Terrified by the chaos of our times, impressed by the need
for order, authority, and the preservation of tradition, some
conservatives are in effect saying: Since it is possible that
a man may cry fire in a crowded theatre, the concept of the
right of freedom of speech is itself false and erroneous. Because
Jacobins and totalitarians have demagogically utilized the idea
of freedom and "the rights of man," it is maintained that any
political theory built upon the freedom and the innate rights

of the individual person leads to Jacobinism and totalitarianism. And where prudence has created a doctrine such as the doctrine of clear and present danger, one capable of defending the foundations of social order while maintaining the integrity of the principle of freedom, they, like the Left, spurn it as hypocritical.

That the dictates of right reason will on occasion seem to conflict one with another in the political arena is a necessary corollary of the fact that we live in an imperfect world. It is no ground for denying the truths of reason. The prudential faculty is given us to make these truths materially viable. If it must be dubbed "hypocrisy"—so be it. But, then, Heaven help the nation that lacks a modicum of "hypocrisy."

Other-Directed Champion of Other-Directed Court

(National Review, August 24, 1957)

Mr. David Riesman, whose sociological study, *The Lonely Crowd*, became a national best-seller, is a rare type among sociologists. Unlike most of his colleagues, he has at one time or another shown considerable imagination and a willingness to stand off from, and critically appraise, the shibboleths of the Liberal atmosphere in which he has his being.

It was therefore with considerable shock that I read in a recent issue of the *New Republic* his unreasoned and intemperate blast directed against anyone who dares to be critical of the line of decisions the Supreme Court has been handing down. The irrational virulence of this attack was matched only by his uncritical adulation of the present Court itself ("the eloquent Chief Justice"—"the great Supreme Court decisions of June 17"—"the recent decisions are more courageous even than the admirable school-desegregation cases").

Mr. Riesman, in addition to being a sociologist, is a trained lawyer. Yet throughout his article there is not a word that reflects an understanding of the structured imperatives that are essential if law is to prevail above opinion. There is no suggestion that the fundamental guarantee established by a compact between sovereign states in a Constitution of divided powers might have relevance for liberty. The "vindication of civil decency and freedom" rests not upon the Constitution, but upon the Court's refusal to recognize the criminal character of the Communist conspiracy and upon the doctrinaire egalitarianism with which it rivals Thaddeus Stevens' attempt to ride rough-shod over state sovereignty.

What is the explanation of Mr. Riesman's enthusiastic acceptance of the Wave of What Everybody Knows To Be Truly Good and Beautiful? After all, he not only popularized the concepts of other-directedness and inner-directedness; he showed a considerable preference for the latter.

It is true that not so long ago he became, along with Richard Hofstadter and Peter Viereck, one of the perpetrators of the "theory" of "pseudo-conservatism," which holds that no one who opposes the Roosevelt revolution can do so from principled and rational motives but must be driven by the devils of a pathological unconscious. Their "authoritarian personality" makes them "pseudo-conservatives," in sharp distinction from the respectable kind of conservative who, like all right-thinking people, naturally accepts statism, collectivism and egalitarianism as the proper forms of the good society.

Still, one had hoped that this was but a temporary aberration on Mr. Riesman's part, an aberration that might quickly be dispelled by the good sense and the ability to see himself and his surroundings in perspective that he has generally displayed in his writings. This hope, it appears, was a vain one. Mr. Riesman now anathematizes as "pseudo-conservatives" all critics of the Court. (Even Mr. Justice Clark "spoke in the recent civil liberties cases with the forceful and unambiguous simplicities of the pseudo-conservative.") He has no need to engage in serious intellectual combat with the principled position of the Right, since those who hold that position are psychopathic, and the sociologist need pay no attention to the content of their fantasies. Protected from rational or emotional challenge by the cozy feeling of "belonging," he can ignore all serious intellectual issues.

But the issues the recent decisions of the Supreme Court raise are not so easily swaddled in cotton wool. Granted the dangers of governmental tyranny over the individual person and granted the complex moral problems posed by the historical development of the Southern states, there remains the fact that American freedom has been based not upon abstract precepts enforced without regard to circumstance, but upon a constitutional structure, created to limit power and *thus* preserve and extend liberty. Both in the understanding of the states that ratified the original constitutional compact and in the constitutional practice that prevailed at least until recent years, the virtue of our governmental system was presumed to arise from the division of powers between the several states and the three branches of the federal government. In the preservation of the tension between them, it has been believed, the guarantees of our liberty were founded.

To assume, as Mr. Riesman and those among whom he moves do, that a single chosen abstract good justifies the destruction of that tension by arrogating power to one or another center— Presidency or Court—has been the political heresy of the 20th century in the United States. To achieve a putative good, the intellectual leaders of the country (whose first responsibility should have been to look beyond the immediate to the fundamental) have been willing to sacrifice that division of power which has been the basis of American freedom. The constitutional tension has been undermined by the invasion of the power of the states and the power of the Congress. The recent decisions of the Supreme Court have carried this invasion so far as to threaten to coalesce the Executive and the Court and leave them the sole repository of decisive power.

The re-establishment of the balance and tension upon which freedom depends calls for the assertion by the Congress and the states of the role envisaged for them in the constitutional compact. Their power still remains sufficient to re-assert that role (not to destroy the power of the Court and the Presidency, but to bring it within proper bounds), provided they possess the understanding and the will to do so.

It is to do what he can to develop this understanding and strengthen this will that the principled conservative—Mr. Riesman's "pseudo-conservative"—raises his voice in criticism of the Court. He is impelled by no Freudian psychic drives, but by a devotion, lost to Mr. Riesman and his friends, to the ancient and rational principles of the American Constitution.

The Constitutional Crisis

(National Review, October 26, 1957)

Looking back upon the first days of the school year in Little Rock, the significance of certain events grows sharper. Many times before September 25, 1957, officers of the United States Army have addressed an assembly of school children. What made that date so different is that it was the first time that an officer of the United States Army, acting under the orders of the President of the United States, addressed such an assembly in a building surrounded by the unsheathed bayonets of his command. Speaking with the sanction of the naked authority of steel, an army officer instructed American students on what they had better accept as the meaning of the Constitution—or else.

In the train of events following upon President Eisenhower's ruthless enforcement of the Supreme Court decision on integration, nothing has symbolized with such terrifying clarity the depths of the crisis into which the nation is plunged— and the nature of that crisis: the essential concept of the Constitution is no longer merely being whittled away, as it has been over the past few decades; it is now directly under attack.

The genius of the American Constitution rests in the institutionalization of the limitation of power, in the division of power so that it is held by a number of separate and distinct organs. But that limitation, that division of power, would be a farce and a mockery if it had been intended that the authority to interpret the Constitution itself should rest in the hands of any specific organ of power recognized under its terms. In whatever hands such authority rested, all power would eventually accrete.

A system of divided powers in which interpretation of the system is not unequivocally the right of *each holder of power* becomes a system in which whoever is vested with the right of interpretation will rapidly become the sole effective power. Therefore, under the Constitution, interpretation of its meaning is the monopoly of no single authority—not the Supreme Court, not the President, not the Congress, not the governor of any state, not the legislature of any state—but rests severally in each of them (and, at the margin, in each individual citizen of the United States).

The Supreme Court exists as a tribunal to make decisions when differences of judgment on the meaning of the Constitution are not extreme and can be more or less simply adjudicated. When profound differences exist, the Constitution clearly envisages a suspension of decision, since no member of the complexly articulated series of constitutional sovereignties can legitimately be forced by another member to accept its version of the Constitution.

This is the settled tradition of the Constitution. But Major General Walker, backed by his bayonets, told the students of the Little Rock high school: "This decision of the highest court in the land is, *of course*, an [*i.e.*, the] authoritative interpretation of our Constitution, is binding on all citizens and government officers, both state and federal . . . we . . . have an obligation in conscience to obey them." With this *Diktat* the laws of the State of Arkansas and the prerogatives of the Congress go crashing to the ground, together with all constitutional limitations upon centralized and concentrated governmental power.

This is the meaning of the course entered upon by the President and his entourage. The Little Rock invasion will be only a beginning unless the constitutional balance is redressed by the responsible organs of the Constitution that still have the power to do so. The remedy lies in the hands of the Congress and of the governments of the several states.

The Congress can, and immediately should, set forth by legislation its authoritative interpretation of the Fourteenth Amendment in the areas now moot. Reaffirming Article IV, Section 4, of the Constitution, it can limit explicitly the power of the Executive to use force without invitation from the state concerned, except in case of danger to its "Republican Form of Government," or in case of foreign invasion. Further arrogation by the Executive or the Judiciary can be met by appropriate legislation forcing them back within constitutional limitations.

The governors and legislatures of the several states under attack also have their recourse: interposition and/or nullification. But to make such vindication of the sovereignty of the states real, it is essential that their militia become what it was in the beginning—forces under the command of the states themselves, not subject to "federalization" on Presidential whim. Discharge of the National Guard, and the organization of a State Guard, solely under the control of the states themselves, would seem to be a prime requisite for the assertion of sovereignty.

The determination of even a single state thus to defend its sovereignty could call a halt to the progressive deterioration of constitutional processes. If such a resistance were associated, in the spirit of John Calhoun, with a call by the governor of the resisting state for a convocation of all the states, to consider the joint assertion of their constitutional integrity, not only might the present crisis be resolved, but much that has been lost in recent years recovered. Meeting the federal government as an equal, the states would be able to prevent the forcing of complex moral and social issues peremptorily to the point of catastrophe. Time and common sense, working within re-established constitutional forms, might solve problems that now seem insoluble.

If the measures here proposed seem extreme, it is only because the danger is extreme. They are very like the measures taken and projected by Thomas Jefferson in the formulation of the Virginia and Kentucky Resolutions at another critical point in the life of the Republic. And no one can say that John Adams and Alexander Hamilton were a worse danger to the Republic than the omnipresent bureaucracy that rules in the name of Dwight D. Eisenhower.

Frank v. Maryland: The Knock on the Door

(National Review, June 6, 1959)

The characteristic image of terror and tyranny in the twentieth century is "the knock on the door," symbol of the unrestricted power of the state over the individual. To whatever degree Continental European law may lack defenses against this horror of totalitarianism, it has been the proud boast of Anglo-American jurisprudence that the citizen's home is a fortress, proof against invasion by officers of government, except upon a warrant issued by a magistrate—and only then (to quote the Fourth Amendment of the Constitution) "upon probable cause, supported by Oath or affirmation and particularly describing the place to be searched and the persons or things to be seized."

So reads the Constitution; and despite occasional violations by authorities here and there our higher courts have always held that agents of the federal government could not enter a man's home without a warrant except in "an immediate major crisis in the performance of duty [when there was] neither time nor opportunity to apply to a magistrate." With the Fourteenth Amendment, these protections against the federal government were affirmed against the states. As recently as 1947 in *Wolf* v. *Colorado* the Supreme Court stated: "The security

of one's privacy against arbitrary intrusion of the police—
which is at the core of the Fourth Amendment—is basic to
a free society."

But on May 4 of this year, in the case of *Frank* v. *Maryland,*
the Supreme Court handed down a 5-4 decision which radically
subverts this security of the person against the agents of government. The substantive issue concerned the owner of a dilapi-
dated house in the city of Baltimore, suspected of being a
breeding place for rats; the refusal of the owner of the house
to allow a city health inspector to enter; and the arrest and
conviction of the owner under a Baltimore city ordinance. No
effort was made by the health inspector to obtain a warrant;
and the trial record reveals that there was no reason except
bureaucratic convenience why such an effort should not have
been made:

> *Q:* Could you not just as well have made your inspec-
> tion one hour or two hours later than at the time
> you demanded entry?
> *A:* I could not. I had two students I had to release
> at three o'clock. I have to be in the office at three-
> thirty every day to take care of my reports.

"Flimsy ground," indeed, as the dissenting Justices wrote,
"for denying . . . the constitutional protection afforded by a
search warrant."

Justice Frankfurter, speaking for the majority, based the
Court's decision voiding the guarantees of the Fourth and
Fourteenth Amendments upon arguments rooted not in jurisprudence but in that kind of sociological generalization and
majoritarian expediency which the late Justice Oliver Wendell
Holmes bequeathed to the Court and which was so notoriously
exhibited in *Brown* v. *Board of Education.* At no point in his
opinion did he allow fundamental principles to bear upon the
essential issue of the case: is it in accord with the dictates of
the Constitution or the preservation of a free society to breach
a doctrine so central to our liberties that John Adams regarded

the struggle in its defense over the Writs of Assistance as the sparking point of the War of Independence?

Justice Frankfurter knows this history and indeed refers to it; but in the case of issue, he slides past it, speciously maintaining the claims of majoritarian opinion and sociological imperatives, in blithe disregard of legal and moral principle. The health inspections, he says, are "welcomed by all but an insignificant few." The rule of law is reduced to the rule of numbers; the "significance" of principle and the Constitution is to be assessed purely by the whims or by the acquiescence of the majority.

Then the sociological argument: Our country has become (you guessed it) so large and complex (and in such a damn hurry) that the feeble vision of those who drafted the Constitution is antedated: "The growth of cities, the crowding of population, the increased awareness of the responsibility of the state for the living conditions of its citizens" become the basis of judicial decision. The safeguards of the Fourth and Fourteenth Amendments, invoked by Mr. Frank, must give way to the prior claims of bureaucratic power: "Time and experience have forcefully taught that the power to inspect dwelling places . . . is of indispensable importance [more indispensable than freedom?] to the maintenance of community health; a power that would be greatly hobbled by the blanket requirement of [these] safeguards."

The decision rests—again in Justice Frankfurter's words— not upon moral and political theory, not upon jurisprudential principle, but upon "history [by which he means sociological opinion about history] and dominant public opinion."

It is not a new story that the Court has forsaken principle for expediency and prejudice. A long record of service to the intellectual fashions of the hour has left its iron marks upon the rights of the person in his property and upon his defenses against bureaucratic tyranny. Judicial precedent and constitutional principle have been broken up by the Court into bits and shards, to be used or rejected in any given argument, to buttress or to undermine an opinion derived from extra-judicial considerations. So it is not to be wondered at, and should in no way palliate the destructive error of Justice Frankfurter and the majority, that the minority opinion was delivered, and forcefully delivered, by Justice Douglas, who has so often subordinated the Constitution to *his* ideological prepossessions.

The fault, as decision after decision shows, lies not primarily in this or that Justice, but in the positivist legal philosophy that is destroying the Constitution and the tradition of law based upon morality. With *Frank* v. *Maryland*, a Court imbued with that philosophy has brought the knock on the door perilously close.

The remainder of this chapter consists of columns from National Review *dealing with a variety of topical issues: welfarism, McCarthyism, social security, crime and self defense, the ideas of Richard Cornuelle, the Negro question, and the draft.*

The Ballot in the Hand

(National Review, December 6, 1958)

In the early days of the acquisitive State, when Lloyd George was rousing the rabble of Britain, one of the campaign songs that sparked his confiscatory attack upon the landowners ran this way:

> The land, the land,
> The land on which we stand,
> God gave the land to the people!
> The land, the land,
> The land on which we stand,
> Why should we be beggars
> With the ballot in our hand?

With appropriate diminution of the appeal to the divine— to the point of zero—and with a transfer of the attack from the landowners to property owners in general, this is the theme upon which all variations of the twentieth-century socialist revolution have turned. It is most blatantly developed by the Communists, who forthrightly demand the total confiscation of productive private property; but in a lower pitch it is the theme of the continuing American revolution in its successive phases: the New Deal that launched it; the Fair Deal that continued it; and Modern Republicanism which has been its stage of consolidation.

The Modern Republicans, their function of making the revolution respectable fulfilled, have gone down to defeat before those who are ready and anxious to carry the revolution to its next stage. The combined forces of the Reutherite trade-union oligarchy and the left wing of the Liberal establishment now dominate the national scene. Their program as expressed in the demands of the AFL-CIO, the proposals the *New Republic* is pressing upon the incoming Congress, and the ideological pronouncements of such stalwarts of the New and Fair Deal as Justice Douglas and Leon Keyserling would make even Franklin Roosevelt startle in his grave. The magnitude of their demagogy is indicated by Keyserling's bland assumption that any family with less than $7,500 a year, any family that cannot "afford trips abroad [and] university educations for their children" is, as the social workers say, "underprivileged."

Keyserling may go a bit farther in his demagogy than others, but he sets the tone of the demands with which the new Congress will be greeted by those who brought about its election: a federal health program, a federal education program, legislation to destroy the effectiveness of Taft-Hartley and entrench the power of the union leaders, sharply increased social-security benefits and public-housing expenditures.

From Lloyd George to Reuther the advance of the welfare state, the advance of the bureaucracy to power, has been almost unchecked. The formula is always the same: "Why should we be beggars [or be content with less than $7,500 a year] with the ballot in our hand?"

What can conservatives oppose to this call to safe and legalized robbery? Certainly not the Modern Republican counsel to rob more slowly and more delicately. It is immoral counsel; and even if it were not, all the me-too election campaigns, including those of the Modern Republicans this year, have shown that it doesn't work.

But neither, I think, can conservatives rely upon the argument which they have too much used, the argument that the socialist or welfarist system, whether in its simple form or in the form of a "mixed economy," will not work, that it will in the immediately foreseeable future collapse. This simply is not true, as theory could have foreseen and history has shown.

It *is* true that the industrial revolution and the immense leap in productivity and the standard of living that accompanied it were only possible because of the capitalist economic system; it is also true that the high standard of living which welfarism can distribute in the United States, and to a lesser degree in Britain, is a distribution of reserves accumulated by the success of capitalism; and it is true that even in the Soviet Union and Communist China, where capitalism had never functioned sufficiently to accumulate such reserves, the economic development achieved depends upon the existence of a technology which was the product of capitalism.

What is *not* true is that, given the historical conditions of the abundance made possible by capitalism, welfarism is certain to collapse in the short or medium run. Welfarism, or any form of socialism not dependent on terror, can survive as long as the fat inherited from capitalism lasts. But even this is not the end. When the fat runs out and the incentives to productivity have been drowned beneath the sea of levelling social policy, the methods of Communism still remain: coercion and the threat of coercion can be substituted for the lost incentives of a free society. In the long, long run the human spirit will indeed rebel against the lowering of the skies. But this is a far cry from depending upon immediate collapse of a welfarist economy as the decisive argument against welfarism.

No, the only ground on which conservatives have to stand is a moral and spiritual criticism of the essential inhumanity of socialism and welfarism: the levelling that, by reducing the person to a statistical number, degrades all men, whatever their capacity or position; the ignominious removal of responsibility for his future and his family from the hands of individual man into the hands of an all-probing bureaucracy; the steady attrition of all separate and rooted centers of power and the massive growth of a single bureaucratic center of state power which from day to day gains more and more control over all the avenues of thought and life.

Upon a platform of opposition to these, the true evils of welfarism, conservatives can firmly stand. To such a platform men of spirit will rally. And if men of spirit do not outnumber those to whom the ballot is a weapon for self-aggrandizement, they overweigh them in will, in intellect and in influence. Once united, they would have the capacity to save the Republic.

The Meaning of McCarthyism

(National Review, June 14, 1958)

Now, a year after Senator McCarthy's death and three years or more after his political execution by the Watkins Committee, it should be possible to assess with reasonable objectivity the meaning of that movement of thought and action which the Liberals dubbed McCarthyism. It is too soon perhaps to grasp its significance *sub specie aeternitatis,* but we are sufficiently removed from the immediate clamors of those extraordinary years between 1950 and 1954 to abstract from the surface aspects, to see beyond the strengths and weaknesses of Senator McCarthy himself, to begin to delineate what it was that lay beneath those clamors and gave so intense a sense of urgency to those years.

Perhaps one way of approaching the problem is to consider what has changed since Senator McCarthy was eliminated from the political scene. Life is a great deal more tranquil. It was tranquil indeed when he was still alive but no longer heard, when in November 1956 we went about our business while our national honor died and the blood of our friends flooded the streets of Budapest. It is reasonably tranquil today (we are somewhat worried about the recession, of course), as we haggle about the conditions upon which we will meet with murderers on some summit, meanwhile rising at the Metropolitan Opera House to honor the murderers' anthem.

The commanding heights of our society are held by those who preach tranquility. There are problems, of course—outsputniking Sputnik; out-propagandizing Khrushchev; winning friends and influencing people—Sukarno, Nehru, Nasser. But it is all part of the game, the give-and-take of coexistence. A few voices are raised, but hardly heard, to warn that coexistence with an enemy sworn to the destruction of Western civilization is an impossibility, that it can only lead to the victory of that enemy and to our defeat. But those voices are smothered by the soothing formulas poured down upon us from the heights where the Liberals of both parties sit.

What was it that in the McCarthy period broke through this mist? What was it that penetrated tranquility and brought the country as close as it has ever been to an understanding of the threatening danger? It certainly had nothing to do with Senator McCarthy's "tactics." They were the small change of American politics—nothing that has not been used on every side of every political controversy for scores of years. It was, I submit, an understanding, sometimes crudely expressed, sometimes shrewdly accurate, of the tragic truth of politics in the United States, as in all the West, in the last forty years: *the integral characteristics of the Liberalism which became increasingly predominant during those years are such that our present leadership can neither resist the infiltration of Communists within nor concert an effective strategy against Communists without.*

It was an instinctive realization of this among large sections

of the American people which Senator McCarthy activated—
a gnawing sense of something wrong, something which they
could not define, but of which they were intuitively sure.
Senator McCarthy, to be sure, did not contribute much towards
definition. What he did was done not by analysis but by
courage, pertinacity, and rhetorical expression of the mute and
strangled common sense of millions of Americans.

Be it said that such an expression of the instincts of a people
is not the best expression intellectually or aesthetically that
could be found nor, in the end, the most effective. Every society
needs intellectuals capable of articulating its fundamental instinct in terms of reason and the accumulated wisdom of tradition. But what is to be done when the immense majority of the
putative intellectual leaders of society go awhoring after strange
gods, whose blandishments both the traditions of their culture
and the discipline of their profession should enable them to
resist? Better by far the rough-hewn truth than a sophisticated
and articulated apology for error.

It is unfortunate that the "treason of the intellectuals," their
desertion of their duty to truth, has created that suspicion of
intellectuality *per se* which gave rise to the ambiguous epithet,
egghead, with all that word implies. It is unfortunate that a
corrupt intellectuality has put intellectuality itself under suspicion. It is unfortunate that, these things being so, the attack of
McCarthyism upon ideas which are dangerous errors and upon
the intellectuals who hold these ideas could be so easily interpreted as an attack upon ideas and upon intellectuals in general. Although it is cold comfort to a society which desperately
needs intellectuals inspired by truth, those who have perverted
their role as articulators of the spirit of their society have only
themselves to blame.

The attack on McCarthy as an uncouth enemy of ideas and
culture was a defensive effort to confuse the issue which he
expressed and dramatized. The normal outlet of Americans who
disagree with prevailing authority, the Presidential election, had
been foreclosed. The critics of established Liberalism, quad-

rennium after quadrennium, saw the Republican Party come under the sway of ideas only superficially different from those of the New Deal Democrats. A quiet and undramatic revolution had, since the early thirties, occupied the decisive positions of American society—not only in politics, but in mass communications which became daily more powerful, in the schools and universities, even in a large proportion of the pulpits. A civilization founded upon the premise of the inviolate primacy of the individual person was being steadily socialized.

For the solid citizen, well grounded in the tradition of his ancestors but unequipped in intellectual dialectics, this was a hard thing to combat, since every step in the growth of socialization was rhetorically defended by specious humanitarian appeals to ideals of charity and brotherhood, noble in themselves. Communism, he could place. With its avowed materialism and its insistence upon an unrestricted use of power to achieve its ideological goal, it was clearly evil. Although the product of the same ideological development as contemporary collectivist Liberalism, it had cast away all the moral inhibitions based upon an intellectually-rejected, but emotionally-held tradition, which Western Liberals not only appealed to in their propaganda but were affected by in their personal ethos.

Correctly, the American people refused to *identify* Liberalism and Communism; but that refusal to identify disarmed them in understanding the nature and danger of Liberalism in its *similarities* to Communism. The distrust remained in large sections of the population; but after the battles of the thirties, after the unification of the nation under Liberal leadership in World War II, it became harder and harder to put a name to that mistrust: Communism was evil; democracy was good; and since the Liberals were not Communists, why were they not, as the Communist threat began to develop after 1945, as much entitled as any one else to lead the nation in the new developing crisis?

The answer to that question burst upon the nation first with the Hiss case in 1948, when overwhelmingly the Liberal Estab-

lishment rallied to Hiss' support. And when, despite all the odds
in Hiss' favor, the single witness of Whittaker Chambers convinced not only a jury but the great mass of Americans that
Hiss was indeed guilty, the issue was posed again, and more
sharply: what are the credentials of the Liberals for the leadership of a free society?

The Hiss case was a sharp blow, but by itself it was not
enough to establish the true character of Liberalism. After all,
Hiss was but one man. He was personable and persuasive. His
associates could well have been no worse than victims of his
personality. The Hiss case did much, but not enough, to drive
home the truth which Chambers so clearly stated in *Witness:*

> [The] drift [of the New Deal] was prevailing to-
> ward socialism, though the mass of those who, in part
> directed, in part were carried along by it, sincerely
> supposed that they were liberals . . . the New Deal
> was a genuine revolution, whose deepest purpose was
> not simply reform within existing traditions, but a
> basic change in the social, and, above all, the power
> relationships within the nation. It was not a revolu-
> tion by violence. It was a revolution by bookkeeping
> and lawmaking. . . . Now I thought that I understood
> . . . how it happened that so many concealed Com-
> munists were clustered in Government, and how it
> was possible for them to operate so freely with so
> little fear of detection. For as between revolutionists
> who only half know what they are doing and revo-
> lutionists who know exactly what they are doing the
> latter are in a superb maneuvering position.

It was this socialist equivalence of the aims of the Liberals
and the Communists, and the inability of the Liberals to protect
themselves and the nation from the deeper and more malevolent
aims of the Communists which Senator McCarthy's activities
dramatized. And it was his ability to express his perception of
that connection existentially, if not analytically, that fixed his

following and gave point and meaning to the vague apprehensions which had so long existed without focus.

It was this—not McCarthy's "methods," which differed not a whit from those of the Teapot Dome investigations and the Black Committee—that brought upon his head the whole accumulated weight of entrenched Liberalism. For a moment it seemed as though for the first time since its establishment in 1932, the Liberal leadership might face a serious challenge.

It is interesting, if fruitless practically, to speculate what might have happened if a substantial number of the intellectual molders of opinion had recognized the essential truth McCarthyism represented and had articulated its meaning in detail: 1) that contemporary Liberalism is in agreement with Communism on the most essential point—the necessity and desirability of socialism; 2) that it regards all inherited value— theological, philosophical, political—as without intrinsic virtue or authority; 3) that, therefore, no irreconcilable differences exist between it and Communism—only differences as to method and means: and 4) that, in view of these characteristics of their ideology, the Liberals are unfit for the leadership of a free society, and intrinsically incapable of offering serious opposition to the Communist offensive.

But such a breach in the ranks of the Establishment did not occur. Except for a small handful, the accepted leaders of the nation were anti-McCarthyite to a man. Most even of those whose record in the fight against Communism was honorable, those who knew that fundamentally Senator McCarthy was right, joined the solid phalanx against him, mumbling that, somehow, he was hindering the fight against Communism.

Senator McCarthy was defeated and he died. McCarthyism, which was never an organized movement, despite the troubled fears of the Liberals, dissipated. After his defeat, before his physical death, the Hungarian shame occurred. This spring we are handing over Indonesia to the Communists without raising a finger. Coexistence, cultural exchange, is the order of the day. We play coy and we jitter-jatter about the conditions of a summit meeting, but we never reject in principle the very concept of meeting in peace with murderers and enslavers, as we would have refused to meet with Hitler.

The Liberal Establishment, its ideological presuppositions being what they are, can make great noises, but it cannot fundamentally and finally regard Communism as an irreconcilable enemy. With appropriate modifications, its slogan is that of the thirties in France: *"Pas d'ennemis à gauche*—no enemies, at least no irreconcilable enemies, to the Left. McCarthyism is more dangerous than Communism."

Is Social Security a Sacred Cow?

(National Review, June 1, 1965)

Since that torn-up social security card came fluttering down the television screens with such terrific electoral impact, there has been a tacit agreement among conservatives that the social security system is a cow too sacred to approach without due reverence. But, as the payroll tax which supports it edges toward 10 per cent (with no firm limit in sight), a serious question is posed. Can an effective critique of the welfare state be sustained if the social security system is to be forever immune from attack? It is a central pillar of the entire structure, a pillar now being strengthened by the addition of the first phase of socialized medicine.

If the principle of governmental action in these fields of insurance is allowed to go unchallenged, then there will remain no *principled basis* for challenging the usurpation by government bureaucrats of any field of private endeavor. The essential issue is not this program or that, but whether the over-all massive weight of government action and the concomitant growth of government power are compatible with the continued existence of a free society.

We sometimes forget that the present situation, in which government at all levels—federal, state, and local—takes from the citizen more than one-third of every dollar of his income, to be spent by a vast bureaucracy, is not the condition under which our institutions of freedom were formed and grew to maturity. Throughout our history, and as short a time ago as the childhood of men now in their forties, a few pennies were the total government take from the citizen's dollar, and the power of government was commensurately small.

It is true that a proportion of the increase is due to the needs of defense against the Communist enemy; but this accounts for only one-third or so of total governmental activity. Far the largest proportion of the fantastic increase of governmental control over the product of the American citizenry represents steady intrusion of governmental power into a province always previously regarded in the American constitutional system as one from which government was excluded and in which the energies of individual citizens and associations of citizens were to be free to express themselves without political control.

Nor should we, looking about us and priding ourselves upon our comparative freedom in a world increasingly totalist, be complacent about the large degree of freedom remaining to us despite the growth of potential power in the hands of government. Thirty years is a short time historically. It takes a while for the potentialities of power to break down habits of freedom, constitutional safeguards of freedom, the inbuilt inertia of 150 years of free society. The men who lived during the transition from the Roman Republic to the Empire saw, many of them, dangers to the commonwealth in much that was happening; but not one signalized the moment at which the Republic died. Men living under Augustus still saw the traditional forms of the Republic operating around them, although the Republic and all it stood for was dead.

We have not reached that point of no return, but the tremendous power now available to government is beginning to be used in alarming ways. I am not referring to the burgeoning increase of that power through legislation that carelessly grasps a billion more here, a few billion there, to push the Federal

Government into education, medicine, urban construction, the life of the region dubbed "Appalachia"—though this is bad enough.

What is more disturbing is the exercise of power and the threat of power by the Executive and the Court without the shadow of constitutional or legislative sanction. A shameful ransom is paid to Castro, and the drug manufacturers are compelled to participate by Executive blackmail; the constitutional structure of the electoral process is transformed to meet equalitarian prejudices, in direct defiance of constitutional provision; the wages and prices of the steel industry are arbitrarily fixed without concern for the market by the mere threat of unnamed governmental action.

All of this would be impossible, were the over-all power of government reduced to its legitimate sphere; but this will never take place until the principles of the restriction of government are re-established. So long as any area of illegitimate government action is considered beyond the discussion, the principles themselves cannot be clarified. Whatever prudence may dictate on the advisability of not precipitantly transforming a situation so established in our lives as the social security system, the principle that insurance for retirement and illness is not a proper function of government remains valid.

This would be true even if substantial benefits enured to the participants. But, as *Barron's*, of April 26, points out in an excellent article on the system, for the great mass of the working population, it is, like so many other government programs, a con game. A worker entering the system at eighteen will, under the new Social Security Bill, contribute and have contributed for him money which, with interest, will by retirement have reached $84,300. He will receive after retirement, if he lives to 79, $25,802. Or, seen another way he could for the same money purchase from a private company a monthly annuity of $634, while he will receive under social security a maximum monthly amount of $312. Under the present law, the figures are: $61,596 against $24,114; or $463 against $254.

Fundamental criticism of the social security system is not only an imperative of principle for the renewal of a free society. It is also politically practicable, in view of the fraudulent nature of the entire enterprise.

The Right and Duty of Self-Defense

(National Review, May 17, 1966)

The present state of affairs in our great cities raises one of the most fundamental problems in political philosophy in the most immediately practical way: the right of self-defense when civil society fails to protect the individual. The most divergent moral and political theories of the West agree that all men possess the inherent right of self-defense when their lives, their persons or their property are forcefully or violently attacked. Under normal conditions of civil peace, that right is, as it were, yielded to the juridical and police organs of the state in order that men may be protected without the constant need of each individual's maintaining his own continual self-protection. But when civil order breaks down, it is all but universally agreed that the right of self-defense reverts to the individual.

I would not, of course, maintain that civil order has completely disappeared in our major cities, but any honest appraisal of the situation as it actually is can only lead to the conclusion that it has partially done so. We are not in what theorists call "a state of nature," in which no law or order exists, but we are, although in civil society, in a situation where too often civil society cannot protect us. Although there exists, in John Locke's phrase, "a common superior," civil authority, to which we can theoretically appeal for defense against the attacker, more and more frequently men and women find themselves in circumstances where their lives and their persons are in danger, with that authority effectively unavailable. It is this condition Locke describes:

"But force, or a declared design of force upon the Person of

another, where there is no common Superior on Earth to appeal
to for relief, *is the State of War:* And 'tis the want of such an
appeal gives a Man the Right of War even against an *aggressor,*
though he be in Society and a fellow Subject." (*The Second
Treatise of Government,* Sec. 19.)

Daily we see crimes of violence mount. Every year mob
actions, whether inspired by ideology or by the senseless savagery of amoral teenagers, become more common. Yet at this
very time our lemming-like leaders proceed to raise a clamor
against the means by which individuals can protect themselves.
The right of citizens to bear arms, as old as the Republic and
older, comes under attack, as the agitation for a fire-arms control
bill gains momentum. When a girl defends herself with a knife
against rape and murder, the District Attorney's office seriously
considers indicting *her.* When the Maccabees in New York City
organize patrols to defend their women and children, they are
castigated as vigilantes.

The Liberal theory is that criminal violence is the product
of "underprivileged" environments, and that the only thing to
do about it is to improve the environment. The Liberal theory
is wrong, but even if it were right, it would take a very long
time—granted the Utopian dream that it could ever be done—
to transform the situation. Meanwhile the citizens of our great
cities continue to face violence and terror in their daily lives.

Nor is the usual conservative response adequate. Conservatives say—and, unlike the Liberals, they are fundamentally
right—that the underlying cause of criminal violence is the
breakdown of moral standards. There is no question but that a
permanent solution of the crisis of crime and violence will be
found only in revitalization of the Western ethos, but this is no
solution to the immediate problem. A renascence of the West
is not something that can be achieved without long and desperate struggle. Some conservatives who recognize this would
attempt to restore order by increasing the numbers and power
of the police, and there is much to be said for such a course,
provided the safeguards of the individual against irresponsible

government action are maintained. Nevertheless that alone will not be enough.

When the standards of morality are broken down, when individual criminals are coddled by the courts, when mass violence is condoned, indeed praised as a civic duty, at the heights of American society, a spirit of disorder is let loose that police measures alone can never control. Order is maintained in a society primarily by the moral outlook of the citizens; the function of the police under such circumstances is to handle the criminal exception to that outlook. When, however, criminality is no longer an exception but becomes endemic in whole groups of the population, it is then more than the police alone can handle.

Self-defense today has become not only a right but a duty. I can hear alarmed cries of "vigilanteism," but the measures that need to be taken can be taken in full cooperation with official law-enforcement agencies. It is time and more than time that—whether through hiring of private policemen or the volunteering of individual citizens—our streets, our parks, our apartment houses, our schools should be guarded by widespread private patrols. Rather than talk of government control of fire-arms, private citizens should be encouraged to arm themselves. Laws like the Sullivan Law in New York State should be repealed. They hamper the criminal very little, but throw masses of bureaucratic red tape in the path of citizens who want to protect themselves, their families and their homes.

It is sad indeed that our country has fallen on such evil days. But fortunately the remedy exists—enunciated by the philosophers of the West, guaranteed by the Constitution of the United States—the inherent right of self-defense.

The Right of the People to Bear Arms

(*National Review*, July 2, 1968)

Since Adam ate the apple, the per capita quantum of violence and potential violence in human society has remained, century in and century out, reasonably constant. Indeed, the third person in the world killed the fourth—or, if you prefer more secular images, primitively there was always present "continual fear and danger of violent death; and the life of man, solitary, poor, nasty, brutish, and short."

What has made the difference between the quantum of potential violence and actual violence has been the power of the moral authority of civilizations to inspire the members of society, and the firmness with which force has been exerted in defense of civilizations against external and internal barbarians. Against external barbarians, sometimes the moral authority of a great civilization has played a part, but primarily it has been force which has held the *lines*. Against internal barbarians, the problem has been more mixed, since a civilization with sufficient moral authority tends to civilize its internal barbarians.

The abysmal ignorance of history, as of the elements of political philosophy, that characterizes so much of the political and intellectual leadership of the United States today is all that can explain, although it does not excuse, the torrent of nonsense about "violence" with which we have been assailed these past days and weeks and months. The simple knee-jerk reactions that pass for high political wisdom might be understandable in a local official of the League of Women Voters; they are proclamations of bankruptcy when they come from men of supposed political or intellectual sophistication.

Violence is bad? Of course: then let us do away with it. Problem; solution: instant Utopia. Guns kill people? Put government control on guns: domestic peace in our time.

Despite its appealing simplicity, this enthymeme conceals a double fallacy. In the first place, violence is not always evil *per se*. In the public sphere it is morally legitimate when employed to resist or overthrow tyranny. In the private sphere it is equally legitimate when employed against criminal incursion upon life or property. For the latter purpose it may fall into desuetude in times when, unlike our own, the constituted authorities are able to keep crime and riot under control. But it is always a residual right, and in times like ours it becomes the citizen's duty to use violence when necessary in his own defense and the defense of his family.

The second fallacy is that weapons or the accessibility of weapons creates violence. Violence, for good or ill, arises from the souls of men. Gun control would have no more effect ultimately upon the quantum of domestic violence than disarmament agreements have had upon the prevalence of warfare. Indeed, in the one case as in the other, the logical effect is only to strengthen the bad guys and weaken the good guys. It was Nazi Germany that was armed, it was Britain and the United States that were disarmed, in 1939. If gun-control legislation at any level were to be enacted in this country, it would be the criminals, the rioters, the insurrectionists, who would find illegal means of procuring weapons; it would be the solid citizens who would be disarmed.

These are the considerations, derived from a philosophical understanding of the nature of man and from practical experience, that make nonsense of the hysterical clamor for gun control now emanating from the serried megaphones of the Establishment. It is a clamor that might be ignored if the basic law of the land were still respected by the judiciary, if the Constitution had not become a paper document to be manipulated into its opposite by the Warren Court. The Founding Fathers whose wisdom was based upon theory and experience, tried almost 200 years ago to defend the United States against such mischievous incitations to tyranny and crime as are invited by a disarmed citizenry. Boldly and unequivocally, the First Congress and the states, in the Second Amendment to the Constitution (Article II of the Bill of Rights), proclaimed that "the right of the people to keep and bear arms shall not be infringed."

The constitutional principle is strong and sweeping, so strong and sweeping that even the present Supreme Court, one hopes, will not be able to work its sinuous way around it—should Congress prove to be so subject to utopian pressure as to pass legislation defying it. The key word is "infringe," and there can be no doubt in common sense or in law that any proposals for registration are direct infringements of the free citizen's right to keep and bear arms. If I may paraphrase an old maxim: the power to regulate is the power to destroy. The patently unconstitutional Sullivan Act in New York State has shown, in its administration over the years, that registration of firearms (in this case of concealable weapons) has made it next to impossible for anyone legally to possess such arms. Criminals and insurrectionists, of course, get hold of them easily. Even the prohibition of sales by mail, while it is less integrally objectionable than registration, seems to be of doubtful constitutionality.

An unarmed citizenry is potentially the victim, first of anarchy, then of tyranny and totalitarianism. The present campaign to infringe the right to keep and bear arms is a utopian assault upon the freedom of American citizens—an assult scornful of the testimony of history, the counsels of morality, and the express mandate of the Constitution.

Richard Cornuelle and the Third Sector

(National Review, February 9, 1965)

One of the most difficult problems facing conservatives in developing and articulating a more concrete program than we have hitherto presented to the American people is the continuing challenge to be "positive." This would be a challenge easy enough to answer if we were prepared, like the Liberals, to use the massive power of the state to enforce a program of fiat and taxation in order to solve any difficulty, real or imagined, in the society. But conservatives have a commitment to preserve the freedom of individual persons by limiting governmental power, and they cannot play fast and loose with that commitment in order to achieve a dubious solution at the expense of a free constitutional political order. But the preservation of the framework of a free constitutional government never has the human appeal of the cry to solve immediate and obvious social problems.

Yet, although the defense of freedom has to be given the first priority in a time like ours, when collectivisms of various degrees of virulence press upon us from within and from without, the question remains as to how real human needs can be met without traversing those principles. Nor is this done by asserting that, given time, the free society will meet such needs automatically. Conservatives are not social Darwinians. Nor do they share with the collectivists a Utopian arrogance towards human beings, if only an abstract ideological pattern can be imposed.

Fundamentally, conservatives have a way out of this dilemma, but the statement of it has been largely general and dry. That way out does assume that, in the long run, a free polity and a free economy will solve, to the degree they are soluble, the problems of human welfare. But it goes further; it posits that immediately, for the living problems around us, the solution can and should come (if government aggrandizement and tyranny are to be inhibited) from the responsible action of individuals and groups of individuals. The difficulty of implementing this solution is that the increasing impersonalism of modern society makes the personal relationships between those who need help and those who want to help them very hard to achieve. It was that face-to-face relationship which formed the foundation of the noble virtue of charity in simpler days. To achieve this virtue today, however, requires more complex effort—an effort to which conservatives, with a few exceptions, have not sufficiently directed their attention. This is understandable when one considers the tremendous drain on energy and imagination required to work to hold back the Liberal-inspired decay of the fundamental structure of society.

Among the few who have concerned themselves with creating a positive program for the meeting of human needs by voluntary action is Richard C. Cornuelle, Director of the Foundation for Voluntary Welfare. A number of years ago, in a series of discussions, he raised the question I have been outlining here. It had long troubled him, and he was then groping towards a way of dealing with it.

His analysis distinguished three sectors of human activity: the "public," concerned with power and the limitation of power —the province of politics; the "private," concerned with production, profit, the achievement of personal economic well-being— the province of economics; and the sector of what he called "service"—the province of the problems I have been discussing. He stressed that from a conservative and libertarian point of view the principles underlying what had to be done in the "public" and "private" sectors, to create a good society, were known, and that the techniques of achieving those principles were being consciously developed. It was his point, however, that in the third sector—the "independent sector," as he also called it—neither principles of action nor techniques for directing altruistic energy in a complex age had been developed.

During the past half dozen years he has set himself to the closing of this gap. His efforts have not been theoretical alone, or even primarily theoretical (although his book, *Reclaiming the American Dream,* shortly to appear, will deal with his overall concept). A few years ago he founded the Foundation for Voluntary Welfare and proceeded through it to carry out his ideas in practice. The most successful of his projects so far has been the United Student Aid Fund which, with the help of bankers, businessmen and administrators, has been able to pre-empt a large part of the area of loans to students that would otherwise have become an additional activity of expanding government. His next project is to take Marion County, Indiana, as a pilot community, and there to enlist all available private resources in an attempt to eliminate hard-core unemployment in that county.

There are numerous fields in which his technique can take hold and add a dimension of the greatest importance to the struggle to reclaim a free America founded on voluntary effort. Mr. Cornuelle's ideas are catching on—to such a degree, indeed, that *Look* Magazine devoted a feature article to them. But the author of that article, Mr. T. George Harris, missed the point. He presented Mr. Cornuelle's efforts as an alternative to conserva-

tive political action, using them as a foil to attack the American
conservative movement and the central ideas of conservatism.
What he did not or would not understand was that the concepts
of Richard Cornuelle could not live in an atmosphere dominated
by Liberal statism, that they depend for their viability on a
society of free economy and limited government. They do not
rival, rather they complement conservative political action.
They add a necessary dimension to the conservative endeavor.

The Negro Revolution

(National Review, June 18, 1963)

So loaded with ideology and sentimentality is the discussion of
Negro-white relations in America today that any critical examination of Negro demands and Negro action has become suspect.
To approach these problems in any terms but the terms of
established egalitarian clichés seems to mean just about automatically that one will be labeled a "segregationist," a "racist,"
or worse.

The events of the past few weeks, however, have raised the
issue to so dangerous a level that, at whatever risk of being
misrepresented, it has become urgent to go beyond the undoubted wrong suffered by American Negroes and the undoubted justice of some of their aspirations, to the overarching
requisites of a free and ordered polity. These weeks have seen
the coming to a head of what, without exaggeration, can be
called a revolutionary situation.

Encouraged by the actions of the President and the Supreme
Court, inflamed by the unmeasured and apparently unlimited
demands of a leadership ranging from Malcolm X and James
Baldwin, through Martin Luther King to the emulatively radi-
calized bureaucracy of the NAACP and the Urban League,
spearheaded by organized rioting masses, a typical modern
revolution would seem to be in the making. The grievances of
a section of the population are being stirred to feverish heights

by ideologues who direct the impact of the forces they have called into existence in such a way that the one certain result of their "success" would be destruction of the constitutional order. Meanwhile, those responsible for the maintenance of that order are so bemused by Liberal ideology that they cooperate in its destruction.

Consider the combination of demagogic threats, Presidential actions and judicial decisions we have been witnessing. The threats range from open ultimata issued by Negro leaders to the white community, invoking rioting and violence unless it accedes to vaguely stated and unlimited demands, down the line to solemn pronouncements from the Secretary of State that unless we acquiesce in these demands our stance against Communism will be fatally weakened. The Presidential and judicial actions range from the invasion of a sovereign state by federal troops in order to terrorize local law-enforcement agencies, which have quite successfully and humanely suppressed mob action, to denial of protection to property owners against trespass and violence, to refusal even to hear the suit of a sovereign state in its attempt to vindicate the constitutional separation of powers.

I would not be misunderstood. I know that the Negro people have suffered profound wrongs—not least in their original enslavement by Northern merchants and Southern plantation owners. But those wrongs cannot be righted by destroying the foundations of a free constitutional society, which is indeed the only basis upon which a joint and lasting solution of their problems is possible. Furthermore, I assume the innate value of every created human being and the right of every American citizen, enshrined in the Constitution, to equal treatment before the law. But for the enforcement of that right there exist prescriptive legal modes—by the use of which enormous advances had been made before the developments of this past decade transformed orderly progress into a clash of communities.

The social, cultural and economic relations of the races, however, are another matter. The multifarious adjustments of the relations of human beings—sensitive and delicate, and above all individual in their essence—can never be regulated by governmental power without disaster to a free society. *Laws* enforcing segregation have always been a monstrosity; and *laws* forcing private citizens to regulate their behavior in an opposite manner, that is, laws against segregation and FEPC laws, are an equal monstrosity. The fact is, however, that segregation laws are today largely dead letters and rapidly becoming completely so, while the reverse interference of government is growing apace.

This problem is one which in the end can only be solved (as Mr. Garry Wills has recently stressed in these pages) by personal encounters in charity. Inevitably when—as now seems to be happening—a single set of wrongs is raised to an absolute, and all the accumulated political wisdom of a civilization and a nation is tossed aside, in the name of righting those wrongs, an atmosphere of revolution is created, such an atmosphere as made it possible for the abolitionist William Lloyd Garrison to call the Constitution "a covenant with death and an agreement with hell."

We are approaching that pitch of frenzy. In the name of Negro rights, under the pressure of rioting mobs, intemperate demagogues and rampant ideology, we are in train of depriving private citizens of the protection of their property; of enjoining, under threat of federal armed power, the police power from preserving order in our communities; of disrupting and catastrophically lowering the standards of an already enfeebled education system; of destroying the constitutional separation of powers, abrogating the sovereignty of the states and yielding unlimited power to a Presidency served by an ideologized Supreme Judiciary.

The situation is becoming starkly revoltuionary and devastatingly dangerous. It is time for sober men of both races to take counsel and establish a consensus that will satisfy the claims of justice *in consonance with the constitutional guarantees for freedom and order*—and for the Congress, exercising its contitutional powers, to implement that consensus.

The Violence of Nonviolence

(National Review, April 20, 1965)

In the *Saturday Review* of April 3, the Rev. Dr. Martin Luther King presents for us the etiology of nonviolence in the ongoing Negro revolution. To achieve his aims (which, as is usual with leaders of that revolution, he does not very clearly specify), it is necessary, he writes, that four things take place:

"1) Nonviolent demonstrators go into the streets to exercise their constitutional rights. 2) Racists resist by unleashing violence against them. 3) Americans of conscience in the name of decency demand federal intervention and legislation. 4) The Administration, under mass pressure, initiate measures of immediate intervention and remedial legislation."

There is much to be learned about the violent essence of "nonviolence" from this paradigm. I should like to discuss it on three levels, from the obvious to the more subtle: nonviolence as the provocation of violence, nonviolence as the use of force against civil society, and nonviolence as violent assault upon representative, constitutional government.

Most obviously (and clearly stated by Dr. King in the second point of his paradigm), the entire tactic of nonviolence depends upon its success in provoking violence on the part of the defenders of existing civil order. The corollary implied by this proposition, since on Dr. King's own witness such violence is an essential element of his program, is that if nonviolent provocations are not outrageous enough to provoke violence, they must be escalated until they do—a theoretical proposition amply borne out by the empirical evidence of the history of the movement of which Dr. King is a leader.

Indeed, a cursory acquaintance with the literature of that movement shows that most of its active agitators are quite prepared, if necessary, to resort to violence themselves.

But this blatant admission, that the aim of the nonviolent

movement is to provoke violence, only exposes the surface. It is not merely in its commitment to the provocation of violence by others that this movement betrays the hypocrisy of its name; it is violent in its very essence, relying as it does upon the terror inspired by mobs to destroy the processes of constitutional government. "Mob" may seem a strong word, but what better word is there to describe an assemblage of persons, themselves a militant minority of a minority, devoted to over-awing constitutional processes, which represent a balance of the rights of the majority and of many minorities, by the threat of creating terror and civil chaos.

As I read Dr. King, I wondered where I had previously heard those accents combining surface virtue with threatening ultimatum. Suddenly I remembered. It was in the writings of Friedrich Engels, denying that the Marxist revolutionaries of his day espoused violence. No, he said, we shall not institute violence; all we shall do is to make the maintenance of existing civil order impossible, and then its defenders will have either to use violence or to surrender. And, parodying the duellist's challenge, he ended: "Bourgeois gentlemen, you shoot first."

This is the meaning of Dr. King's nonviolence: it is more convenient in the mobilization of force against constitutional order to bring it about that the first overt act of violence proceeds from others. It is a tactic, and it is hypocrisy on a grand scale.

All this is not to deny that: there may be circumstances— in the struggle against Nazi or Communist tyranny, for example —in which civil disobedience or open revolt is morally justified. But against a constitutional order with inbuilt modes for the redress of grievances, there is no such justification (even though the necessity of maintaining constitutional procedure and a balance of interest may make that redress slow). Indeed, it is in its recourse to modes of action directed against the very substance of constitutional process that the violent essence of the nonviolent movement is most fundamentally displayed.

This is easy to lose sight of these days when a democratic and plebiscitarian ideology has obscured the meaning of representative government even more thoroughly than it has weakened understanding of the virtue of our constitutional system of checks and balances. As our constitutional system was designed to preserve the rights of individual persons and the interests of minorities, as well as to give expression to the deliberate will of the majority within those limitations, so representative government exists to ensure that the decisions of the majority of the electorate will be deliberate and just. In the American political tradition, as in the English tradition from which it springs, it has always been understood that elected representatives are something more than mere messenger boys required to register the opinion of a majority of their constituents on any issue that arises. Rather, it is their duty to adjudge issues on their merits, refining, as it were, the raw opinions of their constituents by taking account of all factors conducive to the health of the polity and the freedom of its citizens. On this Edmund Burke and John Stuart Mill, usually so opposed in their viewpoints, are agreed—specifically, the one in his *Address to the Electors of Bristol,* the other in *Representative Government.* On this, Madison, Hamilton, Jefferson—all were fundamentally agreed.

The political morality of Dr. King and his nonviolent movement would destroy the very possibility of representative government. For deliberation, adjustment, and justice he would substitute the assemblage of a militant mob, the provocation of violence, the stirring up of mass emotion, culminating in the *forcing* of his ideological prescriptions upon the constituted representatives of the republic. It is a program for government by force and the threat of terror.

The Negro Revolution—A New Phase

(National Review, October 4, 1966)

The Negro revolution is entering a new stage. The most dramatic and obvious sign of this development is, of course, the spreading slogan of Black Power. But this is only one facet of a much deeper transformation in the aims and character of the Negro movement, a transformation which is as pronounced in the integrationist sector as it is in the separatist black-power sector.

I have for some time been reading widely the analyses, pronouncements, polemics, of the protagonists, black and white, of the Negro movement. What emerges is a virtually unanimous conclusion. Sometimes it is expressed in the openly revolutionary rhetoric of Stokely Carmichael, sometimes in the more dulcet welfarist rhetoric of Bayard Rustin or A. Philip Randolph. In either case, and in all the modulations of tone between, the stark fact emerges that the Negro movement has passed over from a program of "civil rights" to a program of confiscatory socialism, revolutionary in its essence.

From Carmichael's threatenings of unfocused violence to Randolph's $100-billion freedom budget to abolish Negro poverty, many and myriad are the changes rung on the theme. Carmichael thunders that "the economic foundations of this country must be shaken . . . a totally different America must be born." Rustin demands "an equitable share of the abundance of the 'great society' "—equitable, from the context of the discussion, meaning that political power must assure the Negroes 12 per cent of the national income whether they earn it or not. Neither faction ever makes clear just how a group comprising that small percentage of the population is to achieve this raid upon the substance of the great majority. The integrationists talk of political power to be achieved by bloc participation in the traditional political parties; the supporters of Black Power propose separate Negro parties holding the balance of political power. But always, whether openly proclaimed or simmering below the surface of the rhetoric, is the threat of blackmail by violence.

It is a threat which the leaders of this country, from Stevenson and Robert Kennedy to Humphrey and Johnson, have made only too real by condoning violence and blaming the worst outbreaks in the history of this country not on the immorality and barbarism of the participants, but on "poverty" and "conditions." While the solid Negroes of the nation are as much concerned with the preservation of law and order (a point convincingly demonstrated in recent studies of Harlem and Watts) as their white neighbors, a Liberal ideological approach has encouraged an alliance of agitators with criminal elements to create a climate of terror on a scale never before seen in American society.

Apart, however, from the civil indecency of this riot and pillage, the threat of its continuation and enlargement has become the main stock-in-trade of the leaders of the Negro revolution, even the more moderate. In the now concluding first stage of the revolution, the so-called civil rights movement, it was used again and again as the final sanction to achieve legislative and judicial decisions, patently unconstitutional and often violative of individual rights. Today, the results of permitting the continuation of this atmosphere of terror can be even more disastrous. Without their reliance upon the threat of violence, the pretensions of leaders who propose a confiscatory revolution against nine-tenths of the population would be seen for the absurdity they are. The Negro community might begin to face the great and difficult task, the shouldering of which is the only course for substantial and permanent improvement of the Negro condition: the establishment of community norms and moral authority, the encouragement of hard work and enterprise, the rallying of the community against its own criminal and disruptive elements.

While the threat of violence is the practical factor that makes it possible for the Negro leaders to dream of confiscatory redistribution as a focus for the chaotic energies of the Negro revolution, an ideological factor, also created by Liberalism, gives that dream apparent rational substance. This is the egalitarian myth that anyone who is in any way worse off than anyone else can be so only because of oppression or distortion arising from evil men or evil circumstances. If individual A fails where individual B succeeds, it is always the fault of external circumstances, never of his quality or his effort or his moral fiber. Similarly, if group x fails to achieve proportion y of the goods of life, it is forbidden to inquire (even after allowing for a harsh history) of the qualities of the group in its average; instead, all the powers of an omnicompetent state must be brought to bear to take from those who have achieved and give to those who have not.

This is the essence of that marriage of egalitarianism with unbridled state power that in its various manifestations is called Communism, socialism, welfarism. When a whole nation takes this road, it finds that it has not abolished inequality; it has only handed the goods of society to the most ruthless and power-hungry, reducing the rest to faceless atoms. But for a small minority to dream of achieving well-being through confiscatory measures leveled at the majority has not even the substance of that nightmare. It can only dissipate the good will that, despite the diatribes of the preachers of black racism, does exist among the majority towards Negro self-betterment and advancement. Worse, it will turn aside the Negro community from that task of self-improvement which is the only answer to its condition.

Showdown With Insurrection

(National Review, January 16, 1968)

Three years ago, when "nonviolence" was all the rage, I had occasion in these pages to analyze an article by Martin Luther King, an analysis which I called "The Violence of Nonviolence." Dr. King had openly stated that the function of nonviolent demonstrations, such as that at Selma which he was currently discussing, was to provoke violence by his opponents. I wrote: "But this blatant admission that the aim of the nonviolent movement is to provoke violence only exposes the surface. It is not merely in its commitment to the provocation of violence by others that this movement betrays the hypocrisy of its name; it is violent in its very essence, relying as it does upon a terror inspired by mobs to destroy the process of constitutional government. . . .

"For deliberation, adjustment, and justice he would substitute the assemblage of a militant mob, the provocation of violence, the stirring up of mass emotion, culminating in the *forcing* of his ideological prescriptions upon the constituted representatives of the republic. It is a program for government by force and the threat of force."

Dr. King, unlike many of the other leaders of the Negro revolution, still wears the fig leaf of nonviolence, if somewhat rakishly askew. But if there were ever any doubts as to his insurrectionary intentions against constitutional government, his program for 1968 dispels them once and for all. What Dr. King has done, after three years of mounting violence culminating in Newark and Detroit, is to announce the organization this spring in Washington of a massive campaign of civil disobedience, that is, an effort to bring the functioning of the government to a stop until Dr. King's ideological program is enacted; in his words, "massive dislocation" of the capital "until America responds."

The methods he has indicated he will use, according to the New York *Times*, include invasions of the Capitol and the White House, transportation tieups, boycotts and demonstrations of various types. It is obvious on the face of it that such actions will have to be met with force unless the government is to surrender to Dr. King. It is equally obvious, considering the history of the past few years, that anything but surrender will spark off uprisings not only in Washington, where an uneasy peace has prevailed these last two summers, but elsewhere. As a matter of fact, Dr. King, according to the *Times*, "acknowledged that the ugly mood of many Negroes in the nation's slums made the campaign 'risky' "—the understatement of the year.

What in essence Dr. King is doing is making a bold play for leadership of this year's insurrectionary developments, which he is programming to begin in April rather than July, and hoping to turn from a haphazard series of events into a coordinated rebellion. He is bringing to a head a crisis that, if it is not met by the firm methods available to constitutional government to maintain itself, can only end in bloody race war, with a resulting movement of government towards that dictatorship which always follows anarchy.

A free constitutional order is a precarious civilizational growth. Once riven asunder, it is not easily attained again. The history of the past few centuries is littered with the corpses of governments that met the challenge of organized mobs with too little and much too late; they went down in a welter of anarchy succeeded inevitably by dictatorial usurpation. Unless early firm action is taken this spring to suppress Dr. King's attack on constitutional government, the outcome in Washington and nationwide could be incalculable disaster. It is also true that preparation for the same type of action is urgently necessary for every city in the country, but it is Washington in April that will set the pattern.

Preservation of civil order and firm defense of constitutional procedures against the revolutionary methods of Negro leaders like King, Carmichael and Brown are measures necessary to the preservation of a free society in the United States; at the same time they are the indispensable prerequisites for any possible future advance of the Negro people.

I would conclude from extensive reading right across the spectrum that the hopes of American Negroes are concentrated on two goals—respect and employment. Nothing significant about either can be achieved by government action, or *a fortiori* by violent pressures to bring forth government action. Fundamentally, as Booker T. Washington understood decades ago, respect and access to jobs must be earned by the Negroes themselves, as a substantial number of individual Negroes have demonstrated. The sooner it is made clear that revolutionary methods will achieve nothing, the sooner the Negro community will set its course on this, the only road to advancement. It is the road that other ethnic groups have successfully taken, and while the difficulties for the Negro are greater, the prejudices deeper, the principle is the same.

There remains as an asset the great fund of American good will towards any group striving to improve itself. That good will still continues despite the excesses of the past few years. But if civil order is not restored quickly in our cities, it will soon vanish.

A decent future for the Negro people, like a decent future for the country as a whole, depends upon the preservation of constitutional order. It is to be hoped that President Johnson in his actions and the Republican candidates for the Presidency in their programs, will address themselves to this overriding crisis, free of ideological prepossessions or self-seeking electoral considerations.

Liberalism Run Riot

(National Review, March 26, 1968)

Judging by the summary of the Report of the National Advisory Commission on Civil Disorders (which is all of the Report that is available as I write), it is one of the most preposterous ebullitions of the Liberal spirit ever seriously submitted to the public. Created to assess the insurrectionary riots of 1967 and to propose measures to avert their continuation, the Commission has put the blame everywhere but where it belongs, everywhere, that is, except upon the rioters and upon the Liberals who, with their abstract ideology, prepared the way for the riots by their contempt for social order and their utopian, egalitarian enticements and incitements. As Richard Nixon has said—and his courage and honesty should be commended: "[The Report] in effect blames everybody for the riots except the perpetrators of the riots, and I think that that deficiency has to be dealt with first. Until we have order, we can have no progress."

This is the heart of the question. The issue facing the United States this summer is the survival of a free society. No society can exist in a state of endemic disorder. Specifically, a representative republic cannot function if its magistrates and its representative assemblies are subject to blackmail by mob violence. Most of the violence has as yet not been so directly applied, although we have seen the invasion of the legislative chambers of California and South Carolina. But Martin Luther King's plans for this April in Washington are openly directed towards the overawing of the Congress. It was with just such tactics that the Jacobins led the mob of Paris to overawe the Assembly and usher in the terrorist stage of the French Revolution.

The Commission was faced with a condition—the condition of incipient revolution. It responded with a theory, the truly utopian theory that if sums massive enough to bankrupt the nation and heavily penalize the productive, tax-paying section of the population were spent, and if simultaneously deep-ingrained prejudices were eliminated, then at some point in the future (even John Lindsay could not have meant this summer, or next summer, or the summer after), everything would be solved.

I waive for the moment the question whether further governmental expenditures along the lines which hitherto have done nothing to moderate strife would have the effect the Commission projects. I waive the Commission's proposed creation of a massive bureaucracy to administer its stupendous program—a development inimical to the freedom of white and Negro alike—and the question of the injustice inherent in massive taxation of already massively taxed producers, white and Negro alike. I waive the cherubic innocence of the Commission's dictate that white "racism" must be eliminated—although it might have anticipated Daniel Moynihan's observation on reading the report, that strongly held ethnic or religious attitudes have never been eliminated in any society of which he knows.

Still, granted the validity of absurdity, granted what I would deny—that the measures it proposes are either appropriate or just—what has the Commission proposed to meet the terrifying immediate situation it was called into being to consider? In a word, nothing.

That situation is a revolutionary situation—though with a difference from most revolutionary situations. Revolution means the seizing of power by force and terror. In the American situation it is clearly impossible for the self-styled leaders of a tenth of the population ever effectively to seize power, but the exercise of force and terror is an integral aspect of the developing Negro revolution. While it could not achieve the true revolutionary aim of seizing power, it could make orderly government impossible. In fact, to the degree that it is not controlled by the legal authorities of society, it will inevitably bring into existence counterforces of violence and thereby subject us to long-lasting, endemic civil war.

No society—least of all a free society—can subsist if the challenge of illegal violence is not met with all the force of legal authority necessary to subdue it. This is the first answer the Commission should have given, before going on to consider the causes which have fed revolutionary violence and to recommend measures to alleviate those causes.

Such a consideration would have required a different spirit, however, than the spirit of Liberalism. It would have put the whole problem in the perspective of the immense gains that a large section of the Negro people have made over the past decades. It would have built on the great insight of Booker T. Washington, that the Negro people will gain respect and status primarily on the basis of their achievement of economic and social skills and disciplines—a truth that hundreds of thousands of solid Negro families are demonstrating in our time. It would have considered how our free economic system could be motivated to assist in this decisive endeavor. Above all it would not have compounded the basic cause of the present crisis.

For that cause is implicit in the Report itself. It is the false hope with which the Liberals have imbued American Negroes, that by an act of government, without strenuous effort, without the time always needed for beneficent social change, instant Utopia could be created. With this promise drummed into their ears by a generation of Liberal ideologues, but with life improving only slowly, the foundation for revolutionary violence was laid. The Commission, with its grandiose escalation of that same Liberal ideology, has only added fuel to the fire it was created to help put out.

Anything Goes

(National Review, June 28, 1966)

It used to be called *raison d'état.* Translated into American, it means: anything goes if the government wants it. This would seem to be the rationale of Secretary McNamara's Montreal address to the American Society of Newspaper Editors. That, at least, is all that one old-fashioned enough to care about constitutional principle can conclude from his call for universal service in non-military activities by all young people not in the armed forces. It is true that Mr. McNamara did not dot his i's and cross his t's as to what he meant by "asking," when he proposed the government's "asking every young person in the United States to give two years of service to his country— whether in one of the military services, in the Peace Corps, or in some other volunteer developmental work at home or abroad."

It was only a trial balloon, after all, and the nasty word "compulsory" might have been quite a leaden weight, but it is hard to know what else he could have had in mind except direct compulsion or some kind of hanky-panky with indirect compulsion through manipulation of the military draft. Senator Javits at any rate drew the logical conclusion—universal compulsory service for anything the government wants, from dentistry in Danang or baby-sitting in Burma to garbage collecting in Gowanus or social work in Waukegan.

It seems to me shocking that, despite all the discussion of the Montreal address, there has been no major outcry against its unconstitutional and totalitarian implications. Whatever the immediate fate of Mr. McNamara's proposals may be, the reception accorded them proves that in the influential circles of the country there is no sensitivity to the constitutional enormity and political immorality they represent.

The primary cause of this deadening of constitutional sentiment and vigilance for personal freedom is the slow attrition of decades of governmental infringement upon the rights of the individual person, together with the erosion of constitutional understanding in the courts and the academy alike. The result is that all proposed governmental actions tend to be discussed purely empirically in terms of their relevance to specific "problems," and without the question being asked seriously whether government in fact has the constitutional right to undertake them. This is the general cause of most of our political woes. But something more specific is responsible for the emergence of Mr. McNamara's proposal as a serious political option. Every attack on constitutional safeguards we have suffered over the years has been founded on some specific pretense at logical justification, however specious and tortuous—and this is no exception.

The constitutional principle—the veritable maxim of the free society—would seem to be clear: the only legitimate reason for governmental coercion of the services of free citizens is military necessity. The reasoning that transforms that principle into a justification of universal service, non-military as well as military, domestic as well as foreign, is a direct reflection of the Alice-in-Wonderland reasoning that shapes our policy in the confrontation with Communism's threat to our survival. That reasoning is thoroughly embedded in the main body of Mr. McNamara's Montreal address. Its central assumption is that we can eliminate the Communist threat not by fighting the Communists, but by "building bridges" to them and social-working the rest of the world.

Since the conflict with Communism is to be won in this way, all sorts of actions far removed from the actual conduct of war become part of the struggle and are justified as essential to national security. Everything is grist to the mill: foreign economic aid unrelated to the strengthening of real allies, all forms of "service" to backward countries, or for that matter "image building" for the swarms of petty diplomats who infest the UN—by crushing Tshombe or embargoing Rhodesia or waging war on poverty at home. Once this pseudo-logic is accepted, the Liberals are in a splendid position to eat their ideological cake and have it too. On the one hand they can retain the high purity of their disdain for the power realities of international politics and continue, with Mr. McNamara, to proclaim reason, not combat, the way to bring Communism to terms. On the other hand they can happily make use of the real threat to our national security and of the constitutional war-making powers to expand their coercive welfarist programs and steadily increase the scope of governmental action.

The pattern that emerges year by year is that of a garrison state—but one whose wartime powers are directed not primarily against an enemy but towards control of the lives and property of its own citizens. The continuing development of this pattern, together with the Newspeak rhetoric that accompanies it, steadily erodes the ground of resistance to ever more outrageous governmental action.

The lack of instant and widespread indignation at Secretary McNamara's proposal is but a further sign of this erosion. It is particularly disturbing, however, since only a few short years ago the very concept of universal service for non-military purposes would have been regarded as totally beyond consideration in a free society; it would in fact have been immediately recognized for what it is, a characteristic of such regimes as fascism and Communism. It is to be hoped that when the clear meaning of the McNamara labor corps begins to emerge from the cloud of rhetoric that enshrouded it at Montreal, the opposition to a program so alien to our traditions and so dangerous to our freedoms will be overwhelming.

The Draft

(*National Review*, August 9, 1966)

In my column of June 28, which was concerned with Secretary McNamara's totalitarian proposal for universal youth forced labor, I wrote, "the only legitimate reason for governmental coercion of the services of free citizens is military necessity." A number of correspondents have objected on libertarian conservative grounds to conscription even in circumstances of military necessity.

I am myself, for reasons I shall go into in a moment, very doubtful whether such military necessity exists under conditions of limited warfare, as in our present engagement in Vietnam, the Korean War, or wars of similar scale. Whenever it is possible to wage the nation's wars by voluntary service, it is the duty of a free government so to wage them.

On the most limited view of the powers of the state, however, I would say that its first responsibility and its broadest powers are those concerned with the preservation of the national safety and interest—ultimately, the war-making powers. Unless one is to take a pure anarchist position and oppose the existence of the state altogether, its minimum functions (which, I would maintain should be also its maximum functions) are: defense against foreign enemies, preservation of domestic order, and the administration of justice.

When a man accepts the civilizational life made possible by the existence of the state, he by that very action accepts the obligation to fight for his country, just as he accepts the obligation to put aside vendetta and private justice, respecting and supporting the organs of internal order and the public justice of the courts of law. Certainly I would maintain that if, in deliberate conscience, he concludes that the moral law demands it of him, he has the ultimate right to secede from his obligation—*but only if he simultaneously renounces the benefits and protections of his citizenship.*

He has the right to become an outlaw, to put himself beyond the law of his country, whether by seeking exile or by becoming a revolutionary. Exile should be his free right, but if chosen it should be permanent and irrevocable, unless in the case of a penance proven by actions above and beyond the obligations he has denied. The choice of the revolutionary road should open him to all the penalties of the law. Our century, like other times of crisis before it, has seen too many unhappy occasions when these have been the only alternatives for a man of conscience; but the man of conscience will take such a decision with open eyes, recognizing that it is moral fraud to reject the obligation to defend one's country in arms or to join in conspiracies or actions to overthrow its institutions, while clinging to the perquisites and protections of the citizen.

The noble name of libertarian is besmirched and degraded when it is used to condone a one-sided repudiation of the contract of civil society, a whining demand for all its benefits, a pseudo-principled rejection of its obligations. If it is not moral depravity, it is invincible moral insensitivity that makes it possible for men calling themselves libertarians to prate in the name of freedom about the civil rights of disruptive practitioners of civil disobedience or the free-trade beauties of commerce with the enemy, or the iniquity of the citizen's military obligation, when the very structure of our freedom depends from moment to moment on the vigilant maintenance of an armed watch that only the American state can provide.

The principle of universal military obligation is justly derived from the constitution of civil society, without which no human freedom could exist. It is therefore one of the pillars of a free society. But since the enforcement of that obligation perforce limits temporarily the free choice of the citizen, a free state has the right to enforce it only when such enforcement is the sole

way to defend the structure of freedom itself—that is, only in
circumstances of paramount necessity. I would maintain that
this has not been the case either during the long stretches of
the cold war or during the limited wars in Korea and Vietnam.
Nor have those who have supported the continuation of the
draft ever founded their position upon necessity. Rather, they
have ignored the necessity of morally justifying the use of the
draft, or they have defended it on specious grounds.

Sometimes their defense is on grounds of ideological preference—for example, that military service is good for people
per se. Such reasons for subjecting free citizens to compulsion are as outrageous as any Liberal ideologist's utilization
of state power to force other men to do what he thinks they
ought to do. More usually, however, the defense is on economic grounds. We simply cannot afford, this argument runs,
the expense of making the armed services an attractive career.

It is hard to get a firm estimate of what the actual additional
cost would be to run our present military establishment on
a voluntary basis. Whenever the question arises, the bureaucratic supporters of compulsion come up with fantastic figures;
but in what was perhaps a moment of unguarded truth recently,
the New York *Times* quoted Pentagon sources as saying that
the cost would come to something like $6 billion a year. Even
if it were twice that, or more, the cost of guaranteeing the
freedom of the person, as we wage our wars in these long
decades of protracted conflict, should take precedence over the
tens of billions we spend on sloppy, politically motivated, and
morally corrosive "welfare" at home and abroad.

A free society can of necessity morally demand universal
military service of its citizens; but when overriding necessity
is not present, conscription is immoral—be the excuse ideology,
convenience, or expense.

Chapter Four

Political Commentary 1956–1968

The columns in this chapter, being in the nature of current discussion of political events, are grouped in chronological sequences. As events have taken place and changes occurred in the relation of political forces, some things that I had written at an earlier date may no longer be applicable in later circumstances. For example, the reader will note that my estimate of Richard Nixon is rather different in the circumstances of 1968 than it was in the circumstances of 1960.

THE EISENHOWER YEARS

Adrift on the Wave of the Future
(National Review, September 15, 1956)

It is a small gain—but a hitherto most obscure point was clarified by Mr. Eisenhower in his acceptance speech at San Francisco: the meaning of "dynamic conservatism." It may be that his recent assiduous reading of Eric Hoffer, Chester Bowles, and—it is rumored—Arthur Larson, has put him into a philosophical frame of mind. At any rate, for the first time, he has made clear the philosophical foundations of his position.

Dynamic conservatism, it turns out, is a brand-new streamlined sort of conservatism, founded neither on tradition and prescription nor on eternal principle, but on the Future. To be sure, Mr. Eisenhower spoke most favorably about principle and had some pretty sharp words to say about expediency. But he made it very clear that when *he* said principle, he did not mean anything old-fashioned or non-progressive, nothing in the nature of unchanging truths that remain true, however repugnant to the materialistic temper of the times, however unfamiliar to a bribed and pampered electorate. No nonsense like that for the dynamic conservative. What is true is what works, what succeeds. Or, in the words of Henrik Ibsen, around which Mr. Eisenhower's entire speech was organized: "I hold that man is in the right who is most clearly in league with the future."

It rather puzzles me that Mr. Eisenhower—or his ghost writer—found it necessary to dig up a sentence from Ibsen, that fusty nineteenth-century prophet of the "expert," that contemner of tradition and enshrined principle, when either William James or John Dewey or Franklin Roosevelt could have provided him with the same thought in much more striking words. But be that as it may, the meaning is unmistakably clear.

Four years of power, four years of association with the bureaucracy of the Establishment, have transformed 1952's somewhat regretful and nostalgic acceptance of the basic structure of the Roosevelt revolution into what the commentators like to call "buoyant affirmation" of it. The Future, which is the source of all principle, as dynamic conservatism understands the word, is a Brave New World of ever-increasing material well-being and security. Astonishingly enough (one had thought Aldous Huxley's satire on this kind of scientistic Utopia had once and for all excised the phrase from serious discourse), Mr. Eisenhower uses the very words, "a brave and new and shining world"—where, it would seem, the human condition has been transformed into one vast pleasure park presided over by a benevolent government "with a warm sensitive concern for the everyday needs of people," and where the Old Adam has been finally cast out:

> Science and technology, labor-saving methods, management, labor organization, education, medicine —and not least [!], politics and government—all these have brought within our grasp a world in which back-breaking toil and longer hours will not be necessary.

> Travel all over the world, to learn to know our brothers abroad, will be fast and cheap. The fear and pain of crippling disease will be gradually reduced. The material things that make life interesting and pleasant will be available to everyone. Leisure, together with educational and recreational facilities, will be abundant, so that all can develop the life of the spirit, of reflection, of religion [the product of "leisure, together with educational and recreational facilities"?], of the arts, of the full realization of the good things of the world. And political wisdom will assure justice and harmony.

In short, the millenium. And not just for the United States, but for the whole world. The Iron Curtain will melt under the warm influence of cultural interchange, and through all the world "privation, oppression, and a sense of injustice and despair" will disappear before the advance of our programs of economic aid.

I submit that this is *hubris*, a *hubris* based upon the scientistic and managerial cult of the Future of Progress. It is dynamic enough, not to say demagogic. Undoubtedly it is the sort of thing that wins votes. But where is the conservatism? Where is there an inkling of recognition that men cannot successfully build the Tower of Babel? Where is the responsibility that rests upon those in positions of leadership, the responsibility to distinguish and define, to recall men to their true destiny?

Some of my best friends are Political Realists, and they would answer me now as they have answered me before: What do you expect? You have to win elections. They may be right in their implication; but I prefer to think that, given a clear choice between ignoble security in the state of slavery of the Brave New World and freedom in a society in which men solve their own problems, with misfortune a call for the exercise of the virtue of charity, not a signal for legal robbery by the state—that, given this alternative, and convinced that it is an alternative, that freedom and statist security cannot exist together, the American people would unhesitatingly vote for freedom.

But even if I am wrong, even if the rot has entered so deeply that truth can no longer prevail in the democratic political arena, it is the nobler course to resist the current in the name of principle than to win a "realist" victory at the cost of the progressive surrender of principle. Then, at least, in Richard Hooker's words: "Posterity may know we have not loosely, through silence, permitted things to pass away as in a dream."

The Ethics of Mr. Eisenhower's Rhetoric

(National Review, February 9, 1957)

Some years ago in *The Ethics of Rhetoric,* one of the few wise books by a contemporary I have had the fortune to find, Richard Weaver wrote: "An ethics of rhetoric requires that ultimate terms be ultimate in some rational sense." As I read Mr. Eisenhower's Inaugural Address, with its insistent repetition of such terms as Justice, Law, Freedom, and as I tried to divine what words could mean to the man who had so recently acted at Suez and failed to act in Hungary, I was forcibly reminded of that sentence of Mr. Weaver's.

These are ultimate terms, words uttered to gain our consent and acceptance by the power of the intricate set of associations they conjure up. The weight of the entire address, with its noble-sounding periods and self-conscious pieties, rests heavily upon them. But are they used ethically, that is to say, with responsibility, so that in their context and under existing circumstances they direct us to a coherent and morally supportable set of attitudes and actions? Or are they, like the tetragrammaton of the black magician and the demagogic slogan of the totalitarian leader, but talismanic incantations, intended to secure our assent not to the high purpose which the words connote, but to other and different policies? Are they, in Mr. Weaver's words, "ultimate in some rational sense"? That is to say, when Mr. Eisenhower speaks of "justice" in international affairs, does he accept the rational implications of the term? Is his structure of belief and policy and action such as to be coherent with its inherent meaning?

To answer these questions should not be too difficult, for— fortunately for our examination of his rhetoric—Mr. Eisenhower is not a private man, the coherence of whose structure of belief and action may only very occasionally be rigidly tested. He is at the head of the most powerful nation on earth, and he has been faced repeatedly, in full view of the world, with the need both to express his beliefs and to act upon them.

"There must," he says, "be justice sensed and shared by all peoples; for, without justice, the world can know only a tense and unstable truce." This is a clear enough statement. Do Mr. Eisenhower's other pronouncements and his actions accord with it so that together they form a unified rational structure?

In the first place, Mr. Eisenhower has made it abundantly clear that he regards war as the absolute evil—and that without qualification. Therefore it follows inescapably that peace is the absolute good—and *that* without qualification. Justice, therefore, on any coherent analysis, must be purely a secondary matter.

And if it be thought too abstract to base my criticism upon this logical contradiction, consider some of his more concrete words and acts. He has continuously, as in this very address, subordinated the objectives of the United States, moral as well as material, and its power to realize them, to the claims and authority of the United Nations.

Now the United Nations can in practice mean one of two things: the power of the Security Council or the power of the General Assembly. If it means the Council, where are the claims of justice, when subject to the veto of the Soviet Union, which by its philosophical outlook denies the very possibility of all non-materialist concepts, justice included?

If it means the Assembly, then also what is the fate of justice, at the mercy of the shifting intrigues of blocs and counter-blocs of states unequal in power, disparate in culture, some understanding and some ignorant of the very concept of justice? With power totally unproportionate to responsibility, with the vote of Libya or Luxembourg lying in the balance with equal weight to that of the United States or the United Kingdom, what becomes of justice, however pleasing such a situation may be to the ideologues of "equality"?

Again, Mr. Eisenhower would agree, one assumes, that the Soviet Union represents the epitome of injustice. What, then, does justice mean to him, when he moves against France and England in defense of Moscow's puppet, Nasser, and stands by while Hungary is murdered? How does it square with devotion to justice to woo Tito and Gomulka, whose system of thought and government, in its fundamentals identical with that of the Soviet Union, is as alien to justice as ever was Stalin's?

A policy based upon the coexistence of justice and injustice, under some higher law of peace at any price, is intrinsically incompatible with the principle of justice. As an ultimate term it has no rational foundation. It is a useful device to gain support for a program, but that program is not a program of justice. The appeal to justice is a moral sham.

And so it is with others of his ultimate terms. Law, for example. "There must be," says Mr. Eisenhower, "law, steadily invoked and respected by all nations . . ." But there can be no approach to world-wide law, even in the smallest things, until the Communist power center, which recognizes no law but power, is destroyed. Yet Mr. Eisenhower by word and deed has made it unmistakably clear that he will do nothing to bring that about. He can reasonably believe in coexistence, or he can reasonably believe in law—but not both at the same time. Of the two, it is certain from his actions to which he is committed.

And freedom? The only meaning Mr. Eisenhower can give to the word is "freedom from grinding poverty," world-wide material well-being, to be brought about by a world WPA. Meanwhile, the Hungarians live in Communist slavery (Kadar-type) and the Poles in Communist slavery (Gomulka-type), and for the Russian people Mr. Eisenhower holds out the hope of "greater security before their own [Communist] laws."

Freedom, Law, Justice: how hollow the words must ring in the gutted streets of Budapest—if anyone in Budapest still bothers to listen to the Voice of America. I have questioned, analytically, the ethics of Mr. Eisenhower's rhetorical terms; but the final proof was there, where they were tested in acid and found counterfeit.

"Slippage" and the Theory of the Lesser Evil

(*National Review*, February 28, 1959)

"Better to win with Eisenhower than lose with Taft"—this slogan of 1952 tore the American Right in two, sounding the death knell of the Republican Party as a conservative force and giving the New Deal revolution an eight-year period to consolidate itself and prepare for the next leap forward towards socialism. A tragically concrete expression of the "lesser evil" theory of politics, it brings into sharp focus the malady that has for many years devitalized American conservatism and inhibited the growth of an effective political opposition to the Liberalocracy that year by year moves us further down the road to totalitarianism.

It is this concentration on "winning" by accepting more and more of the enemy's rules for the conduct of the game that has caused the phenomenon of "slippage," which I discussed in these columns last month*: the continuing surrender of forward positions, the continuing conservative defense of positions farther and farther to the rear.

It is true that it is sometimes necessary to compromise, to accept a lesser evil in order to fend off a greater one, to bargain in the political process when you have to. But it is only safe to do so if a firm, principled position is maintained and the compromise is consciously accepted as a compromise, as a concession imposed by weakness. And it is particularly necessary to maintain this clarity when the lesser evil is not some organization or legislative measure, but a political leader, a man to whom support must be given without endorsing his personality, his views, or his integrity. It is vital that it be perfectly clear that he serves you only expediently, is your ally for the moment only.

But the temptation to conservatives, once committed to the support of such a man, has been to see in the lesser evil a good, to attach themselves to him with enthusiasm, to neglect his basic commitments to the prevailing values of Liberalism, to hail him as a hero of opposition to Liberalism—when all his fair-seeming words mean is that he or his advisors want to trap conservative votes in an internecine struggle within the fabric of Liberalism. Support of the lesser evil can only be given without profound danger if it is clearly understood that the lesser evil supported is *an evil*, that what is being

---

* See "What Price a Patch of Sand?", p. 339.

undertaken is a temporary alliance for reasons of maneuver, not an ideological endorsement of the lesser evil as *good.*

Otherwise, the force or the man to whom conservatives give their support, with the hope of blocking the victory of a greater evil, inevitably becomes not a means but an end. The conservative begins to equate his goals with those of his ally, surrendering leadership to him. What is worse, he begins to see as the decisive field of battle against the Liberal revolution what is only the arena of an inner struggle among those who accept the fundamentals of the Liberal revolution, who differ only upon the extent of its goals and the speed with which they are to be achieved. Under such circumstances, "slippage" towards the Left is bound to occur.

When, year after year, the money, the energy, the enthusiasm of American conservatives is devoted to the success of the political fortunes of Liberals who happen to be somewhat to the right of other Liberals—a Willkie, a Dewey, an Eisenhower—it follows that conservative consciousness will be conditioned to delight in the virtues of a $77-billion budget as over against an $80-billion budget; in a federal educational loan program as over against more direct federal interference in education; in the steady extension of the social-security system, slow only by comparison with the demands of a Reuther or a Humphrey—to delight, in short, in creeping socialism because it creeps instead of leaps.

Nor in the even more urgent area of the fight against Communism have conservatives gained from those whom they have supported. Eisenhower blessed the destruction of McCarthy; sadly bemoaning the murder of Hungary, responded to it by a series of Geneva conferences and cultural exchanges, culminating in the disgraceful Mikoyan tour. The Herculean labors of Dulles, it is true, have done something to stem the tide of retreat, but then Truman acted well when Greece and Turkey were threatened and at the beginning of the Korean War. The net balance of 1959, after six years of an Administration brought into power by the basic backing of conservative votes, registers an immense slippage in our will to resist Communism and in our position *vis-à-vis* Communism.

The tendency is to cry, "We wuz robbed," to blame those whom conservatives supported for deception. But this is unfair. The fundamental affinity to Liberalism of the right-wing Liberals whom conservatives have supported, has never been concealed. The UN rhetoric of Eisenhower, his insistence (in a world darkened by the Communist drive for universal conquest) that "war is unthinkable," his solemn assurance that he did not intend to reverse the New Deal—these were enough to describe the Liberal shape of his vision of the world.

The conservative believes that in a world in which tyranny threatens to destroy us, surrender is the only thing that is unthinkable; he believes that the New Deal represents the breakthrough of socialism and that only by its reversal can a free society in America be guaranteed. He has only himself to blame when he supports those who make clear that they believe the opposite.

If conservatives will judge the men and organizations they support by conservative criteria, instead of allowing their energies to be siphoned off by any right-wing Liberal who wheedles them with occasional words of conservative sound, then a consolidation of conservatism would become possible—and a halt might be called to the continuing slippage we are witnessing. Otherwise, that slippage will continue inexorably.

THE CAMPAIGN OF 1960

The Politics of "The Impossible"

(National Review, November 7, 1959)

Politics has been called "the art of the possible." Interpreted literally, this is of course a truism. All human arts are arts of the possible; the impossible is by definition that which cannot be achieved.

But that is neither the intended meaning of the apothegm nor is it the sense in which it is currently employed. Produced with a triumphant flourish as a final argument against anyone who refuses to accept the present structure of society and the limits of accepted political opinion, it means in reality: "Politics is the art of operating within fixed and determined conditions set by established power. So forget about fundamental principle when it clashes with accepted shibboleths, if you want to be politically effective."

And indeed such a definition of politics as a practical matter would be true at most times and places. When the social order is stable and firm and when an accepted hierarchy of beliefs unites men of all stations of life and of all parties upon fundamental ends, then in the pulling and tugging of political activity towards one emphasis or another within the common agreement upon ends, that definition of politics will hold.

But this is not our situation. We live in a social order uncertain, affrighted, and cut loose from all fixed standards.

We are uncertain before the multifarious signs of social decline: civil peace deeply disturbed by manifold and spiralling crime, largely the actions of the young; family security shattered by the institutionalization of divorce; economic sobriety, personal and familial prudence, mocked at by crushing taxation and a governmental policy of progressive inflation.

We are terrified to the point of constant retreat and shameful appeasement by a foreign enemy, whose only superior weapons are our confusions, our hesitations, and our lack of belief in anything for which we are willing to dare the risk of death.

We are cut loose from all fixed standards and deeply held beliefs, in the train of forty years of violent revolution abroad and insidious revolution at home, of catastrophic wars, of philosophical and technological innovation with social results eating to the very heart of the inherited way of life of the nation.

What is patently wrong is not this or that incorrect emphasis, this or that badly conceived policy, but the entire concept of the ends accepted by those in power. In such circumstances an approach to politics which for practical purposes might be reasonably adequate in normal times becomes hopelessly inadequate. "The possible" can only mean a little more or a little less of the same. Politics, if it is to have meaning beyond an empty game, must be conceived in terms of an older and deeper vision, as an art based upon philosophical principle and devoted to the achievement in the body politic of the conditions of freedom.

It must be an art which, in terms of the accepted norms of a rotten society, is the art of the impossible. It must take as its standards concepts founded in truth and in the tradition of the West, but scorned today by the enlightened: the responsibility of individual men for themselves, their family and their future; the moral evil (not the "sickness") of the criminal; the moral excellence of patriotism; the shame of paternalism and the deep danger of government that amasses power beyond its natural limits.

By prevailing contemporary judgment, a politics based upon such principles is a politics of the impossible. This is the burden of books, articles, book reviews, devoted to criticism of principled conservative opinion—as much in the scholarly as in the more popular press. So intellectually bankrupt is Liberalism today that by and large it no longer tries to come to grips with conservative theory, but, glorifying in its position of power, is contented to characterize its opponents as "impossibilists."

Unfortunately, however, it is not only Liberals who maintain the doctrine of "the possible." Some conservatives, men who by their instincts and deeper intellectual understanding recognize the evils of existing circumstances, nevertheless are hypnotized by the doctrine of "the possible"; and waste their energies attempting to square the circle, to achieve conservative ends while accepting Liberal conditions.

But a politics directed towards decent ends manifestly cannot limit itself to what is "possible" under conditions dictated by the Liberal world-view. How can our country and Western civilization be defended from an aggressively messianic enemy if "war is unthinkable"; how can a free economy be restored, if, to paraphrase the words of Mr. Eisenhower, a reversal of the Roosevelt revolution is equally unthinkable? Or, on an instrumental level, how conduct a politics of conservatism tied to the present leadership of a party that accepts (as the Percy reports amply prove) the fundamental principles of Liberalism, a party which presents as its choice of spokesmen a Janus-faced political operator or a demagogic blintz-eating scion of the New Deal? Or on a deeper level, how develop a true understanding of the nature of man and his destiny without taking an intellectual stand "impossibly" in revolt against the triple doctrines upon which Liberal orthodoxy is founded: the historical materialism derived from Karl Marx, the amorality derived from Sigmund Freud, and the philosophical and moral nihilism derived from John Dewey?

Paradoxically, only that which in the light of contemporary opinion is impossible is possible for the conservative. The role of radical is temperamentally alien to the conservative, but in the circumstances of Liberal domination under which we live, that role is demanded of him. Truth and the traditions of the West cannot seriously be defended without defiance of the doctrines presently authoritative, without philosophical and political defiance of the legend of "the possible."

The Politics of "The Impossible"
II: 1960 Dilemma

(National Review, December 19, 1959)

Between the time I write this column and the time it is published, I shall have participated in the *National Review* Forum in New York, opposing the thesis that conservatives owe their support to Richard Nixon. With my mind on the subject, I cannot resist the temptation to shy two stones at one bird, and also devote this column to the problem of Nixon and conservatism. I am particularly moved to do so, since the position of conservatives in 1960 is a striking instance of the dilemma discussed in my last column, "The Politics of 'The Impossible'" (*National Review*, November 7).

For it is the demand that political action remain within the limits of the possibilities of achieving political power immediately (for someone, it hardly matters for whom, so long as he is a little to the right of someone else) that is the strongest argument—indeed in the end the only argument—that can be effectively brought to bear in defense of the thesis that conservatives should give Richard Nixon their active support. But this argument neglects the overriding question: what use is it to spend energy to achieve political power if the positive result is going to be nothing better than a mild decrease in our rate of growth towards collectivism at home and our surrender to collectivism abroad; if, negatively, energies that might be devoted to building a serious conservative opposition are diverted and drained off from that task?

This is the history of the Eisenhower Administration. It is possible, of course, that under the aegis of a Stevenson we might have moved faster in the direction of statist encroachment upon a free economy, of federal aggression against the rights and privileges of the sovereign states, of subservient accommodation to the swelling arrogations of Soviet power. But I doubt it. Stevenson, it is true, would have actively desired such developments and would have wanted them to proceed at an even faster rate. Eisenhower did not desire them, but, being devoid of conservative understanding and principle, he simply floated with the tide. Stevenson, however, would have been opposed in Congress by the same alliance of Republicans and conservative Democrats that hobbled Roosevelt after his first honeymoon days, and continued to hobble Truman, an alliance which has largely disintegrated with the election of a President supported by conservatives.

Such a Congress would have found ways to keep under control the 60 per cent rise in federal expenditure on domestic programs which occurred during the Eisenhower Administration (in the seven Truman years, the rise was about 10 per cent).

A President in Stevenson's position would never have dared—would indeed have courted impeachment had he attempted it—to invite Nikita Khrushchev to our shores and to propagate the concepts upon which the spirit of Camp David rests; to cease nuclear testing; or to move, as Eisenhower and the Herter-Bohlen State Department are moving, towards an "agreement on Berlin" that can only mean the betrayal of West Germany and Europe and the surrender of the very idea of intransigent American opposition to Communism.

The relevance of all this to Nixon? Like Eisenhower, he is undoubtedly less obnoxious than the alternatives. In contrast to every member of the brood of Democratic hopefuls, he is not an open and principled ideologist, committed to the continuation of the Roosevelt revolution. In contrast to Nelson Rockefeller, a patent case of a New Dealer in Republican clothes, he is not subtly attempting to build an image of himself half-conservative, half-welfarist, in order to grasp power as Mediator of the Nation in the mould of an Augustus.

No, Richard Nixon is no more an ideologue than is Dwight Eisenhower. Like Eisenhower—though for different reasons—he drifts with the tide. In Nixon's case that career of drifting is the result of aiming at the Presidency and subordinating all principles to that aim. Pathfinder for the Khrushchev visit, supporter of the Camp David policy, proponent of the surrender of significant American sovereignty to an international organization, defender of the cessation of nuclear testing, Richard Nixon has shown in his concrete acts, as in the rhetoric of his speeches, that he agrees with Eisenhower that "war is unthinkable"—which, by logical deduction, means that if war is thinkable to the Communist leadership (which it is), surrender is preferable to war.

And he has made it clear, no less unmistakably than Eisenhower, that he regards the reversal of the Roosevelt revolution as equally unthinkable. He stands for the welfare state and has proposed no substantial modification of it. He praises the Warren Court and its invasion of the rights of the states.

On the record, he is no conservative. All the arguments urging conservatives to support him boil down to the argument that there is nothing else for them to do.

But is there nothing else to do? Should not the primary aim of conservatives be to consolidate and strengthen a conservative movement directed towards the recovery of the United States from control by Liberal ideologists? And if, as is clearly the case, there are no available Presidential candidates in 1960 whose election will forward that aim, should not conservatives devote their attention to the support of conservative candidates for the House and the Senate, to the development of conservative organization within and without the directly political area, and to organizing a conscious, principled boycott of the 1960 Presidential campaign? Would not such a direction of activity, begun now and continued over the next years, be the best way of assuring that 1964 may promise a possibility of conservative victory, whether through recapture of the Republican Party or through creation of a new alignment of forces?

Only Four Years to 1964

(National Review, December 3, 1960)

Conservatives should, by the nature of their philosophical outlook, always be able to see immediate events (even events that have roused their passions) in relation to abiding principle, and to assess them in perspective. Thus and thus only can they fulfill their responsibilities and avoid becoming victims of momentary circumstances and transitory groupings of power.

The failure of conservatives over the past twenty years to consider the problems of Presidential elections in this light has been the decisive cause of their continuing political ineffectiveness. Trailing the course of events, quadrennium after quadrennium they have been led captive in the train of Liberal Republican Presidential nominees, from Willkie to Nixon. If there is to be a break in this fatuous record of failure, the meaning of the 1960 election must be apprehended in the light of the four Presidential campaigns that preceded it, and in the light of the ends and purposes of conservatives. With this as a foundation, the general outline of a strategy for 1964 can be developed now; and it is now, not in the year just before the next Presidential conventions, that a strategy will have to be developed, if it is to be effective, if conservatives are not once again to be pawns in an internecine struggle for power among Liberals.

I myself have held the view throughout the campaign that nothing, nothing whatever, of political significance for conservatives was at issue *between* Nixon and Kennedy. There was much that was significant in the manner in which the campaign was conducted and in the role that conservatives played in the election, but conservatives had no stake in the fortunes of the rival candidates.

The *manner in which the campaign was conducted* emphasized with the greatest clarity that on no principled issues did the Republican and the Democratic standard-bearers differ. If there could have been any doubt in advance, Nixon made it perfectly clear in the first television debate, when he stressed his complete agreement with Kennedy on all basic issues, explicitly announcing that he disagreed only on the methods and tempo of achieving Liberal ends.

The *role of conservatives in the campaign* was of significance only insofar as they contributed to the strength of the Republican Liberals. Only in one respect did they make themselves seriously felt—in the largely spontaneous demonstration of sentiment around Senator Barry Goldwater. And that was, for this year, all the Goldwater movement came to—a demonstration of sentiment. This is not to criticize Senator Goldwater's strategy at the convention and in the campaign; considering the continued failure of conservatives to achieve clarity of principle upon the electoral process, their continuing bemused refusal to learn the lessons of previous elections, and their lack of effective political organization, there was probably nothing else for him to do than what he did, so long as he wished to remain an effective political figure.

If the same drab drama is not to be played out in 1964 and 1968 and 1972, if the potential electoral strength of Barry Goldwater is not to go the way of that of other conservative leaders of the past two decades, then conservatives will have to recognize that they have no stake in the Republican Party *as such.* Which does not mean any underestimation of the importance to conservatives of a struggle to capture control of the Republican Party. The Republican Party is an existing vehicle of the American political system, which, if captured by conservatives, could sweep into its support Southern conservatives and create a new majority of the South, the Midwest, the Mountain States, the Far West, and some smaller states of the East. Nixon won no state that a conservative could not carry, and, given the addition of the South, he would have been elected. The struggle for the capture of the Republican Party cannot be lightly cast aside in the name of an abstract third-party purity.

But, on the other hand, so long as conservatives cannot see beyond loyalty to the Republican Party as a condition limiting their entire strategy, they are foredoomed to defeat—and for two reasons. First, if they make it clear in advance that whatever the Republican Party does it will have their support, the logic of politics dictates that the Republican Party will remain a Liberal party. Under such circumstances, the conservative vote is locked in as a Republican vote—which predetermines that the Liberal argument will prevail: "The conservatives have nowhere else to go; so, to win, the Republicans must nominate a Liberal candidate and write a Liberal platform."

Second, if conservatives wish to preserve their political existence, they cannot afford again to support a Liberal candidate; therefore, should they fail to prevail in the Republican convention, their existence as a political entity demands that they be prepared to walk out of that convention and, uniting with

Democratic conservatives, fulfill their duty of presenting to the country a meaningful choice.

True, such understanding and such a strategy will not guarantee a conservative victory in 1964; but it is better to lose in 1964 and win in 1968, than to face another election like those of 1940, 1944, 1948, 1952, 1956 and 1960, in which conservatism was foredoomed to defeat whatever the outcome. It may take beyond 1964 for a clear conservative political leadership to create a winning majority; but meanwhile there are the congressional races of 1962, 1964 and 1966, in which there is no doubt that, at least in the Senate, the existence of a sharp conservative alternative to prevailing Liberalism can produce a totally new political situation in the United States and end the domination of political life by one brand or another of Liberalism.

THE KENNEDY YEARS

Which Way for JFK?

(National Review, February 11, 1961)

One of the more galling by-products of an age of mass television democracy and the loose rhetoric spawned by its educational system is the increasing difficulty we have in judging a public man by his public words. The problem is somewhat analogous to that of a speculator operating in a market with broad public participation. He may know the economic factors involved in a given decision and be solidly prepared to make a judgment and risk his money on that judgment; but the economic factors will affect the market in the short run, only as they affect popular psychology; and the judgment of the speculator therefore must be based not upon fundamental factors but upon the effect of fundamental factors on indifferently informed minds.

The political analyst faces the same kind of problem, if somewhat in reverse. The speeches and official statements of public figures are no longer, like those of a Washington or a Jefferson, a Lincoln or a Douglas, even a Wilson or a Theodore Roosevelt, directed primarily to the most persuasive presentation of a position for an audience whose decisive members possessed at least modest training in logic and rhetoric and almost all of whom had been educated in schools which reinforced common sense rather than devaluing it. Today they are filtered through the techniques of "mass communications experts" and conditioned by a political climate in which imprecision, bland self-contradiction, and grandiose meaninglessness have set the style of public utterance.

With all this said, the fact remains that for any prognosis of the Administration of John F. Kennedy about all we have to go on, as this is written, are his words, primarily his Inaugural Address. His actions, apart from a gimmick or two like the RB-47 stunt, to date consist only in the appointments he has made: a predominant representation of left-wing ideologues (Bowles, Kennan, Stevenson, Schlesinger, Murrow) with a judicious sprinkling of capable bureaucratic technicians from the foundations, education, the managerial stratum (Rusk, Dillon, McNamara).

This amalgam, which at first sight appears somewhat haphazard, is, however, very suggestive of the shape of the Administration when it is taken in conjunction with the rhetoric of Kennedy's pronouncements. The Inaugural Address, which has been hailed by bemused journalists, poets, courtiers of the Establishment—and by many who ought to know better—in the most absurd of hyperbolic comparisons to Augustus, Emerson, Lincoln, was, in fact, a similar amalgam.

There were such unexceptionable statements as "I believe that the rights of man come not from the generosity of the state, but from the hand of God," and "Let every other power know that this hemisphere intends to remain the master of its own house." But when the President came to grips with operative principles, he spoke in the purest accents of Liberalism. He betrayed his own, and perpetuated the nation's, deep misapprehension of the very nature of Communism, when he said: "Let both sides explore what problems unite us instead of belaboring those problems which divide us"; when he called upon "both sides [to] join in creating . . . a new world of law, where the strong are just and the weak secure and the peace preserved"; and when he exhorted us to cooperate to "push back the jungles of suspicion."

The hard truth about Communism which our new President, like our old, refuses to face is that we have nothing, nor can we have anything, that will "unite" us with the Communists; that Communism is absolutely alien philosophically—one might almost say theologically—to the very concept of justice, to the very concept of any peace but the peace of the graveyard where Communism would reign supreme over the world.

Ignorance of the nature of the world struggle with Communism dominates the address and inspires its principal operative concepts: acquiescence in the anti-Western "national" revolution, even support for it; dependence upon a world-wide program of bribery, in the spirit of the New Deal domestic program, as our main reliance for security and survival; abject, blind, all-encompassing rejection of reality—the hard, cold, inescapable reality that the only alternatives open to us are victory or defeat.

Early as it is, and despite the difficulties created by modern political rhetoric, I think one can predict fairly clearly the major lines of policy of the new Administration. There will be much talk of the great challenge of Communism, much drumbeating about frontiers and missions; but there will be no firm anti-Communist policy. Instead there will be a grandiose shadowboxing endeavor in which Communism will be the excuse for massive unproductive expenditures of energy and money in every farflung corner of the globe. There will be no Rooseveltian Hundred Days of dramatic extension of domestic welfarism. Instead the Galbraithian prescription of increasing the sphere of government power and contracting the sphere of the individual's control over his own life and fortunes, will be implemented by

welfarism on a world scale, while in the real war we continue
to lose position after position to Communism. And underlying
everything, the main motif of the Administration will be inexorably pursued: to achieve what the *New Republic's* T.R.B. so
trenchantly and admiringly calls "Kennedy's real goal . . . to
achieve a transition to . . . Presidential rule, . . . to activist government."

New York Conservatives
and the Two-Party System

(National Review, July 3, 1962)

Conservatives who have lived through the Liberal-directed
deterioration of the Republican Party—signalized by the candidacies of Willkie, Dewey, Eisenhower and Nixon—face a serious
dilemma. As conservatives, they respect the tradition of the
American two-party system. Through most of our history it has
served to mediate among groups and factions and to maintain
the spirit of the Constitution. By presenting to the electorate
broad choices, while modulating the irreconcilable passions of
dogmatic ideology, it has enabled us to avoid the dangers of
the multi-party structure of European politics, which magnifies
those passions to a point where the possibility of effective constitutional government is foreclosed.

On the one hand, therefore, American conservatives neither
desire nor demand cleanly-wrought ideological parties; they are
firm, principled supporters of the two-party system. But, on the
other hand, when the leadership of the Republican Party for
years strains every nerve to make it as close a carbon copy of
the reconstructed Democratic Party of Franklin Roosevelt as it
can force upon its Republican constituency, the insistent question arises as to whether what we have today is in actuality a
two-party system.

Although a two-party system has always existed in the United
States, parties have been born and parties have died. They

have died, as the Whigs died, when they ceased to reflect in any significant way—however unideologically, however broadly —any basic differences with the other party on major concerns of the people. The continued life of the Republican Party depends upon whether control of its destinies can be won by a leadership that reflects the conservative spirit animating the citizens who are the base of its support. There is nothing sacred about the Republican Party, nor is there even anything instrumentally good about it, unless it functions as a true alternative to the Democratic Party to constitute a real two-party system.

Clearly, the drive of conservatives to reassert their voice in the councils of the nation would be immensely facilitated if they could regain control of the Republican Party. That is why the sober judgment of conservatives has rejected the third-party road. But if that road is not to become the only possible road for conservatives, then they must fight with all their energies for the leadership of the Republican Party, even to the degree of punishing Liberal interlopers who succeed in securing Republican nomination.

The Republican Party deserves conservative loyalty only to the degree that it is conservative. The issue is simple and clear: a Republican Party conceived in the image of Taft, Knowland and Goldwater, deserves conservative loyalty; a Republican Party conceived in the image of Rockfeller and Javits, Romney and Nixon, has no more claim upon that loyalty than the Democratic Party of Roosevelt, Stevenson and Kennedy. This seems to be the understanding of the conservatives who rolled up 35 per cent of the California Republican vote for the comparatively unknown Joseph Shell against the established prestige and organization of Richard Nixon, and who have made known their determination to support Nixon in November only if he turns his back upon the fleshpots of accommodation to Liberalism.

It is upon these motivations, and in consideration of the special circumstances in the State of New York, that a representative group of New York conservatives (including two editors of *National Review*—William F. Rickenbacker and myself) has become members of the State Committee of the Conservative Party of New York. There is no desire in the minds of the leadership of this party to strike at the two-party system. But, in a state where there is no primary system and where the apparatus of the Republican Party is ruthlessly controlled by Nelson Rockefeller and Jacob Javits—in defiance of the sentiments of the great majority of Republican congressmen, state legislators, party workers and the rank and file of New York Republican voters—we have come soberly and thoughtfully to the conclusion that only by placing before the electorate conservative candidates for Governor and Senator, can conservative sentiment in New York be made articulate enough to rescue the Republican Party from Liberal domination and eventual desuetude.

Further, there is a special political situation in this state. A determined and organized left wing, first under the banner of the American Labor Party and then of the Liberal Party, has forced the Democratic Party to the Left (to such a degree, indeed, that many conservative Democrats are moving towards conservative organization). The pressure of the Democratic leadership's leftward motion has in turn moved the pusillanimous, and in any case Liberal-inclined, Republican leadership more and more to the Left. If the principles of conservatism are ever again to be presented to the voters of New York, if the Republican Party is to survive as a genuine component of a two-party system, the conservatives have no alternative to establishing an independent center for countering the Liberal momentum, and, by the pressure that center exerts, winning back the Republican Party of New York to conservatism.

Kennedy, Cuba, and the Voters

(National Review, November 6, 1962)

All available evidence would seem to indicate that there is one issue of overriding and decisive concern the country over at this election time: Cuba. Whether, however, in the tangled state of American politics today, this deep concern will be clearly reflected in the election returns is another matter. If it is, there can be no question that the Kennedy Administration will suffer a smashing defeat.

By that I do not only—or primarily—mean a Republican victory; I mean that Liberals of both parties (or rather, those Liberals whose ideology determines their stand on foreign policy) will suffer seriously, and that the candidates of both parties who have taken a stand for firm and immediate intervention in Cuba (for the most part, conservatives) will register startling gains. In the nature of things this would undoubtedly mean a considerable increase in Republican representation in both Houses of the Congress; but it would not represent a victory for the Republican Party as such, it would simply reflect the fact that by and large a great many more Republican than Democratic candidates tend toward conservatism.

The overwhelming American sentiment for action in Cuba may, however, not be registered in the election returns because of what I have called "the tangled state of American politics." Several factors are involved here. One (and this is in normal circumstances by no means an altogether bad aspect of American politics) is the tendency of congressional elections to reflect multifarious local issues, thus obscuring basic national issues amid the welter of urgent local concerns. Another factor, which is specific to this election, is Kennedy's determined effort to keep foreign policy out of the election—by specious appeals to "bipartisanship" or, alternatively, by trying to blacken the motives and reputation of all critics of his policy, and by tying up the Congress deep into October in a series of struggles on domestic issues. The effectiveness of these tactics has been greatly magnified by a third factor, the ineptitude of the Republican leadership, which has (with important and notable exceptions) so far allowed itself to be bulldozed into fighting the election on Kennedy's terms—and thereby has failed to fulfill its responsibility for the safety of the country, a responsibility that perforce falls on the Opposition when a feeble and faltering Administration puts the country in danger.

Cuba, nevertheless, is the basic issue—and with good reason. *The American people, with instinctive common sense, realize that in the seventeen years of the Cold War this is the turning point.* The rarefied ideologizing and the parlor-game theory, which the Establishment cultivates to deal with our destiny, may put Cuba on a level with Laos or Lebanon, or even the hydroelectric dams for Hindus and food for Poland and planes for Sukarno; but the ordinary American is not swaddled in the layers of ideology that prevent the Establishment from making contact with reality. He knows that there once was a Monroe Doctrine; that calling crack Russian military units "technicians" does not change the meaning of a highly armed enemy force 90 miles off our coast; that if we do not eradicate a focus of infection so near our vitals it will spread until it destroys us.

This instinctive understanding, which washes away all the ifs, ands, and buts that cripple our policy, leads to a forthright conclusion: the Castro regime must be removed by force at the earliest possible moment. It could have been removed a year ago by a variety of methods; six months ago by blockade; but now it must be done by direct action and at once—that is, before Cuba becomes a powerful thermonuclear base. Cuba must be invaded before the Castro government achieves the power to hit back at our shores with devastating effect and before, as a result of our impotence before Castro, the export of Communism from Cuba confronts us with Communist regimes and Soviet bases throughout Latin America.

The decision to do the only thing that can be done in the circumstances, to invade Cuba and destroy the Communist regime, will come from the Administration only if the sentiment of the American people is so clearly expressed in this election that Kennedy will be afraid to ignore it, and if there is returned to the Congress a large enough group of able and energetic men to articulate that sentiment and force action upon Kennedy.

There are key contests to watch as the election returns come in, to determine whether this is happening—contests which will signify much more than will a gross assessment of the Republican-Democratic vote. Indiana Senator Capehart has made Cuba the main issue in that state. There are contests for re-election to the House of the militant group of Republican "Young Turks" (men like Donald Bruce of Indiana, John Ashbrook of Ohio, Bruce Alger of Texas). In California a number of outstandingly anti-Communist candidates are running for congressional seats. In Arkansas it will be worth watching the showing made by the Republican Dr. Kenneth Jones, who is opposing Fulbright largely on the basis of his Establishment record as Chairman of the Senate Foreign Relations Committee.

And there will be very great significance in the size of the vote achieved by the new Conservative Party of New York, which is making the demand for action in Cuba central to its campaign.

In these contests, as elsewhere in the country, the issue of Cuba is modified and muted by other problems, but, by and large, there as elsewhere, it will be the critical underlying issue. Let us hope that November 6 will register a verdict for immediate and decisive action that even John F. Kennedy can understand.

The 1962 Elections: The Turning of the Tide

(National Review, December 4, 1962)

Great historical tides turn slowly; and in the ruck and tumult of conflict, the moment of their turning may well seem but another moment in a long retreat—particularly to men whose lives and fortunes are engaged in the stupendous effort to turn the tide. The historian, soberly judging events in perspective, can see implicit in the inconclusive cannonade of Valmy, the sweep of France over Europe; or in Saratoga, the independence of these United States; or in the battles of Midway and Moscow, the apogee and the coming destruction of the Japanese and German power. But to the men who fought these wars, the turn was unapparent. After these events they felt scarcely less beleaguered than before; and, indeed, long years of fighting lay ahead before the foreshadowed victory was in their hands.

So, it seems to me, it is today in the bloodless war of conservatism to recover America for its traditions. The elections of this year registered, I believe, a basic shift in the structure of American politics—a shift which has for the first time brought the conservative challenge to Liberalism into the center of the American political arena. It is understandable that the inconclusiveness of the returns, as seen in terms of the immediate electoral battle, has left a good many conservatives discouraged. It is understandable, but it is not, I think, a true estimate of the election. Consider its outstanding features:

1. *The political structure of the election*—the terms in which it has been discussed almost universally by television and radio and press. In a profound change—one which, as far as I know, has gone unnoticed—all the commentators have considered the results of the election in terms of a conservative-Liberal confrontation, and they have done so whether they were trying to prove a victory for Liberalism, or a defeat for Liberalism, or a standoff. This is new political language; it represents a coming-of-age of conservatism. It is true that there was much talk of a vague kind some years ago about Eisenhower's "conservatism"; but no congressional election has been so characterized all down the line, and, what is much more important, this time those who are called conservative are consciously and actually conservative.

2. *The muting of avowed ideological Liberalism.* Except in a few strongholds of ritualistic Liberalism, no serious effort was made to go before the voters with a sharp, clear Liberal position. This was in marked contrast to the conservative candidates, successful and unsuccessful, who everywhere pressed their position as conservatives.

The major last-minute factor in the election on the Democratic side, President Kennedy's Cuban *démarche*, was—on the surface —a conservative gesture. However craven the policy of the Administration may turn out to be and whatever further appeasement lies ahead, in the two weeks before election the image Kennedy felt constrained to present to the voters was shaped to conform a great deal more closely to the image of Senator Goldwater than to that of Adlai Stevenson.

Scranton and Romney, widely touted as symbols of the success of Liberal Republicanism, waged a campaign far removed, whatever their personal predilections, from the Liberal line: Romney presented, as always, two faces, but one of them distinctly the face of the fiscally responsible businessman; Scranton skillfully and pragmatically appealed to the electorate on all levels. Even that whited sepulchre of Liberalism and worse, Jacob Javits, talked so "tough" on Cuba in the weeks before election day that the New York *Times* rebuked him; and in his up-state campaign he was the very Model of a Modern Middle-of-the-Roader.

As for Nelson Rockefeller, still gallantly Liberal: despite all the busy little efforts to sew up the rents in his Presidential panoply, he suffered a serious setback. Instead of the widely heralded 750,000 to 1,000,000 majority, he fell well below the 572,000 of the last election, with a 500,000 plurality over Morgenthau and a mere 350,000 majority when the votes of the Conservative Party are taken into account—and this against the most incredibly inept candidate who has run for the governorship of New York within living memory.

Again, the impressive Democratic wins gave no comfort to ideological Liberalism: men like Congressman Stratton in New York, leaning far to the right wing of the Democratic Party, or Ted (I Can Get It For Massachusetts Wholesale) Kennedy. Here too the Liberal trumpet echoed faintly indeed when the voters were around.

3. *The conservative position in the Congress was significantly strengthened.* In the House, 85 out of 88 incumbents with an 80 per cent or better rating from Americans for Constitutional Action were reelected; and a dozen new firm conservatives joined their ranks. The three incumbents defeated—Rousselot, Hiestand and McDonough—went down before the combined effects of Democratic redistricting in California and the see-

saw leadership of Richard Nixon. (If there is any question as to the meaning of the California election, consider that Max Rafferty, running on an outright conservative platform for State Superintendent of Public Instruction, won by approximately the quarter-million margin by which Nixon lost.)

As for the Senate, the conservatives elected in the Mountain States more than make up for the unfortunate defeat of Capehart of Indiana; and the slight Democratic gain over the Republicans has the incidental advantage of retiring Wiley of Wisconsin, whose inveterate Liberalism has long confused Republican policy on foreign affairs.

4. *The center of gravity of the Republican Party has shifted basically to the Right.* The Republican inroads into the South make the Southern Republicans, who are outstandingly conservative, a new force in the counsels of the party. The strengthening of the "Young Turks" in the House of Representatives—both because they are now no longer freshmen and are therefore able to play a much larger role, and because the newly elected conservatives add to their ranks—makes them a vitally important conservative factor in the party. The political elimination of Richard Nixon and the unimpressive showing of Rockefeller in New York shift the balance further to the Right. The showing of the Conservative Party in New York (close to 150,000 votes, with meager funds and without organization or well-known candidates) is the handwriting on the wall for Liberal domination of the Republican Party in New York, and it is likely to serve as a warning to the Republican leadership in other states that conservative sentiment cannot be ignored.

None of this is a guarantee either of the nomination of a conservative candidate for the Presidency in the Republican convention of 1964, or of his victory in the election if he is nominated. That depends on many factors—not least the vigor and quality of conservative leadership. But this election does signalize, I would maintain, a massive, if quiet, turning of the tide. It does portend the *possibility* of a Presidential victory in 1964, if events and the policy of the Kennedy Administration take the course which seems today likely, and if conservative leadership acts with the understanding and skill the situation demands. It portends the *high probability* of a more and more consciously conservative Congress in the years ahead. And, after all, decisive power rests in the hands of a Congress determined to use that power and conscious of its responsibility under the Constitution.

THE CAMPAIGN OF 1964

Conservatism and the Goldwater Consensus

(National Review, November 5, 1963)

It is now official. *Time, Newsweek,* and the New York *Times* all consider Barry Goldwater "the leading Republican Presidential candidate." At this moment—with the seriousness of Senator Goldwater's candidacy universally recognized and before we enter the gruelling months of campaigning, from January to July and on to November—it may be helpful to survey the road the conservative movement has come these past few years, and to consider its future, particularly its relationship to the broad national consensus that can make Goldwater President of the United States. For, we should make no mistake about it, the conscious conservative movement and the Goldwater following (to say nothing of the potential Goldwater following) are not one and the same thing.

The conservative movement, to begin with, is not limited in its perspectives to the arena of the purely political. It looks towards nothing less than a deep-going renewal of American life in the spirit of the Western and American tradition—a renewal at every level of existence: social, intellectual, philosophical, spiritual, as well as political. Its ends cannot be attained by a political victory alone, important though such a victory is.

I do not wish to minimize in any way the importance of that

victory; without it, nothing else is possible. The driving power of modern government in the hands of ideologues (who have in effect controlled it these past three decades) steadily stifles the energies of free persons within our borders and brings more and more imminently upon us the danger of subjugation from without. The *political* problem is, at this point, primarily a defensive one: to remove from government—particularly the executive branch and the bureaucracy—the dominant influence of ideology, and release the energies of a long-thwarted people.

It will then be the task of American conservatives to give leadership to those energies, to formulate intellectually the sound prejudices of a released citizenry, and to guide its actions. This is a stupendous program—a task not of a year, not even of a single generation; but it is the challenge of this task that has brought into being the American conservative movement of these years. And if the challenge seems overwhelming, let us consider for a moment (before turning to the problem of the relationship of the conservative movement to the election of Goldwater) how far we have come already, in how brief a time.

A dozen years ago there was, in the sense that it exists today, no American conservative movement. The hurricane spawned in 1932 had swept across the country leaving only islands of resistance, uncoordinated and intellectually isolated. There were free-enterprise economists desperately holding the fort in the universities; there was a stubborn rear-guard action in the Congress against the increasing powers of government; there was a widespread anti-Communist sentiment, expressed by a few valiant individuals of whom the archetype was Whittaker Chambers. There was, indeed, a beginning of the articulation of an over-all conservative position: Richard Weaver's *Ideas Have Consequences* was published in 1948; William Buckley's *God and Man at Yale* in 1951; and in the wake of the Hiss case and the McCarthy *démarches*, intellectual activity was beginning to hammer out the shape of American conservatism.

In the brief dozen years since then, the situation has been transformed. "Conservative," from being a curse word, a designation from which all but the most intrepid fled, has become a roaring challenge to the established power and the established aridities of the post-Roosevelt era. In every field of national life, from academy and church, television and press, to school district and Congressional District, the battle between Liberalism and conservatism has become the central issue.

Conservatism, then, has come of age; but it would be utopian to believe that any political victory, even the election of Barry Goldwater to the Presidency, could by itself fulfill the conservative vision. By the same token, it is political shortsightedness of a most dangerous kind to demand or expect that a candidate for the Presidency, whose task it is to create a new consensus to replace the prevailing power of Liberal ideology, should stand in splendid purity as champion of the whole sweep of conscious American conservatism. The task of such a man is to change the direction of political events by leading a consensus united by instinct and broad belief, not to be the intellectual leader of the conservative movement which is the spearhead of that consensus.

If I have in these pages, in 1956 and 1960, opposed the candidacies of Eisenhower and Nixon, it was not out of insistence upon conservative purity, but rather because nothing in their campaigns showed a determination to reverse the general trend of American politics. That, Barry Goldwater has shown and continues to show. So long as he does so, he deserves the wholehearted and energetic support of conservatives no matter how much they may disagree with his pronouncements on this or that peripheral issue or his proposals for the practical implementation of basic principles.

Vigilance is the price of liberty, and it is right that conservatives assess the direction of Goldwater's thought; but they should not mistake his necessary role and demand of him a role which is not his. Let us leave to Walter Lippmann and James Reston the thesis (patently directed towards alienating the right wing from Goldwater) that the statement of basic principles in terms understandable to a broad electorate constitutes a desertion of conservatism.

So long as Senator Goldwater and his advisers, in their effort to create a consensus, do not deviate from the broad principles for which he has always stood, so long as he continues to stand for freedom of the person, limitation of government, and effective resistance to the Communist drive for world conquest, American conservatives will give to his candidacy their unflinching support and untiring effort—support and effort without which he cannot conceivably be elected.

The Goldwater Campaign After the Assassination

(National Review, December 17, 1963)

One would think that after the brutal assassination of President Kennedy, responsible men would have recoiled in horror from capitalizing upon it for ideological ends. Yet, hardly had John F. Kennedy been officially pronounced dead than the Liberal Establishment broke forth in a nationwide television and radio orgy of lynch incitement against the American Right. And when, after a few uninhibited hours of hate-mongering, it became clear that if any ideology motivated the murderer, it was not right-wing but left-wing in inspiration, they were muted but an hour or so, before they regrouped their forces and returned to the charge.

There lay ready in the dark recesses of the Liberal psyche the justification that has been pounded over the air waves and in the press ever since. Syllogistically expanded, it reads:

Major premise: The assassin was an extremist (left-wing inspired).

Minor (enthymematic) premise: The only galvanic extremists are right-wing.

Conclusion: The Right is responsible for the assassination of Kennedy.

No conservative would maintain that because the assassin was an unbalanced man under the influence of left-wing ideology that the American Liberal Left is responsible for the assassination. Even if it should turn out in the course of investigation that this was not the deed simply of an unbalanced individual but the action of the apparatus of the Communist underworld —Soviet, Chinese or Castroite—no conservative would hold the Liberal Left responsible. But so far as I know, not a single Liberal voice was raised to protest against the *auto-da-fé* of the entire Right.

Even the charitable assumption that this outpouring of vituperation was an unmotivated emotional tropism proved untenable. For the second wave of the barrage, which followed fast on the first, revealed with ugly clarity the Liberal motivation (unconscious, semi-conscious, or conscious). Rising to a roar, the bombardment zeroed in on the true target—Goldwater: "Now is the time for 'moderation'" . . . "Goldwater is through" . . . "Goldwater should withdraw."

Why? Why, because a left-wing fanatic has assassinated a Liberal President, is the issue between Liberalism and conservatism any less or any more acute? Is there any reason why Goldwater's principles of limited government, personal freedom, and firm resistance to Communism have a different significance than they had a few weeks ago, or why the American people should now be deprived of normal political debate and of the right to vote upon the issues, why they should be given again another of the meaningless choices of the past thirty years?

It is understandable—if somewhat disgusting—that the Liberal power machine trades on the image of its fallen leader to try to destroy Goldwater. It is also understandable—and to their credit as sentient human beings—that some conservatives have been shaken in their will to victory by the emotional barrage to which they have been subjected. But the artificial storm the Liberals have stirred up will pass away because it is a construction blatantly contradictory to reality; and while the American people can be bemused and manipulated for a time, their solid sense of reality will prevail before long. The only way the Liberals can achieve their aim would be if committed conservatives should falter before the onslaught.

I am too altitudinous, too concerned with principle, neglectful of hard political realities? Let us consider those hard political realities. What have been the elements of Goldwater's strength for the nomination and the election, and what are they now?

1) He is the only candidate with a powerful independent following, for himself and his principles—a following more devoted than any since that of Franklin Roosevelt. Even if temporarily somewhat shocked and bewildered, that following remains firm in its belief in his principles and his leadership.

2) He is beyond doubt or question the personal choice of the great majority of Republican professionals, politicians, workers. Where, after all, are the defections from Goldwater?

3) His appeal to the American people as a whole is the singular appeal of a man as distinct from a field of Madison Avenue constructs and second-raters.

4) One thing alone has changed. Where Goldwater running against President Kennedy would have been certain of the electoral vote of the South, President Johnson can challenge him for it. But Johnson faces an insoluble dilemma. He cannot at one and the same time satisfy both the South and the Northern Liberal and Negro leaders. The issues go too deep. If he satisfies the South, the Liberal and Negro leaders could sit on their hands and so create the margin of difference enabling Goldwater to carry such previously doubtful states as Pennsylvania, Michigan, California, or even such a previously certain Democratic state as Massachusetts. If he satisfies the Liberal and Negro ideologues, then Goldwater will be as strong in the South as ever. Either eventuality can provide the electoral votes which, taken together with his solid strength in the Midwest and the West, would give him an electoral majority.

Against Johnson, as against Kennedy, Goldwater remains the best hope of the Republican Party for victory in 1964, as he is the champion of the American tradition against three decades of collectivist Liberalism and retreat before Communism.

When the Chips Are Down

(National Review, April 21, 1964)

To read the judicious takers of the American pulse who pontificate upon the progress of the Republican pre-convention campaign, the last thing you would think is that the Republican nomination goes to the candidate who gets the votes of 655 delegates. As a matter of fact, this is the first campaign I can remember in which the dopesters and the pollsters and the commentators have failed to give us projection after projection of the estimated delegate strength of the candidates.

Instead the press and the airwaves are saturated with general discussions of the state of mind of the mass electorate (which by and large has little influence on the selection of 90 per cent of the delegates), with abstruse speculation on the duty and necessity of "moderation" in American politics, with sad head-shaking on the "lack of interest" of the man in the street. This—and interminable analyses of Goldwater's weaknesses— drummed insistence that Goldwater is losing strength here, losing strength everywhere. If Goldwater had indeed been losing strength, and at the rate we are told, he would some time ago have joined the walking dead along with Rockefeller.

Actually, any detailed state-by-state analysis of delegate strength shows Goldwater not only the leading candidate, but overwhelmingly the leading candidate. I am not saying the nomination is in the bag. The outcome depends upon the energies exerted between now and July. But I am saying that he is ahead and that with proper effort the odds are with him. Even without California, and without the probable pro-Goldwater favorite-son slates from Wisconsin and Colorado, with an absolute minimum estimate of Goldwater inroads in states like New York, New Jersey, and Michigan, it is difficult, no matter how cautious one's outlook, to arrive at a total of less than 500 presently held Goldwater delegates.

Should Goldwater carry California, its 86 votes would bring him so close to the 655 majority that his reserves, in friendly favorite-son states and among Goldwater sympathizers in other uncommitted delegations, would almost certainly put him over on the first ballot. A victory in California would seem at this writing to be tantamount to victory at the convention. If California should be lost, the outlook would be much less favorable; but Goldwater would be far from defeated. A candidate with 500 votes, and up to another hundred leaning towards him, remains the most likely choice of the convention, particularly when he faces a motley field of rivals, no one of whom has been able to assemble a substantial total of delegates or to seize the imagination of Republican activists.

Both of these, Goldwater has done. His delegate strength I have discussed. And, despite many errors and weaknesses in the earlier stage of the campaign and despite all the prophets of doom, there has been no tangible undermining of his position of Republican leadership. A Gallup poll of Republican County Chairmen the country over, taken *after* the New Hampshire primary, gives Goldwater 878 votes; Nixon, 383; and Lodge, Scranton, Rockefeller 244, 164, 117 respectively.

It is indeed a motley crew; Nixon, the two-time loser, uncertain whether he is a conservative or a Liberal, a New Yorker or a Californian; Lodge, saddled with the Democratic Administration's mess in Vietnam and with every active Republican's knowledge that by his acts of omission and commission he did more than anyone else in the party to defeat the 1960 ticket; Scranton, with a grand total of four years of political experience, an apparent lack of conviction on any political issue, and a personality pallid to the fading point; Rockefeller, his New York delegation crumbling behind him, master neither of his passions nor of his legislature, of whose political fortunes, in charity, the less said the better.

"You can't beat someone with no one." The very freneticism with which the Liberals are looking for "a warm body whose name is not Barry Goldwater" (as Stanton Evans put it) shows the trouble they are in. It is understandable why they are worried, why they are using every device to spread an aura of failure around Goldwater. With the immense emotional pressure the organs of mass communication exert, it is also understandable why some conservatives fail to see the wood for the trees and are affected by setbacks which are inevitable in any sustained campaign. The experience of thirty years of Liberal dominance has created an inordinate fear of Liberal power plays. The political realities of 1964 belie this fear.

The Goldwater movement today is a new political phenomenon, one the Liberals have never faced before. This is not 1944 or 1952. There is no Willkie or Eisenhower behind whom they are organized to blitz to victory. In successive tries they have totally failed to build up any serious support for Romney or Scranton. Now in desperation they are falling back on tactics of confusion. There can be no other explanation of the immense public relations build-up of Lodge, a candidate who has no more chance of being actually nominated than Harold Stassen. The effort is obviously to blackmail the delegates to the Republican National Convention into a stop-Goldwater movement by a synthetic Lodge boom; to throw the convention into chaos; and, in the confusion, to ram down the convention's throat a "compromise candidate" or a dark horse—anybody but Goldwater.

It is a desperate maneuver, but it is not the solid well-planned operation of 1944 or 1952. The *solid* convention strength remains with Goldwater. As things stand now, it is the forces of the Liberal cabal, not of Goldwater, that are in disarray.

Goldwater: The Home Stretch

(National Review, June 2, 1964)

Oregon is behind us; and Rockefeller, rising from the dead, has captured 33 per cent of its vote. Like New Hampshire, it was a famous victory. Oregon gave him 18 delegates, as

New Hampshire gave Lodge 14, with just about the same proportion of the popular vote. The victories pile up: The New York *Times* found Lodge impressive with one-tenth of the Texas vote; Mrs. Smith was the Heroine of Illinois with one-quarter of the vote, and Stassen the hero of Indiana with the same fraction. (Wallace, of course, did very, very badly indeed in Indiana with only 30 per cent of the Democratic vote.) Goldwater completely flopped with one-half of Nebraska and two-thirds to three-quarters of Indiana, Illinois and Texas.

It all depends on how you look at it; it all depends on how sophisticated you are. Two-thirds to three-quarters of the votes of states with 32 to 58 delegates is a defeat; one-third of the vote of states with fourteen or eighteen delegates is a massive victory. When you have to prove that Goldwater—no matter how many delegates he has—can't win the votes of the people, couldn't possibly defeat Johnson, you have to be very sophisticated indeed.

Now that the press and television have waked up to the fact that Goldwater already holds close to a majority of the Republican delegates, we no longer hear, as we did last fall and after New Hampshire, that he hasn't a chance of the nomination. Now, all the enlighteners of the American public— who will vote Democratic in November but who are passionately distressed about the fate of the Republican Party in June— are zeroing in on their new target: maybe Goldwater can get a majority of the delegates, but look, he can't impress the voters, so how can he beat Johnson?

If you put Illinois and Texas and Indiana against New Hampshire and Oregon, the whole argument collapses. The cold, hard facts are that not only has Goldwater something like 575 probable votes on the first ballot, without California, and 75 or more in reserve among delegates initially pledged to favorite sons. *He has also been the outstanding votegetter in every preferential primary he has entered in a major state.* Further, he has achieved this against opponents whose only hope has been a primary strategy, and in spite of the concentration of his own basic strategy not upon primaries, but upon securing delegates.

Against this "delegate strategy" the stop-Goldwater coalition is trying to force a double play. California is their last hope— and not only to prevent Goldwater's winning its 86 delegates and clinching a majority on the first ballot. If the developing gang-up of all his rivals, backed by the unlimited financial resources of the House of Rockefeller, focused on an end-of-the-campaign saturation blitz, should succeed in denying him California, they hope to gain much more than that. Building on the distortion of previous primary results which I have been discussing, they hope conclusively to establish the myth that Goldwater cannot win votes, and so to tear away from him already committed delegates.

Their strategy is a mirror trick. It can only succeed on two conditions. First, they have to win California. Second, and much more important, they have to make their interpretation of the previous primaries stick. Specifically, they have to give such life to this myth that it affects delegates already leaning to Goldwater. Unless they can do that, the entire strategy collapses. And to do that depends upon putting over such absurdities as that a vote of 33 per cent for Rockefeller is of political significance in a state that sends to the Senate Wayne Morse (ADA, 100 per cent; AFL-CIO, 100 per cent; ACA, 4 per cent) and Maurine Neuberger (ADA, 100 per cent; AFL-CIO, 100 per cent; ACA, 0 per cent). This, against the factual truth that Goldwater holds an absolute majority over all—Lodge, Nixon, Rockefeller and Scranton together—when the total primary vote to date is added up.

Nor is this the whole story of Goldwater's vote-getting potential. In the primaries it is Goldwater against the field. When it comes to the November election, he will be pitted against a single man, Lyndon Johnson, and the results of that election will have no relation to the sentiments expressed in the honeymoon polls of the past few months. It will depend upon the ability of the Republican candidate to expose the confusions and the contradictions of the Johnson Administration: the effort to pose both as the symbol of prosperity and as the savior of the country from abject poverty; the double-faced stance of wooing the South and wooing the Negro revolution, with its effective encouragement of both sides to violence; the utter confusion of an Administration which tries to conceal its lack of a foreign policy by proudly proclaiming that it has 120 different foreign policies.

It is a record that can be torn to shreds by the Republican candidate—if, and only if, he stands on a firm platform of opposition to the Administration's demagogy, domestic and foreign; if, and only if, he has the fighting spirit to drive home his position and expose the irresponsibility of the Johnson Administration. But, of all the Republicans who are seeking the nomination, Barry Goldwater alone has these qualifications.

His support in the Republican Party is based on this. It is because they understand this that the delegates to San Francisco will see through the distortions of his opponents, shatter their strategy, and nominate him for the Presidency of the United States.

What Consensus?

(National Review, October 20, 1964)

For years it has been an axiom not only in all "sophisticated" circles but wherever the Establishment could use the mass-communications network to hatch its eggs that the contemporary conservative movement and conservative ideas are "outside the American consensus." And for years it was possible to maintain this myth without doing too much violence to the surface facts. Whatever the underlying attitude of the American people in actuality remained, there was nowhere in the intellectual world, and only peripherally or occasionally in the political world, open or striking evidence to dispute the thesis of American consensus upon the moral beauty and existential rightness of the world that Franklin Roosevelt made.

The development, in the last five or ten years, of a conscious and easily observable conservative movement, and the articulation of its attitudes on a high intellectual level, should have shattered the myth. Still, generally, it was sustained by ignoring the reality of a massive and solidly based opposition to the putative consensus. Or sometimes it was glanced at, only to be brushed aside as a fringe phenomenon, primarily expressing the reactions of persons in one way or another "psychologically disturbed."

Given this state of affairs intellectually and politically, it may have been possible until very recently to retain a semblance of intellectual honesty and still to speak of an American consensus excluding the conservative viewpoint. The underlying attitudes, beliefs and prejudices of a very large section of the American people could be disregarded because they were not articulated at the levels which force attention. The conservative movement could be, if one tried hard enough, conceived as a sport without roots in the body politic, without connections to the held beliefs of significant numbers of American citizens.

In the past couple of years, however, the momentum of the conservative movement has taken on such startling proportions that there no longer remains intellectually honest ground for the contention of a Liberal consensus. Nevertheless reality has failed to impinge. The same self-satisfied insistence that the only serious issues in this country are the issues at stake between different wings of Liberalism, that conservatism represents a perversity totally outside the real life of American society, has continued to prevail in Establishment thought and writing.

Even the nomination of Barry Goldwater by one of the two major American political parties has failed to shatter the myth of consensus. Indeed, a hypnotized acceptance of that myth may have had something to do with the comparative ineffectiveness of the opposition to Goldwater (frenzied though it was) in the campaign for the nomination. The powers-that-be simply could not believe that he and the forces he represents were to be taken seriously. They were blinded by their own rhetoric and rallied too late to present any stronger resistance than the farcical performance they put on at San Francisco.

In the aftermath of San Francisco, however, the Establishment has turned that liability into an asset and worked with all its energy to make it the decisive weapon of the campaign. Immensely fortified by the Liberal Republican rhetoric of the pre-nomination weeks, the Johnson campaign is essentially based on a single theme—a theme which is the translation into popular terms of the concept that conservatism is outside the national consensus. This is the meaning of the charge echoed on every level that Goldwater and the movement behind him represents "extremism." It must be admitted that this campaign is having its effects, particularly in the realm of foreign policy. Indeed, the results of the election, both as to victory and the margin of victory, will largely depend upon how great those effects are.

For thirty years the American people have heard the same Liberal rhetoric from both political parties; their deepest beliefs have never gone along with that rhetoric, but on the surface they have accepted it since nothing else has been offered them. The presentation on a mass scale of an articulated conservative position has precipitated a conflict approaching the traumatic, between deeply held beliefs and a confused sense of shame before the ridicule of the "sophisticated" organs of opinion. This conflict is, I believe, the cause of the widespread national phenomenon of a massive undecided vote. My soundings in half a dozen states indicate what is confirmed by such columnists as Evans and Novak (no friends of Goldwater), that 40 per cent to 50 per cent of the electorate is, at this late date in the campaign, undecided. This is utterly unprecedented. It is, despite all the trumpeting of a Johnson landslide, the most significant aspect of the campaign.

This undecided vote will determine the outcome of the election. Which way it swings will be decided by the answer to a single question: Will the American people vote their inner-

most convictions, or will they still be sufficiently in the thrall
of the decades of Liberal monopoly of all the organs of articulation to feel to do so is somehow wrong, "extremist," un-
American—that is, outside the American consensus?

Whatever the outcome, however, one thing is certain: conservative principles have been put forward on the highest
political level and supported by a substantial section of the
American people. The myth of an over-all American Liberal
consensus, however useful it may have been to Liberalism in
this campaign, will have been once and for all destroyed by
the millions who vote for Barry Goldwater.

What Next for Conservatism?

(National Review, December 1, 1964)

What did the election prove and did it not prove?

First, *what it proved:*

1) The mass-communications network, solidly in Liberal
hands, is even more formidable an opponent than conservatives
had thought.

2) Making all allowances for the effects of the mass-communications network, the progress of the campaign showed
that conservatives have not yet learned how to translate the
principles for which they stand into concrete issues that can
seize the imagination of decisive sections of the voters. Examples in point: the failure to dramatize the Communist issue
around the threat of the Soviet base in Cuba; the inability to
drive home the plain truth that President Johnson's course
towards unilateral disarmament, not Goldwater's concern about
American strength, is the real danger to little girls eating ice-
cream cones; the abstract presentation of the issue of freedom
at home, an issue that could have been made concrete and
compelling in the actual lives of tens of millions of voters by
systematic and vividly factual illustration.

3) It became apparent that the Liberal attack on conserva-

tism as a radical tearing down of established institutions (perhaps—along with the "trigger happy" canard—the most powerful
weapon of the Liberal campaign) has to be confuted. There
is no question but that conservatism is arrayed against the
basic development since FDR; but it has to be made clear
that conservatives by their very nature proceed in all changes
with caution. Further, it is essential to work out and present
a much fuller and more confident specific program for return
to constitutional government than was presented in the campaign.

What the election did not prove is what the whole Liberal
Establishment is attempting to maintain—that November 3
signified a repudiation of conservatism by the American people.
The first and most obvious argument against this conclusion
is the vote of 26 million people for a position imperfectly presented by its proponents and pilloried in the most extreme
terms by its opponents. Despite the caricature of Goldwater's
position, despite the fact that everything was done to make
it appear that the conservative course is extremist, radical,
nihilist, anarchic—still two-fifths of the voters saw through the
distortions and solidly voted for the unthinkable proposition
that there is an alternative to Liberal domination.

Further, although the defection of the Liberal Republican
leaders—essentially, their support of Johnson—was an important
factor in generating the Liberal storm of distortion, their absence
from the Republican campaign did not, apart from one or
two states like New York and Michigan where the knifing
was rampant and open, appreciably diminish the available active
workers for Goldwater. Never have so many people contributed
so much money; never have the Republicans succeeded in carrying out so thorough a canvassing of the voters.

A change has been in the making in the mechanics of American politics for a number of years. It first affected the Democratic Party, as the old-style precinct workers were more and
more replaced by motivated workers from the unions and
from Liberal circles. This year the same process has come
to a head in the Republican Party, with the emergence of

a powerful force of committed conservatives as the decisive sector of Republican campaign workers. This is a strategic fact of the greatest importance. On the one hand it means that American conservatism has moved into the actual political arena, creating an experienced political corps of a kind it has never had before. On the other hand it means (whatever gymnastics take place in ensuing months on the National Committee level) that the Republican Party has become a party which will in practice, outside of a few constituencies, function as a conservative party or will not function at all. The GOP will either go forward as the conservative party or it will disappear, and conservatism will be forced to create another political vehicle.

Most important, nothing that occurred demonstrated anything wrong or weak—morally or philosophically or logically— in the conservative position. Nor, when we consider that the campaign represented but a few months of the first opportunity on a broad national scale to confute thirty years of Liberal indoctrination, can the gaining of two-fifths of the vote be considered a "practical disaster" of "momentous consequence."

The one serious danger to our country and our cause would be any tendency to weaken or dilute the conservative position because of Goldwater's defeat. Conservatives stand today nearer to victory than they ever have since Franklin Roosevelt. A shift in the vote of 12 per cent of the electorate is the goal of the next four years.

To achieve it, three things are needed, and they are all realistically within the capability of a movement that has risen in the past few years from an insignificant minority to its present position. The process of conservative re-education of the American people that culminated in the election campaign has to be intensified. Conservative principle has to be spelled out and made concrete across the whole gamut of issues affecting Americans. Above all—and vital to the achievement of these two tasks as well as to the preservation of the positions of power won in the past year—conservatives have to develop forms of organization both within the Republican Party and in the broad national life, forms that can consolidate and advance the energies released by the 1964 campaign for the achievement of victory in 1966 and 1968.

THE JOHNSON YEARS

President Johnson and the Tides of Ideology

(National Review, January 14, 1964)

We live, unfortunately for us, in an Age of Ideology. The temptation to ignore this is very great; we would all prefer to be living in an Age of Civility. But understandable though it be to yield to this temptation, doing so only condemns the analyst to skim the surface of reality and fail utterly to penetrate its meaning.

The personal style of a political leader, for example, might have been of decisive importance in 18th-century France before the Revolution, or 19th-century England before World War I, or in the early years of the American Republic before the Civil War; but to talk today of personal political style as a decisive factor in political events is to talk nonsense. When a man arises among us who can seriously affect our present trends by his personal force, it will not be because of his "style," but because of his devotion to the principles upon which our civilization is founded, and because of the energy and ability he shows in fighting the ideologies and the ideologists. Men lacking these stigmata are certain—however much their style may differ one from another—to be intellectually the prisoners, practically the administrators, of the prevailing ideologies.

Thus, most of the speculation about what kind of a president Lyndon Johnson is going to be is beside the point. There are certain fairly fixed limits within which a President from the Democratic Party must move if he wants to be renominated and re-elected. For, although the Democratic Party is an American institution and is therefore structurally not an ideological organization, its national leadership since the days of Franklin Roosevelt has been and remains inherently tied to the service of the Liberal ideology.

However much Johnson may differ from Kennedy in personal style, two things are certain. Neither has been distinguished for his principled hostility to Liberal ideology, and neither has shown a haughty disdain for the practical problems of renomination and re-election. It was predictable on November 22 that Lyndon Johnson would continue, with greater or less speed, the Liberal revolution and the Liberal attack upon the Constitution. The gruesome event that made him President can no more change the course of American politics than would the election of a Republican of the Rockefeller stripe.

The direction of his course, I repeat, was predictable on November 22, but it might have been possible to question then how rapid that course would be. The weeks that have passed since, however, would seem to show that it is likely to be very rapid (and I make this prediction writing some time before the State of the Union message, with full knowledge that what I write will be read after that message is delivered). Indeed there is evidence that his course may be more rapid than that of John F. Kennedy.

Nor, perhaps, is this to be wondered at in a man who began his national political career in 1937 as a servitor of the New Deal and a congressional henchman of FDR and has since shown no evidence of any observable ideas deviating from the Liberal ideology. As the Fair Deal followed the New Deal, and the New Frontier followed the Fair Deal, Mr. Johnson well and faithfully served each in turn.

There is, indeed, reason to believe that on the domestic front the new Administration may strike out in a spirit more Rooseveltian than Kennedyian. That the rhetoric of FDR's "one-third of a nation ill-clothed, ill-housed and ill-fed" runs in his head, and in a peculiarly grandiose manner, was demonstrated in Mr. Johnson's speech to the UN, where he extended the concept to the whole world, with promises of a welfare program for "that one-third of mankind that is still beset by hunger and poverty and disease."

Domestically, two "task forces" are at work drafting "a declaration of war against poverty," to be implemented by a "poverty package," which would not only pick up Kennedy's Medicare and domestic Peace Corps but add a dozen other projects ranging from greatly expanded foodstamp and "depressed-area" (read "pork-barrel") programs through various forms of "children's aid" to federal educational and "re-training" activities of all kinds. Just how all this (which, by a modest estimate, could cost a minimum of $5 billion) goes with the much-touted economy drive is anyone's guess—but then, without any additional expenditures, the President has admitted that the new budget will reach 102 or 103 billion dollars anyway. Lyndon Johnson's ranch may be in Texas but his heart belongs to the people he telephoned in his first hours as President: men like David Dubinsky of the ILGWU and James Farmer of CORE.

On foreign and military policy, the weeks since President Johnson's assumption of office give indications even more explicit—alarming indications that the Kennedy policy of appeasement, retreat, and drift towards unilateral disarmament [see "Principles and Heresies," NR, 8/13/63] will continue, and very possibly at an accelerated pace. In his address to the Joint Session of Congress on November 27, as in his address to the United Nations on December 17, he projected, in terms even more unrealistic than those of his predecessor, a view of the world that totally ignores the drive of the Communist enemy to world conquest. On the basis of that conspectus, he confirmed a policy that rejects victory over the enemy as a national goal, filling the void with bombastic and empty talk of "peace" when there is no peace. He has fulsomely proclaimed, as the sustaining elements of this policy, his reliance on the three hollow pillars of the shoddy construction which Liberal ideology has substituted for foreign policy: the United Nations, the world-wide welfarist foreign-aid program, and the Alliance for Progress.

Behind this façade of dependence upon words and upon massive "humanitarian" expenditure, where a realistic answer to a bitter threat is imperative, President Johnson day by day shows his intention of continuing Kennedy's disastrous military policy. The Rostow-Wiesner-McNamara-Whiz Kid program of reliance on a Minuteman-Polaris Maginot Line—combined with a steady liquidation of existing offensive arms and the direction of research and development away from future offensive capabilities is decidedly still in the ascendant. One of Johnson's first acts was to give the death blow to Dyna-Soar; the MOL (Manned Orbital Laboratory), which he put forward as a sop to the Armed Forces, involves much too little energy and expenditure for aerospace defense, while many times its cost continues to be spent on non-military space projects. The old team is still at work; the old ideas prevail.

Lyndon Johnson's "style," Heaven knows, differs radically from Kennedy's; but abroad, as at home, he stands for the same bankrupt ideology. The policies Kennedy represented, which so urgently demanded the victory of the principles of Barry Goldwater, Johnson too represents.

Conservative Strategy Now

(National Review, December 29, 1964)

I am in thorough agreement with those who maintain that it is a prime conservative task now to develop the conservative program in depth and over the entire range of issues that affect the American people. There are dangers, however, lurking in this unexceptionable proposition—and some of them are already becoming evident.

For the health of the conservative movement, a great deal depends upon how this proposition is interpreted and implemented. As long as the endeavor is inspired by the desire to make basic conservative doctrine more understandable in terms of the actual problems of Americans today and to concentrate on those issues which are most clearly demonstrable and urgent to the voter, nothing but good can come of it. But if "closing the gap between conservative doctrine and the voter" becomes another sleazy "me too" device to adjust conservative doctrine to Liberal practice, the idea—excellent in itself—could have the effect of destroying the responsible conservative movement and handing over to irresponsible and ignorantist demagogy the leadership of the opposition to Liberalism.

So far as political action is concerned, there are two essential foundations of any conservative program worthy of the name: in our domestic affairs, the vindication of limited constitutional government for the restoration and preservation of the full liberty of the individual citizen; and, in our relations with the world around us, determined resistance to the assault of international Communism. Both of these positions can be developed in terms much more compelling and convincing than have yet been worked out; but neither can be compromised.

In the first place, to compromise them would be morally wrong; it would mean the surrender of principles that are the very reason for the existence of the conservative movement. Further, it would not even achieve its opportunist aim; it would mean giving up leadership over the 26 million who voted for Goldwater and the millions more whose disquietude with Liberalism needs only translation into understandable terms to turn that 26 million into a majority.

The issue boils down to a simple alternative: are we going to develop and strengthen the conservative position by spelling out its meaning in clear practical terms, or is the word "practical" going to be made an excuse for diluting conservative principle? The dramatic success of Ronald Reagan's broadcast is both evidence that it is possible to make conservative principle understandable and an example of a way of doing it. Mr. Reagan did not soften his indictment of the Liberal way of life. He did not attempt to accommodate himself to the prevailing shibboleths concerning what is true and good and beautiful, even on the vexed issue of social security. Rather, if anything, he toughened the conservative position, but he toughened it with a concrete analysis and a living presentation of the true realities that underlie the Liberal surface.

His is, of course, not the only mode of approach that is necessary. Principle, program and presentation are politically mutually interdependent. It is essential to continue to expound the fundamental principles of conservatism. They are the ground on which conservative action is based, and without them as a ground the force of the conservative challenge is dissipated. And, as a connecting link between fundamental principle and the Reagan-type of mass appeal, a third activity is necessary: a serious and painstaking development of articulated and viable programs across the entire spectrum of issues that confront the country. Without such programs the principles remain abstract, dry, rather empty; without them the liveliest mass appeal will become either opportunist or demagogic—or both.

All three modes are equally vital to the victory of conservatism. To downgrade one or another of them as secondary or unnecessary is a harmful error too frequently committed, particularly when one or another mode has been neglected. It is one thing to insist on remedying such neglect, but it is self-defeating to try to overcome one form of neglect by encouraging another.

The statement of sharp conservative principle which obviously demands deep-going change in the existing situation can sound like irresponsible radicalism if it is not backed up by a sober and conservatively restrained program of gradual, phased transformation. It was this lack of proposals for programmatic implementation of basic principles that made it possible to convince large segments of the voters in the recent election that Goldwater's victory would mean radical and chaotic disorganization of their lives.

There is something in politics analogous to the admonition against gaining the whole world at the cost of one's own soul.

There is need for the kind of program and presentation which will make it clear that conservative opposition to the unlimited state would not mean the cutting off of every social security check on January 21, or that the conservative policy of resistance to Communism would not mean the instigation of nuclear war. But, on the other hand, conservatives cannot, in the interest of mass appeal, turn their backs on the harsh realities of the contemporary world and base their programs on any version of coexistence. Nor can they accommodate themselves to the nostrums of Keynesian economics and its concomitant pandering to mass greed.

The rethinking and reformulation of the conservative program must be based not upon dilution but upon strengthening of fundamental conservative doctrine.

Vietnam—The Republican Performance

(National Review, April 5, 1966)

Granted that our engagement with Communism in Vietnam poses many complex problems of policy. Granted also that President Johnson's position (good though it is when contrasted with the position of such Democrats as Senator Kennedy and Senator Fulbright) leaves much to be desired in terms of consistency, energy, and clarity of purpose. Nevertheless we are engaged under his leadership in a serious confrontation with Communism—a juncture of events which would seem to demand of the opposition party the most responsible exercise of its indispensable function as the balance wheel in a free representative polity.

General support of the President against the forces of appeasement within his own party would in no way tie the Republican Party to the President's coattails, since there is room for the most searching criticism of the weaknesses of his policy and the presentation of a program that would by its energy and realism measure up to the immensity of the Communist challenge now centering in Vietnam. One would the more expect this of a party whose 1964 Presidential candidate campaigned on the basis of just such an understanding, particularly when a considerable proportion of his then so denigrated proposals have become the active policy of the Administration.

Instead, the chief spokesmen of the congressional leadership of the Republican Party have indulged in a display of petty partisanship, apparently devoid of principle and certainly irresponsible in effect, the active content of which is just about limited to gloating over the dissensions on Vietnam in the Democratic Party. True, they have expressed *pro forma* support for the war, but the effective image they have presented to the country is that of side-line spectators of the discomfiture of the party in power.

It would be sufficient cause for concern were these manifestations simply the offhand product of the exuberance of political infighting; but the dereliction of responsibility, unfortunately, goes deeper. The line that has been taken seems to be based upon a deliberate decision. The motivation for such a decision is transparent—to achieve political advantage on a non-principled level by picking up votes from all those discontented with the Administration's Vietnam policy. The political "cleverness" consists of couching the attack in a way that they hope will gain support both from those whose discontent arises out of dissatisfaction with the indecision and erratic course of the Johnson policies and from those whose discontent arises from a totally different source, fundamental opposition to the war, based either on confusion or on outright hunger for appeasement.

Even for narrow immediate political gain, such straddling will not work, as it never has worked when a nation stood at a critical point in its affairs. From a longer perspective, rejection of the demands of statesmanlike responsibility can ring the death-knell of a political party.

What has happened to the Republican Party that a decisive section of its leadership can take such a course? These men are at least as patriotic as their Democratic colleagues; they

have shown over recent decades a much greater understanding
of the dangers of Communism. What makes possible the bankruptcy of leadership we are witnessing?

The answer can be found, I think, in the condition of the
Republican Party as it emerged from the election of 1964.
The defeat of Goldwater accentuated the pre-existing divisions
within the Party and traumatized all sorts of people who should
have known better, throwing them into a state of shock in
which they uncritically accepted the sedulously cultivated
analysis put forward by the Liberal Establishment. The loss
of a battle was construed as final proof that the Republican
Party could never win under conservative leadership. But the
Liberal wing of the Party had so thoroughly disgraced itself
by its sabotage of the campaign that it was effectively disquali-
fied for leadership in the eyes of the majority of active Republicans. There remained the center, untainted by the advocacy
of explicit conservative principles and yet proven in its loyalty
to the Party by its dogged support of the Goldwater campaign.

Inevitably, under these circumstances, leadership passed to
the center, a transfer of power symbolized by the election
of Ray Bliss as national chairman. Some conservatives accepted
this as a happy eventuality, resigning themselves to the idea
that the best that could be expected for the next few years
would be a continuation of the alliance of conservatives with
the center, which had backed Goldwater, but with roles reversed
and the center now in the leading position. Affected by the
climate created by the communications media, they felt that
this was the only realistic political course. Abstractly, this
reaction made reasonable tactical sense, but in actuality the
concept has foundered on the hard fact that leaders must
have some idea of what they stand for and where they are going.

This, the present leadership of the Republican Party lacks.
In the image of Ray Bliss, it seems concerned only with trying
to find ways of winning votes, irrespective of principle. Its
bankruptcy in the Vietnam crisis brings to dramatic focus the
inherent weakness of its position. In the light of this perform-

ance, it would seem that the time has come for conservatives to reassert their leadership of the Republican Party. The great bulk of the Party, including most of those who today manage its destinies, will respond if they are given clear, responsible leadership. But this the center has shown it cannot give. It is up to the conservatives.

The Importance of Reagan

(National Review, December 27, 1966)

The 1966 elections are over. The commentators have commented. The road is open to '68. What are the portents and prospects for conservativism?

One thing is clear: November was a victory for the Republican Party. But what kind of a Republican Party? Here the auguries are obscure. By and large, Liberal commentators drew one set of conclusions, conservative commentators another. Objectively, it was probably a dead heat: On the conservative side, the smashing Reagan success and the election of a number of other gubernatorial and senatorial candidates, put together with the strong conservative complexion of the new Republican congressional delegation; on the Liberal side, victory (outside of California) in the dramatic races—Rockefeller, Romney, Percy, Brooke.

The conclusion that would seem to emerge most clearly has been almost totally obscured in a political generation so obsessed with image that it is oblivious of principle. Liberal Republicans and conservative Republicans both have done well; the Republican prospects for 1968 look a great deal brighter; but there is no indication whatever that those prospects would be dimmed if the candidate were a conservative or enhanced if the candidate were a Liberal. The issue is back where it ought to be, after two years of Republican breast-beating and flesh-pottery: not "who can possibly win?" but "what kind of man do we want to elect?"

Of course, this is the last thing the media discuss. All the talk is of Romney, Percy, Hatfield. Even the Buckley-shattered image of Lindsay is being paraded again. As the election returns are seriously studied, the myth of '64—that conservative Republicans cannot win—is bound to be dissipated. It is particularly important that those conservatives who have over the past year or so allowed themselves to succumb to that myth now have objective evidence to counter it—and to dispel a certain willingness that has been creeping in to settle for any candidate who could win for the Republican Party, no matter how little he would achieve for conservative principle.

I find it rather hard to understand this personal tendency in conservative circles to regard the Republican Party as somehow a good in itself. Of course conservatives want to preserve the two-party system, but the Republican Party is clearly not dying. The alternative to a continuing effort to build towards victory on the basis of conservative principle can only be to put into office an Administration which will differ from the Democratic Administration simply in that Republicans instead of Democrats will be expanding the coercive welfare state. (What is there about Albany these past years that is preferable to Washington?)

As far as foreign policy is concerned, indeed, the position taken before and during the recent campaign by many Republican "moderates" represented so opportunist an effort to gain votes by playing politics at the expense of national security that President Johnson's stand on Vietnam made him seem, to this degree, closer to conservative principle. It happened all over the country, with Liberal Republican candidates making insidious passes at the dove vote, but perhaps most repulsively in Illinois, where instead of recognizing Senator Douglas' magnificent anti-Communist record and taking the issue out of the campaign, the Republican candidate's ambiguous stand was calculated to capitalize on dove dissatisfaction with Douglas' support of Vietnam policy. This sort of pandering for votes is the hallmark of Liberal Republicanism. It is paralleled in

domestic matters by the calls that issue periodically from Rockefeller, Romney, Percy, Lindsay, and miscellaneous Liberal
Republican senators for a "positive" program of *Republican
big government.*

A Republican Party inspired by Liberal and opportunist policies is not worth an ounce of conservative support. But this
is the kind of Republican Party we will have in 1968 if conservatives accept Republican victory in the election as taking precedence over winning the Republican Party for a conservative
program and a conservative candidate. One can admire and
share the abhorrence of the American two-party system for
narrowly defined ideological positions without falling into the
opposite extreme of subordinating principle to meaningless
electoral victory. For American conservatives today there can
be no political substitute for the continuing effort to win a
conservative victory. Not only do their principles demand it,
but if responsible conservative leadership puts a Republican
mystique above conservative principle, it is in danger of handing
over a large section of the growing conservative electorate to
George Wallace, whose right-wing demagogy masks socialist
welfare practice.

What does this require in practical terms? A candidate who
can stir conservative enthusiasm and behind whom a campaign
for delegates to the Republican National Convention of 1968
can be launched. By the principled positions he has taken, and
by his proven ability as a campaigner, demonstrated both in
1964 and this year in California, Ronald Reagan, should he
prove the governor he promises to be, qualifies for this role.
California would seem to prove that against Johnson, Humphrey
or Kennedy, he would be as strong a candidate as the Republican Party can field. In any event, a solid body of conservative
delegates pledged to Reagan would assure that no Liberal
could be nominated, and that, if it became necessary to accept
a man of the center like Nixon or Rhodes, he would be strongly
influenced in the conservative direction.

Accent the Negative

(National Review, February 7, 1967)

We have heard a great deal in recent weeks from the cabal of Liberal Republicans about the responsibility of the Republican Party in the Congress to develop "a positive program," to stop being a "mere opposition." To judge by the first days of the new Congress, the Republican delegation would seem to be ignoring this gratuitous advice and beginning to re-forge a conservative alliance with like-minded Democrats, precisely to oppose the further extension of the Liberal program. In doing so they are remembering the long-standing tradition of the Anglo-American political system—that the most valuable service the opposition can perform for the country is to oppose.

This axiom of practical political wisdom, which is a bulwark of freedom and of a lively polity, is by its very nature anathema to the proponents of consensus and the homogenization of men. But quite apart from their inability to grasp the value of opposition as opposition, our Liberals are, on even more fundamental grounds, deeply committed to the concept of "the positive" in politics, by which they mean, Democratic Liberals and Republican Liberals alike, the unlimited extension of governmental power and governmental supervision of our lives. In their opposition to this concentration of power, which is the paramount political evil of the twentieth century, conservatives— how often have we heard it!—are branded as "negative," and negativism is portrayed as the worst of sins.

It is time this question was faced head on: can the political stance of conservatives be positive in the sense that word has taken on these days?

Liberalism finds in every social situation "problems" to be solved collectively by planned action, almost always government action. Conservatism rejects this "problem" approach to human affairs. It considers some of these situations natural manifestations of the human condition—not problems to be solved at all; others it recognizes as situations that can and should be improved, but only by time and the working of free human energies, individually or in voluntary association. Above all, it considers the outstanding social and political issue of our time to be the increasing provenance and power of government. Therefore, it regards further increase of that provenance and that power a greater evil than the specific evils against which the Liberals call government into action.

Under the circumstances and in the intellectual atmosphere created by regnant Liberalism, in which positive solutions to every conceivable problem are demanded, it is clear why this "negativity" is under constant attack. But if conservatives are to be true to the conservative vision, their program cannot but be essentially negative, insofar as government action to remedy social situations is concerned. They will propose the limitation of government to free the powers and the imagination of the citizenry to go about remedying these situations in their several ways as they see best.

This position can, of course, be made to sound callous, hard-hearted, uncaring. But to maintain that hardships, depriva-tions, social imbalances are not properly or effectively solved by government action is not to deny their existence. Rather it is to call upon the imaginative exercise of voluntary altruistic effort to invigorate a widespread sense of responsibility for social well-being and to guard against the moral degradation of citizens as direct clients of the state or as indirect petitioners for community largesse. Some idea of what could be done in this way has been projected by Richard C. Cornuelle, both descriptively in his book, *Reclaiming the American Dream*, and practically in the work of the Foundation for Voluntary Welfare.

Conservative action of this kind cannot be incorporated in a neat "positive" program for the political arena. Nor does the enormous constructive thrust of private industry, which we have come to take for granted, lend itself to neat political packaging. Yet the creative action of free citizens could and would be multiplied a thousandfold if, in a conservative milieu, men ceased to look to government for solutions and if the corollary shrinkage of government left in the hands of the citizens resources now taxed from them in tens of billions to finance government action.

Even when, however, the charge of callousness to human distress is countered, the more general charge of negativity remains. There is only one answer conservatives can give to this charge unless they wish to descend to unprincipled demagogy. That is, to insist and to demonstrate that a positive program for the preservation of freedom, together with the release and expansion of human energies, calls for a series of negative proposals directed towards the dismantling of smothering government activities. Such a program requires, if it is to be effectively presented, specific analyses of the actuality of government activities area by area; otherwise, no matter how fundamentally correct the conservative critique, it will give the impression of being merely destructive criticism.

Only in the areas in which government is the natural organ for action, such as national defense or the prevention of crime and of any form of forceful or fraudulent interference with the freedom of citizens, can conservative programs be intrinsically positive. Elsewhere it is not to government, but to the energy, the imagination, the civil conscience, the charity of free men that conservatism looks for the development of the good society. If eternal vigilance be the price of liberty, an eternal "No" to encroaching government is its watchword.

The Populism of George Wallace

(National Review, May 16, 1967)

George Wallace, like every American demagogue in our history, is a populist. Populism is the radical opposite of conservatism. Why, then, are some conservatives attracted to his candidacy? Why is he able to enter the national arena as a champion of the conservative opposition to prevailing Liberalism? These questions have to be answered and Wallace's claims to conservative support unmasked, if his candidacy is not to tear apart the American conservative movement and poison the moral source of its strength. The danger is twofold: the distraction of conservative energy from the difficult, but eminently possible, task of defeating Liberalism in the Republican Party, and the distortion of conservative principle by acquiescence in Wallace's simplistic demagogy.

A major outcome of the 1964 campaign is that conservatives, if they organize and work, hold at the least a veto over the choice of the Republican convention. Despite the '64 defeat, they have gained substantial control of large sections of the Republican organization. They may not in 1968 be strong enough to nominate the candidate they would most desire, but if they remain united, they can certainly so act that, in alliance with the professional politicians, they can present the country with a serious and greatly more conservative alternative to Johnson.

Powerful historical currents like Liberalism are not reversed overnight. The Liberals took many decades to achieve their hegemony; patience and hard work should be no more difficult for conservatives, whose view of society respects the complex interrelationships of human beings and repudiates utopian reliance upon instant change.

More surely fatal to American conservatism, however, than the impatient loss of solid political opportunities within the Republican Party would be the integral destruction of moral being that would flow from adherence to the Wallace candidacy. And this returns me to the questions with which I began this column. What is the appeal of Wallace to conservatives, and why is that appeal so dangerous for the future of American conservatism?

The root of the problem lies in the history of the contemporary conservative movement. That movement came into existence under circumstances of Liberal domination of the national scene. Although in its intellectual leadership and development it has been based on firm conservative principle, it has drawn its support to begin with, not primarily from widespread conscious conservative sources but from diverse groups, each of which was in opposition to Liberalism for limited and particular reasons.

Some, who were appalled by the appeasement of Soviet Communism and our retreat before its drive to power, were not deeply concerned by the glacier-like advance of domestic centralization and collectivism. Some, who felt deeply the domestic danger, did not understand, and failed to be alarmed by, the power of international Communism. Some were drawn into opposition to Liberalism by its steady encroachment on the liberties of individual citizens; others, by the paradoxically opposite effect of Liberal theories of government, the decay of law and order.

Diverse, often contradictory, positions of this sort abound in the constituency of the conservative movement. In the brief dozen to fifteen years of its existence in its contemporary form, however, it has performed a massive educational task in broadening the conspectus of those whom it has influenced and in forging a broad understanding based on principle. Still, the original strains exist in many quarters—instinctively, temperamentally, emotionally—and at crucial moments they come to the surface. When they do, those of us who attack certain positions as alien to the spirit of conservatism are inevitably criticized on the grounds that those whom we are attacking are also enemies of Liberalism. What such criticism ignores is that there are other dangers to conservatism and to the civilization conservatives are defending than the Liberal Establishment, and that to fight Liberalism without guarding against these dangers runs the risk of ending in a situation as bad as or worse than our present one.

So it is with the populism of George Wallace. Populism is one of the elements in the opposition to Liberalism, because the arrogant and naked élitism of the Liberals, isolated from the ethics and tradition of the people, is populism's polar opposite. But the polar opposite of a political perversion is not necessarily itself a good. Thus, while Liberalism stands for the imposition of utopian design upon the people because the Liberals know it is right, populism would substitute the tyranny of the majority over the individual, the pure will of "the people," untrammeled by considerations of freedom and virtue. It is in its own way as alien to the American conservative conception of constitutional republican government as is Liberalism.

This populism is the air that Wallace breathes. Every speech he makes, every interview he gives, is redolent of it. Of course, when he talks of Vietnam or of violence in the streets or of federal encroachment, he takes positions parallel to conservative positions. But when it is a question of socialist welfare measures or when he builds a welfare state in Alabama, he is as far from conservatism as any Liberal. His combination of nationalist and socialist appeals, couched in the rhetoric of incitement of the masses and contempt for the intellect in all its manifestations, is radically alien to conservatism.

THE CAMPAIGN OF 1968

Thinking Aloud about 1968

(National Review, June 13, 1967)

Like most conservatives with whom I have talked over the last year or so, I have been much perplexed by the problems of the 1968 Presidential election. Until recently, it was possible to say that it was still early, that the passage of time might clarify the situation; but it is now considerably less than a year to the first primaries and very little more than a year to the conventions—not so very long, as political time goes.

It seems to me that two factors are standing in the way

of clear conservative understanding. On the one hand, there is a failure to see that 1968 is not 1964. The nomination of a conservative candidate this time will not be the result of a mass campaign of the Goldwater type, but rather the outcome of a complex of pressures applied in a more conventional way through the inner processes of the Republican Party, coming to a climax in hard bargaining at the convention itself.

As much as one can predict at this stage, it would seem more than likely that no candidate will enter the convention with anything approaching a clear majority, that in fact the decisive power at the convention will be in the hands of uncommitted and "favorite son" delegations. The true issue of the convention will not be one of personalities; it will be whether the process of gaining conservative control of the Republican Party, dramatically inaugurated in 1964, will be consolidated, in however low a key, or whether the Liberals will regain the control they exercised from 1940 to 1964.

It is here that I think the second factor in conservative confusion comes into play: the failure to recognize the degree to which 1964 represented, despite the electoral defeat, a potential massive victory for conservatism through the rehabilitation of the Republican Party as an available institutional vehicle for conservatism. As M. Stanton Evans said recently (*National Review*, May 30, 1967): "November 1964 generated a natural but misleading sense of conservative despair. In the pale glow of that sulphurous Tuesday, all Barry Goldwater had said and done from 1960 forward was bathed in retrospective gloom. The trick of lighting causes us to forget that the Goldwater candidacy—the mere fact of his nomination— marked an enduring victory for conservatism."

The strategic point at which conservative energy can be applied to achieve the most lasting success is in so working within the Republican Party from the bottom up that the Liberal grip which was loosened in 1964 is permanently broken. This patently does not mean in 1968 an emotionally satisfying pre-convention campaign, such as that of 1964. It means hard patient work that can eventuate in a decisive conservative voice at the Republican convention. It may not bring about the nomination of an ideal conservative candidate, but it can make certain that no Liberal of the stripe of Percy or Romney will be nominated. Furthermore, it will insure that the candidate nominated will be acceptable to conservatives, that he will owe his victory to conservatives and will hold to broadly conservative principles, and that the course of the Republican Party will be firmly set in a conservative direction.

These are the general considerations with which I think conservatives ought to approach the problems of 1968. Still they are only guidelines; they do not answer the question of what candidate or candidates might meet their requirements. It seems to me that there are two questions that have to be answered in this respect: the question of a principled position and the question of fitness for office.

On the question of principle, one can rule out, to begin with, Percy, whose miserable position on Vietnam and on Communist aggression has earned him the support of both Martin Luther King and writers for the *New Republic* as a potential candidate. Romney, who has no discernible principles at all, can similarly be ruled out.

Of all the leading candidates, Reagan obviously has the most consistent principled conservative stand, on both domestic and foreign policy. Nixon has an honorable anti-Communist record and, if he has been somewhat ambiguous on domestic questions at times, he would seem to be, on balance, acceptable to conservatives—*if* he can avoid the temptation to which he has succumbed in the past, the temptation of assuming that the conservatives are in his pocket and therefore distorting his position to court the Liberals.

It is on the question of fitness for office that I have encountered conservative hesitation about Reagan. These hesitations seem to me to miss a major fact. While Reagan's governmental experience may be short, he is the only conservative in a generation who has had the actual experience of carrying solidly

conservative principles into practice in a major state. Furthermore, he is doing it with enough success to gain the grudging
admiration of skilled observers who are far from sympathetic
to his ends. And the objection that he lacks a grasp of foreign
policy was effectively dispelled in his recent debate with Robert
Kennedy on "Town Meeting of the World," an encounter from
which he emerged (again, in the opinion of neutral and unsym-
pathetic analysts) clearly superior.

The solider the support for Reagan at the Republican convention, the greater the possibility that he may be nominated—
but also the certainty that any Liberal candidate can be vetoed;
the assurance that, if Nixon is nominated, he will owe it to
conservative support; and the guarantee that conservative control of the Republican Party will be consolidated.

Ten Days in April

(National Review, May 7, 1968)

The ten days from the night President Johnson ran up the
white flag of surrender in Vietnam to the afternoon Martin
Luther King was buried will, I believe, one day impress the
historian as the most fateful point in American history since
Fort Sumter was fired upon 107 years ago.

I may be wrong, I may be "over-reacting," as a colleague of
mine recently accused me of doing. Events may not move as
fast as I believe they will. The Communists may make impossible
the modicum of face-saving that Johnson is bound to insist upon
in his surrender, and the war may be renewed, perhaps this time
at a level capable of achieving our objectives. The fever of the
Negro insurrection may die down, and the Negro middle classes,
under the leadership of men like Roy Wilkins, may prevail over
the nihilist spirit that presently rides high.

But these are unlikely eventualities. It is far more likely that
the first days of April have ushered in a massive crisis, internal
and external, in the history of the United States—a crisis which

could bring all the inherent pathologies generated by decades of Liberalism to cataclysmic resolution. We are living, I fear, through a climactic moment of that Liberal drive to civilizational suicide that James Burnham has analyzed.

At such a time, I thought the editorial discussion in the last issue of *National Review* (April 23) lamentably lacking in urgency and—in spite of excellent reportage and considerable acute analysis—remiss in failing to show the depth of the two crises and their common origin in Liberal relativism and Liberal nihilism. For both crises reflect relativist disdain for the values of Western civilization and nihilism towards any order, national or international, even an order that makes freedom possible. They are, in fact, a single crisis of moral purpose and civilizational esprit.

The domestic crisis most clearly reflects the breakdown of moral authority. What has been happening in the streets of our cities the last few years is not in any primary sense the result of Negro economic and social conditions. Indeed, insurrectionary violence would seem to have burst forth just when those conditions are rapidly improving. Nor will massive panicky expenditures or constitutional emasculations like the open housing provisions of the Civil Rights Act of 1968 touch the cause of disorder. Such ransom paid to the blackmail of violence is actually more likely to increase than diminish the virulence of the attack on American society.

The tired formulas of Liberalism will be no more effective when they are escalated than they have been in the past. The Civil Rights Act of 1968 will have little effect on the social situation, but it will immensely increase Washington's power over the individual citizen. Programs like that of the Kerner Commission or Rockefeller's $150-billion plan would only mean a massive proliferation of bureaucracy and a crushing increase in the already crushing burden of taxation borne by the producing majority of the population (and let us not forget that there are millions of Negroes in that producing majority).

The cause and the solution of our crisis are not to be found in such economic and social nostrums. Our poor are better off than any in the world, far better off than any in past history. Every official voice, governmental and private, has been raised to do what exhortation can do to lower social barriers—support which other minority groups, from the Irish to the Jews to the Italians, never had as they worked their way forward.

The cause is not social and economic, but moral. It is not by chance that at this point we face these lawless explosions not only from our cities, but from our universities. We are reaping the harvest of two generations of contempt for the constitutional tradition of law and ordered freedom. The consummation of a decade of rapidly mounting crime was the spectacle, telecast the country over, of arson and looting going unchecked while troops and police stood by. This was not local or accidental; as the New York *Times* has revealed, it was a national policy conceived on the highest level of government.

But the moral duty of citizens to government depends upon the social compact by which government guarantees the protection of the citizens and their property against outlaws, in return for which the citizens surrender their right to use force in their own defense. Once the compact is broken, that right reverts to all citizens, and the outcome can only be Hobbes' anarchic "war of all against all."

Our external crisis, like our internal crisis, proceeds from the corrosion of national morale. The prosecution of the war in Vietnam has been vitiated from the beginning by the internal decay of our attitude to world Communism, by our refusal to face the reality of an enduring challenge to our existence and the existence of our civilization. The war in Vietnam was a partial rally from our base and irresponsible retreat before Communism. Surrender in Vietnam will lead to renewed retreat and appeasement on an unprecedented scale—unless the country in its agony finds new leadership and a new morale.

Here and here alone lies the solution to the American crisis at home and abroad. It may be objected that this is an ideal answer, that it will not occur in time, that more immediate and practical steps are necessary. But the fact is that there are no such steps. Only national renewal of leadership and moral authority will meet the crisis. And historically it has happened time and again that solutions which seemed distant and improbable have emerged with startling rapidity from the crucible of crisis.

Why I Am for Reagan

(*New Republic*, May 11, 1968)

When some months ago Ronald Reagan and Robert Kennedy appeared jointly on satellite television to answer the questions of an international group of undergraduates assembled in London, the audience was privy to a foreview of a new alignment in American politics that will dominate the American scene in the next decade or so. I do not know whether in this presidential year Richard Nixon will falter, bringing Reagan into serious competition for the Republican nomination—or, for that matter, whether Robert Kennedy can triumph over the combined opposition of the followers of McCarthy and of the Johnson wing of the Democratic Party. Basic trends sometimes take a long time to achieve full expression in electoral politics, and it might well be that the 1968 election will see Richard Nixon pitted against Hubert Humphrey.

If that is the outcome, however, I venture to predict that it will be the last round of the kind of presidential politics that (with the exception of 1964) has been characteristic of the relation of forces and the handling of issues for some 30 years. It would be somewhat skewed by the multiple crises which beset the country and by the presence of George Wallace in the race. But essentially it would represent, on the one hand, a continuation of the practical politics of the Roosevelt coalition based on the ideological foundation of the Roosevelt program brought up to date, and, on the other hand, a challenge from somewhat right of center which would neither attempt to weld the new coalition made possible by social developments since World War II, nor fundamentally dispute the premises of the aging Roosevelt Liberal settlement.

Under these circumstances the true relationship of forces in the country would not be represented, nor would the central issues of the sixties and the years ahead be brought to focus. Not least among the deleterious effects of a Nixon-Humphrey contest, or any similar one, would be that millions would drop out of the central American political process, because it would seem to them that the issues and symbols presented by the candidates were irrelevant to their concerns. In the one direction there would be an escape to the "peace-and-freedom" type candidate and to extra-political action. In the other direction, large segments would be demagogically drawn into the camp of the Wallace movement's Know-Nothingism.

I should make it clear that this critique does not mean that I am opposed to the American tradition of broad-gauge parties, or believe in the European concept of parties based on sharp and clear ideological commitment. The American mode, by eliminating constant ideological confrontation, has preserved social stability and order, while leaving open the potentialities of reasoned change and development. But the success of the system presupposes a broad consonance between the positions of the major parties and the underlying essential issues of the period. The system cannot survive if the parties cease to maintain relevance to underlying national issues.

This has been particularly a problem for the Republican Party, since, with the exception of the imperfectly executed campaign of 1964, it has so shaped its policies that it has not in any true sense functioned to give expression to the opposition in the country to the Liberal ascendancy that has prevailed since 1932. Now the Democratic Party has begun to suffer from the cumulative irrelevancy of the program for which it has stood since the Roosevelt days.

The formula of governmental, particularly federal action as the solution to all social problems, is coming under almost as intense fire from radicals, and from many Liberals, as conservatives have directed against it for years. I read, in the Liberal and radical press, attacks upon big government and bureaucracy— and not merely from the New Left, but from men of the substance of Daniel Patrick Moynihan and Richard Goodwin—of a sort that a few years ago would have come only from conservative spokesmen. The welfare system, for example, is being attacked from the left, as sharply as it ever was from the right, as a system perpetuating unemployment and poverty. And the imperial power of union leaders has no longer the sacrosanct aura that surrounded it a decade or two ago.

Likewise, as the coherence and congruence of the New Deal and the post-New Deal Democratic program have been dissipating, so also the material political basis of Democratic ascendancy, the Roosevelt coalition, has been coming apart at the seams. That coalition was an alliance of labor, the urban poor, the city machines, the farmers and the South. The South has been alienated from the coalition; the city machines have lost much of their power; the interests of labor and the urban poor are less and less similar; the farmers have, in the first place, sharply declined in numbers, and in the second place are increasingly finding their interests homogeneous with those of the great middle section of the American population.

It is not the farmers alone, however, who are involved in this process of homogenization. The central social fact in America in the years since World War II is that formerly disparate classes are cohering into a homogeneous body that incorporates three-fourths or more of the population. Cutting across and eliminating former regional differences, uniting to a very considerable degree the interests of country and suburb, town and city, this body includes office worker, service worker, and industrial worker, farmer and small owner, technician and salaried executive, in a mode of life varying widely in detail but giving birth to broadly similar attitudes and aspirations.

I do not rejoice in this homogenization; as a conservative I much prefer variety of every kind—regional, cultural, individual.

But it is a social and political fact, which all politics from here on must reckon with. And, while the ethos of this new American society is not one to produce civilizational brilliance, it can produce stability, sober progress, and satisfaction in life. It is an ethos in many ways the modern analogue of the agrarian community upon which the Founding Fathers built.

It is this ethos to which Ronald Reagan, more than any other man on the American political scene, gives expression. In a world buffeted by the storms of ideology, he is sane, decent, moderate. The central themes of his position are moral order in society, personal freedom and national dignity.

On the first theme, the issue identified in the polls as the No. 1 concern of the citizenry, under the rubric of "crime," Reagan would propose the rigorous and just enforcement of the laws against misdoing in high and low places, and a national return to concepts of individual responsibility. Despite the jibes directed against him by his enemies, there is no anti-Negro innuendo here. To begin with, the large majority of the Negro population is as anxious for order and serenity as their white compeers. Indeed, the new center of American political life, about which I have been talking, includes a large number of Negroes, whose hopes and aspirations are not dissimilar from those of the other blue-collar and white-collar groups who make up that center.

Further, Reagan is deeply concerned with the problems of the Negro population and has been meeting all over the state of California with groups of Negro leaders to attempt to find solutions. His conclusion, like the conclusion of all those who have looked into the problem without ideological blinkers, is that the key to Negro advancement is employment, and on this front he has taken vigorous steps in California. He sees violence and the decay of order to be as inimical to the interests of the Negro as to those of the country as a whole.

On the second broad issue, Reagan stands for the largest practicable reduction of the interference of government with the free energies of individuals and associations of individuals, whether that interference comes through governmental taxation or governmental regulation. He has shown as Governor of California his awareness that 35 years of governmental aggrandizement cannot be reversed overnight, particularly by a conservative who understands that too rapid a reorganization of social arrangements—even in a conservative direction—would be as dangerous as any revolutionary dislocation of society. But he has sharply slowed the rate of growth of governmental expenditure; he is driving for governmental efficiency and a reduction of bureaucratic fat; and he has used all the powers of his office to encourage the action of the private sector. His initiatives are limited as the governor of a state, in view of the restrictions by the federal government these days. But as President, he could and would come to grips with the problem of bridling the Leviathan that the federal government has become, to the end of increasing the freedom of the citizenry and releasing their private energies for the national good.

On the third issue, he agrees with the majority of Americans that Communism bodes no good for the United States and for Western civilization. He is as aware as any of us of the dangers of nuclear war, but he believes that under the umbrella of mutual nuclear deterrence the United States must take a firm, consistent and independent course. And further, he believes that once we are entered upon a contest of arms, we must carry it through to the achievement of our objective.

That these are all broad positions, with which I as a principled conservative agree, is secondary to my urgent conviction that the survival of this country requires a leadership which will unite the great producing majority. In a time of deep uncertainty, when the lure of demagogy from right and left creates dangers parallel to those of Germany in the twenties and early thirties, Reagan stands at the central point of American politics, expressing the central trends of society. As presidential candidate against the competing demagogies of a Wallace and a Kennedy, or against the tired nostrums of a Humphrey, Ronald Reagan could, I think, win the support of the American electorate—and, winning it, vindicate the basic theme of orderly progress in a secure society.

When Governors Cease To Govern . . .

(National Review, June 4, 1968)

"Nature abhors a vacuum"—and the same principle applies in society. This is why a state of permanent anarchy has never existed and never can exist. Something always fills the power vacuum. And that something is usually decidedly unpleasant. When moral authority, which is the cement of a society, is dissolved, rarely can anything but raw power recreate the social cohesion and order without which no society can function. That raw power, necessary to pull a chaotic, anarchy-ridden society together, almost inevitably is wielded by dictators and tyrants.

This is not abstract historical speculation. It is a possible, not too distant fate that may face this country. The Liberal leadership which has governed the United States since 1932 has in the last few months driven with catastrophic momentum to the edge of bankruptcy—a bankruptcy always inherent in its principles and its understanding of society and politics, but now becoming imminently real. In its surrender before Communism in Vietnam, as in its surrender before mobs in our cities and our universities, that leadership is no longer merely doing what it has done for 35 years, retreating before Communism abroad and steadily dismantling the Constitution at home. It is no longer merely governing with bad means to achieve bad ends. It is showing an inability to govern at all: abroad, betraying the most fundamental interests of the Republic, and at home letting the constituted power in its trust slip from its nerveless fingers into the possession of self-proclaimed "representatives of the popular will," who burn our cities, desecrate our universities, occupy our capital.

Political developments cannot be timed, and it is impossible to say how soon, if we continue on our present national course, the full descent into anarchy will occur. It could be a year or four or eight, or longer. But what is certain is that this is the direction in which the governing Liberal leadership is taking us. It is possible, of course, that there are enough men in that leadership who will recover their sense of reality and pull back from that course before crushing defeat abroad and endemic chaos at home are upon us. But so deeply has ideology, which blots out reality, invaded the Liberal mind that this is a faint hope.

The brighter hope is in the citizens themselves, who, their instincts and experience undimmed by ideology, recognize the developing anarchy for what it is. In their hands rests the power to throw out the present leadership and replace it with one committed to restoring peace and order at home and vigorously defending American interests abroad. Such a change in leadership would be the happiest outcome—the only possible happy outcome—of the crisis of our society, which is week by week becoming more ominous.

Such a reassertion of constitutional authority and order would not only be a good in itself; the only possible alternatives would bring to an end the freest society mankind has ever known. When anarchy threatens a constitutional polity, order will be restored in one way or another. Men will not brook anarchy indefinitely. Either the society will have the strength to pull itself together and vindicate the genius of its institutions, or some mode of authoritarian rule will restore order from chaos at any cost.

There are two ways such an authoritarian, dictatorial rule can come about. It could overwhelm us in a way all too familiar in this century, through the ascent to power of a charismatic leader who concentrates in a mass movement, and distorts for his own ends, the instinctive recognition of the people that they simply are unable to live reasonable lives with the power of government in the hands of men helpless in the face of chaos, men unable to maintain the minimum conditions of civilizational order. It was in just such circumstances—the nervelessness of Kerensky and the Weimar Republic—that Lenin and Hitler came to power. Likewise, but on a more acceptable level, regimes like those of de Gaulle and Franco—regimes of a revolutionary and authoritarian character, but without the total hideousness of Communism and Fascism—have come into existence out of the inability to govern of the Fourth Republic or the Spanish Republic of the early Thirties.

The second way authoritarianism can be imposed on a country is through a revolution within the forms—a concentration of effective, even absolute, power in the hands of a dictatorial personality, while the formal constitutional structure is maintained. It was thus that Augustus, maintaining all the forms of the Roman republic, transformed that republic into an absolute empire. Formally he was never more than *princeps*, the first among the Senators; actually all effective power was in his hands—and Rome did not even have that formidable magistracy, the American Presidency, with its potentialities for transformation into dictatorship.

One form or the other of such a dictatorial future hangs over us if present trends continue, if moral authority in the spirit of our free Constitution is not soon reaffirmed. The election of 1968 is perhaps not the last chance for such a reaffirmation—though it may well be. Among the potential candidates I would judge that one, Ronald Reagan, certainly is of the stature to re-establish constitutional freedom and order, and another, Richard Nixon, could do so if he has finally put aside the tergiversations that have hitherto marred his public career. The others are either replicas of the men who have created our desperate situation or —one or two of them—demagogues of the mold that in a crisis situation threaten to become dictators.

What Is at Issue in 1968

(National Review, July 30, 1968*)*

It is remarkable how, for decades, the Liberals, and now their left wing and the radicals, have succeeded in determining the ground rules of American politics—establishing ideological chimeras as the basic issues for debate, terrorizing opposition (as they did in 1964) when it raises true issues based on reality, setting up their own definitions of what is "moderate" and what is "extreme."

Thus, despite his horrendous programmatic opposition, Senator McCarthy is somehow presented as a "moderate," while Governor Reagan, who represents the essentially moderate and anti-ideological outlook of the great majority of American citizens—the stable citizenry, with what used to be called "a stake in the country"—is branded as "extreme." So far has this gone that I have heard considerable admiration for McCarthy's tone expressed among conservatives and, also from some conservatives, a fear that Reagan as a candidate "would polarize the country"—which is just another way of calling him extreme.

This is not a matter of personalities. Should Nixon win the nomination and campaign on the only basis on which he can be elected, as a conservative in opposition to the entire record of the Kennedy-Johnson Administration, there is nothing said about Reagan today that would not be said about him. The reason Reagan, not he, is cast as the extremist at this time is that Nixon has continued to display an ambiguity (one might mention his flirtations with Lindsay and Percy) that it is to be hoped he will drop if he attains the nomination. It is because of that hope that conservatives can envisage supporting him if he is nominated; but it is because Reagan's position is clear, while his is not, that many conservatives still hope that it is Reagan who will be the nominee.

Actually, these concepts of extremism and polarization are irrelevant to the reality of American society today. They are reflections of an ideological distortion, which the Liberals and radicals, with the aid of the mass-communications media, have superimposed upon American reality. That reality I had occasion to analyze in a recent issue of the *New Republic*, which had asked me to participate in support of Reagan in a symposium on Presidential candidates:

"The central social fact in America in the years since World War II is that formerly disparate classes are cohering into a homogeneous body that incorporates three-quarters or more of the population. Cutting across and eliminating the former regional differences, uniting to a very considerable degree the interests of country and suburb, town and city, this body includes office worker, service worker and industrial worker, farmer and small owner, technician and salaried executive, in a mode of life varying widely in detail but giving birth to broadly similar attitudes and aspirations.

"I do not rejoice in this homogenization; as a conservative I much prefer variety of every kind—regional, cultural, individual. But it is a social and political fact, which all politics from here on must reckon with. And, while the ethos of this new American society is not one to produce civilizational brilliance, it can produce stability, sober progress, and satisfaction in life. It is an ethos in many ways the modern analogue of the agrarian community upon which the Founding Fathers built.

"It is this ethos to which Ronald Reagan, more than any other man on the American political scene, gives expression. In a world buffeted by the storms of ideology, he is sane, decent, moderate. The central themes of his position are moral order in society, personal freedom, and national dignity."

No Republican candidate who does not give expression to this broad consensus of the overwhelming producing majority of American citizens, white and black, can hope to win. Indeed— and perhaps of even greater importance to the future of the Republic—if no major candidate does give such expression, a tremendous section of this vote can well be captured by the demagogy of George Wallace, with the resultant creation of an extremist movement outside of the traditional pattern of American politics.

The much more dangerous extremism, however, is that represented by the McCarthy and Kennedy forces, who are attempting to mobilize a movement based upon the non-producing sections of the American population, for whose comparatively small numbers they hope to compensate by terrorizing first the Democratic Convention and then the electorate. The reckless demagogy of

McCarthy was typified in two successive days recently, when he proposed, first, the disarmament of the United States relative to the Soviet Union by ceasing work on Sentinel, Minuteman III and Poseidon, and, second, the declaration of a national emergency because of hunger.

Of course, in charity, we owe to the poor and the alienated consideration and help. But that is a very different thing from a politics based upon the blackmail demand that it is they whose wishes should rule a great producing society—or, more to the point, that power-hungry men should be allowed to achieve power, using the poor and the alienated of city and university as their battering ram. It was such tactics that destroyed the Roman Republic, created anarchy, and opened the way to imperial dictatorship.

The blackmail of such men and their supporters cannot be allowed to inhibit the Republican Party from expressing the underlying conservative consensus of the American majority. Whoever is the choice of the Republican Convention, the stand of the party and its nominee can yield to the Liberal-radical ideologues only at the cost of disaster for the party and the country.

A Conservative Convention

(*National Review*, August 27, 1968)

On balance, the Republican Convention was a miracle of sanity in a madly ideological world. Despite the pressures from intellectual fashion, from the media, from a considerable faction within the Convention itself, two themes emerged more and more clearly as the days wore by—both grounded in reality, both reflecting the deep beliefs of the great majority of Americans, and both anathema to the ideology-mongers whose political heroes are Eugene McCarthy and John Lindsay.

The first theme, overwhelmingly applauded whenever it was expressed, was the simple call for order in our society. Whatever one's political beliefs, it should be apparent to all but nihilists that order is the first condition of civilizational existence, the only foundation of freedom and well-being for anyone and everyone. When a few speakers attempted to modify this theme or blunt it, the delegates, by their selective applause, underlined this as their central concern.

Closely related to the overwhelming demand for order—and motivated by the same rejection of anti-civilizational nihilism— was the second prevailing theme of the Republican Convention. What once was the common rhetorical coin of an American political convention, here became, under the circumstances of today, a ringing challenge flung in the teeth of Liberalism. It was the assertion of the greatness and the stature of this country, the denial of the masochistic whining that we are "sick," the vindication of the goodness and power of our institutions, public and private.

And arising from this was another position—more clouded, blemished in my opinion by too much wishful thinking about Communist intentions, but fundamentally sound: the programmatic assertion that peace in Vietnam, or in the world as a whole, can only be won by national strength and the re-establishment of national dignity.

These are fundamentally conservative positions, as they are the sentiments of the great producing majority of Americans. That the Convention would reflect them was by no means clear from its beginnings. The platform laid itself open to a dozen interpretations. The Convention was clearly dominated by the Nixon forces, and it was because Mr. Nixon had not previously made it fully clear where he stood on the most essential points that many of us supported Ronald Reagan, whose stand was unequivocal. But as the Convention progressed, the isolation of the Liberal ideologues became more and more apparent, the sentiments of the Convention clearer and clearer. With the quiet struggle over the Vice Presidency the symbolic issue was decided.

Against every pressure of the New York *Times*, the television networks, the dolorous warnings of the Northeastern Liberals,

Nixon rejected Lindsay, Percy and Hatfield, any one of whom on the ticket would have nullified the conservative direction in which the Convention was moving and reduced the Republican Party's campaign to unprincipled nullity. Spiro Agnew, it is true, has in general had a record somewhat to the left of Mr. Nixon. But his speeches at the Convention showed that he is no ideological Liberal. And, indeed, during the Baltimore riots he earned the undying hatred of the ideologists when he dared to tell the leaders of the Negro community in no uncertain terms that the restoration and preservation of order was their first responsibility. The decisive point of the Vice-Presidential struggle, however, was not Agnew himself, but the rout of the Liberal assault on the integrity of the GOP.

The climax and culmination of the movement of the Convention toward a fundamentally conservative conclusion was Mr. Nixon's acceptance speech. With the exception of what I have referred to above as a doubtful position on the possibilities of negotiation with the Communists, it was firm in content and a fitting challenge to Liberalism in tone. This was a very different Nixon from the always cautious, often trimming, Nixon of 1960. If the rest of the campaign is conducted on this level, conservatives can support the Republican ticket with confidence.

Much has changed in this country since 1964. Where then we could see the causes leading to a crisis of our society clearly developing, today the crisis is upon us. In 1964, the conservative task was to direct attention to these causes and to lay out prescriptions for counteracting them. We were able in 1964 to convince the Republican Party, but not the country, of the validity of our analysis. Today, much is clearer, and the issue is simpler. It has become a stark matter of the survival of the conditions of civilization. Is a great, law-abiding, producing people to be held ransom by small minorities of *lumpen* slum-dwellers and *lumpen* students, aided, abetted and directed by Liberal ideologues turned nihilist? The answer of the Republican Convention to that question is a clear and decisive No.

In the civilizational crisis of 1968 this is a conservative answer on the decisive issue of the time. In a very definite sense it is the harvest of 1964, when it was decided once and for all that the Republican Party would no longer be a pale me-too reflection of the Democratic Party. And that conservative answer is in the deepest harmony with the central concern of the American people. If Richard Nixon holds fast to the course he and the Republican Party have charted, the country will rally behind him, and his Administration will turn the tide of the anarchy that threatens to engulf us.

Chapter Five

Communism and American
Foreign Policy:
Eisenhower to Johnson

*Throughout the years that I have been writing these columns
and articles, a central concern of all conservatives has been
the lack of understanding and purpose displayed by those
responsible for American foreign policy. This chapter contains
a selection of what I have written on foreign policy and particularly on our policy vis-à-vis world Communism, since it is
the Communist drive for world power that defines every world
political problem in these decades.*

*The years 1956 and 1957, when I first began writing my
column for* National Review, *were the years of "de-Stalinization," of the revolts in East Germany, Poland, and Hungary,
of Mao's "let a hundred flowers bloom." The series of columns
that follows concerns these questions and includes some which
derive from a discussion with another editor of* National Review,
*James Burnham, whose interpretation of the significance of
de-Stalinization differed from mine.*

Of Khrushchev, Stalin, and Sitting Ducks

(National Review, July 11, 1956)

There is, if I read the signs aright, great danger that, as we view the dramatic spectacle of the devaluation of Stalin and speculate about the motivations and inner-power struggles involved in it, we shall speculate about everything but the substance of the matter and ask every question but the serious one. That question is the one Communists themselves always address to developments of importance: what is the objective historical meaning of these events?

To guide us in finding the answer, there exists a primary set of data, but one which the "experts" seem systematically to ignore. This is the fifty years history of the politics of the Bolshevik Party, That party, under the Czar, in revolution, and in power, steadily, if not unerringly, has pursued a policy and has more than half achieved a goal, World Communism, always guided by a basic philosophy and a methodology of strategy and tactics—Marxism-Leninism. Protean though its expressions, it has remained in the minds of those who hold it monolithic in its essence. Those who died, denigrated in the purges of the thirties, were inspired by it no less and no more than their master executioner (this is the great insight of Koestler's *Darkness at Noon*).

Their denigration served a functional purpose, irrelevant to their merits or to their service to the Communist cause. It became the symbol (whether necessary or unnecessary, at least necessary in Stalin's mind, in the mind of him who represented the Party) of the establishment of certain policies implicit in Leninism and at that point explicitly demanded by the conditions and the problems of the period.

For the present leadership, facing a new epoch created by the immense victories of Communism since World War Two, the denigration of Stalin serves the same symbolic function in their establishment of a new line under new circumstances— *a new line, not a new philosophy or a new methodology or a new goal.* What happened at the 20th Congress is but the inner-Party manifestation of the shift of line of which Geneva, the reconciliation with Tito, and the general tone of Soviet foreign policy are the manifestation in the field of foreign affairs.

This is no minor turn in the line. A change in the objective world situation as the Communist leaders analyze it, of sufficient import to justify so dangerous a symbolic act as the destruction of the Stalin myth, is undoubtedly decisive enough to make of this turn one of the two or three most far-reaching reorientations of grand strategical plan in the entire history of Communism. Its significance is far greater than the significance of tactical changes such as that, for instance, from the People's-Front line to the Hitler alliance—and its effects will show themselves much more radically.

Rather, it is of the order of the great shift of position in the middle and late twenties, which transformed the perspective of more or less immediate world revolution to that of a long waiting period, in which the national power of the Soviet Union was to become the fundamental strategical concern of Communism. That change was consummated only with the destruction of the political power of nine-tenths of the Central Committee of 1917, with profound changes in the agricultural and industrial policies of the Communist Party, and with a reorientation of the aims of Soviet foreign policy from top to bottom.

There can be no doubt as to what the Communist leadership regards as the great change in the world situation which requires so epochal a reorientation now. It was already indicated in Stalin's last work, *Economic Problems of Socialism in the USSR*: it breathes through every section of Khrushchev's main political report to the 20th Congress. It is the belief that the balance of world power has shifted decisively to Communism; that the period of "capitalist encirclement" is ended and the period of "socialist encirclement" begun; that the inertia of history is now moving in the direction of final victory for the Communists.

Such a situation clearly demands that everything possible be done to avoid the only eventuality that could any longer cause serious difficulties: the development of a dedicated counterrevolutionary force, clear on the nature of Communism and determined to throw it back. All that is needed is to avoid a struggle *à outrance* and, by anti-Stalin "humanizing" gestures, to release the Messianic appeal which Communism, as the only inspired—one might almost say, the only "religious"—materialist doctrine, always potentially holds in a materialist age.

The changes that have so far occurred in Communist tactics are but a beginning. For what is coming as the grand strategical plan unfolds, the Liberal-collectivist Establishment, which forms our attitudes and our policies, is, to put it mildly, a sitting duck. With no understanding of the underlying permanent content of Communism, mistaking strategical and tactical waves for the tide, they have directed all our efforts against the surface and changing manifestations of Communism.

Their materialist, collectivist and social-engineering outlook is at bottom so much in agreement with the Soviet outlook that if the monstrosities to which the *consistent* collectivist policy of Communism leads can be in any way disguised, they are defenseless against it—particularly given some counterposed danger upon which they can concentrate, such as Hitler in the thirties or the threat of nuclear destruction today. Under their leadership we have long fought a withdrawing battle. The new Soviet strategy is designed to turn that withdrawal into a rout.

Communism Remains Communism

(National Review, October 13, 1956)

It is more than three years since Joseph Stalin died. Not for one day since that event has the Communist juggernaut ceased its remorseless advance. The Middle East has been breached; the Titoist schism healed; united-front connections with the neutralist bloc immensely strengthened; the blockade of trade in strategic materials broken; our position in Western Germany and Japan undermined. Most decisive of all, a climate of opinion has been created in which socialists, Liberals and "men of good will" can "see no reason [the words are George Kennan's] why a satisfactory and hopeful relationship should not be established between the United States and Russia, even though the respective social systems and political philosophies remain theoretically in conflict."

It is not a bad harvest for three years of *détente* and "the lessening of international tension"; but it is a different world from the one our hopeful apostles of coexistence have been describing to the American people. Throughout these years— and with accelerating crescendo in the months since the 20th Congress of the Communist Party of the Soviet Union—like the twittering of birds before an oncoming thunderstorm, the voices of the Russian experts, the commentators, and, alas, of the political leaders of both parties, have been heard in the land, confiding to one another and to the public that a new era is beginning, that a great change has occurred. It may take time. We mustn't expect too much too soon. But the bogeyman is dead, and his successors are sensible generals, industrial managers, Russian patriots—anything but dedicated Communists.

With their eyes riveted in fascination upon the anti-Stalin campaign and the clumsy condescension with which Khrushchev and Bulganin allow themselves to be feted in every capital of the Western and the Eastern world, they ignore entirely, as though blinded by perversity or some malignant Fate, the reality which presses upon the seeing eye, a reality manifest on every level, practical, historical, theoretical.

Practical: the continued advance of the Soviet position and the deterioration of our position.

Historical: the firm continuity of Communist aims and essential policy, through shifting tactics and strategical reassessments, from the birth of the Bolshevik Party to its 20th Congress, from an idea in the mind of Lenin and the few obscure revolutionaries of his personal circle to hegemony over 700 million human beings of the Soviet Empire and spiritual leadership of millions beyond its borders.

Theoretical: one might say, metaphysical, even, in a perverse sense, theological: the materialistic dogmatism united with the self-immolating service of a dialectical goddess of History that breathes as strongly in the documents of the 20th Congress as in the earliest polemics of Lenin, a living creed which allows no compromise of its end, World Communism.

This is the reality of Communism—Lenin's Communism, Stalin's Communism, Khrushchev's Communism, the party's Communism. That reality, with its fearful threat to the values upon which Western civilization is founded, will not go away because we want it to. This is not the first time a shift of Communist strategy, or even of tactics, or the savage denigration of a former leader, has diverted and bemused the West.

True, since the successive depositions of Trotsky, Zinoviev and Bukharin, no figure even approaching the magnitude of Stalin has suffered their fate. But then, there has been no parallel change in circumstances, no need for so sharp a reassessment of strategy since the twenties. Then the Communist Party of the Soviet Union recognized that the first great wave of revolution, following World War I and the October Revolution, had begun to ebb, that the prime strategic task was consolidation of the Soviet Union, the strong point of the Revolution, encircled by capitalism. The concept of the building of socialism in one country as a beleaguered fortress from which, in due time, the forces of world revolution might again sally forth, demanded, in the dialectic of Communist psychology, the symbol of the destruction of the images of those who stood against this vital thesis of Stalin's.

Today, Stalin's own achievements have destroyed that capitalist encirclement, shifted the fundamental balance of power in the world, and created a situation of socialist encirclement, in which the inertia of prevailing circumstances innately favors Communism. Only a principled, clear and fearless counter-attack by the forces of freedom can, in these circumstances, stem the tide. Strategically, Communism is on the offensive as never before, but tactically it requires an atmosphere which will disarm its natural enemies and make such a counter-attack unlikely.

Stalin stood as the symbol of a *defensive strategy*, based on capitalist encirclement, and of a *tactic predominantly offensive*. A changed, an *offensive strategical concept*, based upon immense successes and requiring a *defensive tactic*, primarily directed toward disarming the enemy, is symbolized by the devaluation of Stalin.

Thus, the last of the companions-in-arms of Lenin pays to the party the supreme debt that he himself had exacted from so many others: having served the Revolution actively and con-sciously in one phase of the dialectical spiral, he serves it again in his denigration in a succeeding phase.

This is the "change," the auspices of which our augurs are so anxiously examining. A fundamental change in strategy, yes—but one which bodes no good to the cause of the West. An accompanying change in tactical emphasis, yes—one which, however it may alternate between the carrot and the club, will be directed toward lulling us, mesmerizing us, preparing us for a kill to be achieved against the least resistance, with the smallest risk possible. But a fundamental change, a Kennan change, a Lippmann change, which would return us to the happy world of nineteenth-century diplomacy and delicately shifting balances of power—no.

There is no change in the Communist metaphysical faith, held innately and in depth, in a way incomprehensible to the positivists, the instrumentalists, the psychoanalyzers who have taken over the intellectual leadership of the West; there is no change in the uncompromising devotion to the achievement of the goal of world conquest; there is no change in the supreme confidence in the methodology of dialectical materialism, the expression of that metaphysic, as the instrument for achievement of that goal. Communism remains Communism.

The evidence of objective history and of subjective intention openly declared, continuously records its character as an enemy that wills the destruction of our civilization. Why, then, do our oracles and the holders of power among us so unanimously and steadfastly refuse to recognize the truth, dire though it may be, and to propose and frame their policies accordingly? Partly, no doubt, it is the result of the deep corrosion of the Western heritage by a positivism that neither believes in a good for which to fight, nor credits to the enemy the possibility of unstinting devotion to an evil for which he is prepared to fight, come what may.

But this is an intellectual error, one which has only corroded, not destroyed, the foundations of our civilization and our nation. The decisive cause, I am afraid, of the bemusement of our policies, of the refusal to recognize the threatening specter for what it is, is a moral defect, a defect of courage. To stand against evil, to vindicate eternal values, when the grim reality of the world as it is today is once recognized, requires the risk of security, prosperity, life itself.

It is the duty of the leaders of a nation to make this plain, and to make plain the alternative of slavery and dehumanization. The people, it is said, are not prepared to listen to such leaders. I wonder if that is true. I wonder if the American people, inspired by political leaders who placed duty above expedience, and instructed by intellectual leaders who held firm to their vocation to truth and tradition, would fail to respond with integrity and heroism. There was Patrick Henry: "Is life so dear, or peace so sweet, as to be purchased at the price of chains and slavery? Forbid it, Almighty God!" And, in a lower key, the sergeant of World War I: "Come on, you sons of bitches, do you want to live forever?"

I wonder.

An American Tragedy

(National Review, December 8, 1956)

What I have found most depressing during the past few weeks is neither the situation in Hungary nor that in the Middle East, but the American reaction to both. The Hungarian tragedy was relieved by a display of heroism such as the twentieth century has rarely seen; in the Middle East, England and France showed, at least for a moment, that determination and the will to fight have not completely died out in the West. But American opinion, American policy, and American action have presented an almost unrelieved panorama of dimmed understanding, febrilely feeble will, and fundamental lack of courage. To the cosmic eye the posturings of a Dulles, an Eisenhower, a Stevenson, during these weeks, must have seemed ludicrous to the point of bathos. But to the American patriot, bound up in the fate of his country (a country, moreover, which is the last bulwark of Western civilization), it is not bathos, but tragedy.

The locus of that tragedy is not so much present policy itself as the causes of its coming about, causes that—should they continue to operate without effective opposition—are leading inexorably to final disaster. Central among these causes is a disposition, so settled as to approach delusionary psychosis, to deny the continuing and steadfast reality of Communism, in favor of soothing hypotheses derived from flitting changes in the visage of the bear.

It is one of the difficulties of the pragmatically trained (and that includes a very large percentage of those who form opinion and policy today) that they are constantly searching for meaning in "the facts" as they present themselves from moment to moment. The multitudinous facts which in any developing historical situation crowd upon the vision have themselves no meaning to yield up except as they are seen in the context of the underlying forces that produce them. Upon the surface of a tidal wave, transitory currents of air and water create patterns often totally irrelevant to the distant causes or the eventual consequences of the moving mass itself.

So, in these weeks, from President to publicist, those who make or influence American policy have, in their enormous majority, steadfastly turned their eyes away from the solid evidence of the fundamental nature of Communism, to take hope and heart from passing surface developments. Undoubtedly there is a factional struggle in the Soviet empire. Undoubtedly in Hungary, as a result of that factional struggle, forces were released which went beyond the limits of the factional struggle and created conditions favorable to us, *had we struck and struck hard*. Undoubtedly in the Middle East, the Soviet Union lost several hundred million dollars worth of military equipment and was placed in a situation where that key strategic area was on the verge of being repossessed for the West. The enemy, in short, was in a temporarily weakened condition, his tactical counsels divided and his forces facing the need of regrouping.

If a military commander, seeing hostile armies in such a condition, decided that it was a sign that the opposition high command was no longer sure that it really wanted to fight him; if he offered food and aid to contingents of the enemy who differed with that high command only on the mode of effecting the destruction of our forces; if he stood by and watched the slaughter of a mutinous enemy division in the center; if, against powerful forces of his allies, striking at the enemy's flank, he exerted all possible pressure, to bring about their withdrawal if not their defeat; if, to the gathering forces of other potential allies, he recommended disarmament; if, then, to prove his virtue, he pleaded that, had he struck, very great slaughter might have ensued, and, anyway, he had been very kind to a few thousand escaping mutineers from the enemy camp—what would his fate have been?

Yet, without unduly straining the simile, these would seem to be the arguments of the intellectual Establishment that guides our policies and the rationale of the actions of those concerned with the execution of our policies. We assume that tactical differences in the Kremlin high command prove that Communism is no longer Communism, that it no longer wills our destruction. And, in the aftermath, as the box cars roll east from Hungary and the pressure upon the British and French to give back Egypt to the Soviets mounts to almost irresistible proportions, we "analyze" and congratulate ourselves on the difficulties the enemy is having. In the working out of a successful Communist policy toward the satellites between the carrot of Gomulka and the club of Budapest, in the Soviet use of American power to drive England and France from the Middle East, we see—the imminent collapse of the Soviet system.

That what we are observing is not the collapse of that system, but the process in which it is solving new problems, is a concept apparently unavailable to the mind that concentrates its attention upon transitory phenomena and attempts to extract meaning from them. Such a method fails perforce to reckon with the underlying evidence of history, that Bolshevism does not become weaker when it moves to solve difficulties by sharp changes of its tactics and strategy. Bolshevism has always been in difficulties—at the time of Kronstadt, of the famines, of the factional struggles of collectivization, of the German invasion, and again now. But it has always come out of each set of difficulties stronger than before, *because the external world has never taken advantage of those difficulties to strike at it when it was absorbed in solving those difficulties.*

Until we learn to look at the nature of Bolshevism, not its changing manifestations, until we learn that those manifestations are but differing expressions of the same firm, unyielding essence, until we learn that its nature is such that either it or we must die, it will go on overcoming each successive crisis, emerging from each one stronger than before.

"New Ideas" or Old Truth

(National Review, February 2, 1957)

James Burnham's proposals for a new strategy for American foreign policy, as developed in his column, "The Third World War," and in his article, "Liberation—What Next?", are submitted for debate "between men who share," to quote the *National Review* editorial opening this discussion, "the relevant fundamental assumptions: that coexistence is immoral, undesirable, and, in the long run, impossible; that we are dealing with an implacable enemy whose revolutionary fervor burns as hot as ever, and whose designs on the men of the West, and their institutions, remain the same."

That Mr. Burnham arrives at foreign policy proposals so sharply different from those which others of us derive from the same assumptions, would indicate that further assumptions, additional to those we share in common, underlie his thinking. His proposals ("reunification of Germany; negotiation of the eastern German boundary; withdrawal of all occupation [foreign] troops from all of Central and Eastern Europe; military neutralization of the entire area") are of the kind that *National Review* and Mr. Burnham himself have continuously and vehemently criticized. Neither at first sight, nor with further and deeper examination, have I found any reason to believe that recent events have so radically changed the situation as to justify the belief that a policy of withdrawal is any less dangerous this year than last year. If anything, the difficulties in which the Soviet empire finds itself should give greater rewards to a forward policy now than ever. But Mr. Schlamm has written a detailed and, in my opinion, convincing criticism of the content of Mr. Burnham's proposals, and I do not wish to repeat or to elaborate his arguments.

I should like rather to examine the special assumptions, additional to the stock we hold in common, which have made it possible for the author of *The Struggle for the World* and *Containment or Liberation?* to propose a policy of this sort. These assumptions would seem to be two in number, each modifying one of the basic assumptions of *National Review*.

The recognition of the immorality, undesirability, and eventual impossibility of coexistence, he conditions by the proposition that "the Eisenhower axioms" must be accepted (absolutely, it would seem) as part of "the reality of our time," upon which any strategic proposals must be based. Secondly, the proposition that Communism remains Communism is conditioned by a further assumption that Communism has suffered a "colossal defeat" and is in such straits as a result that it *is* capable of "changing"; that it can confidently be expected to dissolve from the effect of its own internal stresses, if only the present American and the potential German pressure is released; and that the Communist High Command is caught in such contradictions that it must willy-nilly follow a policy (if only we do withdraw) which will inevitably bring about such a dissolution.

These two assumptions, I should like to discuss in order.

First, therefore: is it possible to develop a strategy compatible with the basic axioms of *National Review*'s policy which at the same time stays within the limits of "the Eisenhower axioms"? Mr. Burnham does not explain why it is now necessary to accept these limitations in our thinking, when it was not necessary so to do half a year ago. Since, however, he stresses as the proximate cause of his change of attitude that the events of these few months, particularly the events in Hungary and Poland, have created a new situation, it may be assumed that this is the reason for now taking into account limitations that previously had to be ignored by "hard anti-Communists" in their proposals for foreign policy.

Undoubtedly, something *has* happened in these months. President Eisenhower's betrayal of our allies on this side of the Iron Curtain at Suez, and of our allies on the other side of the Iron Curtain in Hungary, has made clearer than ever before the extent and depth of the bankruptcy of his policy.

It is one thing to know logically, in the abstract, as it were, what the objective meaning of a policy is; it is another to see it in living reality. What Asia learned in the last decade, Europe has learned this past year: the rhetoric of our foreign policy contains a reality that is unbelievable until it takes material form. The Hungarian slaughter, the apotheosis of Nasser, the humiliation of Britain and Eden, the surrender of the Mideast to the Soviet Union (the Eisenhower Doctrine is as effective as a sledge-hammer against termites)—these are the realities of our foreign policy of 1957.

Chiang Kai-shek and Syngman Rhee learned the same lesson a little earlier. It is a very simple lesson: the "axiomatic structure" upon which American foreign policy is based is surrender, surrender, and again surrender. Nor is this surprising; it is the logical outcome of Mr. Eisenhower's first axiom: War is unthinkable. For, if war is unthinkable in a world in which there exists a rival power, bent upon domination of the world, to whom war *is* thinkable, surrender is the only possible outcome. The only question is: how long will it take to reach the point of final surrender; how much have we got in the sled to throw to the wolves to slow them up?

There can be no mistake about it: unless we take a stance firmly founded upon a willingness to risk war in defense of truth and freedom, and make it clear to the world that we are prepared to take that risk, no strategy for victory can be constructed. Force, actual or potential, is the only arbiter between those who hold no intrinsic truths in common.

It is the daily coin of those who live within the axiomatic structure of the Establishment that "you cannot fight ideas with bayonets." But there are times when there is no mutually accepted ground upon which ideas can be fought with ideas, when evil ideas backed up with force cannot be fought with anything but force. The alternative is surrender to them. Stalemate is ruled out if, as in our situation, the enemy is inspired by a dynamic Gnostic conviction of his mission to transform the world.

To put it bluntly, there are only two alternatives: the destruction of Communism or the destruction of the United States and of Western civilization. This is, for the purpose of founding a strategy, the decisive center of the "realities of our time." The sense in which the "Eisenhower axiomatic structure" can be considered a "reality of our time" is, compared to this, Pickwickian. Mr. Burnham challenges us to advance a "new idea" that was not thought of before 1949, an "alternative to his proposals" that will be "realistic." To that challenge I can only answer that the basic world situation has not changed since 1949.

That situation is the essence of reality. "The axiomatic structure" upon which our policy has been based is a "reality" only in the sense that it is the efflorescence of external terrorization and internal confusion of purpose. It is impossible to fight Communism without fighting to change that axiomatic structure. This, therefore, is the indispensable foundation of any foreign-policy program: to fight against that axiomatic structure, to educate and to mobilize the forces to change it.

This is high among the aims to which *National Review* is dedicated; but there cannot be, unless by pure chance, a policy (with the beauty of the perpetual-motion gimmick) that will at one and the same time satisfy both the axioms upon which *National Review* was founded and the axioms of our Establishment. Unless, therefore, Mr. Burnham's proposals are of the happy and miraculous character that by chance can reflect the demands of contradictory sets of policies, they must reflect the demands of the one or the other. *Prima facie*, being of the nature of *détente*, of withdrawal, they reflect the demands of the Eisenhower axiomatic structure. The burden of proof to the contrary is heavily upon Mr. Burnham. What evidence does he bring forward to prove that they represent that happy conjunction of opposing principles which he maintains has become the case?

This brings us to his second assumption. Is the Soviet empire in such case that it will dissolve precisely if we act as the Eisenhower axioms dictate? Mr. Burnham's case rests (if the

Eisenhower axioms and the *National Review* axioms are both to be respected) upon the judgment that it is in such case.

I shall not repeat what I have written in *National Review* to confute that judgment. I shall only say that if it is indeed—which I deeply doubt—in such a posture of weakness, now is the time to increase not decrease our pressure, to compound not simplify its difficulties, to take advantage of the "new fluidity" to move toward its destruction, not to help it stabilize, relying upon the questionable possibility of its dying of its own contradictions. If it is not, if it is simply having difficulties which it can overcome, as it has overcome previous difficulties, then also we should increase the pressure to make its solutions more difficult, to force it back in the moment of its embarrassment, to move steadfastly toward the showdown.

Mr. Burnham gambles everything in his effort to find a happy meeting ground for the axioms of *National Review* and the axioms of Eisenhower and Dulles, upon the assumption that, left to itself, Communism will gradually dissipate and go away. But any strategical proposal must be prepared for the least favorable estimate of the enemy's forces as for the most favorable. Any strategy based upon reality (pre-1949 or post-1949) must take account of that factor which is the ideological disposition of the enemy. His capabilities we have no reason to scorn after his conquest of half the world and neutralization of half the rest. When disposition and capability are so combined, a Hungarian rising, that before our eyes is being reduced with Bolshevik single-mindedness (totally unaffected by the moral indignation of the world, unbacked by force), cannot change our fundamental estimate of the strength of the enemy. It proves only that *if we struck*, we should have allies.

A policy of withdrawal, congenial though it may be to the outlook of the current Administration, has enormous dangers if Mr. Burnham's second assumption (the deep inner weakness of the Soviet regime) is untrue. If it is true, it promises no gains that would not be magnified a hundred times by a policy of aggressive pressure.

Furthermore, considering the conditions under which foreign policy has perforce to be developed where a mass electorate is involved, concrete strategical proposals of a large scale inevitably are associated with the production of corresponding moods in the nation. Proposals of withdrawal can only strengthen the pacifism and irresponsibility which the Eisenhower Administration has already done so much to develop. Mr. Burnham's proposals, if adopted in the present atmosphere of pacifism, UN-ism, and American subvention of world socialism, could only weaken our military posture while doing nothing to make our immense foreign expenditures less fruitless than they have been.

There can be, in short, no contrived substitute for the hard choices which we face. It is not possible to create a policy that both satisfies the hopes of an Eisenhower dream of renunciation of war, reliance upon the UN, victory without sacrifice, and simultaneously recognizes, as *National Review* has done, the harsh reality of the irrepressible conflict between the aims of armed Communism and the survival of our civilization and our values.

Nature of the Enemy

(National Review, March 23, 1957)

In two recent columns of the Third World War ("Communist or Russian?" and "Definitions and Distinctions"), Mr. Burnham has begun to develop a position on Communism which explicitly goes beyond the level of strategy and comes to grips with major principled questions. It was my belief, as I attempted to make clear in these pages, that a fundamental position was implicit in his earlier strategic proposals; and I welcome his clarification.

In the first place, it would seem that Mr. Burnham has repudiated the conception he, together with most hard anti-Communists, has long held of the nature of the Soviet power-complex, namely: that its dynamic essence and its danger to the

United States arises from its Communist character. Now, answering his own question: "Is the Soviet state structure . . . primarily *Russian* or *Communist?* It is both, of course, but which has priority?"—he replies: ". . . the relative weight of the two elements shifts from time to time, with now one and then the other predominant."

Mr. Burnham, of course, has every right to change his mind, provided either that new evidence comes to hand or that he finds defects in his previous thought processes. It would have been helpful had he indicated to us what has induced him to do so. Lacking that information, however, it is only possible to restate briefly the considerations which have led me, as they have led most hard anti-Communists, and as they formerly led Mr. Burnham, to a firm conclusion: it is the Communist element that is the decisive shaping force in the "Soviet state structure," in the same way that the soul is the decisive shaping force in a man's being, although the mode of his operation may depend upon specific characteristics such as a musical ear or a surgeon's fingers.

The first and most obvious indication that the essence of Sovietism is not Russian, but Communist, is the immense rapidity with which Soviet power has spread in the forty years of its existence. From precarious control of an enclave between Petrograd and Moscow, it has grown till it rules an empire of 900 million people, and, beyond the borders of its physical sway, challenges with its ideology and influence the ancient religions of mankind in every corner of the world. Nothing like it has been seen since the decades after the Hegira, when Moslem power and Moslem influence spread like wild-fire from a corner of the Arabian desert to become the dominant power from the Mediterranean to the borders of China and the Islands of the Indies.

Secondly, there is the factor so often ignored by our sociological institutes which—for themselves, for the State Department, and for the armed forces—study so assiduously and so aridly, the meaning of Communism: the express, explicit ideology of *all* of the leaders of this movement, on all five continents of the earth, is the militantly atheistic religion of Marxism-Leninism. No mystical doctrine of an Orthodox Muscovite Third Rome, no nationalistic nineteenth-century mystique of Pan-Slavism, can explain the conquest by Communist power of Buddhist-Confucian-Taoist China, can enlighten us as to the ideological appeal of Moscow to the rising power-hungry intellectuals of the Arabic world, or can make intelligible the Communist lodgement in Brazil or Guatemala—or, for that matter, in New York or Chicago or Washington.

Can one imagine a devotee of the Third Rome penetrating our Department of State, going to jail on a charge of perjury with the devotion of a martyr? Can one imagine a Pan-Slavic missionary interesting and intriguing a Dutch-patroon President of the United States and influencing his policies?

It is true that one's conclusions upon the question of Communism or Russianism must be founded in a judgment about reality, that is, in an empirical and dialectical inquiry, not in a moral judgment. But the conclusions reached have a profound consequence not merely for practical and strategic purposes; they deeply affect the application to reality of moral principle. (If, as Mr. Burnham says, "the refusal to make distinctions concerning the actual world because it fails to conform to the Ideal is an offshoot of the seductive and perennial Manichean heresy," the subordination of moral principle, of the "Ideal," to reality, the substitution of pragmatic expediency for prudential application of principle, is *the* modern heresy.)

If the Soviet threat is primarily a Russian threat, then it can be handled by civilized men as the eighteenth and nineteenth centuries handled their disputes—by diplomacy, by pressures, by limited warfare conducted by enemies who nevertheless share a universe of moral discourse. Then it is possible to fight, and live at peace, and fight again, if need be, for limited objectives. That is, then it is possible to coexist with the enemy. Then it is, indeed, deeply immoral to think in any other terms than those of coexistence.

But if the essential dynamic of the enemy is an ideology directed towards the destruction of religion, of freedom, of the very kind of moral being we regard man to be; and if those who hold that ideology are pledged by its very nature to a crusade to make the world over in its image—then it is immoral to base long-term policy on anything less than the destruction of that ideology by all means in our power.

And, *in these circumstances,* I would have to say that I regard Mr. Burnham's statement that "This is not a moral . . . problem," and his further statement that "if morality enters in at all on this point, it is immoral for one nation *not* to try to coexist peacefully with every other—no matter what their regimes," as inadequate to the demands, not only of anti-Communist strategy, but of moral principle as well.

The Relativist "Re-evaluates" Evil

(National Review, May 4, 1957)

Nowhere are the ravages of relativism more dramatically apparent than in the effective attitude towards Communism that has been displayed by the leaders and hangers-on of the intellectual Establishment during the past few months. I emphasize *effective* attitude, for of course everybody is "against Communism."

Effective anti-Communism, however, requires an uncompromising understanding that Communism is evil, in comparison with which and against which our heritage, despite all its imperfections, is good. But the relativist philosophical miasma which penetrates every corner of the Establishment blinds the eye to the very existence of good and evil—and *a fortiori* to the conception of any historical situation as a confrontation of good and evil.

Therefore, since the present historical situation is in fact such a confrontation of good and evil, the relativist mind is totally incapable of dealing with it. Hence, the acres of trash on the subject of foreign policy which have appeared in print in every quarter since the Geneva conference. Only the morbid wit of a Swift could do justice to the intricate pseudo-erudition, the desperately complicated mumblings, beneath which the experts and the journalists bury miles deep the dire issue they pretend to be discussing.

Walter Lippmann, for example, in a recent issue of the *New Republic* fills page after weary page begging us "to try to find our bearings," conjuring us to recognize with due humility that our beliefs have no ultimate foundation, that our "picture of ourselves and of our place in the world and of our role in the history of mankind is no longer valid." In the stock image of relativist rhetoric, he urges on us the parallel of "the change from the Ptolemaic to the Copernican astronomy"—from the benighted time when we considered "the culture, the ideology of the western society" as firm and universal truth to our modern situation when we must recognize that no longer can there be any claim to universality and objectivity for our beliefs. They are only one set of culture patterns among many, and, presumably, no more valid than the others.

At least, the difference between their validity and that of the others ("of Moscow . . . Peiping, Delhi, and who knows, perhaps eventually, also Cairo") is not important enough to fight for. The "terrifying destructiveness of the hydrogen bomb," together with an enlightened Copernican understanding of the relative nature of Western and Christian values, seems to Mr. Lippmann to make President Eisenhower's "historic declaration that there is now no alternative to peace" a self-evident axiom.

The practical conclusions for American foreign policy which he draws from this axiom are what might be expected, and I do not propose to discuss them here. They are the prevalent proposals for surrender before Soviet advance that are being universally put forward by the Establishment: "evacuation of the European continent up to the Soviet border by the Red Army in the East and by the British and American Armies in the West"; "the unification of Germany" (no guarantees of what kind of Germany, of course); and a general American stance against "imperialism" and "colonialism."

Granted the premises, there is not much to be said against these proposals. If we have nothing to fight for, and are mortally terrified of fighting anyway, they are as good as any others. Compared to some other hypothetical courses, they might indeed postpone the day of final surrender and a Soviet America by a few years. But if what we are concerned with is not the date of our defeat, but the choice between the acceptance of defeat and a fight for victory, then it is not to Mr. Lippmann's immediate proposals, but to the beliefs and judgments that form his proposals that we must direct our attention.

In the end, this is a matter of intellectual and spiritual decision—of resolution, of honor, of daring, of all the other outmoded virtues that to a relativist are dangerous impulses, to be measured on some "authoritarian personality" scale. It is a matter of that devotion to truth and right that prepares a man to fight, whatever the risk, whatever the possible holocaust, against ingrained evil.

Such an attitude is a rock upon which to stand, even if in the temporal order there is danger that one may be crushed upon that rock. But Mr. Lippmann, and those who think like him, found their position upon the shifting sands of what they choose to call the realities of the times, that is, upon that which from day to day happens to be the case. Technological developments, sociological fashions, ephemeral political events— these are their realities.

The one reality they will not face is that the deep truths upon which Western civilization is founded are challenged as they have never before been challenged, by an enemy who believes in his error as we have ceased to believe in our truth, an enemy who worships his Luciferian goddess of History with an intensity that demands the total conquest of the world.

The attitude of that enemy is clearly evidenced in the bold threatenings of Khrushchev last week. If we believed in our truth as he believes in his error, our reply would be: 1) Don't worry about our giving aid to Gomulka. We have no intention of giving *any* aid to *any* Communist government, yours, or Gomulka's or Tito's, or Mao's, or anyone else's. 2) We *will* help *anyone* who rises against your tyranny *anywhere*. 3) Since it is East Germany that seems to be worrying you right now, we put you on notice that we have learned our lesson from Hungary and that we are prepared to atone for our betrayal there. We shall do what we think necessary in the event of an East German revolution. Furthermore, if West Germans help East Germans, and you raise a finger against West Germany, we will regard your act as a *casus belli* and will reply to your aggression with all necessary force.

The *Times* Finds Another Nice Communist

(National Review, July 6, 1957)

Hope springs eternal in the breast of the New York *Times*—particularly hope that somewhere, sometime it can find a Communist who isn't really a Communist. Years ago it was Mao Tse-tung and his agrarian reformers; during the war, Stalin almost qualified; then it was Tito, then Malenkov, then Gomulka; and now it is Mao Tse-tung again.

In each instance this enthusiasm has been justified by a distorted interpretation of the statements of the Communist leaders themselves. In each instance in the past, even a moderate understanding of Communist language and of Marxist-Leninist theory, combined with elementary skill in exegesis, in the art of elucidating a statement against its conceptual background, would have been sufficient to establish unmistakably that the pet Communist of the moment was uttering good Communist doctrine, that he remained a Communist—and, by definition, our enemy. So it is now again with Mao Tse-tung.

Last February Mao stood before the Supreme State Conference of China and delivered a speech, "The Correct Handling of Contradictions among the People." It was an able and striking analysis in the classical Marxist-Leninist tradition. Everything he said was firmly based upon Communist revolutionary principle; even the tactical propositions he propounded have their parallel in previous Communist history, notably in the period of Lenin's New Economic Policy. Only the particular application to China was new—that, and the peculiar grace that Chinese phrases translated into English always carry.

On June 18 the text of the speech was released, and the next day printed in full in the New York *Times*. That day and the day after the *Times* published several articles and an editorial commenting on the speech. Mao's unexceptionable Communist teaching, directed toward the instruction of the Chinese Communist Party and its followers at a specific tactical stage of the Chinese revolution, is hailed as a new doctrine, a break with totalitarian conceptions, an endorsement of "democratic freedoms."

What precisely did Mao say to bring about this dancing in the editorial rooms of the *Times*, this excited preparation of the fatted calf—with a seat in the UN Security Council, to boot? Nothing heretical, nothing that Lenin had not said again and again, that has not been repeated a hundred times in Communist classes and training schools. He enunciated the Hegelo-Marxist truism that everything existing moves by contradiction, unification, and new contradiction. He repeated with brilliant formulation and illustrations the classical theory that some contradictions can only be resolved by violence ("antagonistic contradictions"), while others ("contradictions among the people") can be resolved by ideological struggle.

What Mao is saying, in language that has been heard for decades in every Communist Party, is that the same measures must not be applied against "misguided elements" as against "the enemy." But who is "the enemy"? Quite frankly and openly Mao says that it all depends upon the strategical and tactical goals of the Party leadership at any particular time:

> The term "the people" has different meanings . . . in different historical periods. . . . During the Japanese aggression, all those classes, strata and social groups that opposed Japanese aggression belonged to the

category of the people, while the Japanese imperialists, Chinese traitors and the pro-Japanese elements belonged to the category of enemies of the people.

During the war of liberation, the United States imperialists and their henchmen, the bureaucrat-capitalists and landlord class, and the Kuomintang reactionaries . . . were the enemies of the people, while all [who] opposed these enemies belonged to the category of the people.

At this stage of building socialism, all [who] approve, support and work for the cause of Socialist construction belong to the category of the people, while those social forces and groups that resist the Socialist revolution . . . are enemies of the people.

The "people," then, are those who go along with the line of the Party at any given moment. They are the ones with whom one uses peaceful coercion; "enemies," "counter-revolutionaries," one "suppresses." Now that 15,000,000 of the latter have been murdered, there are, for the time being, comparatively few around; and the emphasis shifts to the more peaceful modes of dealing with those who do not understand every detail of what is expected of them. But, should the line change again, so that people who are now "people" become "enemies," or should a new crop of intrepid resisters arise, even under the present line, Mao's emphasis on the "non-antagonistic resolution of contradictions among the people" will quickly shift to "ruthless revolutionary action against the counter-revolutionaries."

Limited discussion among those who support "the socialist path and the leadership of the Party," emphasis for the time being upon bringing greater unity into the ranks of those supporters, rather than upon the earlier task of physically exterminating the most determined opponents of Communism: this, the New York *Times* calls "a recommendation for a 'blossoming' of democratic freedoms among the people."

Even granted that this tactical turn, this de-emphasis on violence should last for a while, what, we may ask the *Times*, is the cheering about? If the regime consolidates its power with fewer lynchings and fewer firing squads, if less blood shows, is the agony any less for the millions who die of internal hemorrhage under the tightening pressure of totalitarianism? And as for the United States, we are still explicitly foremost among the "enemies," against whom violence is the proper tactic.

How, in a word, on any basis is there anything in Mao's speech to justify celebration? Why does the *Times* present the most able of living Commnist leaders as a prophet of sweetness and light?

In 1958, as confusion on the Communist issue became worse confounded, I attempted to analyze the possible courses of American action.

Dilemmas of Foreign Policy

(National Review, March 29, 1958)

A curious air of unreality seems to pervade what is said and written these days on American foreign policy. And this quality is as pronounced in the thoughtful studies of a Kennan or a Kissinger as in the simple nostrums of an Eisenhower or the hysterical whinings of a Norman Cousins. What is lacking is not awareness of crisis, nor even (for example in Kissinger) honest and careful effort to analyze its aspects and prescribe instrumentalities with which solutions might be achieved. What gives the discussion, the analyses, the proposals, that air of unreality which (to my mind at least) seems to pervade them is the refusal to face simultaneously all the principled issues involved, simultaneously to see both sides of our dilemma, no matter how fearful the contradiction that may be disclosed.

This refusal takes several forms: a desire to simplify what

cannot be simplified, to grasp one or the other horn of the dilemma of freedom or peace; or a concentration upon means and instrumentalities with such single-mindedness that the principled issues are simply ignored.

There are two kinds of simplification, of which the first is greatly the more dangerous. In the first, the horrors of modern military technology are so central to the mind that freedom and the values of Western civilization become secondary to biological survival. In the second, there is full recognition that freedom and the good must always be fought for if they are to survive, but the power of the enemy and the terrible potential results of the measures necessary to defeat him are minimized: the patent facts of technological reality are pooh-poohed, and the immensity of the moral determination necessary to the defense of freedom is reduced to a simple paradigm.

But more prevalent than these escapes from reality, these simplifications, is the instrumentalist approach which simply ignores the principled issues, while the abilities of powerful minds are diverted to weaving a scholastic web of argument about means: tactical nuclear weapons, little wars, "relaxation of tension."

These evasions of the issue are understandable enough. A powerful instinct urges flight from full awareness of the problem. A fear exists below conscious expression that it may be of such a character and magnitude that no satisfactory solution can be achieved by the human intellect; that the defense of the freedom and the values which the West has always felt to be the way and the end of man's existence may be impossible without the risk of the extermination of the human species, of the race that has borne witness to those values.

To this fear it is not enough to answer as one is impelled to do: if a choice must be made between the claims of the good, and of the freedom essential to human movement toward the good, and the claims of survival, then freedom and the good, being transcendentally based, take absolute precedence in the hierarchy of values over the survival of the species, over bio-

logical ends. It is one thing for a person to decide for the good
at the risk of death for himself—the right and noble decision
of a virtuous man; it is another thing to will that decision upon
tens of millions of other men, women and children. A moral
problem exists—as desperate a one as human beings have ever
faced. If only war, with all it means today, can vindicate the
truths for which it is man's function to live, and if the means
necessary to that vindication are, or will shortly be, as destructive of human life as rational examination would seem to indicate, what is the moral and political duty demanded of us?

One thing is clear: There can be no retreat from the primary
duty of standing for the right. If the Soviet Union is not merely
a foreign imperialist power, strong, threatening, inimical to our
national interests, but is the state form taken by a materialist
faith determined to rule the world and wipe out on the earth
the very memory and image of man as a free being called
to goals beyond material power and material satisfaction—then,
the destruction of this state is a clear duty.

It is no answer to say that the vice that Communism represents has eaten in another form into our own vitals, to ask what
right we have, ourselves half committed to socialism and materialism, to set ourselves forth as champions of human freedom
and the human spirit. If we can raise ourselves to view steadily
and wholly the moral crisis at which we stand and to act in the
full light of our understanding, then the inner corruption will
be purged away in the very act of recognizing the true reality
of the external corruption and of girding our will to stand
radically against it.

There is no question or doubt of the clarity of the enemy on
the basic problem. It is expressed throughout the canon-
ical writings of Communism; it is implicit in the very being
of Communists. Materialists though they are, they do not
concern themselves with survival as an end. It is an older
and a blacker materialist vision than the pallidities of relativism
that inspires them: to seize the wheel of history, to wipe out
the heavens, to remake the world and man; and they are com-

mitted either to victory in that struggle over whoever stands against them or, in Marx's words, to "the common ruin of the contending classes."

Nor can our responsibility be lifted from our shoulders by reliance upon the magical transformation of the "uncommitted third of the world" into a bulwark that will somehow stop Communism without action upon our part—a bulwark to be raised by world-wide WPA and world-wide fireside chats broadcast in forty languages by the Voice of America. Even if the ancient civilizations of Hinduism, of Buddhism and Taoism, of Islam, were not departed from their foundations, it is not their visions of reality, however profound, that could stand against the Communist assault upon the autonomy of the person. It is Western civilization that has grasped, by understanding and by grace, this, the highest concept of man in the history of the race. It is Western civilization that has imperfectly, hesitantly, with contradictions and manifold setbacks, moved towards expressing it in practice. Upon the West and the West alone rests the responsibility to destroy Communism. And in the West it is only the United States that has the power and—however sapped— the will to champion in action the civilization of which it is the latest son.

The responsibility to decide is on our shoulders, and however we turn and squirm, like an uneasy Atlas, we cannot shake it loose. No tolerant mother or skillful father is going to open the nursery door and say, "You've tried to solve that problem long enough. This is the way to do it."

Nor can we take refuge behind the self-warming thought that we are not aggressors, that we want peace; and if the Soviet Union is as bad as some people say, one day it will attack us, and then we can fight with full assurance that we are the aggrieved party and have taken no steps to bring about the disaster. The Soviet Union will never attack us so long as we yield to it (as we have this dozen years, step by step and point by point) everything it wants, from Peiping to Budapest to Cairo, because "nuclear war is unthinkable." From the Middle East through Africa and Latin America, from Indonesia through India and Pakistan, from East Germany through West Germany and Western Europe, the ice sheet, sometimes slowly, sometimes faster, will cover the world. As long as we do not recognize the sheer evil that is advancing for what it is, we shall retreat step by step.

What then, when Communism stands at our boundaries? The next era might be long, but unless at that late hour we reared up and—aggressively—struck out against the evil at long last recognized, there would still be no war. A Sovietized UN would bring ultimatum after ultimatum against us, designed to destroy all forces of resistance. Each would seem, if we retained our present attitude towards Communism, too small a thing (like Budapest) to endanger the survival of the human race. Unless we recognize the character of our enemies and take the initiative, we shall be defeated. The one thing we dare not do is to await supinely the unfolding of their plan of campaign.

But what, to return to what I have said earlier, of the moral problem involved in taking that initiative and risking the unleashing of total nuclear war? If that evil and the greater evil of Communist world domination are held simultaneously in the mind, and if wishful thinking and concentration upon arid instrumentalities are eschewed, only two moral alternatives remain, I believe.

One course would be to take up the championship of the world and, by ultimatum after ultimatum, drive the Kremlin forces back to their narrowest limits, prepared each time to fight at any risk if our ultimatum were denied, until finally we destroyed by ultimatum or by force the very center of the Communist power. This is the only meaning implicit in our rhetoric of "liberation," a rhetoric which is not forgotten in the moral realm nor in the hearts of the enslaved peoples, however convenient it may be to use it in an election campaign and then forget it. But this, the strength and the character of our enemy being what it is, would almost inevitably result in world-wide nuclear warfare.

Or, if that eventuality is one that we cannot accept, if, recognizing clearly the great evil of Communist domination, we refuse to will the lesser evil of biological extermination, then it would seem time to stop sneering at the concept of Fortress America as a Neanderthal survival of a pre-Roosevelt age.

It is only children's games to pretend that anything but the ultimate weapon restrains the Soviets. And present technological developments have brought about a situation in which that weapon will shortly be as effective based in the continental United States (and on our naval forces) as in any "advanced bases." If, on deep moral grounds, we are not prepared to act aggressively, let us retreat to our own borders, decide the boundaries, whatever they may include (our own territory and Latin America alone, or with it the islands—England, Japan, Formosa —or even the peninsula of Western Europe), that we regard as essential to the survival of the Western spirit. Standing within our boundaries, let us state that if this line is breached, we will fight with all our power. If we cannot accept the responsibility of bringing upon the world the immediacy of modern warfare, if we hope that time and Providence will somehow display a solution other than those which now starkly face us, then at least let us draw back from our shameful promises to the oppressed, from our expenditure of money and men in far-flung endeavors that have no aim and only swell the power of bureaucracy. Let us settle in our own sphere, devoting our resources to building a free life, emblazoning on our flag the old American motto of the rattlesnake flag: "Don't tread on me."

Either of these policies—aggressive attack or Fortress America —would be open-eyed, clear upon the issues, devoted to the preservation of freedom and the essential being of man. But the policy upon which we proceed today, and most of the discussion of it, indeed the very atmosphere within which all discourse upon foreign policy is conducted, is characterized by a painful shuffling, is blind to the realities that overshadow all our choices. Such blindness is a form of madness, of emotional rejection of

the world as it is. And it has been written: Those whom the
gods wish to destroy, they first make mad.

The years 1959 and 1960 were those of Mikoyan's and Khrush-
chev's visits to the United States, of the "spirit of Camp David,"
of the Geneva Conference, of "coexistence" rampant.

What Price a Patch of Sand?

(National Review, January 31, 1959)

The triumphal tour of Anastas Mikoyan brings into startling
and excruciating focus the accelerating decay of the American
will to resist Communism. Through the length and breadth of
American society—by the President and the Vice President, by
Senators and Congressmen, by the editorial writers of our great
newspapers, by leading industrialists and state and local officials
in Cleveland, Chicago, Detroit, San Francisco, Los Angeles,
New York, everywhere he has gone—he has been received like
a conquering hero. The few protesting voices—a George Meany,
a Congressman Judd, a General Trudeau, the Archbishop of
St. Augustine—have only served, like the isolated bands of
pickets whose strangled protests have been raised here and
there, to point up the slavering good-will with which the leaders
of our country, politicos and capitalists alike, have greeted this
architect of slavery.

Disgraceful though it would have been at any time, what
makes this exhibition of abasement so frightening is the realization that it could never have occurred before, that we are witnessing an almost unanimous refusal, on the part of those to
whom the nation has a right to look for leadership, to see evil
as evil, a celebration of abandonment of self-respect and of the
confidence in the rightness of our traditions and our institutions
that once enabled us to call an enemy of God and man, an

enemy of God and man. Even during World War II, when an uncritical emotionality glorified "our Soviet ally," nothing like what has happened in recent weeks would have been possible.

The Mikoyan episode lights up, as with a lightning flash, the steep and precipitous road we have step by step descended. It is one of those events, not so intrinsically dramatic in themselves that register and mark the development of a historic trend. More dramatic things have happened in the past few years —the strategy of defeat in Korea, the shameful flirtations with Tito and Gomulka, the American betrayal of the Hungarian revolt; but each of these involved a series of complex judgments and decisions, judgments and decisions made on a high and cloistered level, where reasons and counter-reasons complicated the issues. Grand strategy, Machiavellian design, the dictates of prudence, might be adduced in support of a series of actions which seemed to conscious conservatives to constitute a pattern of slow surrender; still, it was a matter of deducing from the pattern of top-level decisions a conclusion as to the extent to which the leading circles of American society were permeated with the suicidal anti-Western concepts of Liberalism.

Mikoyan's royal reception, however, was not primarily the result of a top-level decision. It was not conceived with some purported subtle Machiavellian purpose or dictated by the needs of a grand strategical maneuver. It was a spontaneous outpouring, an unconstrained reflection of the understanding the great majority of the leaders of American society have of Communism and the Communist threat to civilization. It represented an eager willingness to buy any patch of sand in which to bury our heads, to do almost anything to avoid facing the hard necessity that separates right from wrong.

This is the differentiation we refuse to make. We look for accommodations, comfortable compromises that require no sacrifice—and as the years slip by, we find ourselves compromising and accommodating ourselves to deeper and deeper retreat.

It is not only in foreign policy that this "slippage" occurs. A dozen domestic examples could be cited. We hail Eisenhower for his "economy" in proposing a near-80-billion-dollar budget when a few years ago (as Mr. Bozell has pointed out in these pages) we castigated the statist danger of a much lower Truman budget. The 1952 choice between a Taft or a MacArthur on the one hand, and an Eisenhower on the other, has become the 1960 choice between a Nixon and a Rockefeller—and not even Mr. Nixon's strongest supporters among conservatives would, I think, deny the decline in conservative standards that this represents.

Constant slipping of the issues of the struggle more and more in the direction of the enemy—whether it be Soviet Communism externally or Liberal statism internally—is the result not of a predilection towards corruption on the part of those of solid conservative instincts, who nevertheless find themselves always surrendering forward positions and attempting to defend positions further to the rear, but rather of a fundamental error in their understanding of the situation in the world today.

The Communists abroad, and the collectivists in our midst, are each in their different ways fully committed to ideologies that cannot be resisted piecemeal by a process of give-and-take and accommodation. The one ideology operates with terror and force based upon the Soviet state machine; the other operates domestically by intellectual and political pressure: both challenge the continued existence of Western civilization and traditional American society.

The desire for accommodation, the suspicion of sharp ideological struggle, which in a normal age would be the justified attitude of conservatives concerned with the maintenance of the fabric of society, become, under these circumstances, a recipe for defeat. Against determined ideological challenge, the only defense is firm, ideologically conscious resistance and counterattack.

The "slippage" of national understanding and national morale lit up by Mikoyan's tour, like the "slippage" in conservative resistance to domestic collectivism, can only be overcome by a conservative leadership that states its position boldly and stands upon it uncompromisingly, instead of constantly searching for a lesser evil with which to block the progress of a greater one.

The Tune Is Wrong

(National Review, April 11, 1959)

A friend of *National Review,* a man for whose contributions to the fight against Communism I have the greatest respect, writes to challenge my negative estimate of Harry and Bonaro Overstreet's book, *What We Must Know about Communism (National Review,* February 28). Their book is, he thinks, "the best job that has yet been done on the subject from the viewpoint in which it was presented."

That viewpoint is the viewpoint of Liberalism and relativism, and I would maintain that what the Overstreets do is certainly far from the best that has been done, even from that position. Sidney Hook and a whole battery of writers for the *New Leader* have long since pressed the dialectic between Liberalism and Communism as far as it will go. To the degree that it is possible to mobilize determined resistance to Communism on the basis of the Liberal outlook, they have done it.

But it is not because there have been better critiques of Communism from the Liberal point of view than the Overstreets' that I criticized it as I did. There have been worse ones too. The Overstreets have done their homework reasonably well; their book shows acquaintance with the mass of documentation on Communism that has been accumulated in recent years; and even though their citation of Communist sources is largely from secondary authorities, and sometimes vitiated by the psychologism of such interpreters as Nathan Leites, the material quoted is relevant.

Despite all these good features, however, the net effect of the book, either as a presentation of what Communism is or as an instrumentality for the strengthening of our anti-Communist action, is unsatisfactory. Many of the details are right, but the over-all result is wrong. It is as though the Overstreets were singing a song, all the words of which they had learned but the tune of which they simply could not grasp.

No matter how much they read, they cannot understand Communism because a dry and bloodless philosophy shuts them off from an understanding of what Western Christendom has been and what it still can be, from an understanding of the nature and the destiny of men, from an understanding of what the titanic struggle with Communism is about. Certainly, when we are approaching the sharpest crisis in the war of Communism on the West, when what is demanded of us is firmness and a willingness to die if need be, understanding of the enemy will not be enhanced, nor the kind of desperate determination we need be inspired, by the pallid preferences the Overstreets offer us.

What is missing from their presentation of Communism is both its evil and its strength. And this for good reason. Like all the scientistic, they cannot grasp its evil because their scientism blinds them to the impiety that puts man in the seat of God, the impiety expressed in the central Marxist statement: "Philosophers have previously thought about the world; the point, however, is to change it."

To think about the world, to understand as best one can the truth given to men by their Creator and to try to live by it: this is the content of the high tradition of the West, as, with less exalted consciousness, it has been of all civilization. It is something to live for and to die for. Against it, the Communist faith—that man can make himself and his world—stands as an absolute opposite. But this too is a faith—an evil faith, but still a faith—and from this faith the strength of Communism proceeds.

To the Overstreets, however, this confrontation of two faiths— one true, the other false; one glorying in creation, one bent on twisting and turning the world to the specifications of an overweening ideology—to the Overstreets this confrontation does not exist. What they would bid us see as the glory of our civilization is its "methods," and what they concentrate upon in their indictment of Communism is its methodology. Granted, some of the methods they see as the characteristic virtues of our civilization are good methods ("the parliamentary process," "federal structure"); but some ("reform," "multiple experiment centers") are meaningless unless they are related to substantive ends, ideals, values. And all are secondary to the fundamental beliefs which have made the West and which alone can justify resistance to Communism *à outrance* in an atomic age. Who wants to die, why *should* anyone want to die, for "multiple experiment centers"?

From the beginning of the book, when they speak of Communism as an enigma, to the end when, basing themselves upon Norman Cousins, they propose as our primary goal something called "inclusiveness" (that is, it would seem, a globalled equalization of everybody's experiment centers), the Overstreets never come to grips with the basic issue.

"A strange new force has entered our world," they write, "the strangest and most enigmatic in all history." But there is nothing enigmatic about the meaning and the values of Communism, however contradictory and devious Communist tactics may seem to be. In the *Communist Manifesto* Marx and Engels wrote 110 years ago: "Communists disdain to conceal their views and aims. They openly declare that their ends can be attained only by the forcible overthrow of all existing social conditions." And no Communist has ever repudiated those words.

Their goal is clear, and their tactics would be ineffective if we, basing ourselves upon our own values, would always keep before us our duty to destroy so sworn and open an evil. Our tactics *should* be the easier and the more effective because the ends of our enemy are so openly expressed—but they *will* be only if we keep the issue clearly in mind and stand firmly for those ultimate values upon which our glory has been raised. Books like *What We Must Know about Com-*

munism, emanating from minds that grasp neither the ultimate good of our heritage nor the ultimate evil of Communism, confuse the issue and blunt determination.

They Cry "Peace, Peace," When There Is No Peace

(National Review, October 10, 1959)

The cold war is officially over. The President of the United States has grasped the hand of the Jailer of All the Russias in vows of friendship, and together they have issued a joint declaration of peace. The peace of the purge, the peace of the slave camp, the peace of the murder of nations receives the sanction of the United States.

Without the firing of a shot, we have suffered the greatest defeat in our history. By our recognition of the Communist tyranny as a legitimate and integral participant in the comity of civilized nations, we have surrendered our honor, betrayed our moral duty to the enslaved peoples of the world, and— the character of Communism being what it is—we have immensely assisted it on its road to world conquest.

This fateful step down the road to surrender is the consummation of a process that began in July at the time of the first session of the Geneva conference. There, in abjectly agreeing to discuss Khrushchev's brutal ultimatum on Berlin, the course was set. An immoral decision was taken—a decision springing from a deep illness of the American soul. As I wrote at that time in these pages:

"The issues of life and death come home in the end to nations as to the individual persons who make up nations. Since neither individuals nor nations can live forever, since there is a temporality about their fate that is beyond human control, the problem confronting them is not primarily whether they will live or die, but whether their mode of action is such that they comport themselves with honor and valor and virtue, whatever the outcome may be. The horror of life today is that the very meaning of these ends is almost forgotten. Therefore, the direction of American statecraft heads not toward heroic victory or tragic defeat, but toward a whimpering amalgam of farce and pathos."

The farce of Geneva has been followed inevitably by the pathetic spectacle of the President's invitation to Khrushchev and the *Bruderschaft* talks at Camp David. Unless a radical change in the inspiration of American foreign policy occurs— a change which will take a miracle of resolution on the part of the American people and a complete change of leadership to bring about—the Summit, the many Summits that follow will be successive steps upon the road to the death, "not with a bang, but a whimper," of the United States and of Western civilization.

More dramatically than Geneva, than the Camp David talks, even than the future Summits, the triumphal tour of Nikita Khrushchev through the United States stands as symbol of the new age we are entering—the age of coexistence in which we fawn upon and adulate our executioner. For the first time in the history of the United States, a sworn and implacable enemy has been brought to our shores—and in objective historical terms, he has been brought here for one reason and one reason alone; to assuage him, to pay him blackmail, in the trembling hope that if we pretend that Hungary and East Germany and Berlin and the tens of millions of victims of Communist purge and forced starvation and slave camps do not exist and have never existed, we might avoid the necessity of acting like men, of standing against him, of risking war and death.

No one can say how far in this direction it was intended our retreat should go, once the decision was taken to negotiate with Khrushchev under his ultimatum and to invite him here. But after the key decision was made, everything else followed from the inner logic of the situation.

Consider the sequence of events. Those who understood

the meaning of the visit spoke out. Mr. Robert Welch and the Committee Against Summit Entanglements, Freedom House, the Allen-Bradley Company, The International Rescue Committee spread calls to resistance across the pages of our newspapers. The Committee For Freedom For All Peoples, bringing together an incredible spectrum of Americans of all domestic political beliefs, organized its local committees throughout the country and spread its call for national mourning to press, radio and television, breaking through the miasma that preceded the visit.

And the American people in their good sense responded—in Washington and New York and Los Angeles Khrushchev was met with silence and hostility. Stung by his mass reception, by the sharp hostility of the leaders of American labor, by the pointed remarks of such men as Mayor Poulson of Los Angeles, Khrushchev was spoiling the design, revealing his true rocket-rattling, world-conquering identity.

Then the White House and the State Department swung into action. The press was dragooned. The notables who wined and dined him were persuaded to change their tune. A travesty of truth was hastily created to placate the tyrant once again. It is hard to see what underlying motive can explain this progressive placation on the part of the powers-that-be (and, it must be admitted, the receptivity of a large section of the American people to their urging), but ignoble fear.

Two generations of the relativist teaching that denies the existence of values transcending the temporal life of a man seem to have done their job. Ironic as it is that Camp David, where Eisenhower met in Munich-like negotiation with one tyrant, was the Shangri-La from which Roosevelt fought an earlier and punier tyrant, it is perhaps more ironic that it was a Communist and an atheist, La Pasionaria, who during the Spanish Civil War proclaimed, "It is better to die on your feet than to live on your knees," while we, the most powerful nation the world has produced, grovel in fear of death, "negotiating" with an enemy devoted to our destruction. And yet it is we, to whom eternal truth has been opened, who should—inspired by our tradition—be devoted to *his* destruction, not to slothful hopes of survival at any cost.

Saved by the U-2

(National Review, June 4, 1960)

A total loss of perspective, akin to the disorientation from which astronauts are expected to suffer, is the inevitable result of attempting to judge moral and political matters by relativistic criteria. The absence of firm principles grounded outside of the flux of events leaves men at the mercy of events, constantly astounded, baffled and buffeted by them.

Thus, the set of events beginning with Khrushchev's blast at the United States before the Supreme Soviet on May 5 and culminating in the degrading spectacle of an American President publicly castigated in gutter language at Paris, overnight became the reality of the confrontation of Communism and Western civilization—replacing the set of events beginning with the Geneva Foreign Ministers Conference last summer and culminating in the Khrushchev trip to the United States and the idiotic manifestations of the "Spirit of Camp David" that followed it.

In the aftermath of a few days of national solidarity around the vilified and insulted President, the Democratic Advisory Council and most of the Presidential candidates of the Democratic Party have reacted with a shocking willingness to accept the campaign line Khrushchev worked out for them, while the Administration (apart from Eisenhower's capitulation on the U-2 flights in the face of Khrushchev's blustering) has so far shown an unaccustomed firmness of spirit. But the point is that both are reacting to what they conceive to be a great and dramatic change.

Yet nothing has changed. Nothing has changed since 1945 (in a sense, nothing has changed since 1917)—except the steady expansion of Communist domination, while with our superior power we stand by, ignoring the permanent reality, bewitched by the kaleidoscopic play of events.

As in our fatal fencing with shadows while Eastern Europe, China, key sections of the Middle East (and now Cuba) fell under Soviet sway, so both in our recent mood of coexistence and in our present scandalized reaction to the change of Soviet tactics, we have based our whole policy upon surface phenomena, oblivious to the hard continuing substance of the Communist battle plan and innocent of the kind of analysis and action demanded of us, were we guided by principles, not hypnotized by each new set of events.

As a result, things get turned into their opposites: if only Khrushchev had been willing to meet at the Summit, it would have been a great victory; the U-2 flights over Russia are the instrument of a great defeat.

In the light of reality, the reverse is the truth. The U-2 flights, which, like the tip of an iceberg, have revealed the immense military strength of the United States and shattered the myth of Soviet technological superiority, symbolize the only factor in the real situation which has prevented disasters much greater than those that have occurred and which gives promise of ultimate triumph, if we ever adopt policies based upon reality. However bungled the handling of the issue, and whatever the cause of the capture of Powers' plane, the whole affair represents a spirit of the offensive almost unique in the public manifestations of American policy in the last fifteen years.

It is this offensive spirit—centered, as Khrushchev has so violently insisted, in the Pentagon and even, it would seem, to some degree in the CIA—that alone explains why Khrushchev, despite his brutal ultimatum of November 1958, despite our cringing reactions to it (epitomized by the invitation to him to soil our land), despite all the apparent signs in his favor, has not dared to force the issue on Berlin and has now for the third time postponed his ultimatum another six months.

It is not through their strength that the Communists have made their advances, but by pouring into vacuums created by our timidity and by our acceptance of each new situation as an issue to be discussed in its own surface terms unrelated to the underlying reality, which is the certainty of victory or defeat for one side or the other.

That is why there is nothing to be concerned about, no "failure," no "diplomatic defeat" in the break-up of the conference at Paris. It is true that the circumstances were humiliating to our President, and through him to our country, but that humiliation would never have taken place had we not made the initial error of going to the conference. Will the tempo of our arming be any slower as a result of the break-up of the conference? If anything, it will be faster. Will Communist penetration of the Middle East, of Southeast Asia, of the Caribbean and Latin America, be affected one way or the other? Or the growth of European neutralism? Have we lost anything substantive through not having sat down at the Summit with Khrushchev?

On the other hand, consider what we might have lost at such a conference—lost because there was no single item on the agenda which bore any relation to our interests in the world struggle. What interest have we in disarmament and the end of nuclear testing, when our only hope of survival and ultimate victory—175,000,000 facing close to a billion—depends entirely upon superior technical military strength? What interest have we in discussing the status of Berlin, when the terms of the discussion rule out the liberation of Eastern Germany and Eastern Europe, the only conditions under which we could with honor remove our forces from Berlin? And cultural exchange? What is there we have to exchange with the masters of a slave society except our innocent tourists for their MVD operatives?

These were the subjects for "negotiation." Let us be grateful the discussion did not take place. "In six or eight months" Khrushchev offers us another opportunity. If we have learned anything, our answer will be: "Not in six or eight years—not until Communism ceases to exist."

The Mirage-World of Liberal Ideology

(National Review, July 2, 1960)

Concepts, ideas, beliefs, are the decisive factors in human history. They are, under the dispensation of Providence, the instruments with which men and nations and civilizations assert their primacy over brute nature and vindicate human destiny.

But concepts, to have this power, must more or less truly reflect reality. When a nation bases its policies upon concepts totally false to reality, sooner or later it pays a portentous penalty—and more probably sooner, when such concepts guide the foreign policy of a nation faced with an inveterate and powerful enemy determined upon its destruction. The fifteen years since the end of World War II have already seen the United States' world position decline from one of unchallengeable supremacy to a point where today a third of the world is in the camp of our enemies, and another third, the euphemistically entitled "uncommitted nations," is basically hostile to everything we stand for, while the leading nations with whom we share the heritage of Western civilization graciously put in the field a tithe of the military force which they fielded in 1914 out of a considerably smaller population.

Our retreat has been steady, punctuated with periods of catastrophic rout, such as the physical loss of China in 1949 and the moral loss of honor in Hungary in 1956. Another such rout now seems to be developing, with the crumpling of our northwestern frontier in Korea and Japan and the penetration of the Caribbean by the establishment of a Soviet base in Cuba.

The fact that we have allowed the events in Cuba and in Japan to take place brings into the sharpest of relief the role of concepts false to reality, the Liberal concepts upon which our policies have been based. Certainly for fifteen years we have had the power in Japan to make it into a firm bastion against the Communist world. The helplessness of the legitimate government of Japan, even against internal Communist terror, is not unrelated to our policies and our influence. Nor is there the faintest doubt that we have and have had the power to enforce the Monroe Doctrine in the only way that is significant today, by making certain that no government friendly to Communism exists in this hemisphere.

The refusal to recognize the true power relations between such countries as the United States and Japan or Cuba is the direct result of carrying into action the Liberal concept of the equality of all nations, compounded in the case of Cuba (as in Korea and the Dominican Republic) by the concept that it is in the interest of the United States to support any putatively popular movement against an existing government, irrespective of the position of that government in the over-all struggle with Soviet Communism.

If Japan is neutralized and our Western Pacific frontier is turned and crumpled; if the islands of Cuba and Santo Domingo become a Soviet *place d'armes;* if the Middle East and all Africa slip area by area into the Soviet grasp, until Communism rules from Capetown to Kamchatka—it will be the direct fruit of the application of policies based upon the Liberal concepts of the abstract equality of nations, the abstract evil of the prewar regime of Western domination of the world, and the abstract virtue of "national revolutionary movements." If we are drawn further and further, as now seems the case, into the quagmire of disarmament agreements and find ourselves facing a regimented regime controlling a population of a billion or a billion and a half, with a weapons technology no more powerful than theirs, it will be the result of the Liberal concept which regards "peace" as a goal of national policy in a world that contains a great empire messianically devoted to world conquest.

The truth of the situation is that we are living in a world in which only victory over the Soviet enemy can preserve our nation and the civilizational order for which it stands. No concepts that are not based first of all upon this reality can save us from disaster. All governments, parties, movements, throughout the world, have essential meaning for us only in relation to this reality.

Furthermore, we must rid ourselves of two Liberal concepts which, although they are contradictory, simultaneously guide our policies: 1) that we are so rich and powerful that we can bear the whole burden of defense of half the world and in addition support the socialist and welfarist economies of two-thirds of the world; and 2) that we are so weak that we must subordinate our policy to the demands of the nations we support and defend. The truth is that we are not so strong that we can do the former; but that we are comparatively so much stronger than the other nations of the non-Communist world that on us the responsibility of command in the struggle against Communism rests. If we are successfully to prosecute that struggle on the world-wide scale to which we have committed ourselves, then we shall have to restrict our expenditure to essentials and insist that the nations of Western Europe bring into being a hundred divisions, proscribe their Communist parties and cease to flirt with neutralism. Alternatively, we can only say, since we ourselves wish to survive, that we will have to husband our resources and limit our responsibility to the defense of an American fortress.

Whatever may be the case in the mirage-world of Liberalism, in the real world these are the three possible alternatives: an imperial policy of full responsibility and full command, based upon the realities of power relations in the world; a Fortress America policy, based upon the realities of our unaided strength; or the disaster towards which we are proceeding under the guidance of Liberal concepts.

As I have read over the material for this book, I have been pleased that there is very little I have written which I would not stand by today. My analysis in 1961 of the developing

Sino-Soviet conflict is, however, a definite exception. In what follows, it is true I was primarily concerned with analyzing the significance of Khrushchev's speech at the Moscow Conference of November, 1960—and that analysis I still hold by insofar as Marxist-Leninist Communists are concerned. *But the events of the last two or three years have made it clear to me that what is happening in China is outside the universe of Marxism-Leninism.*

It would be a rash man who, on the basis of the information we have today, would attempt to explain the full meaning of the policies of Mao Tse-tung and his followers; but one thing would seem to be obvious, the ideology which guides Mao's faction and the Red Guards is something utterly new in the Communist world, derived more from Bakunin than from Marx and Lenin. The Marxist-Leninist faction may still win out in China. In that case, I think it will be seen that my analysis will hold. But if those presently in the ascendancy continue to hold sway, that part of what follows which concerns China is dead wrong.

I reprint this material nevertheless, partly because it would be pusillanimous not to do so and partly because I think the basic analysis of Communist strategy is vital to an understanding of orthodox Soviet Communism in this period.

Communist Doctrine, Strategy and Tactics

(Modern Age, Summer, 1961)

Although Mr. Andrew Gyorgy in his article, "Relations within the Soviet Bloc: A Note on 1960 Developments," in the Spring, 1961 issue of *Modern Age*, provides many perceptive and stimulating insights, I would suggest that there is a most important dimension missing from his analysis. The theoretical continuity and world-wide universality of the Communist movement and of the ideology, theoretical and operational, which is integral to its every act and motion, must be constantly held in mind if the play of events within the Communist world—the shifts of positions and personalities—is to be understood in its true significance.

In my opinion, the various tonal developments which have occurred in the Communist world since Stalin's death are fundamentally without significance. It is as tonal developments, and only as such, that I would judge the various changes of leadership and "conflicts" of emphasis, which have occurred, which continue to occur, and to which, for the year 1960, Mr. Gyorgy devotes his attention. The great event, from the Communist point of view, of 1960 was the meeting of the 81 Communist Parties in Moscow in November. The Statement of that Conference and Khrushchev's Report on it, delivered in Moscow on January 6 of this year, constitute together proof that the Communist world still moves, as it always has moved, on the basis of a fundamental monolithic outlook and that the differences which exist within that world continue to be resolved, as they always have been resolved, on a principled basis derived from the ultimate Communist goal of world conquest under unitary leadership—in this case, the leadership of Nikita Khrushchev.

Every indication is that the November meeting was in effect the second Congress of the new form the Communist International has assumed (the first was held in 1957); that the Statement of the eighty-one Parties is equivalent to the Resolutions adopted by the seven Congresses of the Communist International; and that Khrushchev's Report is equivalent in political weight and authoritativeness to the major Reports of these Congresses. Therefore, this Report must be taken in the context of the major Communist documents of the last ten years: the main Reports to the 20th and 21st Congresses of the Communist Party of the Soviet Union and the material of the meeting of the international Communist Parties in Moscow in 1957.

Communist documents cannot be considered as *ad hoc* reactions to current situations, but only as the continuing development of a major medium-term line—established for "the period"—in the light of the particular developments of events. Interpretations of the recent Statement and Report which regard them as primarily reactions to possible Sino-Soviet strains, or to changes in the immediate technological-military situation, or to inner conflicts in the Kremlin, inevitably miss the point as that point is understood by the Communists for whose guidance the documents are issued and as they are understood as guides to action by the ruling circles of the Communist world.

From 1917 until approximately the end of World War II, the continuing Communist strategical position was founded upon a strategic estimate of the situation summed up in the phrase "capitalist encirclement of the socialist world." They considered themselves the smaller segment of the world, the less powerful segment of the world, totally surrounded by those whom they wished to conquer. On the basis of that estimate, the determining strategy was a defensive strategy: to consolidate forces and strengthen the position of Communism, and to work by every means of subversion, conspiracy and diplomacy to secure the material base (the Soviet Union . . . the doctrine of "socialism in one country") from which to move forward.

The years since World War II have constituted, from the Communist point of view, a new strategical period, a period of *offensive strategy.* It is not possible to date the origin of this new strategy too closely. Essentially it begins with the moment that the victory of World War II was assured. The major outlines of the new strategical estimate and the offensive strategy based upon it were contained in Stalin's last major work, *Economic Problems of Socialism in the USSR,* written shortly before his death. With the 20th Congress of the Communist Party of the Soviet Union, what had been developing in Communist consciousness was crystallized—sharply and clearly stated—as the guiding analysis for the period ahead:

The second phase has begun, the phase of socialist

encirclement, the period in which the power of Communism is moving forward ever faster, in which those
who resist are in retreat and on the defensive. This
is the phase of strategic attack, of the strategic
offensive.

The Communists have, in their view, entered the final phase
of the struggle for world domination.

While Communist tactics and methods of action vary from
day to day and hour to hour, depending upon the immediate
situation, the fundamental direction of their tactics is always
derived from their strategy.

During the first strategical phase, the phase of "capitalist
encirclement" and of the *strategic defensive,* Communists relied
primarily on *offensive tactics*—like a boxer who senses that
his opponent is stronger and attempts to hold him off with
jabs and footwork, to keep him off balance as much as possible.
During this period the tone, the attitude, the public directives,
the very mode of existence of Communism was primarily
offensive. Their stance bristled with constant emphasis upon
the irreconcilability of Communism with Western society.

As they have moved over to the *strategic offensive,* however,
the tactical emphasis has reversed. In this period the *strategic
offensive* demands *defensive tactics,* and for a very good reason.
There is only one development that in the Communist view
can interfere with the continuing forward march of Communism:
the consolidation in the West (which means primarily in the
United States) of an understanding of the totality of the
Communist threat; the consolidation in the West of a force
dedicated to the destruction of Communism; the emergence
in the West of a will which places the defeat of Communism
as decisive. The mode of their advance in this period of their
strategic offensive demands that we sleep.

Therefore, the *defensive tactics* (pointed up from time to
time with threats and blackmail and *démarches* which they feel
will not be seriously resisted) are dictated as modes of immobilizing and disarming us. The fundamental concept of these

tactics is the *concept of coexistence*, a concept which is central to all operations of the Communist movement today, to be achieved by every possible method—by propaganda, by diplomacy, by cultural exchange, by infiltration, and above all by influencing opinion in the West so that our clarity of vision and our will to resist will be paralyzed. The tactic of coexistence is an absolutely necessary corollary of the strategy of "socialist encirclement."

It is in the light of this strategical and tactical general line that the statement of the eighty-one Parties and Khrushchev's Report can be understood for what it is. This was not an emergency meeting called because of some intensification of the struggle between Russian and Chinese Communists. It was the second full Congress of the New Communist International, and it reaffirmed and carried forward the general line of world Communism as developed over the past decade.

It is true that certain differences of emphasis undoubtedly existed between Khrushchev's position and the "left" tendencies represented not only by the Chinese Party but by elements throughout the Communist Parties, including the Communist Party of the Soviet Union. It is equally true, although less attention has been paid to it, that differences existed between Khrushchev's position and "revisionist" positions, for which Tito was made the whipping boy, but which would not have received the attention they did were they not reflected in more "legitimate" circles. But those disagreements were resolved and absorbed into the main line of the Statement, Khrushchev's line, on the basis of reaffirmation of the policy of strategic offensive, tactical defensive.

The first, the doctrine of the strategic offensive, is contained in the analysis of "the balance of forces" in the world and the continued vaunting of Communist superiority; in the sharply stated aggressive position on Berlin and Germany; in the aggressive statement of policy for Cuba and Latin America; and in the assertion of a profound contrast between "local wars" and "wars of national liberation."

The second, the doctrine of defensive tactics, is contained in the placing of coexistence, the prevention of general war, and disarmament as the major line of the Communist movement.

It is made perfectly clear that the errors of the "revisionist Right" consist in the transformation of tactical doctrine into strategical doctrine, namely dependence on "coexistence" and "peaceful transformation" to bring about automatically victory for Communism; it is made equally clear that the errors of the "left" consist in the failure to understand that the tactic of coexistence is vital to success in a strategically offensive phase, and therefore to put dangerously aggressive tactics, which run the risk of awakening the West, in the place of the necessary masking tactics of coexistence and disarmament.

The concrete program which embodied the resolution of the different emphases (not a "compromise" of them, as it has been called) is expressed in four major points: (a) to further the widest possible movement throughout the world for "co-existence" and Western disarmament; (b) to threaten to transform any local war carried out by the West in its own defense into a general war (a new tactic—Communist "deterrence"); (c) to proclaim all-out support for all "wars of national liberation," that is, for *aggressive local wars against* the West; (d) to consolidate the balance of power in the Eurasian continent and decisively disrupt the Western alliance by carrying out under the umbrella of coexistence a determined campaign for the capture of Berlin and the neutralization of West Germany.

On the basis of the theoretical analysis of the strategical and tactical situation and by the promulgation of a practical program based on that analysis, a unified policy for the international Communist movement was hewn out; the ideological authority of Nikita Khrushchev as the leader of international Communism in all respects was confirmed; and a clearly directed if flexible program for the immediate future was laid down. That program, which is being carried out before our eyes, can be translated succinctly into: press the Communist advance in Asia, Africa, the Middle East and Latin America through "national revolutionary" movements and drive towards the neutralization first of Germany, then of Europe, while diverting the attention of the West—above all, of the United States— by a world-wide campaign for "coexistence" and disarmament.

The remaining columns in this chapter deal with a series of foreign policy issues of the Sixties—the Congo, Cuba, Vietnam, and problems of nuclear-missile strategic armament.

Abdication of Responsibility

(National Review, April 8, 1961)

The present outbreak of chaos and barbarism in the Congo (Independence for An Aspiring Nation, to the reverent brethren of the press and the State Department) is a shameful regression in human history, for which the responsibility rests not upon the Africans, but upon the West—and principally upon the paramount power of the West, the United States. It is one more portent of the whirlwind that we shall continue to reap unless we cease to sow the wind.

We do not blame children if they act like children, immaturely, intemperately, dangerously, when they are deserted by adults who are responsible for their guidance: we should not blame barbarians if they act like barbarians when they are deserted by those who have taken upon themselves responsibilities for raising them to civilization, and in doing so, have disrupted and destroyed the ancient continuity of their pre-civilized mode of existence.

This responsibility the West took for Africa when it still had confidence in itself and in the incomparable treasure its civilization carried with it. Having done so, there is no way in which it can morally relieve itself of the responsibility it assumed.

It has become fashionable to laugh at the phrase, "the white man's burden," but in the laughter what is forgotten, perhaps purposefully, is that the hegemony of Western civilization was indeed a burden, the assumption of which (despite all the imperfections and secondary motives in human action) represented high purpose, and confidence that the truth by which the West lived was the highest truth known to man. Behind all the self-congratulatory encomiums to which we treat ourselves about the "dissolution of colonialism" and the "end of imperialism," is the hard truth: decay of belief, failure of nerve and confidence, an immoral casting aside of burdens, a sloughing of responsibility.

The result of our abdication, under the conditions which exist in the world today, can only be Soviet domination, Communist slavery. But even if it were not for the Communist drive towards world domination, that abdication of responsibility by the West could result in nothing but chaos and decay. Not only is this true of areas of the world that have never progressed beyond barbarism, it is also true of the areas of ancient civilization—China, India, Islam. Those civilizations fell under the hegemony of the West, partly because they were decadent, partly because even at the time of their highest achievement, they represented a lower order of civilization than the civilization of the West with its glorious tension between belief in absolute transcendent value and belief in the terrestrial primacy of the individual person.

For China and India and the Perso-Arab world, as for Africa, the outcome of the West's failure to regain its self-understanding would be Communist lordship over a cemetery of the human spirit—and the moral responsibility would rest squarely upon us of the West who have put our hand to the plough and then looked back in spiritual weakness and intellectual indolence.

If it should be objected that this may be true of the West in general, but has no relevance to the United States, which was never a "colonial power," I would answer on two levels. In the first place, the United States is a child of the West grown to man's estate, and as such bears the responsibility of the civilization to which we owe our being. In the practical sphere, whether the Dutch were to remain in Indonesia and the British in India after World War II, whether today the French are to remain in Algeria, the Belgians to return to the Congo, the English and the Afrikaners to remain in South Africa, depended and depends upon our power and our decision.

But, in the second place, what of the American experience itself? Did we not make this nation by driving across a continent from sea to sea? Did we not in our earliest years assume hegemony of all the Americas? Did we not, with the Open Door policy, take upon ourselves the quasi-guardianship of China? Did we not in two World Wars vaunt ourselves champion of the values of Western civilization? Historically regarded, we may be no more guilty of retreat from responsibility than the older nations of the West, but we are in no position to plead a lesser guilt on the grounds of innocency.

The stark political realities of Western retreat are the direct product of decades of cultivation of characterological weakness on the basis of a sedulous propagation of the philosophical error which goes under the name of relativism: the doctrine that no truth in reality exists; that whatever a culture believes is as good as what any other culture believes (cannibalism or human sacrifice are not wrong, only "culturally relative" modes of human action); that therefore the West has nothing of which to be proud, nothing for which to fight, nothing worth dying for.

The reasons projected by the cultural relativists as foundation for their theories vary from year to year like Paris fashions. Anthropological discoveries, deep psychiatry, nuclear power, automation, the intellectually unwashed "insights" of the beatniks, space exploration—everything and anything is grist to the mill that grinds out theoretical justification for the constant demand for "a new look," any look that will spare the stern necessity of a return to the truths of our tradition. This is the smoke barrage that must be cleared away if we are to survive

and fulfill our potentialities—potentialities as glorious as they
are fraught with challenge to our spiritual and intellectual stamina.

The Myth of "The People's Revolution"

(National Review, July 29, 1961)

The spectacle of the United States, materially the world's
strongest power, allowing the enemy of all civilized humanity
to establish an armed base 90 miles off our shores, and thousands of miles from that enemy's center of power, is so politically preposterous—in a historical sense, so incredible—that
if it were related of a similar situation in the past, trained
historians would flatly deny its occurrence. The texts, they
would say, must have been corrupted, or the evidence presented was suspect or had been tampered with by later editors
desirous of making a tendentious point.

Yet it is happening right now; there can be no doubt about
it; the bitter and determined enemy of the United States,
of all the West, has with total impunity installed its agents
a few minutes by jet plane from Florida. There they sit, and
all we have done, even as gesture, to remove them is to send
a few hundred unsupported men to die in atrociously unequal
battle—and then to send Adlai Stevenson as the President's
herald to the countries of Latin America to apologize for
having even to this degree disturbed the equanimity of the
bearded Cuban commissar.

The entire situation remains incredible. One has to pinch
oneself to accept what is happening as reality. Nor can it be
explained simply by talking in general terms of the refusal
to face reality and the facts of power that are so characteristic
of the Liberal outlook which forms and guides our foreign
policy. After all, if you set up a machine gun a few hundred
feet from a Liberal's home and announce your undying affection and affinity for a powerful gang which has repeatedly

made clear that its intention is to rub him out at the earliest possible moment, even the Liberal would ordinarily take some steps to eliminate you—unless, of course, you could prove that you were a certified juvenile delinquent, whose actions were a helpless response to "an unfortunate social environment" and whose subservience to a murderous gang was all that one could expect, given the failure of society to provide everyone with a guaranteed annual income, a college degree, and a happy married life.

Ideological images can always blind the Liberal to reality. As a sadistic criminal becomes a "juvenile delinquent," to be "understood" and sociologized when the magic words "underprivileged," "deprived of love" are uttered, so a thrust forward into our vitals by the international Communist power machine becomes a phase in the great world revolution of the "underprivileged peoples." True, many of the Liberals have had second thoughts about Castro and the Movement of July 26. They do begin to recognize that something has gone wrong with their rosy dreams of Caribbean George Washingtons and Thomas Jeffersons. But these are peripheral thoughts; they do not dispel in the slightest the fog screen set up by the magic slogan, "people's revolution."

The proof? In the eating. Imagine the reaction of the Liberal Establishment if Hitler had similarly seized a West Indian island in 1937. The tranquility of Liberalism in contemplation of the "national revolutionary" advanced prongs of the Soviet drive towards world domination, its pusillanimity when it is moved to something like action, stem from the same kind of ideological bewitchment that leads to treating heartless murderers and rapists as cases for the social worker and the psychiatrist. The Cuban revolutionists who would play their part—puny in detail but vital to the far-flung plan of Communist world conquest—in destroying the civilization of the West are not treated for what they are because they represent the great "revolution of rising expectations," the upsurge of "the people."

This myth, which is rendering the Liberals spineless not only against Castroism, Nasserism, Lumumbism and Sukarnoism, but equally against the openly declared Communism of Lenin, Khrushchev and Mao Tse-tung, bids fair to become the winding sheet of Western civilization. The Liberals are its victims because they share in its profits. There was no "people's revolution" in Lenin's Russia or Hitler's Germany or Nehru's India, or in the multifarious springing toadstools the UN recognizes as "new nations." These regimes were created not by the people's desires, but by the inveterate urge for power of ideologically entranced intellectuals, treasonous to their culture, masking their ends behind the myth of the "people's aspirations." Likewise, the American Liberals themselves, heirs of Franklin Roosevelt and his transformation of American society, are the beneficiaries of the same kind of operation, much less violent, less extreme, but still a massively deleterious operation of ideologues touting themselves as representatives of "the people."

No wonder the Liberals are immobilized before the current mode of Communist advance, which is the development and exploitation of "national people's revolutions." Their own heritage of anti-Western ideology, projected as the democratic mandate of "the people," makes it impossible for them to recognize and act against the danger.

The Liberals cannot defend America in this its hour of crisis, for they accept as truth the immobilizing concepts behind which the enemy advances. To borrow a slogan from one of their own heroes, the order of the day, if America and the West are to live, must be *"Écrasez l'infame"*—"Wipe out the scandal." That scandal is first of all a Communist fortress in the Americas masquerading as a people's regime.

Enough of This Nonsense!

(National Review, August 26, 1961)

It is a military axiom that there is deadly danger inherent either in underestimating or in overestimating the enemy. Judging by the reactions of the American press, and of responsible American leaders generally, to the two major events of midsummer in the Soviet world—the publication of the draft of the new Program of the Communist Party of the Soviet Union and the putative multiple circumnavigation of the globe by Major Titov—we are managing the remarkable feat of underestimating *and* overestimating the Communist enemy at one and the same time.

With wild abandon, half enthusiastic, half masochistic, the Soviet "feat" in rocketry was celebrated in a bacchanalian press orgy. The New York *Herald Tribune,* the most abjectly hysterical of the newspapers I saw, under a massive across-the-page headline projected the movie hero mug of Titov in the largest picture I have ever seen in a non-tabloid (four columns across and nine inches deep), with a screaming caption: "I Am Eagle. I Am Eagle." And under it, in exploded type, the text of "What the Eagle's Saying to Earth." Other headlines: "A Cold War Victory for Khrushchev"; "A 'Red Star' Over the U.S." In the lower left-hand corner the only note of sanity: "City's Strollers Unaware, or Skeptical of Spaceman."

That sanity of the man in the street is what is so egregiously lacking in the assessment of the Titov episode by official American society. At the very worst, and taking Soviet claims (unconfirmed by independent verification) at face value, the space probes by the Soviet Union and the United States over the past couple of years would seem to show that only in one area, the development of massive thrust, are we behind, and there only by a year or so. In every other area—in sophistication of instrumentation, in complexity, in a multi-valued program—we are obviously far ahead.

For the future of rocketry, Tiros and Samos represent achievements of far greater potential. For contemporary military purposes, the Soviet "achievements" are meaningless, since with the gamut of our weapons systems presently available—SAC, Polaris, Atlas, Titan—we are more than sufficiently equipped to pulverize the Soviet empire.

But consider how little we made of Tiros, compared to the

multiple amplification we lent to Khrushchev's propaganda in the affair of Major Titov or to all the other Soviet space vauntings, from Sputnik I through the lost and now conveniently forgotten Venus probe.

This is the one side—*overestimation* of the physical power of the enemy—of the double error in our understanding that is steadily eroding our world position before the Communist drive towards universal domination. It is a fantastic acceptance, going beyond the military to the more extravagant domestic production claims, of the material power and success of the Communist system.

The other side—an equally disastrous *underestimation* of the enemy—is reflected in the attitude we have shown towards the most important ideological event in the Communist world in many years: the publication of the new Draft Program of the Communist Party of the Soviet Union. This is a remarkable *summa* of the Communist ideology as it has developed to this historical moment. It has a grandeur of concept, within the universe of Communist discourse, that calls for the most serious consideration as a manifesto of evil incarnate.

We have seemed incapable of rising to the challenge. Our criticism has been, not to put too fine a point upon it, limited to nitpicking. Instead of scarifying with scorn its dark vision of a juggernaut society moving from material triumph to material triumph by the subjugation and transformation of the individual human person, we have entered into a feeble contest of boasting about our material achievements as compared to theirs.

The whole point is missed. Television sets and vacuum cleaners and refrigerators are only symbols to the Communist mind. It is not with consumers' durable goods that they appeal, but with the concept of collectivist Man as the maker of heaven and earth.

Ourselves caught in the degeneration of the Western ethos, we are already half defeated. If perchance the Communists can achieve their goals, how can we, sunk into a materialist and proto-collectivist stupor, say them nay? As Brent Bozell wrote in these columns recently [*National Review*, August 12]: "The Christian West, especially the United States [has been] arguing its case in materialist terms . . . while materialistic Communism, with its teaching about the meaning of history, and the opportunity for controlling history that comes from such knowledge, was exciting the mind and spirit of men. The danger [is] that the West [will] be unable to see the struggle in any other terms."

It is here that the underestimation of the enemy arises. Forgetting our own origins in respect for the authority of God and for the immutable value of the individual person, we unguardedly enter the universe of the ideological outlook of materialist Communism, but on the lowest and pettiest level of creature comfort. We fail to see that at this game Communism must, by the inexorable logical extension of materialist premises, inevitably win. Its overweening materialist spirit, universal and militant in its pretensions, cannot be countered in its own terms.

Enough of this nonsense! The West can survive and conquer, but only if we cease to cower before the concepts of our enemies and assert again, proudly and resolutely, the truths of our heritage.

What Is Under the Bed?

(National Review, April 10, 1962)

It is the stock-in-trade of the respectable ostriches who populate the posts that influence and command American policy, to shriek in unison at the anti-Communist: "Seeing Communists under the bed" . . . "conspiracy theory of history" . . . "hysterical paranoia." Of course, if these gentlemen had ever looked under the bed and verified that there was nothing there, instead of standing with their heads buried and their rumps in the air, they would deserve to be listened to with attention. For it is quite true that to see things under the bed when there is nothing there, to suspect conspiracies where they do not exist, is most unsteadying to the intellect and dangerous to the health of the social order—almost as dangerous as not to see things when they *are* there.

Decades of Liberal pooh-poohing of the reality of the Communist conspiracy have created an atmosphere where it is *de rigueur* for the Left to deny the possibility of conspiracy ever having any serious effect on history (other historical eras in which conspiracy played a conspicuous role are conveniently ignored). On the other hand, in sections of the Right, the true existence of conspiracy as a decisive and inescapable fact in world events sometimes tends to be exaggerated out of all proportion. This misestimation is carried in some circles almost to the point of neglecting completely the other factors which, by their own forces and by interaction with conspiracy, have in this century prevailed so disastrously against the traditions and the fabric of Western civilization.

Indeed, at the margin, the idea of conspiracy has so passionately seized the imagination of some that they are not content with the hideous existence of the actual, documentable, powerfully functioning Communist conspiracy, but must needs conjure up still deeper, more devilish conspiracies, hatched in the murky regions of the intellectual underworld—conspiracies encompassing Communists, international bankers, Freemasons, Jews, Catholics, and Heaven knows whom else, all directed by some mysterious "They," some arcane "Invisible Government."

Even when conspiracy is understood in a limited and legitimate way, avoiding murky imaginings and concentrating upon the actual Communist conspiracy, the same tendency to underestimate the danger of non-conspiratorial factors exists and plays havoc with the attainment of a true understanding of the forces arrayed against us and the development of an effective battle plan to combat them. Actually, there are three forces with which American conservatives must contend: the Communist world enterprise, with its military, political and worldwide subversive powers; the American Communist conspiracy, which is a detachment behind our lines of that enterprise's multi-dimensional army; and—on a very different level—the corrosive ideology of American Liberalism, which eats away at the foundation values of our civilization and our Republic.

Each of these has a specific weight of its own; each has specific characteristics which require that the struggle against them be conducted in a specific way. No one of them alone has created the situation with which we have to deal. As a matter of fact, the purely conspiratorial element, the domestic Communist conspiracy, is intrinsically the least formidable of the three. If it were not for the power it derives, as a parachute division in our rear, from the massive army in our front, it would pose little serious danger. Even then, if it were not for the confusion in our counsels and the debilitation of our will that Liberalism sows, the conspiracy would be unable effectively to function.

It goes without saying that it should be exposed, harried, persecuted, that we should take the necessary steps to destroy it just as if it were an armed contingent in the rear of a fighting army. The Communist movement in the United States is in effect, if not strictly legally, treasonable; and all that would be necessary to prosecute it under the treason statute would be for the Congress of the United States to recognize the fact of the war prosecuted against us by international Communism for the past four decades. Short of the improbable event, however, of official recognition that a spade is a spade, the intensification of informed private activities of exposure, and of public prosecution under existing statutes (and under any other constitutional measures that are found necessary), should be sufficient to deal with the conspiracy.

But that done, the task of the defenders of the Western and American tradition would be only begun. There remain two problems of very different characters: First, to turn our retreat before the Communist world power into intensified counter-attack, carried forward until we have achieved victory. And, secondly, by entirely different methods (because here we are dealing not with a determined enemy, but with confused and misguided fellow citizens), by education, debate, public activity of all kinds, political organization, to win from the Liberal Establishment the commanding heights of the nation. This latter is necessary not only because the internal recovery of our constitutional institutions and the ethos of Western civilization demand it, but also (as I attempted to show in these pages recently—"The Liberal Veto," February 27), because the Liberals are innately incapable of leading an effective fight against Communism.

These are the decisive elements of our conservative responsibility. The fight against the detachment of international Communism that is the American Communist conspiracy, is integral to our total problem; but it constitutes only a part of that problem, and not the most important part.

Just War in the Nuclear Age

(National Review, February 12, 1963)

The primary causes of the paralysis of American foreign policy in the face of the Communist drive for world conquest are clear. The inconsequence of our world stance (if the conglomerate of noble words and base appeasement that passes for our foreign policy can be called a stance) derives directly from the blindness to reality and the enfeeblement of will of the Liberal leadership.

This conservatives have by and large thoroughly understood. But granted the achievement of direction over the destinies of the nation by men purged of the Liberal infection and determined to conduct, with manful purpose, the struggle Communism has forced upon us, do there not remain serious moral problems in the conduct of that struggle under the circumstances created by the monstrously destructive power of thermonuclear weapons with quasi-instantaneous means of delivery? Do not the problems raised in men's minds by this portentous power contribute to the comparative ease with which acceptance is won for Liberal policies that ignore reality and move with inexorable logic towards surrender? And have we conservatives sufficiently come to grips with the moral problems that the determination to win victory over Communism brings in its train in a nuclear age?

The Soviet Union possesses nuclear weapons and delivery systems which, however far behind Communist propaganda claims they may in fact be, are more than sufficient to force submission upon us if we should ever renounce nuclear warfare ourselves when it is necessary for our national survival and the survival of Western civilization. At this point most argument with proponents of American nuclear disarmament becomes a fruitless occupation, because they refuse to recognize the single-minded devotion of the Communist leadership to the conquest of the world and its radical rejection of any moral standard for its actions except the duty and necessity of bringing about Communist control of the world. "Mutual nuclear disarmament" is, therefore, an impossible concept, since there is no way, however strict inspection agreements might be, of enforcing disarmament upon a Communist totalitarian society, and there are no moral sanctions that would constrain the Communist leadership—as there is no way in which the free and open society of the United States could or would evade fulfillment of such an agreement. All proposals for nuclear disarmament are in reality, that is to say, proposals for unilateral nuclear disarmament.

In order to put the moral problem created by nuclear weapons realistically, the ostrich-like refusal to accept the reality of Communism must be ignored and the question posed in its starkest form: granted the certainty of Communist conquest of the world if we repudiate the use of nuclear weapons, is the use of such unimaginably devastating weapons nevertheless immoral? If not, under what circumstances and with what limitations is their use morally justified?

The only way this question can be satisfactorily answered is by driving to bedrock. It is necessary to push aside the impreci-

sion and sentimentality which have obscured discussion, and
face the question on moral grounds—by the use of reason
grappling with the new problems created by twentieth-century
technology on the basis of the traditional wisdom of the West.

The teaching of Western civilization, developed over centuries by patient application of moral wisdom and rational
analysis to war and warfare, asserts that if war is conducted
for a just cause and if the intention of those who conduct it is
not perverted by secondary evil motives, then the morality of
the measures used must be judged by two essential criteria:
1) they must not be intended directly for evil purposes, and 2)
the principle of proportionality must be observed—that is, the
force used must not be greater than absolutely necessary, and
any evil effects attendant upon the use of that force must be
proportional to the gravity of the aim (*e.g.*, though the destruction of the Communist regime in Cuba is undoubtedly demanded morally, it would be far out of proportion, and therefore immoral, to use thermonuclear weapons against Cuba).

Let us examine our problem in the light of these criteria.

The justice of our cause is categorical: for 45 years Communism has waged a relentless and unceasing war against all
human civilization, particularly Western civilization. For the
past 15 years at least, that war has been directed against the
United States as the only force capable of standing in the way
of the Communist goal of world domination. There can be no
question of our moral obligation to resist, to counterattack, to
destroy, this powerful and proclaimed enemy of man and God.
Indeed, the immorality of which we are guilty resides not in
the degree to which we are determined to fight for his destruction, but in the confusion of purpose and the pusillanimity we
have hitherto displayed. That immorality has been registered
on the streets of Budapest and the shores of the Bay of Pigs,
in the slave camps of China and the bloody puddles beneath the
Berlin Wall.

Nor need we, after due search of our conscience, find ourselves guilty of any evil secondary intention in wholeheartedly

conducting the war that has been thrust upon us. Perhaps never in history has there been a nation so powerful as the United States with so little desire to dominate others.

It may be that our Liberals have a prurient itch to tell other people how they ought to live, but this is the poking finger of the social worker—unpleasant, but far removed from the plundering cruelty of the conqueror. Our entrepreneurs, it is true, are anxious for markets, but their desire is trade, not rapine. What the American people want above all is to be left alone.

Given the justice of our cause and the cleanliness of our intentions, however, the question still remains: is the use of nuclear weapons with their horrific effect a morally justified measure in the prosecution of the war that has been thrust upon us?

To begin with, two questions that are often confused with the question of the morality of nuclear bombardment should be cleared up. First, the possession of preponderant power can never justify a war aim of "unconditional surrender," because such an aim is inevitably out of proportion to the necessities that justify war. The effective removal of a leadership devoted to aggression for evil, yes; but the unconditional surrender of a nation as a whole, no. Unconditional removal of the Nazi leadership yesterday and the Communist leadership tomorrow, yes; but unconditional surrender of the German or the Russian nation, no. The demand for unconditional surrender is the *hubris* that transforms the justice of a cause into injustice.

Second, measures of war directed to the obliteration of populations as their central purpose are always and everywhere immoral, whether they are the action of the Athenian *demos* armed with sword and bow, or the bombardment of Rotterdam and London, of Hamburg and Dresden, with high explosives and incendiaries—or of Hiroshima and Nagasaki with nuclear bombs.

The issue is not the character of the weapons, but the direction and intent of the blow. The force used must not be greater than the minimum necessary to achieve the objective, and that objective must be destruction of the enemy's military power, not terrorization and slaughter of civilian populations.

Of course it goes without saying, considering the character of nuclear weapons, that every other method of achieving victory should be utilized first, with the aim of making the use of nuclear weapons unnecessary: peripheral warfare with every available resource (*e.g.*, an attack on the mainland of China by Chiang Kai-shek's troops; armed support to our friends, of the sort we should have given Tshombe); black political warfare directed to developing sabotage and insurrection behind the Iron Curtain, together with armed support of revolutions, such as those in East Germany, Poland, and Hungary, when they occur; defense of areas against which Soviet aggression is directed (*e.g.*, enforcement of the Monroe Doctrine, with arms where necessary); and, when the strategic situation makes it necessary, direct engagement of the land, sea or air forces of the Soviet Union.

Our aim should be to drive Communist power back to its original borders by such measures, and then to preside over the dissolution of the Communist regime. It is clear, however, that in carrying out such a strategic program, the risk of the Soviets using nuclear weapons for a counterblow will always exist. If and when the issue of nuclear warfare is forced upon us, the only moral question remaining—given the justice of our cause and the necessity of nuclear force to its victory—is *how* we use nuclear force.

By the moral criteria developed, it would seem here that so-called counter-force strategy, directed against the enemy's air and missile delivery systems, is morally justified, since injury to the civilian population would be secondary, not directly intended, but a by-product. But counter-force strategy by its very nature requires that we be prepared to strike the first nuclear blow, for once Soviet nuclear bombs have been delivered, there is little meaning to an attack upon their delivery systems. Yet we rightly shrink from the idea of initiating nuclear warfare. The only alternative, however, is so powerful a threat of counter-attack on the population of the Communist countries, if they do attack us with nuclear weapons, that they will be deterred from ever doing so.

Neither nuclear strategy is free of moral problems: counter-force strategy requires that we initiate the attack; deterrence requires that we coldbloodedly make the civilian population our target. But it would seem that the counter-force strategy is far the more moral course. In defense of a just cause, uncontaminated by impure intentions, strictly proportional in force employed to the purpose (destruction of the enemy's nuclear power), a first-strike counter-force nuclear blow, minimal in its effects upon the civilian population, meets every moral criterion. A strategy of second-strike deterrence, intending as it must—if it is to be believed and to be effective—an attack upon the civilian population, would seem to be immoral *per se*. The only justification for such a strategy is the hope that it would prevent nuclear warfare altogether. If the policy of deterrence by threatening annihilation of population cannot deter, then that policy is profoundly more immoral than one based upon first-strike attack on the enemy's military-nuclear potential.

The morality of either course, however, depends upon an underlying recognition of the moral duty of defending civilization by destroying Communism, and upon the determination to move towards doing so by every available non-nuclear means first.

It may be said that I have ignored the question so often raised, whether any use of nuclear weapons, so devastating by their very nature, is not immoral, no matter how proper the target against which they are directed. To this I can only answer that, even granted the most horrendous estimates of the effects of their use, the preservation of human life as a biological phenomenon is an end far lower than the defense of freedom and right and truth. These the victory of Communism would destroy. These it is our duty to defend at all costs.

What Does Kennedy Mean?

(*National Review*, July 16, 1963)

So absurd does the rhetoric of Liberalism seem when judged in the light of reality that the sober conservative tends to discredit it as pure flourish. No American in his senses could conceivably mean what the words issuing from the mouths of Liberal spokesmen patently say; it must be ritualistic titillation for the satisfaction of ideological sentiment. Thus, President Kennedy's speech at American University last month has largely been considered in terms of its concrete programmatic statements: cessation of atmospheric nuclear tests, and high-level test-ban discussions in Moscow. What has not been seriously considered is the meaning of the speech as a whole with its underlying assumptions.

Let us examine this speech by considering its key statements in a logical order and analyzing their import. If they form a coherent whole and if the actions of the Administration confirm in practice the ideological pattern that whole expresses, it would seem that we are dealing with something more significant than rhetorical flourishes.

Kennedy on the determining political reality of the mid-twentieth century, the drive of the Communist leadership to world conquest in the name of an encompassing ideology: "... *Let us re-examine our attitude towards the Soviet Union. It is discouraging to think that their leaders may actually believe what their propagandists write. ... It is our hope—and the purpose of allied policies—to convince the Soviet Union that she, too, should let each nation choose its own form, so long as that choice does not interfere with the choices of others.*" But it is precisely the essence of Communism that propaganda and action, philosophical system and conflict-doctrine, the political-military and the agitational-revolutionary elements of its being, express a single unified purpose and reflect a deeply held faith. It would be heresy to that faith to "let each nation choose its own form."

It is pathetic to hope, as President Kennedy does in this speech, that "*if we cannot end now our differences, at least we can help make the world safe for diversity.*" Diversity is just what the Communists, with their vision of a collectivist, controlled, engineered and utopian world, strive by every means at their disposal to eliminate. To posit "diversity" as the basis of a possible compromise with Communism is the historical equivalent of a Norman Crusader proposing to a Moslem leader acceptance of the doctrine of the Trinity as the basis for agreement between them.

This utter lack of understanding of the phenomenon of Communism and of the extreme challenge it poses to the West is the foundation of the structure of Liberal foreign policy that President Kennedy is developing. Like Franklin Roosevelt at Teheran and Yalta, he can conceive the Communists only as a rougher and cruder species of Liberal, with whom we can have "common interests." This conflict between us, in Kennedy's ideology, does not spring from the principled devotion of Communism to the destruction of Western civilization (the civilization of the free person and the transcendental moral law) and of the American Republic (the polity based upon the sanctity of the free person and the norm of the moral law). It is the result of a parallel guilt on both sides: *"We are both caught up in a vicious and dangerous cycle, with suspicion on one side breeding suspicion on the other, and new weapons begetting counterweapons."*

We have, it would appear, in President Kennedy's view, *"a mutual deep interest in a just and genuine peace"* and in *"increased contact and communication."* But "justice" in our tradition is derived from the objective reality of the moral and metaphysical order; to the Communist it is that which serves the victory of Communism. And "contact and communication," which is to us the stuff of civilized intercourse, is to them a weapon of war.

This radical failure to understand the historical significance of Communism as an alien and inimical force bearing down upon the West is central to the suicidal program Kennedy presents in this address. The focus of this program is that *"our primary long-range interest . . . is general and complete disarmament"*—or, to spell it out in the words of the specific program of his Administration introduced at the sixteenth General Assembly of the United Nations in September 1961: "The disbanding of all national armed forces and the prohibition of their re-establishment in any form whatsoever other than those required to preserve internal order and for contributions to the United Nations Peace Force."

Given the fearsome dangers of contemporary weapons, it is easy to understand why men grasp at straws. But it would be hard to understand how even the Liberal mind of a Kennedy could look with hope towards a world in which all force was centralized in a United Nations Army, if one did not understand his utter incomprehension of what the West and the United States stand for. His address makes clear his total failure not only to comprehend the impossibility of a world authority based simultaneously upon our ideals and the ideology of Communism, but also to comprehend the impossibility (even if Communism did not exist) of maintaining the virtues and triumphs of our civilization under the centralized power of any world monopoly of force.

President Kennedy's address is no compound of rhetorical flourishes; it represents a homogeneous ideology which is antagonistic to the American tradition of freedom, and, as a result, blurs our vision of the enemies of freedom and abysmally lowers our guard against them.

The Khrushchev-Kennedy Treaty

(National Review, August 13, 1963)

Averell Harriman, the Hero of Laos, has negotiated and initialed the nuclear test-ban treaty. John F. Kennedy, the Hero of the Bay of Pigs, in a nationwide television speech, has opened the barrage designed to smother sober consideration and criticism of the treaty in a welter of emotion. Nothing now stands in the way of establishing it, substantively and symbolically, as the settled policy of the United States, except to secure the advice and consent of the Senate. Rarely has the utmost deliberate consideration been more demanded of the Senate, yet every device available to the Administration is being pressed into service to bring about a precipitate, unconsidered and emotional ratification.

Kennedy's appearance on television was the climax of the first phase of this campaign—a phase in which the press was filled with inspired stories of every sort and description. Henry Cabot Lodge was dragged from his grave as a portentous warning to the enemies of Presidential wisdom, and the Chinese bogeyman was paraded across the stage to terrify those who doubted Khrushchev's sincerity and peace-loving nature.

In the second phase of this campaign, beginning now, the pressure on the Senate will mount to further heights. That pressure the Senate must resist—not only because it is its constitutional duty to consider treaties in calm deliberative process; not only because the treaty is highly questionable in itself; but primarily because this is the first opportunity the Senate has had to pass upon a consistent Administration program (previously implemented by Executive actions alone), the effect of which has been steadily to weaken our military stance vis-à-vis the Soviet Union (apparently in implementation of the Rostow doctrine of appeasement of Communism by military-technological retreat).

Consider the record: *abandonment of the RS-70 (reputedly the first fruits of Rostow's visit to Moscow in late 1960); phased withdrawal of the B-47s from Europe and elimination of European-based IRBMs; planned obsolescence of the B-52s and B-58s, intensified by the scrapping of Skybolt; the decision not to develop nuclear weapons in the 50+ megaton range; downgrading of the nuclear plane project and Dyna-Soar; grotesquely distorted emphasis on space exploration and NASA civilian-centered projects at the expense of military rocketry; the Administration's official Maginot-line policy of concentrating all our strategic force in Minuteman and Polaris, weapons whose warheads are ineffective against enemy offensive nuclear power and are therefore limited to a purely deterrent, a statically defensive role.* It is true, of course, that any one of the decisions to relinquish this or that weapons system might be justified on specific military-technological grounds; but the series of decisions taken together adds up to a policy of appeasement, retreat, and inherent weakening of the military stance of the United States.

That this *is* the policy of the Administration is confirmed both by its actions in the face of Soviet aggression (the loosening of the embargo on trade in strategic items with the Communist empire; the Hungarian negotiations; the farcical Laos agreement; the shameful and perilous retreat in Cuba) and by its words. Blindly ignoring the character of Communism, to say nothing of the revolution of envy sweeping the "colonial" sector of the world, the Administration projects as the goal of our policy a disarmed United States subservient to an international authority, an authority which, things being as they are, would inevitably be controlled by the Communists in manipulative alliance with the envious.

Kennedy expounded this policy in his American University speech (which I have analyzed in these pages [*National Review*, July 16]) and the State Department has solemnly introduced proposals to implement such a policy in the General Assembly of the United Nations. Now Kennedy has, in his television address, reiterated it, proclaiming his "ultimate hope for general and complete disarmament." The preamble of the test-ban treaty, which the Senate is called on to ratify, declares that the signatories "[proclaim] as their principal aim the speediest possible achievement of an agreement on general and complete disarmament under strict international control in accordance with the objectives of the UN . . ."

There are strong enough arguments against the substantive terms of the treaty, of course. In the first place, outer-space testing is, in the view of scientists, almost as difficult to detect as underground testing, and this may well become in a few years the most important kind of testing. More immediately, atmospheric testing is of the utmost importance if we are to surpass the Soviets, not only in very high yield weapons and in acquiring the necessary knowledge of the effect of major nuclear explosions on communications vital to the effectiveness of our strategic striking force, but most decisively in achieving a breakthrough at the key frontier of military technology, the antimissile missile.

These arguments alone indicate the danger of the Khrushchev-Kennedy treaty. But, in the light of the consistent military and diplomatic policy of this Administration, it presents to the Senate a manifest opportunity, by rejecting it, to call a halt to appeasement and retreat. Those senators of both parties and many persuasions who have understood the disastrous consequences of this policy—Goldwater, Tower, Russell, Thurmond, Stennis, Symington, Jackson, and many others—have the strength, standing together, to rally the Senate against a willful President and bar the road to continued retreat.

Reflections on Vietnam

(National Review, February 22, 1966)

A conservative is put into something of a quandary when it comes to discussing the war in Vietnam. Just the fact that we are fighting the Communists somewhere is a tremendous step forward after years of retreat under the slogan of "coexistence." One does not want to do anything to weaken national support for President Johnson insofar as his actions are actions of confrontation rather than retreat.

Nevertheless the policy that guides our engagement in Vietnam is so obscure, the conduct of the war so ambiguous, and the goals for which Americans are fighting and dying so uncertain, that discussion and clarification are imperative, if more is not to be lost than won on this extended salient of our frontiers. For a profound contradiction exists between the fact of serious warfare in the jungles of Southeast Asia and the assumptions of national policy that still guide the administration. It is the contradiction pointed out by James Burnham discussing our NATO policy in the February 8 issue of *National Review*—

the contradiction between the assumption of peaceful intentions on the part of the Soviet Union and common interests between us and the Soviet Union on the one hand, and the maintenance of NATO as a war alliance or the prosecution of actual war in Vietnam on the other hand.

The Vietnam contradiction is further intensified by an additional twist in Liberal thinking, the idea that while Chinese Communism is still bad, Russian Communism is somehow good. So prevalent is this last attitude that Edmond Taylor, in an excellent report from Vietnam in the *Reporter* for January 27, finds it the key to the bogging down of our efforts there. In interview after interview with leading officials he finds the theme reasserting itself until, as he says, one gets the impression of Alice in Wonderland, or rather "a mixture of Alice and Walter Lippmann." It is as if we were accepting "paralyzing restrictions on our conduct of the war in Vietnam simply to enjoy the privilege of seeing Russian rather than Chinese bullets kill American soldiers."

Indeed, to go beyond Mr. Taylor's thesis, it may well be that it is precisely this peculiar contrast in our attitude to Russia and China that had led to a most strategically unfortunate choice of place for our armed encounter with Communism. Both from the point of view of essential national interest and from the point of view of tactical and logistical advantage, it would seem that Cuba, not Vietnam, should have been the scene for a serious rollback of Communist aggression. Be that as it may, it is in Vietnam that we are presently engaged, and if this is far from the ideal spot for an encounter, it is nevertheless here that the direction of our policy—whether towards resistance or towards further retreat—will be determined.

But no good for the United States can come out of Vietnam unless our engagement there is recognized for what it is—one battle in the continuing war with Communism. There can be nothing but sorrow in return for our sacrifice of blood unless the *Through the Looking Glass* approach of *rapprochement* with the Soviet Union is abandoned. So long as we fail to understand that the Vietnam struggle is but a battle in a larger war it will not be possible to have any clear objectives, any clear definition of what we could regard as victory.

Once we understand Vietnam in its proper context, it should be possible to select any one of a number of possible aims, depending upon the degree of involvement we wish to accept in this particular theater and upon our intentions to press the war on Communism in some other more likely theater. But at whichever level we place our objective, it must be one which registers a sharp clear setback for Communist power.

There are, it seems to me, three possible objectives in ascending order of necessary commitment and expenditure of men and *matériel*. These levels, however, cannot remain totally distinct because the effort to achieve a minimum objective may, depending upon the commitment of the enemy, require escalation to the next higher objective if the first is to be achieved at all. These possible objectives, as I see them, are: (1) the destruction of the Vietcong and the sealing off of South Vietnam, to permit the establishment of a firm anti-Communist regime in South Vietnam—a "Korean solution" for Vietnam; (2) the overthrow of the Hanoi government and the establishment of an anti-Communist government in all Vietnam; (3) in case vigorous prosecution of warfare directed towards (1) or (2) should bring the threat of Chinese intervention, the welcoming of war against China as an opportunity to destroy its nuclear potential and set back its development as a serious military power for years.

Since the Asian continent is hardly the ideal strategic arena for American arms, it may well be that the first of these objectives is to be preferred—but only if it is fully understood that we are prepared to face enemy escalation that would force us to the second or third level rather than fail to achieve the objective of the first level. Indeed, such escalation is quite possible, since it would seem that only actions of the magnitude of a blockade of all Vietnamese ports and land attack against the head of the Ho Chi Minh trail from our bases in Thailand could achieve the complete pacification of South Vietnam. In any case, whichever be our objective, nothing less than a clear statement that we see it as part of the broader war with Communism and that we are prepared to take all steps necessary to achieve it—whatever the Chinese *or* the Russians do—can lift the Vietnam war from its present obscurity and confusion.

The McNamara Policy: Road to Disaster

(National Review, August 8, 1967)

Phrases like "strategic doctrine" and "military policy" have a certain distant and abstract quality that tends to deprive them of political sex appeal. Yet there is no issue—not even Vietnam or the disorder in our cities—which is of such intimate importance to every living American as the conflict over the strategic doctrine and military policy that have come to be associated with the name of Robert McNamara. What is at stake is, quite literally, the lives of three out of every five Americans, to say nothing of the survival of the United States and of Western civilization.

The issue is too serious to be discussed, as it often is, simply in terms of the personality of McNamara. He is no doubt the principal executor of current policy, and if that policy is wrong, as I believe it is, his removal would be a necessity both practically and symbolically to make way for a reconstitution of our strategic stance. But McNamara, although he is one of the architects as well as the principal executor of present policies, is not primarily responsible for them. This responsibility rests first of all, of course, with the President and his predecessor, but more fundamentally it is lodged in the Liberal outlook on world politics with its insistently suicidal refusal to face reality.

The effect of this outlook is disastrous for the basic requirement of all strategic thinking—estimate of the enemy's intentions and estimate of the enemy's capabilities. On the level of intentions, it produces a wilful blindness to the open and continuous proclamation of the philosophico-political doctrine of world Communist rule—a doctrine from which the Communist leadership in its fundamental statements has never deviated for fifty years, whatever its immediate tactics. But the self-induced blindness goes further. Even were it not for the underlying Communist doctrine, even were the Soviet Union simply an expansive great power in a bi-polar world, how would it be possible safely to ignore the Soviet military doctrine—freely available in every Soviet military journal—which uninhibitedly puts primary reliance on a sudden nuclear-rocket first strike?

Communist intentions, both philosophico-political and military, are clearly and unreservedly aggressive. Since we are deeply committed to a second-strike-only policy and since our strategic potential is shaped to this policy, our sole defense against a Soviet knockout blow that would kill 120 million Americans is based on the concept of deterrence—that is, sufficient *believable* power to retaliate after a Soviet first strike with great enough force to inflict upon the enemy what the analysts call "unacceptable damage," an equally terrible destructive blow. It is obvious, therefore, that the very existence of the country depends upon such unquestionable superiority in our striking force that under no circumstances would the enemy dare to carry through his avowed intention of striking a pulverizing blow at the United States.

This misjudgment of the enemy's intentions is matched by a systematic underestimation of the enemy's capability, that is, his power to carry out his intentions. Whether as a result of the general Liberal inability to deal realistically with questions of force, or whether as a result of a natural human propensity to buttress one error with another, persistent misreading of Soviet intentions has for some years now been compounded by steady underestimation of their capabilities. A true assessment of those capabilities, and of the actual dynamic balance of force between us and the Communist world, has been made difficult for the informed observer by the complexities of judging technological possibilities and has been complicated still further by the classified status of so much of the information, as well as by McNamara's systematic obfuscations of the issue. It has nevertheless become increasingly clear over the past few years that our superiority, and therewith the credibility of our policy of deterrence, has been steadily deteriorating.

And now, whatever lingering doubts may have existed about the danger of the McNamara policy have been authoritatively set to rest with the publication by the American Security Council of a report prepared for the House Armed Services Committee: *The Changing Strategic Military Balance, U.S.A. vs. U.S.S.R.* (American Security Council, 1101 17th Street N.W., Washington, D.C. 20036, $1.50). It was prepared by a committee headed by General Bernard A. Schriever, recently retired Commander, U.S. Air Force Systems Command, and including General Curtis E. LeMay, former Chief of Staff of the Air Force, General Thomas S. Power, former Commander, SAC, Dr. Edward Teller, and Professor Stefan T. Possony. Based entirely upon unclassified information, but written by men whose previous access to the highest classified material has undoubtedly shaped their judgment, it gives a grim picture indeed of the strategic situation.

In sum, the report indicates that by this year, 1967, our former superiority in decisive areas has fallen to equality and that by 1971 the Soviets will possess strategic superiority. In 1962 the United States possessed massive superiority; by 1971 "the U.S. and the U.S.S.R. will have reversed their role in a ten-year period"—*unless present policies are drastically revised.* Although the study covers all aspects of the strategic situation but refrains from making specific proposals for action, four conclusions would seem to be dictated by its analysis as essential for national survival in the 1970s.

1) An immediate crash program to install a full anti-ballistic missile system, in order to save the lives of at least 50 million Americans in case of attack and to make our second-strike deterrent policy credible.

2) Full-scale upgrading of missile and plane delivery capacity

and of the megaton yield of our warheads, in order to equal and surpass potential Soviet megatonnage for 1971, which is projected on the basis of present policies as 30,000-50,000 megatons against 5,000-15,000 megatons for the United States.

3) Immediate revision of the nuclear test-ban treaty and the resumption of nuclear testing to catch up with the Soviet knowledge gained from the 1961 and 1962 tests, which may have given them capabilities of seriously crippling our ICBM retaliatory force and which certainly have placed them far ahead in anti-ballistic missile defense and multi-megaton weaponry.

4) Meeting the Soviet challenge in the military utilization of space, an area where our present enormous expenditures are overwhelmingly non-military.

Nothing less than these actions would seem to be consonant with the imperatives of national defense.

Part Three

Ideas, Forces, People

Chapter Six

On History

The roots of conservatism lie in the history of our civilization, and an understanding of historical processes is essential to the conservative critique of prevailing norms. The columns, articles, and book reviews assembled in this chapter represent a continuing effort to come to grips with some of the key historical questions that have seemed to be relevant to the endeavor of recovering and developing our heritage.

Review of *The Taming of the Nations: A Study of the Cultural Bases of International Policy*, by F. S. C. Northrop

(Freeman, February 23, 1953)

Reputations are strangely made these days. Since the publication of *The Meeting of East and West,* Professor F. S. C. Northrop has been widely and extravagantly hailed as a distinguished philosopher who brings deep spiritual and intellectual insights to bear upon the problems of our time. But a careful reading of his books, a little checking on his more obscure references, leaves the unhappy impression that to his self-appointed task of harmonizing the differences between nations and cultures he brings little more than enthusiasm and good will.

His mind appears to have been trained exclusively in the contemporary disciplines of scientific method and the "philosophy of science." He seems incapable of the most elementary understanding of the content and meaning of the philosophical and religious concepts of East and West which he so blithely tosses about; and of the historical development of the cultures he discusses he is appallingly ignorant.

In *The Taming of the Nations,* his latest book, his stated purpose is to discover a cultural basis for the framing of international policy and an international law. He insists that "internatonal relations must become more than . . . an art. It must also be a science. . . ." But he modestly questions whether it is possible for it to be a science. "Are we not in the presence of imponderables?" Yes, he says, we are, but let us not despair. There is an answer, "imponderables can be specified"—and once they are specified, the problem is solved. "Specifying the imponderables" of civilizations will enable us to control international relations in the same way that analyzing the qualities of chemical elements has made it possible to predict the reactions of chemical materials.

A happy thought. But who can bell the cat? Civilizations are not objective physical entities which can be studied and known by the experimental scientific method. Professor Northrop, however, seems to think that when he has characterized a civilization with a string of words ("specified the imponderables"), he has exhaustively analyzed it in the same way that the natural scientists have exhaustively analyzed the chemical properties of an element. He reduces all the richness of man's histories to a series of fat phrases and then endows these corpulent entities with autonomous being.

Thus, India's culture is based on "attachment . . . to the intuitively felt, all-embracing immediacy in its timelessness and formlessness." "Spiritual, experimental, naturalistic universalism [is] the soul of the people of the United States." Western civilization generally is based upon "the abstract, logically formulated, theoretical way of thinking about naively observed, personally sensed and felt natural phenomena, which requires quantitatively exact experiments for its verification."

A Spengler or a Toynbee might momentarily stress an insight into one or another facet of a great culture, but a few pages later he would enrich it with another insight. But once Professor Northrop has achieved his little vision, he avariciously hoards it up in a formula. This formula becomes a counter in a game, or more exactly, an algebraic symbol which he manipulates and combines and re-combines with other similar symbols. Such simple reductions of the complex reality that makes up a culture of living men can lead to nothing more than what logicians call "agreement between propositions." The significance of such an agreement depends on the original validity of the insights which led to the propositions. Professor Northrop's insights may sometimes agree with themselves, but, being one-sided and often blind, they can say nothing about human civilizations.

The aridity which is the manifest weakness of such an approach has usually at least the merit of its defect—a stringent sense of logic. But Professor Northrop manages, even in the combination of his abstractions, to be maddeningly untrammeled by any logical scruples. He recognizes one of the basic principles of law and jurisprudence, that what he calls "living law"—the basic attitudes of a society, the social norms—underlies and gives substance to all legislative enactments, "positive law." Therefore, positive international law can only become possible when there exists an international "living law" on which it can be based. But there does not exist an international "living law." There is no international norm. There are only a series of different, often contradictory, social norms. The logical conclusion would seem inevitable: there can be no positive international law. The stage would seem to be set for an intelligent and biting critique of all the assumptions of one-worldism, for a defense either of the concept of the balance of powers, or, if that be impossible in this Soviet-infected world, of a Pax Americana.

But, no, Professor Northrop calls the many cultural norms of the many civilizations "living law pluralism" (which, of course, is simply another way of saying they are "many"). Then he takes the phrase "living law pluralism" and gives it independent being. International law, he says, is entirely possible: the only thing is, it must be based on "living law pluralism."

What conceivable meaning is there to this word juggling? All it can possibly mean is that international law must be based on many different social norms, contrary and contradictory. But many different norms, contrary and contradictory, equal no norm; therefore there is no possibility of international law today. *Quod non erat demonstrandum.* Which is, indeed, the opposite to what he was trying to prove.

There is no room in this review to treat at length his errors of fact, insight, and interpretation—historical, philosophical, and theological. I have noted down some twenty-seven of them; a sampling will perhaps suffice. *Item:* The Logos, neither in the Neo-Platonic nor the Christian cosmos, is a "concept of scientifically known, theoretically conceived man and nature." It is the Immanent God in this world—the mystical principle of creative form. *Item:* The "Yin and Yang" concept is not Confucian but is immemorial in the Chinese outlook, while its philosophical development is primarily the work of Tsou Yen and the "Yin-Yang experts."

Item: Indian civilization is not divided sharply into a Vedic Aryan segment and an aboriginal Dravidian segment. The two are as inextricably combined as the Greek and the Hebraic are in Western Christendom. *Item:* Hellenic society certainly does not move "from the immediately felt relations of the joint family and the village elders . . . direct to the Western state universal." Professor Northrop apparently has never heard of the Greek city-state, the political form of Hellenic society in its most glorious period.

Enough. Ideas and words to Professor Northrop are what he wants to make them. As Humpty Dumpty said, "There's glory for you!"

"I don't know what you mean by 'glory,'" Alice said.

Humpty Dumpty smiled contemptuously. "Of course you don't —till I tell you. I meant 'there's a nice knock-down argument for you!'"

"But 'glory' doesn't mean 'a nice knock-down argument,'" Alice objected.

"When *I* use a word," Humpty Dumpty said, in rather a scornful tone, "it means just what I choose it to mean—neither more nor less."

"The question is," said Alice, "whether you *can* make words mean so many different things."

America: No Imperial Rome

(National Review, September 14, 1957)

It is hard to think of a European who has ever written about America as it is. In European thought the United States always plays a pat role—hero or villain—designed to promote a moral in whatever intellectual or psychic drama is afoot. Even so great a book as *Democracy in America* distorts the American reality in order that America may play its proper part in Alexis de Tocqueville's magnificent dramatic tragedy upon the theme of democracy in Western civilization.

I am not denying, I would strongly affirm, that America is of the West. I am not proposing the thesis that the United States is wholly new and different. We are so much of the West, so deeply of the West, that it is here that the fate of the West will be decided—*but* in the form we have given to the Western heritage, not on the terms decreed for us.

We have been cast in the role of the lower millstone to the Russian upper millstone; of the technological messiah; of the noble savage regenerating an enfeebled Europe. But most frequently in late years we have been iron, soulless Romans, administrators who come at the late summer of a culture to preserve order and civilized forms when the creative heart has gone out of society. Europeans, who see Europe as the Greece of Western civilization and themselves as late Greeks (mysteriously, through some trick of fate, deprived of energy) grudgingly concede to America energy, but only energy. America can play the role of a fierce or a lovable (depending on the writer's mood) watchdog, guarding the decaying mansion of the West; but that is all.

This "Roman" theory of America is usually connected with one or another of the cyclical views of history, of the kind that in the twentieth century has been powerfully projected by Oswald Spengler and Arnold Toynbee. On the whole, the place of America in these constructions has been only broadly and generally indicated. The architects of these historical systems have seemed content to let the America of their imagination stand as a symbol in their ideological structure, as though they were a little afraid to look too closely at the reality, in case it should fail to conform to the required image.

Recently, however, a young Frenchman, with a head full of Hegelian and Spenglerian ideas, has attempted to come to grips with the American reality and to force it willy-nilly into the Roman image. Some pages from Amaury de Riencourt's *The Coming Caesars* have been published in *National Review* (June 1, 1957); the book itself has been widely and admiringly reviewed.

M. de Riencourt brashly skims over Classical and Western history, picking and choosing bits of fact and pseudo-fact to develop his case: that America is Rome, and Caesarism is its destiny. His manifold historical errors of fact could be ignored, were it not that his pretensions of scholarship, uncritically received, have given prestige to his fundamental thesis.

A small sampling of those errors: *Item.* John Adams was *not* a member of the Virginia dynasty. *Item.* Marbury vs. Madison did *not* "firmly [establish] that the Supreme Court was the one and only interpreter of the Constitution." *Item.* "Jefferson was as much dazzled by the last days of Europe's ancien régime as the Romans were by Periclean Athens." Jefferson was *not* dazzled by the France he saw, he was highly critical of it; no Roman but a semi-civilized tribesman of the Sabine Wars yet existed to look at Periclean Athens.

But these errors, I repeat, would be comparatively unimportant, were it not for the fundamental error that arises from the attempt to make a mechanical parallel between the development of Classical civilization and Western civilization, thus ignoring the essential characteristic of Western civilization: the Christian vision of the innate value of the person and of his freedom under God.

The Roman genius was in truth, in relation to Greece, only an administrative and military one, holding together in dull but orderly existence a world inspired by Greek ideas and insight. America has been something else in its relation to Europe. It has been that place in the West where a political constitution, limiting government and protecting the freedom of the person, has matched the philosophical vision of the West, where an adequate political structure has carried that vision to its highest *political* expression.

America is not, as M. de Riencourt and the school he represents would maintain, the representative of the forces of egalitarianism, massocracy, and Caesarism against the refined and spiritual culture of Europe. As a matter of fact, America has till now resisted those forces more energetically than has Europe. It is Europe that has been the source of the theories of the "general will," of egalitarianism, of socialism—not America. In Europe they are close to their decisive victory; in America the issue is still to be decided.

The same struggle, however, between freedom and tyranny, between a God-like and a worm-like view of man, goes on on both sides of the Atlantic. If the Caesars come, borne on the wave of mediocrity, it will not be because America imposes them upon Europe, but because in neither continent have there been enough men dedicated to truth and freedom to resist them.

George Washington is, in the astigmatic eye of M. de Riencourt, the shaper of America and the prototype of its Caesarism;

but it was George Washington who said: "Government, like fire, is a dangerous servant and a fearful master." This is a truth that is a necessary political corollary to the Western and Christian understanding of man's nature. It is one that, unhappily, Europe never understood. America once did, and enough remains of that understanding to give some hope for a future American era of Western culture which will be not Caesarist, but free.

Ferment Among Historians

(National Review, July 5, 1958)

The eyes of the world are upon the tremendous ferment in the technology of the physical sciences; but less dramatic, yet in the end perhaps more fateful for our future, is the ferment in the philosophy of history. The way in which we see ourselves and our historical role will in the end shape our will. It will affect our being a great deal more deeply than the material instrumentalities with which we implement our will.

Western civilization, to a far greater degree than any other civilization of which we know, has been deeply concerned with the problem of history, with the passage of men through time, where "every moment is a new beginning" and freely willed thought and action are fraught with immense responsibility and portentous outcome. To none of the other great civilizations has this sense of man's responsibility in his course through history been so present a condition of consciousness.

Though we see this consciousness today primarily in the distorted form of the scientistic and progressivist arrogance of the post-Christian *Weltanschauung,* it is a consciousness that came into being, and could only have come into being, on the basis of the sublime paradox of faith that created the West: the penetration of the Transcendent *into* history, vindicating the freedom of men *in* history. This folly to the determinist, this scandal to the relativist, has made it possible for Western man to grasp, as men of no other civilization have, the possibility of ultimate spiritual freedom. Neither the monism of materialism nor the monism of philosophical idealism can withstand the critical impact of the deep certainty of the West that man's existence is not wholly reducible to the *resultat* of material forces or the fixed and predetermined dictates of fate.

The relativism that has characterized the dominant thought of the West for the past century or more can in this context be seen as a desperate and distorted attempt to deny the threatening determinism of material forces that seemed unchallenged in a world from which the transcendent had been exiled. But the relativist denial of essential reality, which reduces the roll of the ocean, the aroma of the orchard in spring, the clarity of mathematical achievement, the fullness of faith, the ephemeral symbols of ephemeral relations—this the Western spirit could not stomach. It affronted the Western sense of history.

The reaction flung wildly to the other extreme. The lyric determinism of a Spengler, the hesitant determinism of a Toynbee, the subtle Hegelian monism of a Collingwood, destroyed the feeble pretensions of relativist history. But it was a leap from the frying pan into the fire. The free will of the individual person is lost as hopelessly in their great systems as in the futility of relativist history.

In the past dozen years—the result perhaps of the latest stage in the immense and wracking crisis in which Western society has been gripped—a new spirit has been precipitated out. The towering genius of Eric Voegelin, the insight of Percy of Newcastle, the critical acumen of Herbert Butterfield are but the highest points in a developing movement of thought which rejects the two extremes of historical determinism and historical relativism, returning to the fundamental Western understanding of human history as the free acting of men, moving towards a transcendent destiny, in the conditions of a material world.

It is not only, however, in the work of these men and of many others who are explicitly proceeding along the same path (one could mention such works as Leopold Kohr's *The Breakdown of Nations* or Marie Swabey's *The Judgment of History*) that the sign of a great turn in the philosophy of history can be discerned. Great changes in modes of thought also carry along men who are striving deeply for an understanding of reality even when they are not prepared as yet to recognize that their ultimate terms of philosophical reference depend upon unsound premises. Two examples, drawn from widely different ideological worlds, may suffice to illustrate this tendency.

Professor von Mises, although he is without doubt the world's greatest living economist, has always shown a utilitarian bias on philosophical and historical questions, which carried to its logical conclusions could only lead to relativism. The power of his grasp of reality, however, which has enabled him to avoid relativist futility in his analysis of the laws of the economy, seems now to have affected his outlook on history. In *Theory and History* the utilitarian bias is still strongly apparent in his formulations, but the judgments that he makes on critical problems of history break beyond the bounds of those formulations and show an astonishing affinity to the line of historical thought I have been discussing.

Much farther from this stream of thought than Professor von Mises is Karl Popper. His *The Open Society and Its Enemies* has been for some years quoted—at least in its title—as a manifesto for Liberalism. But whatever may be made out of that book (and much of it, be it said, cuts harder against the contemporary collectivists than against their critics), there is little in his newly published *The Poverty of Historicism* to please the Liberal mind. However different his ultimate philosophical attitudes are from those of Eric Voegelin or Herbert Butterfield, his historical criticism is a powerful intellectual weapon against determinism, whatever its origin.

A strong tide is moving, and it is not only sweeping the main channels, but working its way into all sorts of unexpected places. More than in any other area of intellectual endeavor, the trend of thought in the philosophy of history is a promising one.

Review of *Oriental Despotism,* by Karl A. Wittfogel

(National Review, June 22, 1957)

The first months of 1957 have produced two books that, taken together, may well form the foundations of a profound counter-revolution in a decisive ideological area, an area underlying and giving form to the politics of the century. Eric Voegelin's *Israel and Revelation* (the first volume of his projected five-volume *Order and History*) has already been reviewed in these pages (March 2, 1957). Karl A. Wittfogel's *Oriental Despotism, A Comparative Study of Total Power,* like Dr. Voegelin's book, is directed toward the destruction of the prevailing theories of history that have played so large a role in bringing about the agony of our time.

Dr. Voegelin and Dr. Wittfogel are very different men. Their starting points are far apart. But the impact of their criticism hits from different directions upon the historical myths that are the complement of relativist scientism and that, with it, determine the shape of the age.

The interplay between these two phenomena requires some explanation, if the significance of these two books is to be fully appreciated. The character of the last 200 years has, in the first instance, been determined by the triumph of rationalism and then of scientism over that balanced tension between the authority of tradition and the claims of reason which had characterized the mode of thought of Western civilization from its beginnings. With scientism, which attempts completely to destroy man's awareness of a divine purpose and meaning to his existence, the process reached its culmination. The proper consciousness now is swept clean of the unconditioned, the mysterious, the absolute. Everything is relative, useful, instrumental.

But there seems to be a law of compensation in the psyche

that forbids such violence being done to the structure of reality. Men cannot live in an antiseptic universe, inhabited only by gadgets and by human beings who are nothing but particularly clever gadgets. So, as if this vacuum of meaning had called into existence myths to furnish out the dry emptiness of a soulless universe, the age of rationalism and scientism has been at the same time the age of the deification of the forces of History.

From Hegel to Marx, and on to Spengler and Toynbee, powerful minds, rejecting the inspiration of their tradition but unable to believe in the meaninglessness of human life, have created these myths. They differ immensely among themselves, both in the distance of their removal from the integral tradition of the West and in the intensity of their impact upon the practical. But they have in common a double act of denial: to individual men, the denial of innate being and freedom of will; to God, the denial of transcendent being. History subordinates men to *its* being and replaces God, or drags Him down to a vague immanent "principle."

The contribution of Dr. Voegelin to the destruction of these myths has been to raise over against the prevalent approach to history a structure of interpretation of the destiny of man, firmly based upon the philosophy and theology of the West. Dr. Wittfogel's contribution is of a different kind, though of a vital importance to the disestablishment of the reigning historical myths. He approaches them, not from the outside, as it were, but as one who has had to work his way out of their influence. As he did so, he found it necessary to convince himself by a meticulous sapping operation directed toward the leveling of the decisive strong points that barred his way to freedom. The analysis of history displayed in *Oriental Despotism* is in a sense the record of that operation, as it is an unrivalled critique of the foundation of twentieth-century historical myth.

An historical scholar of eminence, one of the century's outstanding students of Chinese history, Dr. Wittfogel brought to this task an immense erudition at the service of a forceful intellect. To grasp the breadth and power with which he undermines the cant of contemporary historiography, it is necessary to read the book itself. Here it is only possible to summarize the heads of his achievement:

He has conclusively shown:

1. the similarity of the great irrigation-based despotisms of ancient and Eastern history to modern industrial-based totalitarianism;

2. that these tyrannies are not determined by economic necessity but are the result of a failure of "moral responsibility" in open historical situations;

3. that no evidence exists—that all the evidence is to the contrary—for the fatalistic unilinear interpretations of history that reduce men to the status of puppets of social forces and deny them moral autonomy;

4. that the essential difference between despotic, that is, "managerial," society and free society is the difference between single-centered and multi-centered power;

5. that, therefore, "strong private property" (that is, private property which exists in its own right and not by virtue of the grace of the state) is the sign and the guarantee of a free society; so that

6. in direct contradiction to the Marxist myth (which has penetrated far beyond Marxist circles), feudalism and capitalism are by their very character free societies, while all bureaucratic, "managerial," single-centered societies, whether those of ancient and Oriental despotism or those of modern socialism, are in their essence tyrannical.

On the basis of these conclusions, Dr. Wittfogel develops a many-sided refutation of the Marxist theory that "ruling classes" exist only on the basis of their control of property. Rather, Dr. Wittfogel shows that the holders of *political* power that goes beyond the minimum needs of any ordered society are the true tyrants. Ironically he turns Marx's description of ancient despotism as "general slavery" against the totalitarianism he fathered, maintaining that, in a way which even the worst of the ancient societies never approached, "general slavery" is the apt and accurate description of contemporary managerial totalitarianism.

It is Dr. Wittfogel's leading proposition that this fearful danger of the descent of general slavery upon all mankind is not "historically determined," is not the inevitable result of economic and social forces, is not a wave of the future that no man can resist. To the pervasive myth that history moves like a juggernaut that cannot be stopped by men, he counters: Historic situations are open situations, subject to the action of free men, of beings characterized by freedom of the will, accepting or rejecting their moral responsibilities.

Review of *Order and History*, Vol. II, *The World of the Polis;* Vol. III, *Plato and Aristotle*, by Eric Voegelin

(National Review, August 16, 1958)

The second and third volumes of Eric Voegelin's monumental *Order and History* (*The World of the Polis* and *Plato and Aristotle*) continue the grand development of his theme which was introduced in the first volume, *Israel and Revelation. Order and History* is a theory of history as the continuing and recurring struggle of men to realize their free being under God. But it is more than a theory of history; it is projected "not as an attempt to explore curiosities of a dead past, but as an inquiry into the structure of the order in which we live presently," as "one of the means of establishing islands of order in the disorder of the age."

Professor Voegelin has no less a goal than to controvert the two related theories of history which have created the world view that dominates our age: Marxism and the Liberal theory of progress. Both of them he sees arising from a rejection of the finite conditions of human life—ideologies which would substitute for the truly human end of "the love of being through love of divine Being as the source of . . . order," a Utopian drive to redesign the world in the image of a pattern of "perfection," distorted in its shape and hideous in its consequences because of the finite limitations of the human designer.

The essence of Professor Voegelin's interpretation of the drama of history was presented some years ago in *The New Science of Politics,* and more briefly in the Preface and Introduction to the first volume of *Order and History.* In reading each successive volume as it appears we must depend on these for the large outlines of his interpretation until *Order and History* is completed. The present volumes are immensely rich in their representation of Greek history and politics, epic and tragedy, religion and philosophy; but it is in the light of his larger design that they become transparent with a meaning not simply interpretive of the age of Hellas, but of all human existence in history and of the particular crisis in that history in which we live today.

The history of man, Professor Voegelin is saying, is the history of his understanding of his being and of the "symbolizations" in which that understanding has been expressed—on the one hand, in myth and poetry, philosophy and sacred writings, and on the other hand, in the structure of political and social institutions.

To summarize the main modes of that self-understanding, with a brevity that runs the risk of doing violence to Professor Voegelin's insights:

1. In the immemorial millennia of the great early civilizations in which conscious order was first born—Egypt, Mesopotamia, China (before Lao Tze and Confucius), India (before Gautama Buddha and Jainism)—the ultimate truth of man's being was felt and understood in such identity with the factual presence of civil rule and social existence that the soul of the individual person remained undifferentiated from the society around him. By consequence, the transcendent, the Eternal Ground of being and of truth, was inconceivable. God and King, Heaven and Earth, Truth and Representation, were

grasped in a unity that left no possibility for the emergence of the soul of the individual person or for recognition of the transcendent.

2. Almost simultaneously in Israel and in Greece, although in different ways, there burst through this undifferentiated primitive consciousness a new form of consciousness, a new "symbolization." This "leap in being," as Voegelin calls it, broke through the unity in which the social order below and the cosmic order above were conceived, so that both Greek and Jew were suddenly able to perceive an immense chasm. In Israel it was by the direct grace of Revelation; in Greece (with grace no less the effective cause, I think Professor Voegelin would say), by the effort of philosophy. In their different ways each civilization became aware of the tension between what is and what ought to be, between the immanent play of events in the world of actuality and the transcendent source of reality and ultimate value.

But deep as this revolution in ways of thought was, it stopped short of the confrontation of the individual person with the final Source of his being. The chasm that had appeared between God and man was too great, and the individual soul took refuge in collective unity with the *polis* (the city state) or "the Chosen People," which became, instead of the person, the moral link between immanent existence and transcendent value.

The temptation was to return to the unity of the cosmological empires by forcing upon society a pattern derived from the finite human understanding of the transcendent. But the consciousness of Hebrew prophet and Greek philosopher at their highest—but only at the end, when the civilizational order around them was in decay—caught a glimpse of the ultimate reality. Deutero-Isaiah and Jeremiah, Plato and Aristotle, broke beyond the containment of consciousness in a collective, however hallowed, and saw that "God is the measure" by which, without benefit of civil institution, the individual person is to be judged and must judge himself.

3. But this sublime insight remained the possession of philosopher and prophet. It could not become common to men and

thereby mediate an outlook on existence and a set of institutions without a more concrete and at once more profound solution of the contradiction between the transcendent and the immanent. Only with the ultimate act of grace, the Incarnation, "the flash of eternity into time," was it possible for the individual soul truly to recognize itself and its simultaneous existence in two worlds, the world of eternity and the world of time. And thereby it became possible for human persons, drinking deep of the source of their being, to create an historical order inspired by understanding of the transcendent but aware that earth is not heaven and that human life, though inspired by transcendent understanding, "must remain adjusted to the order of mundane existence." This understanding created our great tradition, which recognizes and is based upon "the tensions, frictions, and balances between the two levels of attunement, a dualistic structure of existence which expresses itself in pairs of symbols, of *theologia civilis* and *theologia supranaturalis,* of temporal and spiritual powers, of secular state and church."

4. In challenge to this balanced tension which is the high world view of the West, there has arisen in recent centuries a new outlook, at first obscure and clothed in religious terms, then more and more open and radically man-worshipping in philosophical content. This outlook Voegelin calls "gnosticism." Now dominating our world in its two forms of Communism and Liberalism, it threatens to destroy the wonder of man's discovery of his being under God in the conditions of a finite existence and the balanced institutions that reflect that understanding. This world view of "gnosticism" begins with a refusal to accept the conditions of mundane existence, with an overweening pride in the glimpsed image of perfection distorted by the limits of man's understanding, and with a determination to enforce it upon the world, come what may. It ends in the bloody terror of the Lubianka cellars or the dry terror of social-engineered conformity.

Until *Order and History* is finished, one cannot speak with assurance of Professor Voegelin's counsel to the West at this moment when our ancient and integral heritage is so mightily assaulted from without and from within. But judging both from his work as a whole, so far as we now have it, and from these latest volumes where the Greek experience of civilizational decay and spiritual rebirth is so vividly presented, it is possible to be reasonably certain. What he would seem to be saying is that our fate hangs in the balance and will depend upon the degree to which we are able not simply to recover the understanding of our ancestors, but to enrich it and deepen it so that it may live triumphant in an idiom that speaks to contemporary man.

It may be objected that this is the enterprise not of men of action, but of philosophers. Perhaps it is, and perhaps only that enterprise can save us. If so, Eric Voegelin will be long remembered as one of the foremost of those who defeated the forces of infamy.

Review of *The Might of the West,* by Lawrence R. Brown

(National Review, November 3, 1964)

In *The Might of the West,* Lawrence Brown has made a most impressive contribution to the understanding of the history of Western civilization and of the crisis of the twentieth century. Challenging the accepted assumption of received historical opinion by its forthright rejection of historical egalitarianism, it is not likely to be very well received. But then, this is not the first time in human experience that an immense gulf has existed between the true scholars of the epoch and those who succeed in imposing upon society as intellectual leaders. It has happened before that the norms of "educated" opinion are solidly based upon fallacies, long painstakingly exposed by the best thought of the age. But in this respect our age is one of the worst; in the whole area of thought about the nature and destiny of men, about their relations with each other, about their political, social and economic institutions, the greater part of what is taught in our schools and colleges, and preached through our omnipresent communications media, is decades behind the work of serious scholarship.

One could cite field after field, from the simplistic relativist ethics that our social workers and juvenile criminals alike soak up from their "education," to the vulgar semi-Marxist, semi-Keynesian economics that instruct our present course towards national bankruptcy. Nowhere, however, is the gap between true scholarship and received opinion more profound than in the field of history. And nowhere, perhaps, is that separation, between men intent on the search for truth and ideologists intent only on advancing their panaceas, more fraught with danger. For our sense of identity as participants in the fate of our nation and our civilization depends upon our sense of the history of that nation and that civilization.

A sense of the history from which our institutions and traditions have been derived is vital at every level of the social scale, even (possibly most importantly) at levels where it is understood only in the most general terms, only "mythologically." It is just this sense of identity, however, that the prevailing "educated" historiography of our time has devoted itself to pulverizing. The vulgarity of its anti-historical history, shallow enough at its source, becomes something close to pure drivel in the "social studies" of the schools. But at every level it substitutes sociological cant for historical insight, and relativist culture-egalitarianism for the national and civilizational pride that arises from an understanding of one's own past.

Meanwhile, over the recent decades in which this mummery has held the front of the stage, a truly tremendous feat of scholarship has created a corpus of work in the philosophy of history that is one of the outstanding intellectual achievements of Western man. The massive contributions of Spengler, Toynbee (in his early volumes, before he sold his historian's heritage for a mess of international pottage), Wittfogel, Voegelin, are the most impressive part, but a part only, of this colossal scholarly endeavor embracing hundreds upon hundreds of books and monographs.

The Might of the West is the most recent of these contribu-

tions. It is also one of the most stimulating. Like Spengler
and Toynbee (in his earlier phase), Lawrence Brown sees
history not as a linear development of an abstract "mankind,"
but as the life courses of a number of discrete civilizations,
such as the Egyptian, the Chinese, the Classical, the Western.
Like Spengler, but unlike Toynbee, he burns with a fierce love
of our own civilization. Unlike Spengler, however, he insists
that the fate of the West, like that of other civilizations before
it, rests in the hands of men, not in a mystic Destiny that
inexorably determines its dying and its death. Much though
he owes to Spengler, in fundamental concepts as in detailed
interpretations, the very title of his book, *The Might of the
West*, is a ringing challenge to Spengler's *Decline of the West*.
The unique quality of this book arises from Mr. Brown's ability
to combine an objective study of civilizations as civilizations
with commitment to our own civilization.

I suppose that anyone who is deeply concerned with the
problems of the interpretation of history will always have serious
criticisms of any one else who has the courage systematically
to commit his understanding to the printed page. Much though
I have learned from *The Might of the West*, I have nevertheless
many disagreements in detail with it and one or two major
criticisms of it. In the space available here I can only indicate
briefly what these latter are.

In the first place, although Mr. Brown has a vision of the
grandeur of the West of a kind that is missing in Toynbee
and is too narrowly circumscribed in Spengler by the dogma-
tisms of his system, he nevertheless seems to me to give far
too large a role to the technological excellence of our civilization
in his definition of its character and too small a role to what I
would regard as its essential genius and the characteristic distinguishing it from all other civilizations—the centricity of the
person in its world view.

This weakness of Mr. Brown's analysis seems to me to be
closely related to two other aspects of its historical thought: his
displacement of the Christian vision of man's fate as the decisive

force in the forming of the Western ethos and his derogation of the influence of Classical Civilization on the West. Both this displacement and this derogation in turn arise from an element in Mr. Brown's historical view which is in itself one of the great strengths of his work. That is his view of what he calls Levantine Civilization (roughly what Spengler called the Magian Civilization), the civilization he sees arising in late Roman times, in which early Christianity developed and which gave birth to Islam. His concept of this civilization is magnificently developed; but, in my opinion, he exaggerates its influence upon the West. It is this exaggeration which causes him to see Christianity as primarily a Levantine religion and to miss the tremendous significance of the development of Latin Christianity both for Christianity itself and as *the* forming influence of the West. It is also this which leads him to derogate the influence of Classical Civilization upon the West, since he maintains (although I think he by no means proves) that what we regard as Classical in our heritage is so distorted by transmission through Levantine Civilization that it is, in essence, not Classical but Levantine.

It is a mark of the power and insight of *The Might of the West* that, in spite of these weaknesses, it is a historical work of the utmost importance. Mr. Brown's searching and imaginative mind, his wide-ranging interest in all the facets of human life, give his book substance and depth. His firm commitment to Western Civilization, combined with a delicate historical sense, give it force and direction.

Western Civilization:
The Problem of Political Freedom

(*Modern Age*, Spring, 1968)

Western civilization arose in southern and western Europe on the ruins of the Roman empire, the final political form of Classical civilization. It is and has always been unique among the great civilizations of the past 5000 years, whose existence is the substance of recorded history. It is unique not simply in the sense that each civilization—the Egyptian or Chinese or Classical—is manifestly different from all the others, but in a much more profound sense. In its most important characteristics it stands apart not merely from each of them but from all of them; it is differentiated from them by almost as sharp a leap as differentiated the other civilizations from the pre-civilizational cultures of the Neolithic age. This is, I know, a disconcerting, even a shocking, statement by the standards of the cultural relativism that prevail in 20th century historical thought. I can only ask my readers to bear with me while I attempt to sustain it with a brief discussion of the civilizational history of mankind and the place of the West in the sweep of that history.

The significance of any civilizational order derives from the way in which it organizes the life and outlook of the individual persons who compose it in their relations to the universe in which they live—that is, in the way it relates the person to moral values, spiritual forces, the material environment, the other persons who make up the society. The various civilizations have done this in discernible styles. It is that style which defines their specific character.

For the first 2500 years of recorded history men lived in civilizations of similar styles, a style for which the Egyptian may stand as the type. These cosmological* civilizations conceived of existence so tightly unified and completely fashioned that there was no room for distinction and contrast between the individual person and the social order, between the cosmos and human order, between Heaven and earth, between what is and what ought to be. God and king, the rhythms of nature

* I take this term from Eric Voegelin's epoch-making *Order and History* (Baton Rouge, La.: Louisiana State University Press; Vol. I, 1956, Vols. II and III, 1957). I owe as well the concept that underlies this section to his work, but—as I have said previously in my *In Defense of Freedom*— I have developed that concept according to my own lights and he is certainly not responsible for the result.

and the occupations of men, social custom and the moral imperative, were felt not as paired opposites but as integral unities. The life of men in these civilizations, in good times and bad, in happiness and unhappiness, proceeded in harmony and accord with nature, which knows no separation between what is and what ought to be, no tension between order and freedom, no striving of the person for individuation or the complement of that striving, the inner personal clash between the aspirations of the naked self and the moral responsibilities impressed by the very constitution of being.

Exceptions, modifications, to this basic mode of human life there undoubtedly were. Man in his essence has always been, as Aristotle long ago saw, part animal, part spiritual. The clash at the center of his nature was never totally stilled. We have indeed documents from Mesopotamia and Egypt which show the stirrings of the impulses that shaped later ages. Nevertheless these are but stirrings; they do not express the age, or affect the essential character of the cosmological civilization. They are but premonitions of what is to come.

When it came, it came with historic suddenness. It came in different ways and for different reasons among two peoples of two new civilizations—the Greeks of Classical Civilization and the Jews of the Syriac Civilization. The way of its coming was as different as the character of these two peoples was different, but the new understanding was in essence the same. It shattered the age-old identity of the historic and the cosmic. It burst asunder the unity of what ought to be and what is. It faced individual men for the first time with the necessity, nay, the possibility of deep-going moral choice. In a word, it destroyed the unity of what is done by human beings and what they should do to reach the heights their nature opens to them. And, in doing so, this understanding created, for the first time, the conditions for individuation, for the emergence of the person as the center of human existence, by separating the immanent from the transcendent, the immemorial mode of living from its previous identity with the very constitution of being. The arrangements of society were dissociated from the sanction of ultimate cosmic necessity; they were desanctified and left open to the judgment of human beings. But that transcendent sanction remained the basis of the judgment of human life. The transcendent was not destroyed; it was re-affirmed in terms more profound and awesome than ever. The earthly immanent and the transcendent heavenly remained; but how now were they to be related each to each?

The nexus, the connecting link between the transcendent and the immanent, between the eternal and the historical, could be no other than the human person. Living in both worlds, subjected by the demands of his nature to transcendent value and at the same time maker of history and master of society, he was suddenly (suddenly as historical process goes) revealed to himself as a creature whose fate it was to bridge this newly yawning gulf.

I am not saying, of course, that the multitudes who made up Hellenic and Judaic society thought in these terms or even dimly glimpsed them conceptually. I do maintain two things: first, that the inspirers of the two societies, the prophets of Judah and Israel and the philosophers of Greece, grasped this new condition of mankind, grasped it in fear and trembling; and, secondly, that their understanding shaped the enduring *ethos* of their societies as surely as the *ethos* of the Pharaoh God-King shaped the society of Egypt.

This common understanding of the Judaic and Hellenic cultures was expressed, of course, in radically different forms— so different, indeed, that these cultures have been more commonly conceived as polar opposites than as different expressions of the same stupendous insight. This is not to deny what is sharply opposed in the two cultures, most especially their different understandings of the relationship of man to the transcendent. But the overriding fact is that in both these cultures, at their highest level, there emerged a clear distinction between the world and the transcendent, as well as the startlingly new concept of a direct relationship between men and the transcendent.

In the Hellenic civilization it was the philosophical movement culminating with Socrates, Plato and Aristotle that raised to the level of consciousness this new understanding of the nature of men and their relations to ultimate things. The sense of the individual, the person as over against society, had been inherent in the *ethos* of the Greeks from the dim beginnings of Hellenic civilization. Such a sense is apparent already in Hesiod and Homer. It inspires the human scale of their archaic temples, as contrasted with the monstrous inhumanity of scale of ziggurat, pyramid and sphinx. But this inherent tendency of the Greek spirit did not, for a number of reasons, decisively shape Hellenic society. In the beginning, in the Northern war bands from which it arose, the collectivity of the pack contended always against the individual spirit; also, from that heritage it drew a religious practice and a pantheon of gods almost devoid of transcendence. Further, Hellenic civilization developed in its youth under the looming influence of the great cosmological civilizations of the East, and when the aridity of its inherited pantheon drove men to search further, the mystery religions which arose were saturated through and through with Eastern concepts. Finally when the civilization reached maturity, the classical social form it assumed was the *polis*, the city state, which was a tight unity of society, government and religion. Despite the fact that within that form there was immeasurably greater room for the development of the individual personal consciousness than in the older civilizations, the shadow of the past and the limiting shackles of the life of the *polis* smothered and distorted the full emergence of the new consciousness.

It was the contradiction between the inherent Hellenic awakening to the possibilities of a new state of being and the trammels of the inherited old with which the Greek philosophers wrestled. What they created out of their struggles was the first systematic *intellectual* projection of an independent relationship between free men and transcendent value. (I stress "intellectual" because nearly simultaneously, in the Israel and Judah of the Prophetic age, there emerged another form of the same understanding, expressed not in intellectual but in existential and historic terms—a development I shall be discussing shortly.) The power and analytical depth of the Hellenic intellectual achievement were so great and profound that it has remained ever since a firm foundation for the philosophical and political thought of men who have been concerned with the freedom of the person and the authority of transcendent truth. But, as essential as the work of the Hellenic philosophers has been to the growth of this understanding, they were limited and their thought was distorted by two factors. That limitation and distortion prevented, particularly in their political theory, the fullest confrontation with the radical independence of human beings before earthly institutions, their dependence only upon the transcendent. Of these two factors, the first, the problem of what might be called Utopianism, is best considered after we have discussed the Judaic Prophetic experience, since it is a factor that affects it as well as the Hellenic philosophical experience. The second factor was the effect of the life of the *polis* upon the consciousness of the Greek philosopher.

The mode of being of men living in the *polis* was effectively constrained by the character of that community. As I have said, the *polis* was at once state, society, and religious cult, all wrapped up in one. The citizen of such a state was truly, as Aristotle called him, "a political animal," that is, an animal of the *polis*. It was the *polis* that gave him human stature; outside of it, he was only potentially human. Such men the Greeks called "barbarians"—making little distinction between uncivilized tribal peoples and the subjects of the great civilized empires of the Middle East.

There was reason in this disdain in which the men of the *polis* held the cosmological civilizations of the Middle East.

Although the form of the *polis* stood between its citizens and their full achievement of freedom by independent individual confrontation of the transcendent realm of value, it did so in a different way and to a far less degree than did the cosmological societies. Hellas had broken loose from a world in which human existence was completely absorbed in the cosmos, in which the earthly and the transcendent were so merged that the person could not stand free, clearly and sharply delineated from the surrounding universe. But this new consciousness of the Hellenic spirit was bound still by the necessity of expressing itself through a collectivity—no longer the cosmic collectivity of the Middle East, but a socio-political collectivity, the *polis*. It was, indeed, a great leap forward toward men's consciousness of their personhood and their freedom, because now the limiting form on individual freedom and individual confrontation of transcendent destiny was a collectivity composed of the subjective spirit of men, not the objective, totally external, roll of iron cosmic fatality. Nevertheless, the Hellenic philosophers who expressed this spirit at its highest level always had to struggle, in their farthest penetrations towards the meaning of human existence, against the circumstances of being and thought created by *polis* society.

The Judaic experience was extraordinarily parallel to the Hellenic, although its content was very different. The Hebrew prophets, like the Greek philosophers, expressed, at the highest level, the consciousness of a people broken loose from cosmological civilization to confront transcendence. As *Exodus* is the symbol of that breaking away, the content of the Judaic experience of transcendence is the belief in a unique, personal, revealed God.

But here also, as among the Greeks, a social structure distorted the individual experience of transcendence. The potentialities for full individuation inherent in the concept of a God of Righteousness were collectivized. The concept of the *b'rith*, the compact between God and the Chosen People, placed the collectivity of the Judaic people, rather than the individuals who made up that collectivity, as the receptor of the inter-change with transcendence. The Prophets strove mightily with these circumstances, as the Greek philosophers struggled with the circumstances of the *polis*. Future events have taken from them both an inspiration and an understanding that are derived from the thrust of their struggle towards individuation, but neither the philosophy of Hellas nor the prophecy of Israel ever completely threw off the conditioning influence of their social and intellectual heritage.

At the heights of the philosophical and Prophetic endeavors, in a Plato or a proto-Isaiah, as occasionally among their prede-cessors and followers, the vision cleared and a simple con-frontation between individual men and transcendence stood for a moment sharply limned. But at these heights of under-standing another problem arose, one I have referred to above when discussing the Hellenic experience and have called the problem of Utopianism. A clear vision of the naked confronta-tion of individual men with transcendence created a yawning gap in human consciousness. It was something of the effect of eating the fruit of the Tree of the Knowledge of Good and Evil. On the one hand stood the perfection of transcend-ence, and on the other the imperfection of human existence. The temptation was enormous to close that intolerable gap, to grasp that understood transcendent perfection and by sheer human will to make it live on earth, to impose it on other human beings—by persuasion if possible, by force if necessary.

The same temptation beset the Hellenic philosophers at their highest reach of vision. The effect of this temptation was portentous for the future, because of its continuing impact upon both the Hellenic and the Judaic traditions, the twin sources from which our Western civilization derives so much of its content. Its effects can be perceived in the most diverse areas: in the effect on Western thought of the concepts of moulding human life implicit in the Utopian society of Plato's *Republic* or in the dictatorial powers of the Nocturnal Council in his somewhat less rigid *Laws;* or in the actual political absolutism, derived from the Judaic tradition, of such polities as Calvin's Geneva or Spain of the Inquisition or Cromwell's England. Secularized with the passage of time, the Utopian desire to impose a pattern of what the imposers consider perfection becomes ever more rigid, total and terrible, as in the all-powerful Nation of the French Revolution or the Dictatorship of the Proletariat of the Communists.

The Utopian temptation arises out of the very clarity of vision that tore asunder the cosmological world view. Released from the comforting, if smothering, certainties of identification with the cosmic order, men became aware of their freedom to shape their destiny—but with that freedom came an awesome sense of responsibility. For the same leap forward that made them fully conscious of their own identity and their own freedom made them conscious also of the infinite majesty and beauty of transcendence and of the criterion of existence that perfection puts before human beings, who in their imperfection possess the freedom to strive to emulate perfection. A yawning gulf was opened between infinity and finity.

There are two possible human reactions to the recognition of this reality.

On the one hand, it can be accepted in humility and pride—humility before the majesty of transcendence and pride in the freedom of the human person. That acceptance requires willingness to live life on this earth at high tension, a tension of men conscious simultaneously of their imperfection and of their freedom and their duty to move towards perfection. The acceptance of this tension is the distinguishing characteristic of the Western civilization of which we are a part, a characteristic shared by no other civilization in the world's history.

On the other hand, the hard and glorious challenge of reality can be rejected. The tension between perfection and imperfection can be denied. Men conscious of the vision of perfection, but forgetting that their vision is distorted by their own imperfection, can seek refuge from tension by trying to impose their own limited vision of perfection upon the world. This is the Utopian temptation. It degrades transcendence by trying to set up as perfect what is by the nature of reality imperfect. And it destroys the freedom of the individual person, by forcing upon him conformity to someone else's limited human vision, robbing him of freedom to move towards perfection in the tension of his imperfection. It is in form a return to the womb of the cosmological civilization, in which the tension of life at the higher level of freedom was not required of men, in which they could fulfill their duties in uncomplicated acceptance of the rhythms of the cosmos, without the pain or the glory of individuation. But Utopianism is only similar to cosmological civilization in form; in essence it is something different, because cosmological civilization was, as it were, a state of innocence, while Utopianism comes after the eating of the fruit of the Tree of Knowledge of the persons of God and men. It is a deliberate rejection of the high level at which it is now possible for men to live, and as such it distorts and oppresses the human spirit. Yet it has remained, ever since the Hellenic and Judaic break through the cosmological crust, an ever prevalent historical factor. In particular, as Western civilization is the civilization that accepts and lives with the tension of spirit, Utopianism has been a constantly recurring destructive force within it.

Indeed, the history of Western civilization is the history of the struggle to carry forward its insight of tension, both against the remaining inherited traumas of the cosmological attitude in its social structure and in its intellectual outlook and against the continuing recrudescence of Utopianism. For Western civilization inherited, as the Hellenic and Judaic did before it, much continuing influence from the long eons of cosmological life. And, although the forms of its thought and the content of its spirit rise directly out of the Hellenic and the Judaic themselves, it broke as far beyond them as they broke beyond the cosmological civilization. It founded itself, in its inmost core, on acceptance of the tension between the transcendent and the

individual human person and on the reconciliation of that
tension implicit in the great vision of the Incarnation—the flash
of eternity into time.

The history of Western civilization, since it came into being
out of the fermenting remnants left behind by the death of
Classical civilization, is distinguished by a preeminent regard
for the person. This is not to say that this regard has always,
indeed generally, been ideally reflected in its institutions and
social reality; but it is to insist that, at the heart of the concept
of being that forms the limiting notions by which the West has
lived, the preeminence of the person has prevailed. And this is
true of no previous civilization. It is of course a concept, a view
of reality, at the opposite end of the scale from that of the
cosmological civilizations. But it also goes radically beyond the
intermediate experience of the Hellenic and Judaic civilizations.
Although they, each in their own way, broke through the
cosmological unity, they did so not in the name of the person
as such but rather in the name of collectivities of persons, the
polis and the Chosen People.

It was given to the West to drive to fruition the insights
glimpsed in Greece and Israel. Its consciousness founded upon
the symbol of the Incarnation placed the person at the center
of being. From this very deepening of the understanding of
the person there arises, even more than in Greece and Israel,
a Utopian temptation; and that Utopianism has been expressed
right down to our own day in more and more extreme forms.
But while the factors we have discussed, which lead to Utopianism, are by the very nature of the Western concept of
transcendence more intense than ever before, the symbol of the
Incarnation that has made possible that concept and the temptation ensuing therefrom, also offers a resolution of the pressures
leading to Utopianism, a resolution that did not exist in Greece
and Israel. The simultaneous understanding that there exists
transcendent perfection and that human beings are free and
responsible to move towards perfection, although incapable of
perfection, no longer puts men in an intolerable dilemma: the

dilemma either, on the one hand, of denying their freedom and their personhood and sinking back into cosmological annihilation within a pantheistic All, or on the other hand of trying by sheer force of will to rival God and, as Utopians, to impose a limited human design of perfection upon a world by its nature imperfect. The Incarnation, understood as the "flash of eternity into time," the existential unity of the perfect and the imperfect, has enabled men of the West to live both in the world of nature and in the transcendent world, without confusing them. It has made it possible to live, albeit in a state of tension, accepting both transcendence and the human condition with its freedom and imperfection.

It is that tension which is the distinguishing mark of Western civilization. Of course, to say that for the West alone has it been possible to live in that state of tension, to rise above both cosmic absorption and the temptation of Utopianism, is not to say that either the men of the West or the institutions of the West have always, or even generally, existed at the heights that were open to them. It is only to say that in our civilization alone has such a conquest of these twin pitfalls of human history been possible. Further, it is to say that the direction of the understanding of the West has been towards a grasp of this insight, that the institutions of the West at their best reflected it, and that the men of the West at their highest moments were inspired by it. The West has strayed often, indeed constantly, towards the fleshpots of cosmic authoritarianism, as towards the false paradise of Utopianism. The history of the straying in the one and the other direction is the history of the West. But always there remained in the reservoirs of Western consciousness a solution not given to other civilizations, a way out from the impasse of previous human history, the way of its genius—life at the height of tension.

The characteristic concepts, institutions, and style of the West, where they stand in the sharpest contrast to those of other civilizations, are shot through and through with tension. And this is true from the most matter-of-fact levels of existence to the most exalted. Everywhere, impossible contradictions maintain themselves to create the most powerful and noble extensions of the Western spirit. At the most mundane level, the economic, the Western credit system takes leave of hard matter, etherializing money, the very foundation of production and exchange. The Gothic cathedral, thrusting to the heavens, denies the weighty stone of which it is built, while rising from the center of its city it affirms the beauty of materiality. The doctrine of the Lateran Council, central to the philosophical tradition of the West, proclaimed, after a thousand years of intellectual effort, the pure tension of the Incarnational unity, in radical differentness, of the material and the transcendent. This is the mode of the West at its highest and most typical. But always the human heritage of the cosmological civilizations has pressed upon it, distorting its understanding, exerting a pull dragging it down from the height of its vision.

Nowhere was the effect of this force more profound in stifling and destroying the development of the Western genius than in the political sphere. It is here that the vision of the West should have been translated into actual relations of power that would have made the revolt from cosmologism real through and through the lives of individual men.

The state in the cosmological civilizations, reflecting the overall world-view of these civilizations, was the sanctified symbol of the cosmos. In it resided both earthly and transcendent meaning, unified in a grand power that left to the individual person little meaning or value beyond that which adhered to him as a cell of the whole.

In radical contrast, the vision of the West, splitting asunder the transcendent and the earthly, placed their meeting point in tension, in the souls of individual men. The individual person became, under God, the ultimate repository of meaning and value. That world-view demanded a consonant political structure, one in which the person would be primary, and all institutions—in particular the state—secondary and derivative. But Western civilization in Europe never achieved this in serious measure, either in practice or in theory. The continuing heritage of cosmologism, which again and again, in all spheres, arose to resist, weaken and destroy the Western vision, here, in the political sphere, combined with the natural lust of men for power to maintain in large measure the age-old sanctification of the state.

The Western spirit broke through, of course, so that neither the state nor thought about the state was purely cosmological. In their thought, Christian men could never fully divinize the state; and in their practice, they early created two sets of tensions which divided power, thus effectively preventing the full re-emergence of the cosmological state and creating room for the existence of the person to a degree impossible in cosmo-logical civilization. Those two sets of tensions were, on the one hand, the separate centers of power represented by the Church and secular political power—Empire or monarchy—and, on the other hand, the broad decentralization of secular power inherent in the feudal system. Nevertheless, both the holders of hierar-chical churchly power and of secular power (first, the Holy Roman Emperors and then the emerging territorial monarchs) moved with all their strength to re-establish cosmological unity. The inner spirit of the West resisted and for long centuries the issue swayed back and forth in the balance. Only, indeed, in the 16th, 17th and 18th centuries, with the subordination of church (whether Protestant or Catholic) to state, with the increasing subordination of feudal and local rights to central authority, with the emergence of the absolutist monarchies of Bourbon, Tudor and Habsburg, was the Western drive towards diversity and separation of powers tamed. Never, in fact, was cosmologism, even in the political sphere, established in the West. It took cosmologism's twin, Utopianism, in the form of the mass egalitarian nationalism of the French Revolution, to make the decisive break towards mystical statism, to sow a harvest which was fully reaped by the totalitarianisms of the 20th century.

All this is not to maintain that the political forms of the West were ever in a deep sense cosmological or even that the Utopian state in its grim parody of cosmologism, approached totalism until the emergence of the Communism and Nazism of our time. It is, however, to assert that Western civilization in its European experience did not achieve political institutions fully coherent with its spirit.

Likewise, the basic thrust of Western political theory on the European continent (and in England, though to a lesser degree) was bound always within the categories of the Hellenic philosophers and the Hebrew prophets. Neither of these influences allowed the expression of the full drive of the Western spirit towards the primacy of the person and the limitation of political powers. The one, bounded by the *polis,* could only conceive of full freedom of the person in the emancipated flight of the philosopher beyond temporal conditions; the other, inheriting the concept of the Chosen People—even when it enlarged that concept to all humanity in the manner of a proto-Isaiah, could grasp the freedom of the person only in other-worldly relationships between man and God. Both the Hebrew and the Hellenic influences bore strongly against the development of a political philosophy that would provide the basis for a political structure solidly based on the primacy of the person and directed towards achieving the greatest possible freedom of the person.

It is true that the underlying *ethos* of the West again and again moved in this direction. Much of the thought of mediaeval political philosophers and legal theorists, some of the arguments of writers on both sides of the Papal-Imperial struggle, the tradition of the common law of England, drove in this direction. But these efforts, while they broke ground for the future, never rose to the creation of a truly Western political philosophy of freedom. And when, in the ferment that culminated in the French Revolution, it seemed as though such a concept might break through, it was swallowed up in the communitarian outlook typified by Rousseau, in the egalitarianism of the collective Nation, and by the Revolution itself and the nationalisms that followed in its wake throughout the continent.

In England, both in practice and in theory, there arose out of the conflicts of the 17th century and the relaxation of the 18th, something closer to a society of personal freedom and limited government. But the drag of established ideas, institutions and power held that society back from achieving the political potentiality towards which it was moving.

Thus the stage was set, when the American experience reached its critical point and the United States was constituted. The men who settled these shores, and established an extension of Western civilization here, carried with them the heritage of the centuries of Western development. With it they carried the contradiction between the driving demands of the Western *ethos* and a political system inconsonant with that *ethos*. In the open lands of this continent, removed from the overhanging presence of cosmological remains, they established a constitution that for the first time in human history was constructed to guarantee the sanctity of the person and his freedom. But they brought with them also the human condition, which is tempted always by the false visions of Utopianism.

The establishment of a free constitution is the great achievement of America in the drama of Western civilization. The struggle for its preservation against Utopian corrosion is the continuing history of the United States since its foundation, a struggle which continues to this day and which is not yet decided.

Chapter Seven

On Education

Deweyism in American Education

(Freeman, September, 1954)

The symptoms of deterioration in our educational system—long apparent to serious observers—have become so obvious that the fact of deterioration is now a matter of public concern. Everyone except the educational bureaucrats, whose vested interest is under fire, and the "liberals," to whom any attack on any state institution is impermissible, agrees that something has gone wrong. But what? Why is it that the school graduate accumulates so little learning from the years invested in the modern school? And why is he so devoid of any sense of values?

Starkly, in the corruption of our children, we stand face to face with the truth that "ideas have consequences," that philosophical thought is not a dreamer's luxury but the most powerful of forces. The present state of American education is the direct consequence of the pragmatic-instrumentalist philosophy of John Dewey. Applied to the educational process and transmitted to the American educational system through a network of associations, training schools and publications, these theories have, in little more than a generation, annihilated the education which for a thousand years formed the men who made Western civilization. This education, inherited from classical Greece and transmuted by Christianity, molded the framers of our Constitution and the leaders of the Republic in its early years.

It was based on the assumption that the function of the school is to train the mind and transmit to the young the culture and tradition of the civilization—leaving everything else necessary to the raising of the new generation to the family, the church, and other social institutions. This assumption, of course, implied the acceptance of certain other assumptions of a philosophical kind: that there is such a thing as truth; that the tradition of Western civilization embodies the conclusions of countless generations in the search for truth; that value resides innately in the individual, so that the claims of society and the state are secondary to and derived from him. It implied definite social and political beliefs: that, although all men are created with certain inalienable rights, individuals vary in capacity and ability; that, therefore, in the name of equality, to deprive the able of the opportunity to realize their ability is as great an oppression as to enslave the many for the benefit of the few. And it implied an important psychological presupposition: that, like everything else worth having, education can be acquired only at the cost of work and pain.

Today, one can examine volume after volume of the proliferating official literature which prescribes the practice of our educational system and find scarcely a trace of the great concepts of Western education. It is not that the training of the mind and the transmission of the truths asserted by our civilization have been forgotten; they have been deliberately and consciously eliminated. Those who have done the eliminating have made no secret of their intentions. From the writings of John Dewey himself down through all the literature of the "philosophy of experience," as Dewey liked to call his instrumentalist pragmatism, these concepts are branded as reactionary obstacles to the development of the New Education.

For the instrumentalist there can be no cultural heritage worth transmitting; values are a superstition left over from the

Middle Ages; what is right and good is what serves as an instrument to achieve adjustment to the society immediately around. Therefore, the aim of education must be "life adjustment" and the method, "life experience." Above all, the teacher must "impose" nothing. His role is not to teach the wisdom that a great civilization and a great nation have created, but to "cooperate" with the child in gaining "acquaintance with a changing world," where "experience" and "free activity" will somehow magically educate him. Thus he will grow up free of the "stifling authoritarianism" of the old education, and become independent of mind and will.

Now, as a matter of fact, it is nonsense to assume that because the child is not taught values and drilled into habits of thought he will spontaneously develop an educated independence of thought. What will happen instead is what is happening. The teacher, freed from the responsibility of teaching "abstract values" in a disciplined manner, must fill the gap with something. Being under pressure to bring about "adjustment" to the environment, he fills it with the current prejudices of his environment, and the prejudices of a contemporary educationist or a teacher trained by educationists are certain to reflect the fashionable collectivism of the day.

This nihilistic method not only ends thus in collectivism; it destroys the very ability to think clearly about anything. To learn to think requires effort and pain. There being no pressure to exert effort or to undergo pain, the mental habits of run-of-the-mill students are simply slovenly, while the bright ones develop into brash youngsters in whom flashes of brilliance only emphasize lack of intellectual development. That there are still a few hard-thinking young people about can only be put down to the remaining vestiges of home influence and the providential survival of a few good teachers in the interstices of our educational institutions.

This is a tragedy, first of all because it dwarfs the true potentialities of man. It makes scarcer and scarcer, year in and year out, the development of individuals strongly rooted in the wisdom of the past and capable of standing on their own against error, whim and fashion. But it is also a social tragedy. Such individuals are the only kind of men who can give society the leadership it must have if it is to solve its problems in the spirit of right and justice, to reject facile and erroneous solutions, and to survive as a free association of individuals.

The primacy of society and the state over the individual, which is the essence of collectivism, can never be enforced so long as such men exist in reasonable quantities. The New Education, by destroying the possibility of rearing such men, by inculcating "adjustment to society"—which can only mean subservience to society—has been perhaps the most important factor in making possible that widespread acquiescence in collectivism with which the body politic is today so deeply infected. It has left its students bereft of any defense against the fallacies of collectivism, unable to think their way through political problems, and with a vague uneasy feeling that anyone who puts the individual above the group or the state is somehow evil. Its effect has been catastrophic, and that catastrophe is the direct outcome of the philosophy of John Dewey and his followers.

But the question still remains: what were the political and social conditions which made it possible for this philosophy to prevail? In my opinion, the conditions for the triumph of Deweyism in our schools and the consequent decay of education were created by a process which set in a hundred years ago or more. The invasion of the field of education by public tax-supported authority was the first great breach in the concept of a government limited in its powers to the maintenance of internal and external order, the concept upon which our Republic was founded.

The movement for universal free compulsory state education begins simultaneously with the emergence in American history, in the person of Andrew Jackson, of the type which Franklin Roosevelt brought to perfection, the demagogic "leader of the masses." By the turn of the century the movement was largely successful. The decay of the quality of American education had already been signalized by many eminent observers, and the foundation had been laid for the debacle of the past thirty years.

If all must be educated equally and in the same way, and if education must be "produced" without competition under the monopolistic control of a bureaucracy, then the very idea of quality in education will go by the board. What is wanted is not the development of the spirit of man but its acclimatization to the mediocrity of the mass. To such a system of "education" Dewey's theories were well adapted; when quality and differentiation were rejected, his ideas were bound to win out.

Education in the true sense, the opportunity for every individual to develop himself to the limits of his ability, is the most valuable thing a father can provide for his children. Had the spirit of the American Republic been fulfilled in this field, is there any reason to doubt that, with the increase of wealth in the last 150 years, there would have been as multifarious, diverse and brilliant a growth of educational opportunities under the enterprise of private individuals and independent groups, as has taken place in other fields? Under such circumstances, if the false theory of Deweyism had gained influence in some institutions in a competitive educational network, its obvious inferiority would soon have put them out of business. Or, at the least, it would have restricted their patronage to those who could not recognize a superior product. Nor can it be alleged that this would have restricted good education to the wealthy. Competition would have made educational opportunities as common as it has made the automobile.

The entrance of the state into education, however, moving inevitably through quasi-monopoly toward monopoly, crushes all differentiations. Its leveling effort to assure that no unworthy son of a wealthy father shall receive an education he does not deserve, has made it certain that no one, rich or poor, shall receive an education pitched above the dead level of the mediocre.

For the achievement of the mediocre, for the destruction of individualism, for the transformation of a Republic into a mass state, the philosophy of Deweyism has created the ideal educational system.

The Wrong Alarm

(National Review, August 1, 1956)

There has been a good deal of to-do in the press lately about the rate at which the Soviet Union is training scientists and technologists, and about our "dangerous lag" in this respect. Eminent educationists shake their heads gravely about it, as they agitate for federal aid to education. Columnists and bureaucrats dwell upon it as evidence of "the new challenge to American democracy in the epoch of coexistence."

Neither the reliability of Soviet statistics nor the motivations of the Americans who keep drumming on this theme are sufficiently above question to lead one to react to this latest ringing of the Establishment's alarm bell with very serious concern. It is hardly likely that the field upon which the United States of America will be defeated is the field of technology, of production, of the pragmatic.

But in the rhetoric with which this campaign is conducted there is strikingly revealed a matter which is of the greatest concern. The "production"—the word recurs repeatedly—of technologists and scientists is equated with the highest aim of education. Our educational system is condemned not because it creates, as it does, intellectual and moral dwarfs, but because it is not even more efficient than it is in producing robots for the research laboratories. As in the Johnny-can't-read furor of the past year or two, the whole concentration is upon techniques.

An age which is dedicated to the proposition that knowledge is power has drawn the logical corollary from that maxim, and has more and more limited its definition of knowledge to that which gives power. With ever increasing acceleration it has transformed education into training. Now, brute animals, which apparently are created without the need for education—that is, for indoctrination in tradition and development of the reason—can benefit from training pure and simple. But human beings, necessary as is training to enable them to play their roles in the workaday world, whether as bricklayers or lawyers or atomic physicists, must, to be men, also be educated, each in the light of his capacities and to the highest degree that circumstances make possible.

Training is secondary to education; and when the ends of education are lost sight of, the true nature of man is dwarfed. Indeed, to judge by the cries of alarm that are now rising from those who are concerned primarily with the training of men to harness power, the degradation of education would seem to bring in its wake a decay in the very process of training itself. The Deweyan thistle is, of course, not bringing forth figs. That it could not be expected to do. But in its sterility it seems to be failing more and more to bring forth even thistles.

It will be a long time, however, before the efficiency of our *training* lags so badly that we need seriously worry about being surpassed by any nation on earth in the sphere of the technological and the practical. It is in the sphere not of training, but of education, the sphere of the moral and intellectual understanding that should control and direct technological power, that our physical no less than our spiritual survival is threatened. There is no need to emphasize what is happening to the second generation of those exposed to the radiation of the theories of relativism, the generation for whose amorality the cant phrase is "juvenile delinquency." It is only necessary to look at the moral concepts which inspire the dominant national policies of the day to recognize what the prevalent intellectual attitude, contemptuous of serious consideration of the being and end of man, has brought forth.

No one, of course, could accuse either Dwight D. Eisenhower or Charles E. Wilson of being in any direct sense a product of Deweyan thought; but the "experts" who surround them, and who fill their mushy platitudes with whatever content they have, are almost to a man representatives of the trend of which Dewey is the outstanding symbol. They are sons of "the revolt against formalism," that is, of the denial of objective truth and of objective moral values.

The answer of the Eisenhower Administration to the trumpet call of the heroic uprising at Poznan was typical of the instrumentalist outlook, to which good and evil are but relative reflections of the *mores* of differing cultures, and honor an outmoded superstition. To the aspirations of the insurgents—our allies—for freedom, it responded with silence or sophism; and, taking pity upon their material desperation, it offered food —to their oppressors, the tyrants of Warsaw. As that gallant gesture faded into defeat, and the bloody, systematic repression of a police state began to grind its remorseless course, Secretary Wilson, testifying before a Senate Committee, expatiated on the "liberalization" of the Soviet Empire, and amiably discussed the Soviet leaders as if they were the executives of some rival Ford or Chrysler corporation.

The greatest technological triumphs are powerless in association with such a moral paralysis and intellectual blindness, which, to purchase a moment of peace and prosperity, bemuses itself as to the nature of the enemy and shirks the hard duty of confronting evil uncompromisingly. It is this flabby and unprincipled attitude, which smiles benignly on evil and promotes "cultural interchange" with it, that gives substance to the dark and ominous foreboding that ours is the "losing side." If this is not to be, it will be not upon an increased "production" of scientists, a more efficient training for technical proficiency, but upon a new—and old—understanding of the ends of human life, upon education for intellectual clarity and moral insight, that the issue will depend.

More of the Same Won't Help

(National Review, January 25, 1958)

The guided uproar about the training of scientists and technologists that is now sweeping the country is based upon arguments which at first sight have a certain simple plausibility: *major premise,* the Soviets have apparently made an impressive breakthrough on an important technological front; *minor premise,* the Soviets are training *x*-thousand more scientists and technologists per year than we are; *conclusion,* to meet the Soviet threat we must train *y*-thousand more scientists and technologists than we are now training. Therefore, the way to save the country is to direct our entire educational system toward the production of scientists and technologists.

Like most simple arguments about complex problems, the present favorite formula of pundit and President abounds in fallacies. To treat the more obvious ones first:

1. There is no proof whatever that Soviet advances in the rocket-missile field are due to the superiority of their scientists or their technologists; rather it would seem that they are the result of a political-military decision to concentrate the maximum of money and scientific manpower on the problem. Here, the Administration of a Chief Executive who believes that "war is unthinkable" concentrated its economies upon military development while "welfare" expenditures continued to expand.

2. Even if it could be proved that we have suffered from a shortage of first-class personnel available for decisive technical projects in the military field, this would by no means prove that scientists of the highest ability did not exist in sufficient quantity in this country. It has been clear for a number of years that a well-directed and highly organized strike and sabotage operation against scientific development in the military field has been conducted by an important group of scientists, aided and abetted by other sections of the Liberal Establishment. One need only mention such instances as Einstein's widely publicized advice to a young scientist to go on strike; Oppenheimer's sabotage of the hydrogen bomb; Norbert Wiener's refusal to participate in military projects.

3. The crowning absurdity of the argument arises from the pleasant thought that the Soviet leaders are playing for marbles. If we really had fallen disastrously behind in the technological

race because we simply did not have the scientists and technologists to equal the Soviets', if therefore the Soviets were moving rapidly toward a technological supremacy to which our only answer was the education of the next generation— what kind of Communists would they be who would hesitate for a moment to smash us? If the situation were indeed so bad, the education of a new generation of scientists would be totally irrelevant. There could be only two logical conclusions to the argument: surrender, or immediate all-out war while we still possessed general superiority or parity.

But all these fallacies are relatively minor compared to the fundamental fallacy. That is the assumption that our overriding problem is a technological one. Granted we do have such a problem; granted the Soviets have made immense advances. But suppose tomorrow we reported a stunning technological triumph —an impenetrable anti-aircraft and anti-missile defense, or the conquest of the principle of anti-gravity—what would we do with it? For almost a decade after 1945 we possessed paramount technological power and available military predominance in decisive weapons sufficient to guarantee the success of any principled and steadfast foreign policy. What did we do with it? During those years an additional third of the world was conquered by the Communists.

There is a kind of macabre logic in the current concentration of interest upon the educational system. The failures of that system do have a great deal to do with the present travail of the nation—but not because it has failed to train scientists and technologists. Predominant educational theory has been all too scientific, all too technological. It is not scientists it has failed to produce, it is men. It is in the education of men imbued with the intellectual and spiritual heritage of Western civilization that it has failed desperately. And without such men, is there any wonder that the will to defeat the Soviets, the will to utilize our strength, has disintegrated?

The education of men as intellectual and spiritual beings is logically and existentially prior to any training of specialized capacities. Only an educational system based upon the vision of man as a creature destined to ends beyond the utilitarian can contribute to the making of such men. No education based upon the scientific outlook and method can meet this criterion.

The scientific outlook, impressive though its triumphs have been in the past century and a half, is concerned only with control and manipulation. It explores nature in order to create instrumentalities for the control of nature. When it turns to men, as in the "social sciences," it is to create instrumentalities for the control of men. It is pragmatic to the core, totally unconcerned with the ends of existence, with the destiny of man, with the very meaning of the Good.

Our stupendously footless educational system was sired by John Dewey out of Teachers College under the sign of the pragmatic and instrumentalist scientific method. It has been a major factor in the creation of a society dedicated to the proposition that everything is instrumental and relative, that there is no good or evil, no high or low, no noble or ignoble.

Certainly our educational system must be recast from top to bottom if we as a nation and the champions of a civilization are to survive. But what is needed is not more emphasis on science and the pragmatic, but less. What is needed is a return to education based upon what Alfred North Whitehead called "the habitual vision of greatness," an education that displays to men the grandeur of their destiny, the nobility of their duty.

The New Dark Ages: "Book" as a Four-Letter Word

(National Review, May 9, 1959)

I read enough of the specialized academic, educational and publishing-trade press to have supposed I was no longer susceptible to shock. But a report in *Publishers' Weekly* of the American Textbook Publishers' 1959 management conference shattered my assurance that I knew the worst. The session was devoted to "new developments in educational materials and media of instruction" and was well bolstered with some twenty-five "guest experts" from the Fund for the Advancement of Education, the National Advisory Committee on the National Education Act, the National Education Association, and various universities and school systems.

What was exposed at this session was a glimpse of things to come, things partly already here, in the Brave New World of the intellect which the Liberal worship of the instrument—of technology—is building for us. The up-and-coming planners of the intellectual and educational future, who dominated the conference, proclaimed the theophany of the gadget, the conquest of mind by machine—the victory of television, the electronic calculator, and "mass communications technique" over the spirit. And no one in the assemblage, as far as one can find out from the published report, rose to say them nay.

Let me be clear. I am not denying the auxiliary value of television and "audio-visual aids" in the training of students in some technical subjects, any more than I would deny the value of diagrams in a technological manual. But the challenge laid down at this conference—and not only here, but wherever the Liberal view of education is today put forward, as in the *Saturday Review*, in the *College Board Review*, increasingly in the educationist press—is of a different order. It is the claim for these gadgets not as auxiliary, but as central; not for the purposes of training (which is the conditioning of operators), but as the essence of education (which is the civilizing of human beings and the opening of souls). Though, of course, neither to these men nor to their Deweyite predecessors is there any distinction between the two functions.

What we are seeing now is the second stage of the Liberal and Deweyite revolution in education. The first substituted man for God and whim for value. This second abolishes man in turn, and with him, his whims. No longer do we hear of "child-centered education" as the foundation of educational theory, but, instead, the talk is of "the technological revolution in communication which is shaking the roots of modern society," of impersonal processes, of the inexorable movement of science, of "the wave of the future." A materialist determinism, as inhuman as it is ignorant and scornful of the divine, buries the very concept of education as the exaltation of the young to truly human status, through their initiation and indoctrination in values permanent in time and beyond time.

The educationist servitors of this determinism threatened the assembled publishers: either accept the future or "be carried kicking and screaming into the new educational era." The sanction was economic: if the books they publish are not reduced to the level of auxiliaries to the central process of electronic education, they will go bankrupt. "Your books look too permanent," scolded Philip H. Coombs, Secretary of the Fund for the Advancement of Education. "The better job education does in stimulating new scientific and cultural developments," said John E. Ivey Jr., executive vice president of New York University, "the faster it makes its curriculum, study materials and teachers obsolete." Poor Socrates.

True education depends upon the interplay of mind with mind, of soul with soul. It has nothing to do with masses, with audiences, even with groups as such. The true teacher moves the members of his class severally. Ideally, education is the relationship of one teacher to one student; and the nearer the approximation to the ideal, the better the teaching.

The only substitute for that direct relationship is the voice of a teacher communicated through the book to the solitary student. Both modes, personal teaching and the book, depend upon the word (human analogue of the Word). For it there is no substitute. It is the carrier of reason, as it is the stuff of poetry. The glory of the West has rested largely on its understanding of this; and the descent of the West into barbarism can be measured by the degree to which it forgets this.

But the word requires, to be effective, the personal dialogue between two minds which is the essence of education. Mass classes with visual aids, mass student audiences for television "educational" presentations, though they may help train technicians, move regressively farther and farther from educating men.

The hair-raising concept of Professor Zacharias of MIT, presented at the publishers' conference, that one satellite orbiting at the same speed as the earth rotates could broadcast "educational programs" to more than half the earth's surface, approaches the absolute opposite of education. All that would be necessary to make the horror complete would be to have another satellite on the other side of the earth broadcasting the same program. The teacher and the book would be finally subordinated to planet-wide gadgetry and its manipulator servants.

"A good book," wrote John Milton, "is the precious life-blood of a master-spirit, embalmed and treasured up on purpose to a life beyond life." And again: "As good almost kill a man as kill a good book: who kills a man kills a reasonable creature, God's image; but he who destroys a good book kills reason itself."

Edward P. Adkins, the national coordinator of NBC's *Continental Classroom,* generously conceded to the publishers' conference: "In education 'book' is not yet a four-letter word." Not yet.

Equality Ad Absurdum

(National Review, November 15, 1966)

A recent dispatch in the New York *Times* informs us that the College Entrance Examination Board is undertaking a full-scale review of "the foundations upon which [its] tests have been based for the last 30 years." One can understand that a review of these examinations (which are used by the highest-ranking American colleges as an aid in admission of their incoming freshman classes) should be undertaken from time to time to improve their efficiency in discriminating between more able and less able students.

So when the eye meets a headline, "College Board To Study Tests," the first reaction is to assume that the article describes an admirable, if not particularly noteworthy, activity—"Good. They're tightening up standards"—and pass on to the next item. It would be a mistake. The headline is a trap for nineteenth-century minds. The article reveals the full glory of the twentieth century. The aim of the review is to counter "criticism that the tests [are] geared towards the middle classes and that the culturally deprived [are] not taken into consideration."

Let us leave aside the demagogic class-warfare rhetorical implication of "middle classes" and get to the guts of the sentence —which is that the College Entrance Examination Board examinations ought to be so distorted that they will no longer discriminate against those who now fail them because they are too ignorant to pass them. "Culturally deprived" is nice soapy sociological jargon, but all it means is "ignorant." The examinations separate the sheep from the goats, the educated from the ignorant? Down with the examinations!

Translated into another medium, the absurdity shouts. Why should Sandy Koufax pitch in the World Series when there are hundreds of others who would like to and are just athletically deprived?

But absurd though this proceeding is, there is method in the madness. Among the thousands of American colleges that serve as playpens and little more, the few hundred who make use of the College Entrance Board's examinations are those which have preserved some standards, some sense of quality. These examinations are one of the criteria by which they manage to get a superior student body, and the evidence over some period of time has been that college performance is well predicted by their results. If the examinations can be transformed so that they fail to distinguish between the educated and the ignorant, it will become that much more difficult to discriminate between superior and inferior. We may hope that if this should happen, the best of our universities will throw the CEEB results into the waste-basket, but one less standard to weed out the inferior will exist; the mediocre and the shoddy will have chalked up one more victory over excellence.

We are witnessing the full flowering of egalitarianism, that perversion of the Western and Christian belief in the ultimate worth and dignity of each individual person. Egalitarianism is a perversion because it transforms that belief in the incommensurable, unique value of every created human being into the assumption of measurable equal capacities (if only everybody's environment and opportunities can be homogenized). It transforms the metaphysically grounded right of a human being to freedom from coercion by others, in order that he may develop his capabilities and pursue his destiny, into the pseudo-right (since every man is by definition of equal capability with every other) to equal rewards and equal respect.

For a long time the egalitarian doctrinaires directed their fire against all institutions and human conditions that stood in the way of the achievement of their perfect environmental equality. The Age of Rousseau believed that if only the evil designs of "priests and kings" were circumvented, the equal capability of all men would be displayed. All through the nineteenth century and up through the twentieth, it is this concept of the nature of man that has maintained the zeal of the leveling attack upon tradition, prescription, civilizational absolutes.

By the middle of this century, much of this program has been accomplished. American society today is far closer to the open, classless ideal of their dreams than all but the most sanguine of the eighteenth- and nineteenth-century reformers concretely envisaged. The advanced countries of the rest of the world are rapidly approximating to the same state. It is not perfect yet, but enough of the leveling program has been achieved to put the ideology of equality to the test.

Alas for the dogma, the more things change, the more they remain the same. That upon which folk wisdom, common sense, and philosophical demonstration have always agreed remains the verdict of reality: men are unequal—unequal in intelligence, in ability, in vigor, in moral stamina. So now we pass to a new stage of egalitarianism. If, despite the leveling of opportunity, inequality still raises its ugly head, then there is nothing to be done but to destroy the standards that measure difference.

The College Entrance Examination Board's egalitarian fervor is only one of a thousand straws in the wind. Crime becomes "delinquency," morality becomes "situation ethics." Relativism comes to the aid of egalitarianism, and the very concept of standards, criteria, hierarchy of value, is repudiated. But to distinguish, to make judgments between the better and the worse, to live by standards, is the essence of culture and civilization. It is, moreover, the foundation of justice, without which a well-ordered society cannot exist. Egalitarianism, with the destruction of standards it demands, leads inexorably to barbarism and darkness.

Chapter Eight

On Men, Famous and Infamous

In this final chapter I have collected a series of observations on various figures, some famous, some infamous—economists, psychologists, statesmen, novelists, poets. Diverse though these critiques are, I hope the reader will find a common thread running through them—a continuing vindication of the tradition of Western civilization.

Review of *Tomorrow and Tomorrow and Tomorrow, and Other Essays,* by Aldous Huxley

(National Review, November 3, 1956)

At first glance these new essays would seem to demonstrate no more than what has been apparent for some years: the decline of Aldous Huxley. Once an unrivalled satirist of his age, he has become in late years a moderately entertaining highbrow journalist and a semi-slick novelist.

In *Tomorrow and Tomorrow and Tomorrow* he touches upon a potpourri of subjects—from activated sludge and do-it-yourself (of which he approves) to Dante, Shakespeare and T. S. Eliot (of whom he disapproves). The mode of his style has not changed in thirty years, but the life has gone out of it.

The turned phrase just misses the mark; the association of incongruous ideas that in *Antic Hay* or *Mortal Coils* exposed in a brilliant flash some absurdity of twentieth-century civilization is now too often slightly on the hither side of banality, and sometimes degenerates into sheer bad taste.

At the immediate level of criticism, then, this appears to be but another instance of what has happened before and will happen again, the recurring pathos of

> Runners whom renown outran
> And the name died before the man.

But why, in this instance? It is an enquiry worth pursuing, if only as an act of piety; for upon many of us who came to consciousness in the twenties, Huxley exerted an influence second only perhaps to that of T. S. Eliot in opening our minds to fundamental philosophical problems.

The influence was, it must be admitted, iconoclastic, but *pace* Messrs. Babbitt and Kirk, there are times when there is immense value to iconoclasm. When the icons are not only images of false gods, but stuffy to boot—and Heaven knows they *were* in the years after World War I—the road to truth and to the recovery of tradition will inevitably pass over the debris of shattered images. Other roads, it is true, also pass over the same field of shards, some leading to the shrines of gods as false and infinitely more malignant, some leading nowhere, petering out in wastes of meaninglessness.

And here is the crux of the matter. Unlike Eliot and others who shared with him the mordant criticism of an era, Huxley has never been able to regain the high road of Western civilization. Fascinated by all sorts of "modern" scientistic problems—garbage disposal, soap and sanitation, "population control"—yet unable to accept the materialist philosophy of a scientistic age, he has constructed a fantastic position compounded of bits and ends of Eastern philosophy, remnants of Western aestheticism, and scattered pronouncements derived from the more lurid of the prophets of science. Consistent in its inconsistency, this patchwork "philosophy" is projected at the most unexpected moments into whatever he may be discussing.

It is a sad end for so gifted a mind. But it is a self-willed end. For, despite his stance of the seeker after truth, there is one place Huxley has never been willing to look for truth—in the traditions of his own civilization. Always, in all his thinking there has prevailed an almost pathological hatred of the Word. Reason and revelation, as the West has known them, are alike anathema to him. And the vaporings of a California mysticism —neither Eastern nor Western, but an empty pseudo-religiosity —are all he has to fill the void.

The Uses of Modern Poetry

(National Review, March 7, 1956)

Undoubtedly the most characteristic, if not the gravest, vice of the Liberal mind is the eager monkey-like busyness with which it pries into and tries to organize other people's affairs. But lest we as conservatives look in our own eye too complacently, we ought to recognize that we too have a characteristic vice. Our enemies call it smugness. I should prefer to call it laziness: the spiritual laziness of the servant in the parable, who kept his talent laid up in a napkin.

To know that primary Truth exists, that men have had and have, through reason and intuition operating within tradition, many inklings of it and some blinding insights, is something for which to be humbly thankful; but for each man and each generation, this is a beginning, not an end. The multiplex possibilities of human circumstances and of the human consciousness require not new truths, but new ways of approaching and understanding the same eternal Truth. It is here that the parable of the conservative servant applies. To preserve is not enough (although in times like these it is a great deal); it is demanded that the understanding passed on to us by tradition be used, not hoarded, that it be increased in depth and meaning.

I have long thought that the hostile attitude of many conservatives toward the contemporary tradition of American and English poetry—an attitude that identifies its difficulties and obscurities with the general spirit of the age—exhibits a failure to discriminate which arises from this characteristic self-satisfaction. I have been impressed again with this thought in reading two articles that have appeared recently in the quarterlies. Each in its way seems to me to place brilliantly the virtues and limitations of contemporary poetry. The one, by Allen Tate, "Reflections on American Poetry: 1900–1950," was published in the *Sewanee Review* for Winter, 1956; the other, by Charles G. Bell, "Modern Poetry and the Pursuit of Sense," in *Diogenes*, No. 10, 1955.

Aside from this article, I know nothing of Mr. Bell except that he is an Assistant Professor of the Humanities at the University of Chicago and a poet; but Mr. Tate speaks not only with the broad authority of a poet and critic of the first excellence, but also as one whose twenty-five-year record in the intellectual Resistance to the dominant trends of modern thought gives him a special authority, to which conservatives at a minimum should pay the tribute of careful attention and consideration.

Implicit in both Mr. Tate's argument and Mr. Bell's is an assumption which I believe to be essential to an understanding of poetry and its place in human endeavor: that it is neither simple enjoyment divorced from other meaning than its own, nor ornament upon the soberer business of life, but an independent and serious mode of understanding. If it does not, in the strict sense, give us knowledge, then at the least, in the words of Eliseo Vivas,

> it ought to be recognized that it is prior in the order of logic to all knowledge, since it is constitutive of culture, which is one of the conditions of knowledge. [For] the girders of culture are seldom formulated by [man] in the abstract way in which theologians, philosophers and scientists discuss them. They

are expressed in mythopoetic terms . . . by the artist at a given juncture in history, in terms of the factors of a culture which, when he starts his work, is already a going affair, but which would not survive for long if it did not have the benefit of his renovating ministrations.

It is my contention that the poets of the last generation or two have played in this regard an heroic role, that they have preserved and deepened the true lineaments of the image of man, under the most adverse circumstances and in fierce defiance of the accepted norms of the intellectual milieu. The obscurity with which they are taxed is, for the best of them at least, a necessary outcome of their contingencies. To a small degree it is a smokescreen and a diversionist provocation, to draw off the fire of the enemy, as, for example, in the eccentric typography of E. E. Cummings. But this is minor. The obscurity and the difficulty of their writing stems primarily not from perversity, but from the very virtue of an intransigent insistence upon creating nothing less than that which mirrors reality as personally perceived, despite the accepted manner in which conformity presumes that all right-thinking men must perceive it. This is the point to which Mr. Tate is directing our attention when he says:

> What poets know and how they know it are questions that go beyond the usual scope of criticism, for what a poet of the past knows is viewed historically, not ontologically and we take it for granted. But with a poetry which is near us in time, or contemporaneous, much of the difficulty that appears to be in the language as such, is actually in the unfamiliar focus of feeling, belief, and experience which directs the language from the concealed depths that we must try laboriously to enter.

Such labor is not without its reward. The gnarled form which so much of the very best writing of our time takes bespeaks the effort to reach truth in circumstances little conducive to that

search. More open ages, ages which in their generality respect
truth and beauty and the search for them, give nurture to a
style which spreads generously, like a single oak or maple alone
in an open field; in an age, however, which denies the very
existence of truth and beauty, the desperate effort of the poet
to recover identity and meaning creates a form with a different
grace, the knotted grace of the apple tree, whose every fruiting
is a frustration and a new beginning. So also the reader in such
an age has himself a harder labor to perform—and, just because
insight is so rare in the effusive jungle of mass communications,
a commensurate reward.

If he prefers, he may save expenditure of labor and dismiss
this poetry as "too obscure for the common man"; he can still
be gently titillated by B. B. D. & O. or Norman Corwin. But
if he wants the pleasure and the insight contemporary poetry
can give him, he must work for it. "This state of affairs," Mr.
Tate acidly observes, "is frequently reprehended by the common
man, a person of our age who can be either 'educated' or
merely arrogant." But there is no way out of it in a society
like ours without giving up poetry completely. The "difficulty"
is implicit in the situation. Even the poetry of Robert Frost,
which is sometimes brought in evidence as an example of simplicity over against the central tradition of Pound, Eliot, Tate,
Stevens, Cummings, Auden, is "difficult" in its own way:

> He is just as sophisticated and modern as anybody,
> and his way of being sophisticated and modern is to
> pretend in his diction that he is not: he is quite as
> self-conscious . . . as the late Hart Crane, or Wallace
> Stevens himself.

I am not—nor, do I believe, is Mr. Tate—making a case for
obscurity as a virtue; I would maintain, indeed, that the very
greatest poetry, while it too has its share of the obscure (think
of *Antony and Cleopatra* or *Measure for Measure*), has a grand
public quality. The point is not that the first half of the century
has been a poetic age to rival, for example, the Elizabethan,
but that, in our circumstances, we are fortunate to have had

any poetry of quality, and very fortunate to have had such consistently fine poetry. By contrast, consider the poverty of imagination and values of, say, the philosophers or the statesmen of the same half century.

Actually it is the very state of affairs these latter have created which has forced its peculiar private mode upon the poetry of the time. This has been an era where by and large the man of sensitivity has been forced into a posture of private resistance if he wished to preserve his integrity. And the poet in that posture is the poet we know. The "high contemporary tradition" is, therefore, as Mr. Tate points out,

> not a tradition of the grand style or of the great subject. But it has resisted the strong political pressures which ask the poet to "communicate" to passively conditioned persons what a servile society expects them to feel. . . . The common man in a servile society is everybody; modern society is everywhere servile; everybody must accept the servile destruction of leisure and of the contemplative life if he would live without alienation. . . . The liberal, utopian, "totalitarian" mind assumes that one must give up alienation at any cost. High on the list of costs would be poetry; and if we would sacrifice it, in the illusion that its sacrifice alone would propitiate the powers of darkness, we should forfeit along with it the center of consciousness in which free and disinterested men must live. There are some things from which man, if he is to remain human, must remain permanently alienated. One of these is the idolatry of the means as the end.

If there have been points of light in the murky fog generated through decades of "idolatry of the means as the end," it is the poets who have kept a great many of them burning. And the form their message has taken is that of a Declaration of Alienation from the public compulsions of a servile society. This is both their glory and their limitation—the limitation, again in Mr. Tate's words, of "the aesthetic consciousness aware of its isolation at a moment of time."

As we enter the second half of the century, we are approaching the end, I believe, of this tradition, with this particular glory and this particular limitation. Perhaps it is because the very growth of the all-pervasive monster state and octopus community of the norm has reached the point where it begins to enter the most private recesses, that the very struggle for the preservation of personal identity requires a more public commitment to the vindication of values. Whatever the reason may be, there is every sign in the air that we are at the end of one style and, if we are fortunate, at the birth of a new one. A consistent reading of the literary journals will show that the best poetry is being produced by men in their fifties and sixties and seventies. The younger poets who write in the tradition of Pound and Eliot are many of them good, but not good enough.

What can we expect, what kind of thing may come next? Mr. Tate thinks that this is a question that "nobody can know or ought to think that he knows."

Mr. Bell rushes in where angels fear to tread; but his article, concerned very largely with precisely this question, has so many good things in it that he is very convincing, if not as to what the new poetry will be, at least as to what it could be. At the end of a style like the one we have been discussing, as the energy and the justification expire, it can well become, and in many cases has become, what Mr. Bell justly describes as "a last extension of fragmentation and disease." The search for violent image and for relations ever more dissociated, which in its origin had good ground in the revolt against a muddled leveling of thought and value, moves beyond the point of salutary criticism of misused reason to the disavowal of reason itself. But, as Mr. Bell says,

> that a poem transcends its rational content in prose
> is such a commonplace, not only of our generation
> but of others, that I doubt if anyone would be found

> to deny it. But if somewhere in poetry the reason
> must be abandoned for that leap into the unknown,
> the radiance, the symbolic and associative light,
> there must still be some kind of a jumping-off place,
> and the reason plays a part in getting us there.

Nothing can detract from the value of the great poetry of the half century, of what Mr. Bell calls its "magic of the unservile image." But I tend to agree with him that more than that is now required:

> The creation of a responsible art, as of a respon-
> sible freedom, depends on one thing: the regenera-
> tion . . . of a belief in man and the organizing uni-
> verse, a relation of human values to eternal values.

As he is more daring than Mr. Tate would allow, he is, I am afraid, more sanguine than sober consideration of circumstances might warrant, as to certain birth of such a poetry. But the direction he points is the right one, and his enthusiasm is infectious:

> . . . the spirit of a new poetry is also the spirit of
> renewed freedom, being the wisdom and will to live
> affirmatively in the highest drama of mind . . . it may
> be difficult of access. . . . Its complications, how-
> ever, will be those of responsible profundity, opening
> to reason, involving the explicit and affirmative core.
> Such is the fruit that will appear, and its token and
> sign will be wholeness.

Review of *Freud and the Crisis of Our Culture*, by Lionel Trilling

(National Review, February 22, 1956)

A recent little essay by Lionel Trilling, *Freud and the Crisis of Our Culture,* reflects with a rare clarity the pathos of the

Liberal intellectual mind at its best and gentlest, its least smug and arrogant. Although the essay is based upon a lecture delivered as the Freud Anniversary Lecture of 1955, it is not for any light that Mr. Trilling throws on Freud that it is of interest. That tormented Promethean had for ill or good a stature far beyond the comfortable ken of Morningside Heights. He was one of those "terrible simplifiers" who, with sword or word, from time to time appear in history to end one epoch and begin another. A Napoleon of the intellect, he left nothing as he found it. Although his vision of man's being is of a Stygian blackness unrelieved by grace or spirit, he shattered with a single blow the prettification of man and the materialist vision of him as the potential creator of Utopia.

After Freud, it is still possible to deny the spiritual essence in man; what it is no longer possible to do is to screen with the smiling image of omnipotent and beneficent man the dark void that denial leaves. Not possible to do—I should say not possible for the searching mind, willing to bear reality, to do. And reality being a hard thing to bear, Freud's bleak prophetic vision has been transformed by his followers into a melioristic instrument called Freudianism; or it has been adapted by such epigonoi as Karen Horney and Erich Fromm out of all recognition, to hide the agony of man's alienation from God in the busy task of overcoming man's "alienation from society" by changing the material world.

It is this pallid likeness of Freud which Mr. Trilling celebrates. Someone has said that certain historians write history as though nothing ever really happened. It is characteristic of the milieu out of which Mr. Trilling writes that he speaks of men, including himself, as though they never really existed, as though they were only the constructs which "prove" or "disprove" the arid abstractions of the social scientists' "model." To such a mind, the passionate negations of Freud, that nether image of Augustine, become counters in a tidy parcheesi, as the drama of man's fate is reduced to a quiet little game played out where nothing is at stake, not even real pennies.

What, then, is Freud to Mr. Trilling? How does he translate and soften those searing prophecies into modestly balancing counters in his intellectual exercise?

To begin with, Freud's concrete and existential picture of man must be changed into an abstraction and a resultant of abstractions—the meeting point of "biology" and "culture." Biology, the sense of one's self "as a biological fact," is the happy contribution of Freud to rescue mid-twentieth-century man from the oppression of an over-demanding community. For Mr. Trilling, to do him credit, is disturbed by the merging, in the outlook of the "educated middle class," of the "sense of self" with the culture conceived as possessing

> . . . a new sort of selfhood bestowed upon the whole
> of society . . . having a certain organic unity, an
> autonomous character and personality [so that] men
> . . . think of their fates as being lived out not in rela-
> tion to God, or to individual persons who are their
> neighbors, or to material circumstance, but to the
> ideas and assumptions and manners of a large social
> totality.

He is distressed by this outlook, although as far as one can tell, given his professional "we," he never dissociates himself from it, but accepts it as a sort of fate from which he can only be rescued by another abstraction. The affirmation of his existence as a person, through the direct love of man for God, or of man for man, never seems to occur to him as a way out; nor does that other darker affirmation of personality which the living Freud, like others before him, threw with defiant challenge at an empty and godless universe. The only escape he can conceive is by way of another abstraction, by subsuming himself under another generalization, the biological, to balance the societal, to ward off the danger of total absorption into the community, against which fate the flicker of selfhood left reacts with an instinctive, if most judiciously expressed, abhorrence.

It would never do to say, "This is wrong," or "This is right." Everything must be balanced to a point where no "objective" scientific reader could say that he has rudely asserted a value drawn from a realm beyond the purview of measuring instrument and electronic computator. Mr. Trilling can, indeed, be devastating in his criticism of the pressure for conformity and adjustment to the norms of the culture:

> We cannot really imagine non-conformity at all, not in art, not in moral or social theory, certainly not in the personal life—it is probably true that there never was a culture which required so entire an eradication of personal differentiation, so bland a uniformity of manner.

But the "we" here is a genuine "we," the whole essay shows; it includes Mr. Trilling himself. He cannot tear himself loose; he depends too much upon the very concepts he castigates. There is no moral basis outside of him, in which he can find foundation for his existence. The situation which overwhelms him is, after all, derived from material categories he will not deny:

> Our culture is in process of revision, and of revision in a very good and right direction, in the direction of greater socialization, greater cooperativeness, greater reasonableness.

Despite all this, still the pressure is too great. He feels himself ground by "the unified and demanding culture." Here it is that the simulacrum of Freud he has created for himself presents him with a sanctified and acceptable, a certifiably scientific "countervailing" abstraction: ". . . we may think of Freud's emphasis on biology as being a liberating idea. It is a resistance to and a modification of the cultural omnipotence."

Materialist man, shrinking in desperation from himself as artifact of society, looks not upward but downward for salvation. Unable to bear himself as nothing but a social animal, he finds hope of freedom in the purely animal. Perhaps in a distorted and feeble way, this is the gospel of St. Freud after all. At any rate, it is a sad solution to "the crisis of our culture," a pathetic end to Mr. Trilling's journey.

Norman Mailer's Culture Hero

(National Review, July 27, 1957)

Time is wearing away the moral capital, inherited from an earlier age, which has thus far prevented the champions of relativism from acting like the beasts their philosophy envisions men to be. John Dewey personally lived, I am sure, an upright life. Followers of his, such as Sidney Hook, on particular issues very often display exemplary moral attitudes, totally at variance with their philosophical teaching, a teaching corrosive of all values except the successful achievement of random emotional desire.

Only lately have we begun to see serious practical signs of the emergence of the type of human being logically to be expected from that teaching. The generation of children brought up by teachers whom the relativists have trained and by parents whom they have influenced has for some time been producing an alarming number of depraved and criminal adolescents. Unwilling to face the obvious conclusion that the denigration and destruction of the moral values which guide and discipline the growing human being will result in dehumanization, in an approach to the condition of the beasts who live without values, the authors of this degeneration of man call the phenomenon "juvenile delinquency." They consider it a clinical problem to be solved by the "scientific" techniques of sociology or psychology.

But their methods will avail not at all. Indeed, so long as they endure, the evil will grow. This "juvenile delinquency" is not the mischief, the watermelon stealing, the petty vandalism, of the young of earlier generations; it is brutality, uncontrolled sexuality, violence for violence's sake. It is the foretaste of the fruit that we shall inevitably inherit unless the philosophical offensive that is eating away at the values upon which civilization is based is beaten back.

Nor does it matter greatly whether the harvest takes the form of unrestrained ravaging by hordes of wolf-like men or the equally brutal "order" of the totalitarian state. Men bereft of moral values, without the inspiration of a vision of human destiny beyond the given and the seen, will remain beasts, whether they prey as anarchistic individualists or in the name of order and the state—and however imposing and powerful their scientific control over nature.

While it has long been clear to the eye of theoretical understanding that this was the inevitable end towards which the prevailing philosophy of the age was tending, and while such phenomena as "juvenile delinquency," concentration camps and total war have given us some taste of what a world without the sanctions of transcendental values could be like, hitherto no person of intellectual pretension has seen and gloried in the goal towards which this post-Christian secularist religion of relativism has been ineluctably directed. Men like John Dewey and Sidney Hook, to repeat, living on the moral stock inherited from the Western tradition, have personally regarded their intellectual endeavors as conducive to the flowering of virtues, although their own philosophy has no way of distinguishing virtue from vice. Even so horrendous a specimen of the social engineer as Professor B. F. Skinner (the Harvard psychologist who would create Utopia through a conditioning of men comparable to Pavlov's conditioning of dogs) projects as his goal a society whose members seek some ends which are virtuous and none which are vices *per se*.

It is, therefore, with the horror one experiences in an inexorably logical nightmare that I read in the current issue of *Dissent* an article by Norman Mailer, glorifying as the end of human existence the full expression of the most brutal impulses of lust and violence. It should be noted that this was not Mr. Mailer in his role of best-selling novelist, shovelling in the smut that brings the sales. It was Mr. Mailer writing and publishing as a serious thinker, for the *avant-garde* of the Establishment, in a journal which represents the left wing of the Establishment, a journal which, despite its criticism of the stuffed-shirt aspects of Establishment thinking, shares every fundamental theoretical position of the Establishment.

Considerations of taste prevent me from reproducing Mr. Mailer's thesis with its full stench; but I shall do what I can within the limits of my prejudices. His subject is the "hipster," the devotee of the cult of jazz and marijuana, raw sex and violence. The hipster, it is his thesis, is a "philosophical psychopath," and while there are as yet only perhaps 100,000 of them in the country, there are 10,000,000 psychopaths. On the future of the psychopaths, on their maturing to the philosophical level of the hipster, it is necessary to depend for the final overthrow of "the slow relentless inhumanity of the conservative power" of civilization and its values.

No longer is it John Dewey's social engineer or Karl Marx' economically and politically oppressed proletarian who is to be the demiurge of the future where man makes himself. It is "the sexual adventurer deflected from his goal by the implacable animosity of a society constructed to deny the sexual radical." It is "the psychopath [who] murders—if he has the courage —out of the necessity to purge his violence, because if he cannot empty his hatred, then he cannot love."

One may thank Mr. Mailer for exhibiting so clearly the fearful, devilish lineaments of the ideal man, product of the teaching that human capabilities have no function but as instrument to desire. Ideas, as Richard Weaver has said, have consequences; and the positivist attack upon the structure of values that has made our civilization leads straight to the jungle—or rather to something much worse, for the animals of the jungle, possessing no spiritual essence, cannot become incarnate evil.

Out of the Frying Pan

(National Review, February 27, 1960)

"Forward-looking" has a brave fine sound. Who wants to be stigmatized as "backward-looking," singled out as a counsellor of retreat? And yet, what virtue is there in going forward when the road has been found to lead to disaster? Is not true courage then the willingness to turn back, to retrace one's steps as far as need be until the point is reached where the false turning occurred? Mountain-climbers, explorers, the most intrepid of men, do no less when their boldness is coupled with the wisdom that transmutes boldness into courage.

In a wider arena this is the decision that must be taken if the West is to recover wholeness and strength. Conservatives, understanding that such a return to the sources of truth is the only hope of salvation from the multiple disasters towards which our revolutionary age is moving, have steeled themselves against the *mystique* of the new, the prevailing prejudice that only innovation is valuable, that salvation arises from innovation.

When, however, a man who has followed the collectivist dream of forcing human perfectibility becomes aware that what he believed would lead to paradise on earth is leading only to the dead ashpits and living torment of totalitarian tyranny, his agony of search for meaning in life is compounded by the *mystique* of the novel. Some do turn back to their heritage, but more take refuge in a variety of ideologies which, whether they are modern constructions of the Western intellect or importations from other civilizations, are all alien to the central tradition of the West. The existentialism of Sartre and Heidegger, Indian Vedanta, Zen Buddhism—the particular fashion changes, but all these intellectual refuges have in common a rejection of that high tension between the freedom of the person and his responsibility to transcendent truth which is the Western heritage.

And, alongside of these succeeding fashions, Sigmund Freud's vision of the human condition has continued to exert a strong attraction upon the dispossessed of collectivism. I do not here refer to Freud's techniques of mental therapy, or to that watered-down Freudianism which has served for a generation or two as substance for drawing-room chit-chat, or to the gospel of adjustment derived from neo-Freudian sources that has been so usefully absorbed into the collectivist armory of social control. It is not these aspects and derivates of Freud's thought, but his essential dark metaphysical vision that attracts the homeless intellectual.

Freud is at the other pole from the melioristic Utopianism of the collectivists. He sees men caught in a narrow strait, without exit, between primitive instincts whose full satisfaction alone will make us whole, and the pressures of a civilization without which we cannot live but which represses those instincts and cruelly distorts our being. This is a vision of men condemned, a perverse concept of original sin in a world without transcendent truth and without the freedom with which to choose truth, a world closed, dour, without grace.

Given the emerging realization that men suffer from some primordial imperfection—a truth which presses itself upon those who have become disillusioned with modern Utopias—and given a refusal to accept the existence of transcendent Perfection, this metaphysic makes a strong appeal. But only the sternest and most stoical can live with it. No wonder, therefore, that effort after effort has been made to modify it, to smuggle in some gleam of hope.

The latest and most ambitious of such efforts is a book which is likely to have a most profound influence upon the intellectual consciousness of many of those breaking free from collectivism, but unwilling to return to the sources of their tradition. Published a year or so ago by Wesleyan University Press, it got little notice at the time, but recently it was made the selection of the Mid-Century Book Society, with a glowing recommendation from Lionel Trilling and the other judges, and it has now been selected by Modern Library for paperback publication this spring. Its author, Norman O. Brown, explicitly states that his thinking is derived from an awareness of the "superannuation of the political categories which informed liberal thought and action in the 1930s."

The book, *Life against Death,* represents a tremendous intellectual effort to retain the Freudian analysis of man's nature and a wholly materialist view of existence, while reintroducing hope—hope for human action directed towards a new Utopia. Mr. Brown's project is to cut Freud's Gordian knot by abolishing civilization and freeing the instincts. Stated simply so, it might seem that I distort or exaggerate, but this in sum is the substance of his argument, an argument that is pursued with an erudition, subtlety and force that might well give this book an impact today such as Nietzsche had in the late nineteenth century.

The destruction of civilization, the release of the instincts, he believes, would release Eros, creative love, and rescue man from all his agony. But this is a program for perfect creatures, not for men. Common sense and traditional wisdom alike testify that the relaxation of the bonds of civilization releases not love, but savagery.

What is there to say when such an analysis of man's condition (and such a solution) is raised and accepted with intellectual seriousness? Revolt against the distortion of civilization that collectivism represents is understandable enough today. But surcease from present evils will not be found in flight to other extremes, but in a return to the tradition of the West with the balance between the freedom of the person and the authority of the truth that civilization transmits from generation to generation.

Why Conservatives Reject Keynes

(National Review, July 30, 1960)

I yield to no one in my admiration for the wide-ranging intelligence, the trenchant wit, and the intellectual courage of

Ernest van den Haag. But when he proposes to conservatives
("Must Conservatives Repudiate Keynes?" *National Review*,
June 4) that they should embrace the economic doctrine of
Lord Keynes as potientially consonant with their purposes,
as a mere means, "politically neutral," I must take exception.

As has been demonstrated again and again in the critiques
of Keynesism so brilliantly and meticulously developed by
Ludwig von Mises, F. A. Hayek, Henry Hazlitt, and others,
there can be no question as to the central theme of Lord
Keynes' doctrine: it is that "we" (read, "the state"; the same
"we" Professor van den Haag, following Keynes, invokes) can
achieve a better society than can individual persons in their
individual capacities as producers and consumers, bringing
their individual wants and profferings (their demands and
their supplies) into relation with each other through the
functioning of a free-market system.

Let us be perfectly clear here. The issue is not primarily
whether the Keynesian model will "work." Many economic
systems "work," granted the ends towards which they are
directed. Tribal economy worked. Oriental despotism worked,
Socialism works, Communism works. But for the conservative
who rejects all theories, however attenuated, which presume
the determination of human existence by material forces, economics must be subordinated to moral and political philosophy.
He demands not only that a given economic system work,
but that it serve proper ends.

When I say that economics is a subordinate discipline, I
do not mean that in its own sphere it should be censored in
its methods of inquiry or in the objectivity of its conclusions.
Economics is the nearest to an exact science of all the disciplines that study man and society. It is at the same time the
farthest from philosophical competence, the most removed
from a capacity for the establishment of value. Economics can
neither establish nor confute the validity of a moral system
or the virtues of a political system. What it can do is to
demonstrate what the results of alternate courses of economic
action will be. The choice between these sets of results (and

therefore between the economic systems which lead to them) is beyond the prerogative of economics. It is a moral and a political choice.

It is therefore not the narrowly economic question of whether or how the Keynesian system can work that primarily concerns the conservative. A prior question is decisive for him: what political ends does the system propounded by Keynes serve? and how do these ends relate to the political ends to which the conservative is committed?

The conservative has no blueprint for the reconstruction of society; he recognizes no "we" with a mission to regulate, directly or indirectly, the lives of individual persons. He moves towards no Utopia; indeed he denies the possibility of a Utopia in this, our imperfect state of being. Recognizing the authority of no revolutionary ideology, he subordinates himself politically only to "the laws of nature and of nature's God." He looks with the greatest of suspicion upon self-constituted secular prophets and their followers, who would, by capturing and making use of the power of the state, impose their ends upon other human beings.

Conservatives believe that the true locus of value in the political sphere is the individual person. He—not some collective pseudo-organic entity called "state" or "society"—is the touchstone by which political and economic systems are to be assessed. Within the limits of the physical order necessary if men are to exist as human beings, the good systems are, therefore, those which enable him to live uncoerced, subject to the authority of truth alone, not of force. The limits are: the protection of the nation from foreign enemies; the preservation of internal physical order; and the concomitant existence of a system of justice to judge the disputes of man with man. These are the necessary functions of the state. Since to carry out these functions, the state must possess a monopoly of violence, it remains always a dangerous servant, constantly to be circumscribed to its sphere—a servant which, as Washington said, is as useful as fire and as dangerous as fire.

In our time that danger is peculiarly great. Even if we did

not have as warnings the ravening totalitarianisms which have arisen around us, we could grasp its essence from consideration of the conditions of modern life. The immense development of technology has placed as the primary danger control of the economy by the state. To add to the monopoly of violence any further power is fraught with the greatest peril to the liberty of the person; but to add to it control, direct or indirect, of the massive resources of modern technology is to create a Leviathan monstrous beyond the possibilities of earlier less technically developed ages.

Division of power, which the framers of the Constitution thought so vital in regard to political power itself if liberty was to be preserved, is today decisive as between political and economic power. Control by the state over the economy, over the property of individual persons and their free utilization of that property, is the highroad to twentieth-century tyranny.

The problem of state control of the economy is the decisive point at which conservatism confronts Keynesism. For Keynesism is in its essence but an alternative to Marxism as a mode of state control of the economy. Slower than the methods of Marxism, more indirect in application, it has proved far more successful than Marxism itself in promoting the cause of statism in countries with advanced economies. Only in backward countries, or where, as in the case of Czechoslovakia, Communist physical force has prevailed, has the road to statism been the Marxist road of nationalization of the means of production. Not only has the movement in the statist direction in advanced countries prevailed almost entirely with Keynesian methods under the slogans of "progressive capitalism" or "the mixed economy"; the very Socialist parties of such countries have given up their Marxism to embrace the more effective Keynesian methods of "welfarism," of state interventionism.

Those methods include: 1. state control of credit and of the interest rate, either directly or through state-dominated central banking systems; 2. "a somewhat comprehensive socialization of investment"; 3. "measures for the redistribution of incomes," primarily through taxation; 4. "the euthanasia of the rentier [that is, the painless (to whom?) doing away with those who have acquired capital either through their own efforts or through inheritance] and, consequently, the euthanasia of the cumulative oppressive power of the capitalist to exploit the scarcity-value of capital"—which, since the scarcity-value of capital cannot itself be eliminated, means that a monopoly of the usufructs of capital will be gradually transferred to the state.

With some of this Professor van den Haag is presumably in disagreement. He writes that he omits "a number of points with which I disagree, but which are of little interest to the general reader." How much of it he wants the conservative to swallow is not entirely clear. But the essence of Keynesism— the control of the economy by the state through credit manipulation, taxing policies and subsidies—he enthusiastically recommends to us, in the innocent guise of a technical method of combatting the economic cycle.

However much he hedges his Keynesian bets, however much he may limit his concept of Keynesism to exclude this or that of Keynes' specific prescriptions, he accepts wholeheartedly the basic Keynesian concept—state direction of the economy— and presses it upon conservatives as a "neutral" technique, as useful to conservatives as to Liberals or Socialists. This is like telling a surgeon that a revolver will serve him as well as a scalpel. No techniques that aggrandize state control of the economy can be neutral to the conservative who is engaged in a desperate struggle—a struggle which today has priority over all others—to reduce and limit the power of the state.

Of course, as Professor van den Haag writes, since the beginnings of the free-enterprise system, "The government has always spent money, created money and taxed." But when the principles of limited government prevailed, these activities were generally restricted to the financing of the government's legitimate activities; and even when these powers have been used with other and illegitimate ends in view, they have been justified (since the days of Mercantilism) either by specious arguments based upon these legitimate powers or by pleas of emergency. Keynesism, on the contrary, justifies an open and unconcealed use of these and other powers to give the state a directing control over the economy. On the basis of the application of Keynesian policies, Liberalism has in the past three decades created the massive bureaucratic state under which we live.

The techniques of Keynesism, originally popularized as cures for depression, can be as readily employed for their true purpose—statist and bureaucratic aggrandizement—in prosperity. John Kenneth Galbraith condescends to Keynes as old-fashioned; but the measures he would use to bring a still larger share of the national income under the control of the state are the same measures of fiscal manipulation and taxation which the influence of Keynes institutionalized in the "mixed economy." Where Keynes thought the capitalists did not know how to invest and "we" could do it better by state manipulation, Galbraith thinks consumers don't know how to spend and "we" can do it better for them by transferring purchasing power to "the public sector," that is, to the state.

As Liberalism, through Roosevelt and the New Deal, used Keynesism in bringing about the first stage of its revolution, so it is moving today to use the new Galbraithian form of the same doctrine in carrying its revolution to another stage. The Democratic platform of 1960 exudes these concepts; Nelson Rockefeller propounds them in his every utterance on national policy; and even the Percy report, on which the Republican platform is supposedly to be based, is far from free of them.

The doctrines of Lord Keynes and the heirs of Lord Keynes lead directly to the siphoning off of a large proportion of national wealth into the hands of the state and to the steady deterioration of free citizens into dependents of the state. The conservative can be neither "neutral" towards them nor tolerant of them. They are the economic doctrines of Liberal statism. They are the economic form of the Liberal collectivist ideology against which he is arrayed.

Teilhard de Chardin: The Attack on Man

(National Review, July 13, 1965)

I do not know what the newly elected General of the Jesuits meant when he said at a recent press conference that "the positive elements" in the work of Teilhard de Chardin were far more important than "the negative elements or those which are questionable." Nor would I, as a non-Catholic, argue with him on Catholic theological grounds. Philosophically, however, Teilhard's thesis would seem to me to be directed squarely against the concept of the integrity of the human person, which is the foundation of Western civilization.

A sort of amalgamation of theological evolutionism and cosmological mysticism, Teilhard's system presents us with a universe in which the human person—and, for that matter, the person of God—is absorbed to the point of disappearance within a great "spiritual" evolutionary force. He sings a paean to that force proceeding impersonally and irresistibly to the "Omega" point where God, man, and the whole of existence are fused in a featureless unity much more akin to Brahma or Nirvana than to anything in Classical, Hebrew, or Western Christian thought.

Despite its "spiritual" trappings, Teilhardism is but another variant of the corrosive predominantly materialist century-old attack upon the autonomy of the person. That attack has many aspects, which differ widely in their specific content but are all characterized by a common prepossession, a prepossession which might be called "reductionism." Marxism, Freudianism, the philosophical evolutionism which would turn Darwin's scientific observations into an ideology—all of them try to suck life and meaning out of the rich and multiple spectacle of creation, reducing the whole of being to nothing more than a pale reflection of the chosen ideological force. More particularly, each of them reduces the person to a mere unit determined by that force.

Marxism reduces existence to the play of matter in motion and human beings to pawns manipulated by the development of the forces of production. The Freudian analysis of men in the final reckoning makes of them only more or less complex products of biological instincts and forces. Biological evolutionism, raised to the level of a philosophy, destroys the very meaning of the individual, subsuming him as a mere cell of the species. From these and from a dozen variants on the theme, there has developed the predominant form of contemporary intellectuality. This is expressed in multifarious ways, but fundamentally it is a denial, on the one hand, of the virtue, the freedom and the glory of the individual human person, and, on the other hand, of his responsibilities and duties.

Recognition of this assault on personality, which pervades the intellectual atmosphere of the age, makes intelligible the common origin of the two phenomena (on the first glance so different in character) which dominate the current social scene: grandiose Utopian schemes and campaigns; degenerate decadence of manners, morals and culture. Public life is saturated with the most idealistic visions and appeals—the Great Society socially, the New Era economically, internationalism, egalitarianism. All the imperfect modes by which imperfect men have managed to live in civilization are scorned; but the more loudly the idealisms are proclaimed, the more our social life itself degenerates.

Statistics and common experience alike show a catastrophic rise in broken families, juvenile criminality, narcotics addiction. Our great cities are infested with violence and rapidly approaching a state where the preservation of civil order will be in doubt. The moral vacuity and intellectual frivolousness of three decades of our educational system are now raising their second generation. Our fiction—and the visual arts of movie and television that draw from it—projects an image of man confused, feeble, ignoble. We are enveloped in an *ethos* that gives support neither to the sober virtues of day-to-day duties fulfilled nor to the display of nobility and heroism.

Between the ambitious ideologies and the grimy actualities, the common link is philosophical. As is so often the case (though the philistine, like the pragmatist, cannot abide the idea), the surface phenomena of our life have their origins in fundamental movements of thought. When immense impersonal forces are apotheosized as the only significant reality, so that the moral and political power of the individual person to affect reality is utterly denied, what else can result than what we see occurring about us? The two apparently incongruous aspects of that scene are only two sides of the same coin. Abstract and collective visions and movements monopolize the exercise of energy as they career across the social scene, destroying the landmarks of civilization, for the same reason that the actual life of human beings becomes empty, purposeless, amoral. If the individual person lacks all significance, if he is but a determinant of suprapersonal forces, then only the forces and their development can have meaning, and it matters not a whit what a man does with his own life, or how much it approaches the merely brutish.

It is the disservice of Teilhard de Chardin to have given a quasi-religious aura to the philosophical outlook that has brought about this crisis of civilization. He stands, despite the verbiage in which his concepts are clothed, in direct opposition to the long philosophical tradition of the West. That tradition, fusing the insights of Greece and Israel in the transcending understanding of Christianity, has always placed the person as the ultimate and decisive reality. The recovery of that central truth is essential if our civilization, or any civilization, is to survive the storms of this age.

Lincoln without Rhetoric

(National Review, August 24, 1965)

Sometimes there are judgments at which one arrives that one hesitates to state publicly, out of respect for deeply held beliefs and prejudices. I have over a number of years come to think that the general admiration for Abraham Lincoln is ill founded. Particularly recently, in the course of work I have been doing on a book on American history, it has been borne in upon me more and more that his pivotal role in our history was essentially negative to the genius and freedom of our country.

It would undoubtedly have been wisest all around had I delayed any public expression of this judgment until I could fully state the reasons for it in my forthcoming book; but an excellent study of Lincoln's repressive measures during the Civil War, *Freedom Under Lincoln,* by Dean Sprague, crossed my desk and I gave it a brief review (*National Review,* June 15, 1965), in which I expressed skepticism of the accepted attitude toward Lincoln. A few weeks later, in the issue of July 27, a Letter to the Editor took me severely to task. Further, the letter was sharply seconded by my colleague and friend, Mr. William F. Buckley Jr. Under these circumstances I cannot in candor do less than set down here some of the considerations on which I base my judgment.

The issue is not really the one my critics raise: whether Lincoln was or was not a humanitarian. So far as this is concerned, suffice it to say that against Lincoln's magnificent language and his personal acts of individual kindness there must be placed in the balance the harshness of his repressive policies and his responsibility for methods of waging war approaching the horror of total war.

Granted that Lincoln was a complex person, that his well-known spells of depression and his self-searching, combined with his undoubted personal charity, display a man complex in the extreme. I do not pretend to judge Lincoln as a person; to so judge any man borders on impiety. But men who live by politics in the forefront of history can and will be judged politically and historically.

Such a judgment of Lincoln requires an evaluation of the role he played in our history. That history is the history of the exalted attempt, through the Constitution in its original form, to establish for the first time in human experience political mechanisms to guarantee the liberty of the individual person by limiting the power of government. Essential to this constitutional concept was the establishment of what has usually been called "checks and balances," but is more accurately designated as the setting up of a state of tension between all the political centers of power so that effective final power rests in none of them. Confounding almost every school of political theory, the American Constitution rested sovereignty nowhere (unless it were in every individual citizen), by establishing such a state of tension that no political body in the constitutional structure could accrete to itself sovereign power.

At the very center of this structure of tension was the tension between the several states and the national government. Until the Civil War no one knew whether a state could secede as its last sanction, and this was of the utmost necessity if the federal government were not to grow so strong as to destroy the tension that guaranteed liberty.

In 1860 the question was truly raised whether a "nation so conceived and so dedicated can long endure." It remained to Lincoln vigorously to attack that conception and that dedication. It is true that others, in the South as in the North, were as determined as he to shatter the subtle tension of state and national powers. But he alone had the power to reaffirm the constitutional balance. Instead, under the spurious slogan of Union, he moved at every point (no matter that he would have preferred to achieve his ends without war; so would every ideologue) to consolidate central power and render nugatory the autonomy of the states.

It is on his shoulders that the responsibility for war must be placed. Had he been less the ideologue, he could have let the seven states which seceded before Sumter go, and thus hold Virginia (the key to future unity) and the others in the Union, relying upon the passage of time, the congruity of natural interest, and the exercise of statesmanship to reunite the federal structure.

Nor, once battle was engaged, did Lincoln wage the war in a manner calculated to bring about the conditions of reconciliation. He waged it to win *at any cost*—and by winning he meant the permanent destruction of the autonomy of the states. We all know his gentle words, "with malice toward none, with charity for all," but his actions belie this rhetoric.

Total war is war conducted to achieve victory neglecting every other moral end. It is least excusable, moreover, in a war between brothers. Nevertheless this was Lincoln's pattern of war leadership: in the North, a repressive dictatorship; against the South, the brutal meat-grinder tactics of "Unconditional Surrender" Grant and the brigand campaigns waged against civilians by Sherman; in war aims, no effort at reconciliation, only the complete triumph of central government.

Were it not for the wounds that Lincoln inflicted upon the Constitution, it would have been infinitely more difficult for Franklin Roosevelt to carry through his revolution, for the coercive welfare state to come into being and bring about the conditions against which we are fighting today. Lincoln, I would maintain, undermined the constitutional safeguards of freedom as he opened the way to centralized government with all its attendant political evils.

Again on Lincoln

(National Review, January 25, 1966)

In his critique (*National Review,* September 21, 1965) of my discussion of Abraham Lincoln (*National Review,* August 24, 1965), Professor Harry Jaffa makes two major points. The first is that I am wrong in my interpretation of the American Constitution as establishing a government of sharply limited and radically divided powers with sovereignty settled in no single center. The second is that I have failed to understand that the concept of equality is central in the American tradition, and with this, that I have ignored Lincoln's role in the eradication of slavery. To this second indictment I plead guilty, and I shall return to a defense of my position after first considering Professor Jaffa's other major point.

What is at stake between us here is the 175-year-old dispute between the "loose constructionist" and the "strict constructionist" interpretations of the Constitution. Professor Jaffa is, of course, entitled to his loose-constructionist position; he has distinguished company, men so different in other respects as Alexander Hamilton, John Marshall, Andrew Jackson, Franklin Roosevelt and Lyndon Johnson. It does seem rather odd to me, however, that, considering the honored antiquity of both positions, Professor Jaffa should imply that all constitutional tradition is on his side of the argument. Perhaps because (before a rather checkered political career) I was raised by an old-time strict-constructionist, tariff-for-revenue-only Democratic father, I had rather supposed that until the days of Franklin Roosevelt the strict-constructionist theory predominated in the tradition— although battered from time to time by the power grabs of an Andrew Jackson or an Abraham Lincoln.

The issue beween the two interpretations of the Constitution is brought to a head by Professor Jaffa himself when he writes: "The principle of a free constitution rests not in any particular distribution of the powers of government, but in the recognition that *all* men have rights which *no* government should infringe." A happy thought—the only problem is what to do about government when a "particular distribution" of power lands all the power in the hands of a government that *does* "infringe." It is the genius of the American Constitution, understood as a constitution of radically divided powers (the strict-constructionist view) that it provides, for the first time in history, guarantees that no one shall have sufficient power to infringe upon the freedom of the individual person. Professor Jaffa's airy and cavalier lack of concern with how power is distributed leaves him with no defenses, except hope, against the innate tendency of government to concentrate power and to ride roughshod over the individual. It fully explains his admiration of Jackson, Lincoln, *et al.*

The essential guarantee that power will remain divided is that sovereignty is divided; this was the tacit agreement on which the federal compact was achieved. And sovereignty in turn implies the right to secede. Only the concentration of all sovereignty in the national government could negate that right. On the other hand, an easy certainty of the exercise of that right could have led to an early loss of all the goods of federal union. The Constitution was silent on this issue precisely in order to maintain the tension between federal and state power—a tension which could be broken only by shattering the federal union or by so concentrating power at the center that separation of powers was fundamentally undermined—and with it the genius of the Constitution in its defense of liberty. This is what I meant when I wrote "until the Civil War no one knew whether a state could secede as its last sanction. . . ." Lincoln, in words and deeds, before and after his election, provoked and intensified a challenge to the tacit acceptance of tension, and thereby struck at the heart of the Constitution.

Professor Jaffa, since he regards the division of power as irrelevant to the "principle of a free constitution," does not begin to grasp the incalculable damage for which Lincoln is responsible. He brushes aside the gravamen of my contention and raises as the center of his defense of Lincoln the question of slavery, regarding it as astonishing that I did not deal with it in my treatment of Lincoln. I did not deal with it because both Lincoln himself and most of his defenders (including Professor Jaffa in this essay) deny that the abolition of slavery was ever Lincoln's intent. To this degree even they respect the settled doctrine of the Constitution that slavery was understood by all parties to be the province solely of the several sovereign states.

The moral objections to slavery are manifold and I fully share Professor Jaffa's sorrow at its historical existence in the United States. But Professor Jaffa, ignoring all the unexceptional moral grounds for the hatred of slavery, chooses to base his critique of American slavery on the proposition that the American polity is in its essence dedicated to equality—and to center his vindication of Lincoln on Lincoln's role as the champion of equality. Nothing in my opinion could be further from the truth than this view of the American polity. The freedom of the individual person from government, not the equality of individual persons, is the central theme of our constitutional arrangements. Nor is this merely a matter of two different emphases. Freedom and equality are opposites; the freer men are the freer they are to demonstrate their inequality, and any political or social attempt—like those so frequent in the twentieth century—to enforce equality leads inevitably to the restriction and the eventual destruction of freedom.

When I write of equality, I am not, of course, speaking metaphysically or theologically of the innate worth of every human being in the eyes of God; and I would always affirm the principle of equality before the law and before government. The equality which I regard as the opposite of freedom is the abstract, overarching, unmodified concept Professor Jaffa employs. The ideological drive to enforce such equality upon men, always unequally endowed, is the primrose path to tyranny.

Professor Jaffa's Lincoln is the champion of equality. The Lincoln of whom I originally wrote is the creator of concentrated power, the President who shattered the constitutional tension. They are one and the same man.

The LSD Syndrome

(National Review, March 21, 1967)

The spreading cult of LSD seems to me to have significance rather deeper than simply as a further extension of the growth of the use of narcotics. LSD, unlike the morphine-derived "hard drugs," is largely being used by an educated, often intellectual and *avant-garde* sector of the population. So far as one can determine from reading the burgeoning literature on the subject, the central characteristic of the LSD experience is a destruction of intellectual discrimination, the creation of an unordered sea of kaleidoscopic impressions. What is destroyed when under the influence of the drug—and what those who take it seek to destroy—is the intellectual ordering of experience, which is the fruit of millennia of civilization. The consciousness retreats to the state anthropologists and psychologists attribute to primitive man—or even further, to that undifferentiated sea of images posited of the new-born infant.

But the hard-earned achievement of civilization—most specifically of the highest forms of civilization, the Classical and the Western—is the differentiation and ranging of the elements of experience in their essences, together with a controlled and objective consideration of their interrelations. It is true that this can be carried to an extreme, where thought is abstracted from life, as in the farther reaches of eighteenth-century rationalism or in some of the fearful ideologies which have devastated the twentieth century.

It was in reaction to this degree of arid abstraction that the existentialist philosophers of the nineteenth and twentieth centuries developed their mode of thought, and in doing so supplied a much-needed corrective; but even the best of them tended to throw out the baby with the bath water, to go beyond their critique of abstract and desiccated thought and attack the foundations of the conceptual discipline which holds Western civilization together. If this was a tendency among the philosophers (and what has been said of existentialism might with equal force be said of the various forms of positivism, pragmatism, instrumentalism, in their anti-civilizational effects), it became, as it affected the main stream of Western intellectual consciousness, a pervasive agent of corrosion.

I do not want to give philosophers more than their due (although the practical effects of their thought are far greater than we currently tend to allow). When a mode of consciousness begins to pervade a society, it comes from many sources at once; nevertheless, distorted philosophical activity has played a major role in this epoch, by tearing down the defenses of civilization and by giving shape and license to what is occurring.

The LSD cult is only a symptom, a far-out episode in the broader retreat from civilization. Yet it is symbolic of an entire intellectual movement. And its slogan is an apt slogan for that movement. "Turn on, tune in, drop out." Turn on the attack on civilizational restraints, tune in on the animal and instinctual, drop out of civilized society. It epitomizes the rejection of structure, differentiation, order.

In small things, as in large, this syndrome manifests itself throughout our culture. One can pick at random: the jellyfish sloppiness of mind and body which characterizes the *avant-garde* youth; the permissive disdain for the genius of the English language that takes expression in contemporary linguistics or in the Third Merriam-Webster; the radically amoral stance of our courts. The catalogue could be continued indefinitely. It may be more illuminating, however, to attempt to fill in the outlines of the syndrome I have described by considering briefly three writers presently exerting predominant influence on the intellectual world. Norman O. Brown, Marshall McLuhan, Leslie Dewart—each of these men represents a different aspect of the dissolution of the structured forms of civilized thought and life.

Brown is the most straightforward; his *Life Against Death,* which has had a continuing profound effect in literary and scholarly circles for almost a decade, is an attack across the board on all restraints, moral, customary, psychological, which stand in any way opposed to the unbridled reign of the instincts. His thesis simply stated may sound absurd, but it is backed up with resources of erudition and a power somewhat akin to Nietzsche's: relieve us of the burdens of civilization, release the instincts, particularly "polymorphous sexuality," and man will be rescued from all his agony. It is a formula for a return not merely to the primitive, but beyond and below it, to elementary forms of animal life.

McLuhan's attack is more sharply directed. His enemy is the word—in all its connotations. It is the word, the essence of language and the bearer of thought, upon which civilization is built, which carries from generation to generation knowledge and tradition. McLuhan would deny meaning to all this. The content is nothing. Everything dissolves into the momentary mode of presentation: yesterday, the printing press; today, television. Nothing remains but the flashing image—PR raised to a philosophy and a theology.

Dewart, a Catholic, can stand for an entire school, Protestant and Catholic alike. God and our understanding of God is his target. He would divest Christianity of its entire Hellenic heritage, i.e., of its intellectual structure, and thereby divest God of his Personhood, leaving only a whirling Scotch mist.

For these three, as for the intellectual trend they represent, the dissolution of distinction, form and structure (analogue of the LSD experience) is the goal. Its achievement would constitute a surer assault upon civilization than the Hun or Goth before the gates of Rome.

The Medium Is The Medium

(National Review, April 18, 1967)

Since the appearance of my column, "The LSD Syndrome," I have received a number of letters questioning the criticism of Marshall McLuhan, whose work I characterized, along with that of Norman O. Brown and Leslie Dewart, as an intellectual analogue of the LSD experience, a primitivistic attack upon civilization. While the specific content of these objections varies, there is a common element to all of them. Esentially what my correspondents are saying is: isn't McLuhan describing what is actually taking place, and shouldn't we all catch up with it and learn to live with it?

This objection totally misses the point. It absolves the intellectual—as it does the artist, the statesman, the entire elite of society—from the responsibility of his role, to bring tradition and reason to bear upon the flux of events, not passively to float on the wave of the present. The rejection of that responsibility is the *trahison des clercs*, the treason of the intellectuals, of the twentieth century.

From the intellectuals, who should be the guardians of the high thought of civilization, that treason has spread to the poll-guided political leaders who renounce their responsibility for the maintenance of a free constitutional order to pander to the prevailing passions of the least common denominator. It has spread to the artists and novelists and dramatists and film makers, who have betrayed their calling to give form and beauty and meaning to existence, substituting an uncritical representation (however decked out with complex claims of artistic subtlety) of whatever is most distorted, decadent, dismal in our society.

To attack this phenomenon is not to ask for chromo-art, for pollyanna intellectuality, for ignoring the realities of a society simultaneously suffering from a deep spiritual malady and from the disruptions of breathless technological change. It *is* to accuse those who form the ethos of society of perpetuating and accelerating the malady. It is to accuse them of utterly failing in their responsibility to build that spiritual strength which could direct the human effect of technological change, absorbing the disruption, putting order in place of distortion, giving meaning and joy to life.

It is on these grounds that I cited McLuhan as a prime exemplar of the *trahison des clercs*. I shall not discuss the solipsistic weavings of his literary and intellectual style. Hugh Kenner has done that with an unerring precision I could not hope to approach (*National Review*, November 29, 1966). Rather, I should like to discuss the objective significance of his position so far as it is possible to determine that position as it erupts out of the barbaric incoherencies of his prose.

The first point to be observed is that Mr. McLuhan is a crank and, like all cranks, has a single explanation for everything. In his case it is a fanatical extension of one of the heresies of modern thought, technological determinism. More specifically, it is determinism by the technological development of the modes of communication. All history is divided into three parts. There was the tribal era when direct vocal communication determined every aspect of human life; there was the era beginning with the invention of the alphabet and coming to its climax with the invention of printing; and now there is the electronic era. So runs the reiterated sermon of *The Gutenberg Galaxy* and *Understanding Media*.

Nothing substantial results from the conscious will of men. The fruits of reason, the intuitive sweep of human imagination, men as conscious agents mastering their environment—all these are subordinate to technological development. Thus the concept of civilization is meaningless to McLuhan. That which has been the glorious construction of ages of human endeavor becomes a tropism, the reflex of a technological quirk in the means of communication. The gradual emergence of the human person from the cosmological collective is but the chance product of mechanical innovation. Aristotle, Chartres and Shakespeare, Aquinas, the Parthenon and Dante, become but emanations indistinguishable on any scale of values from the totems and ceremonies of tribal existence.

And now, in our time, McLuhan's home-made history dooms civilization and all things civilizational. By another twist of technological fate—the emergence of electronics with its television and computers—we are being returned to tribal society on a world stage. The discrimination and differentiation that constitute civilization, which was nothing but a byproduct of passing technology, must be submerged in an interpersonal, electronically linked collective of "cool" togetherness. The human race is to become a giant jellyfish swaying in the amniotic ocean.

There are those who say McLuhan is only describing a tendency, not championing it. That would be bad enough, if he dscribed it without speaking out against it in the name of the human spirit. But even this defense falls before his own attack upon the discriminations of tradition and reason: "The mark of our time is its revolution against imposed patterns. . . . There is a deep faith to be found in this new attitude—a faith that concerns the ultimate harmony of all being. Such is the faith in which this book [*Understanding Media*] is written."

Both as analyst and as advocate he is hopelessly misreading the human condition. The medium is the medium—no more. Whatever its protean technological changes, the human spirit will use it for good or evil. The fate of men is in their own hands—in their understanding of the wisdom of tradition and their mastery of the gift of reason.

Index

Acheson, Dean, 68
Acton, Lord, 25, 45
Adams, John, 29, 69, 181, 182, 396
Adkins, Edward P., 440
Adorno, T. W., 68, 97
Agnew, Spiro, 306
Alger, Bruce, 250
Anschutz, R. P., 32
Aquinas, Thomas, 480
Aristotle, 22, 53, 135, 406, 415, 480
Ashbrook, John, 250
Auden, W. H., 449
Auerbach, Morton, 54–56
Augustus, 194, 243, 301

Babbitt, Irving, 445
Bakunin, Mikhail, 354
Baldwin, James, 204
Bell, Charles G., 447, 451, 452
Bell, Daniel, 58, 99, 100
Benedict, Ruth, 101, 102
Berns, Walter J., 51, 136, 137
Beth, Loren P., 167–169
Black, Charles L., Jr., 135–138
Black, Hugo, 51, 52
Bliss, Ray, 279
Bohlen, Charles, 238
Böhm-Bawerk, Eugen, 28
Boorstin, Daniel, 58
Bowles, Chester, 129, 224, 243
Bozell, Brent, 29, 38, 43–51, 83, 113, 118, 119, 136, 341, 367
Brooke, Edward, 280

Brown, H. Rap, 214
Brown, Lawrence R., 408, 410, 411
Brown, Norman O., 461, 477, 478
Brownell, Herbert, 153, 154
Bruce, Donald, 250
Buchanan, James, 154
Buckley, William F. Jr., 136, 138, 145, 255, 281, 470
Bukharin, Nikolai, 313
Bulganin, Nikolai, 312
Burke, Edmund, 33, 68, 69, 143, 209
Burnham, James, 85, 121, 292, 308, 319, 320, 322–327, 382
Burton, Harold H., 53
Butterfield, Herbert, 399, 400

Calhoun, John, 180
Capehart, Homer, 250, 253
Carmichael, Stokely, 210, 214
Castro, Fidel, 195, 249, 364
Chamberlain, John, 136
Chambers, Whittaker, 86, 191, 255
Chardin, Teilhard de, 467, 469
Christie, Richard, 98, 99
Churchill, Winston, 69
Clark, Tom, 176
Cleveland, Grover, 92, 154
Cohen, Eliot, 122
Collingwood, R. G., 399
Confucius, 405
Constantine, 46
Coombs, Philip H., 439

Cornuelle, Richard, 184, 201–204, 284
Corwin, Norman, 449
Cousins, Norman, 333, 344
Crane, Hart, 449
Cromwell, Oliver, 46
Cummings, E. E., 448, 449

Dante, 444, 480
Darwin, Charles, 467
Dawson, Christopher, 25
Decter, Moshe, 122
deGaulle, Charles, 300
Dewart, Leslie, 477, 478
Dewey, John, 63, 92, 101, 225, 236, 427, 428, 430, 432, 433, 437, 438, 456–458
Dewey, Thomas, 84, 232, 245
Dillon, Douglas, 243
Diocletian, 46
Disraeli, Benjamin, 59
Djilas, Miloslav, 116
Douglas, Paul, 281
Douglas, Stephen, 243
Douglas, William, 51, 52, 184, 185
Dubinsky, David, 273
Dulles, John Foster, 127, 232, 316, 323

Easton, David, 101
Einstein, Albert, 435
Eisenhower, Dwight D., 58, 78, 84, 86, 87, 92, 121, 127, 128, 153, 163, 178, 181, 224, 225, 227–230, 232, 233, 236–238, 245, 251, 256, 262, 308, 316, 320–324, 328, 333, 341, 347, 348, 433, 434
Eliot, T. S., 444, 445, 449, 451
Emerson, Ralph, 243

Engles, Friedrich, 208, 344
Evans, M. Stanton, 44, 54, 261, 289
Evans, Rowland, 267

Farmer, James, 273
Franco, Francisco, 300
Frankfurter, Felix, 52, 182–184
Franklin, Benjamin, 29
Frenkel-Brunswik, Else, 97
Freud, Sigmund, 236, 452–456, 460, 461
Fromm, Erich, 122, 453
Frost, Robert, 449
Fulbright, William J., 126, 129, 131, 250, 277

Galbraith, John K., 28, 74, 117, 466
Gallup, George, 143
Garrison, William Lloyd, 206
George, Lloyd, 184, 185
Gerth, Hans, 105
Glazer, Nathan, 100
Goldwater, Barry, 67, 70–74, 86, 128, 240, 241, 246, 252, 254–270, 274–276, 279, 289, 382
Gomulka, Wladyslaw, 229, 318, 329, 330, 340
Goodwin, Richard, 296
Gyorgy, Andrew, 354, 355

Halle, Louis J., 123
Hamilton, Alexander, 29, 181, 209, 473
Hand, Learned, 169
Harlan, John Marshall, 164
Harriman, Averell, 68, 379
Harris, T. George, 203
Hartz, Louis, 58
Hatfield, Mark, 281, 306

Hayek, F. A., 28, 74–77, 462
Hazlitt, Henry, 462
Hegel, Georg Wilhelm Friedrich, 402
Heidegger, Martin, 459
Henry, Patrick, 315
Herter, Christian, 238
Hesiod, 415
Hiestand, Edgar W., 252
Hiss, Alger, 86, 190, 191, 255
Hitler, Adolph, 137, 193, 300, 310, 311, 364, 365
Hoffer, Eric, 224
Hofstadter, Richard, 68, 96, 99, 176
Holcombe, Arthur N., 155
Holmes, O. W., 101, 167, 173, 182
Homer, 415
Hook, Sidney, 122, 342, 456, 457
Hooker, Richard, 227
Hoover, Herbert, 154
Horney, Karen, 453
Housman, A. E., 88
Hoyle, Fred, 108
Hughes, Charles Evans, 162
Hughes, H. Stuart, 122
Humphrey, Hubert, 210, 232, 282, 294, 295, 298
Huxley, Aldous, 225, 444–446

Ibsen, Henrik, 225
Ivey, John E., Jr., 439

Jackson, Andrew, 163, 430, 473, 474
Jackson, Henry, 382
Jackson, Floyd Louis, 156
Jaffa, Harry, 472–475
Jahoda, Marie, 98, 99
James, William, 225

Javits, Jacob, 218, 246, 247, 252
Jefferson, Thomas, 29, 163, 181, 209, 243, 364, 396
Johnson, Lyndon, 159, 210, 215, 259, 263, 264, 267–274, 277, 281, 282, 286, 291, 294, 302, 308, 382, 473
Jones, Kenneth, 250
Judd, Walter, 339

Kahn, Herman, 131
Kai-shek, Chiang, 321, 375
Kariel, Henry S., 171
Kendall, Willmoore, 132, 136, 158
Kennan, George, 68, 115–117, 123, 243, 312, 314, 333
Kennedy, Edward, 252
Kennedy, John F., 86, 121, 127, 128, 130, 131, 159, 163, 240, 242, 243, 245–253, 257, 259, 272–274, 282, 302, 376–382
Kennedy, Robert, 210, 277, 291, 294, 298, 303
Kenner, Hugh, 479
Kerensky, Alexander, 300
Keynes, John M., 28, 75, 461–466
Keyserling, Leon, 185
Khrushchev, Nikita, 39, 127, 130, 131, 188, 238, 309, 310, 312, 313, 329, 339, 345–350, 354, 355, 358, 359, 365–367, 379, 380, 382
Kilpatrick, James Jackson, 160
King, Martin L., 204, 207–209, 212–214, 216, 290, 291
Kirk, Russell, 30, 31, 34, 35, 445
Kissinger, Henry, 333
Kluckhohn, Clyde, 101–106
Knight, Frank, 74
Knowland, William, 246

Koestler, Arthur, 309
Kohr, Leopold, 400
Kolb, William Lester, 105
Koufax, Sandy, 441

Larson, Arthur, 133, 224
Lasswell, Harold, 108
Latham, Earl, 166, 167
Leites, Nathan, 342
LeMay, Curtis, 387
Lenin, V. I., 300, 313, 314, 331, 354, 365
Lincoln, Abraham, 87, 163, 243, 470–475
Lindsay, John, 216, 281, 282, 302, 304, 306
Lippmann, Walter, 58, 106, 129, 157, 256, 314, 328, 329, 383
Lipset, S. M., 100
Locke, John, 58, 196
Lodge, Henry Cabot, 261–264, 380
London, Jack, 105
Lubell, Samuel, 143
Lukacs, John A., 123

MacArthur, Douglas, 95, 341
McCarthy, Eugene, 294, 302–304
McCarthy, Joseph, 68, 95, 96, 136, 138, 152, 153, 187–189, 191, 192, 232, 255
McDonough, Gordon L., 252
McKinley, William, 92
McLeod, Scott, 96
McLuhan, Marshall, 477–480
McNamara, Robert, 218–221, 243, 274, 385, 387
Madison, James, 29, 56, 209
Mailer, Norman, 456–458

Malenkov, Georgi, 330
Marshall, John, 473
Marx, Karl, 28, 59, 63, 92, 236, 336, 344, 354, 402, 403, 458
Mason, George, 29
Mead, Margaret, 96, 97
Meany, George, 339
Meiklejohn, Donald, 167–170
Menger, Karl, 28
Metternich, Prince Klemens von, 68, 69
Mikoyan, Anastas, 232, 339–341
Mill, John Stuart, 30–35, 209
Mills, C. Wright, 105
Milton, John, 440
Mises, Ludwig von, 28, 74, 400, 462
Morgenthau, Hans J., 122, 123
Morse, Wayne, 264
Moynihan, Daniel, 216, 296
Murrow, Edward R., 146, 243

Nasser, Gamal Abdel, 90, 188, 229, 321
Nehru, Jawaharlal, 188, 365
Neuberger, Maurine, 264
Newcastle, Percy, of, 33, 399
Newman, Cardinal John Henry, 120
Newman, William, 56–58
Nietzsche, Friedrich Wilhelm, 461, 477
Nisbet, Robert A., 123
Nixon, Richard, 133, 215, 236–238, 240, 241, 245, 246, 253, 256, 261, 264, 282, 290, 291, 294, 295, 301, 302, 305–307, 341
Nkrumah, Kwame, 90
Northrup, F. S. C., 104, 391–394
Novak, Robert, 267

Oppenheimer, Robert, 115, 435
Overstreet, Bonaro, 342–344
Overstreet, Harry, 342–344

Parry, Stanley, 59–67
Parsons, Talcott, 100
Pell, Robert, 128
Percy, Charles, 14, 280–282, 290, 302, 306, 466
Pfaff, William, 123
Philip II, 46
Plato, 22, 406, 415, 418
Podhoretz, Norman, 122
Polanyi, Michael, 116–118
Popper, Karl, 400
Possony, Stefan, 387
Poulson, Norris, 347
Pound, Ezra, 449, 451
Power, Thomas, 387
Powers, Gary, 349
Pritchett, C. H., 169

Rafferty, Max, 253
Rand, Ayn, 45
Randolph, A. Philip, 210
Reagan, Ronald, 14, 275, 280, 282, 290, 291, 294, 297, 298, 301–303, 305
Reston, James, 256
Reuther, Walter, 185, 232
Rhee, Syngman, 321
Rhodes, James, 282
Rickenbacker, William, 246
Riencourt, Amaury de, 396, 397
Riesman, David, 68, 99, 116, 122, 175–178
Ripper, Jack the, 137
Roche, John P., 167, 168
Rockefeller, Nelson, 14, 125, 129, 131, 132, 238, 246, 247, 252, 253, 260–262, 264, 272, 280, 282, 292, 341, 466

Romney, George, 125, 246, 252, 262, 280–282, 290
Roosevelt, Eleanor, 112
Roosevelt, Franklin, 63, 69, 87, 90, 92, 132, 154, 158, 162, 185, 225, 237, 238, 245, 246, 259, 265, 269, 270, 272, 294–296, 347, 365, 378, 430, 466, 472, 473
Roosevelt, Theodore, 243
Rostow, Walter, 129, 274, 380
Rousseau, J. J., 425, 442
Rousselot, John, 252
Rovere, Richard, 68
Rusk, Dean, 243
Russell, Richard, 382
Rustin, Bayard, 210

Sartre, Jean P., 459
Schlamm, Willy, 319
Schlesinger, Arthur A., Jr., 68, 243
Schriever, Bernard, 387
Schwartz, Benjamin, 105
Scranton, William, 252, 261, 262, 264
Shakespeare, William, 444, 480
Shell, Joseph, 246
Sherman, W. T., 472
Shils, Edward, 147
Skinner, B. F., 171, 457
Smith, Adam, 28
Smith, Margaret Chase, 263
Socrates, 22, 415, 439
Spengler, Oswald, 61, 66, 393, 396, 399, 402, 409–411
Sprague, Dean, 470
Stalin, Joseph, 137, 229, 309–314, 330, 355, 356
Stassen, Harold, 262, 263
Stennis, John, 382

Stephen, James Fitzjames, 31, 32, 34, 35
Stevens, Wallace, 449
Stevenson, Adlai, 68, 69, 84, 129, 133, 210, 237, 238, 243, 246, 252, 316, 363
Stillman, Edmund, 123
Stratton, Samuel, 252
Strout, Cushing, 135–138
Sukarno, Achmed, 90, 188, 249
Swabey, Marie, 400
Swift, Jonathon, 328
Symington, Stuart, 382

Taft, Robert, 68, 95, 230, 246, 341
Tate, Allen, 447–452
Taylor, Edmond, 383
Teller, Edward, 387
Thurmond, Strom, 382
Tito, Marshal, 229, 310, 312, 329, 330, 340, 358
Titov, Gherman Stepanovitch, 366, 367
Tocqueville, Alexis de, 395
Toledano, Ralph de, 83, 84
Tower, John, 382
Toynbee, Arnold, 60, 61, 393, 396, 399, 402, 409, 410
Trilling, Lionel, 452–456, 460
Trotsky, Leon, 313
Trudeau, Arthur G., 339
Truman, Harry, 153, 154, 232, 237, 238, 341
Tse-Tung, Mao, 308, 329–333, 354, 365
Tshombe, Moise, 375

Van den Haag, Ernest, 462, 465
Veblen, Thorston, 101
Viereck, Peter, 67–70, 100, 176
Vivas, Eliseo, 447
Voegelin, Eric, 33, 62, 86, 399–402, 404–409, 412

Walker, Edwin, 179
Wallace, George, 263, 282, 285–288, 294, 295, 298, 303
Warren, Earl, 51, 52
Washington, Booker T., 214, 217
Washington, George, 29, 154, 243, 364, 397, 398
Weaver, Richard, 33, 225, 228, 255, 458
Welch, Robert, 347
Whitehead, Alfred North, 437
Wiener, Norbert, 435
Wiesner, Jerome, 274
Wiley, Alexander, 253
Wilhelm II, 123
Wilkie, Wendell, 84, 232, 240, 245, 262
Wilkins, Roy, 291
Wills, Garry, 206
Wilson, Charles E., 433
Wilson, Woodrow, 243
Wittfogel, Karl, 55, 401–404, 409

Xerxes, 88
X, Malcolm, 204

Zacharias, Jerrold R., 440
Zinoviev, Grigori Evseevich, 313